Kurt Weill on Stage

Kurt Weill on Stage

FROM BERLIN TO BROADWAY

Foster Hirsch

LIMELIGHT EDITIONS
NEW YORK

First Limelight Edition   October 2003
Originally published by Alfred A. Knopf in 2002

Published in the United States by Proscenium Publishers, Inc., New York

ISBN 0-87910-990-4

Manufactured in the United States of America

Library of Congress Cataloging-in-Publication Data
available from Proscenium Publishers, Inc. upon request

Contents

CONTENTS

Acknowledgments

Walter Alford, Alan Anderson, Hesper Anderson, Quentin Anderson, Mordecai and Irma Commanday Bauman, Eric Bentley, Sheila Bond, Phoebe Brand, Carmen Capalbo, Margaret Cowie, Danny Daniels, Gemze de Lappe, Jonathan Eaton, Fred Ebb, Alvin Epstein, Michael Feingold, John Fuegi, Kitty Carlisle Hart, Gerhard Henschke, Mr. and Mrs. Al Hirschfeld, Jane Hoffman, Anne Jeffreys, John Kander, Joan Bartels Kobin, Kim H. Kowalke, Miles Kreuger, Pearl Lang, Robbie Lantz, Paula Laurence, Jo Sullivan Loesser, Bob Lydiard, John Mauceri, Laura McCann, Allyn Ann McLerie, Karl-Hans Möller, the late Scott Merrill, Ruth Nathan, the late Robert Pagent, Estelle Parsons, Harold Prince, Jan Rothenberg, Julius Rudel, the late Sylvia Sidney, the late Anna Sokolow, Jim Stuart, Arnold Sundgaard, Lys Symonette, Michael Wager. At the Kurt Weill Foundation for Music in New York, Brian Butcher, David Farneth, Elmar Juchem, Joanna Lee, Dave Stein, Carolyn Weber; for research assistance, Ian Cook; for expert musical analysis of Kurt Weill's scores, composer Herschel Garfein; at Alfred A. Knopf, Victoria Wilson.

Kurt Weill on Stage

ONE

Overture

Two opening nights. Two hits. Two cities. Two continents. One composer.

Berlin, August 31, 1928: *Die Dreigroschenoper (The Threepenny Opera),* a collaboration among Bertolt Brecht, adapter, Caspar Neher, scenic designer, and Kurt Weill, composer, opens at the Theater am Schiffbauerdamm.

New York, January 23, 1941: *Lady in the Dark,* a musical play by Moss Hart in collaboration with Ira Gershwin, lyricist, and Kurt Weill, composer, opens at the Alvin Theatre.

Based on John Gay's *Beggar's Opera,* produced in London two hundred years earlier, *Die Dreigroschenoper* is set in a naïve, imaginary version of Victorian London that holds a mirror up to "wicked" late-Weimar Berlin. An irreverent musical comedy with its heartbeat attuned to the zeitgeist, *Die Dreigroschenoper* is political theatre in the broadest, most audience-friendly sense. *Lady in the Dark* has a narrower but equally purposeful didactic intent: a show about the romantic and emotional problems of the editor of a high-fashion magazine, it advocates Freudian analysis. *Die Dreigroschenoper* is deeply Germanic; *Lady in the Dark* is just as irreversibly American: a Broadway artifact.

3

For all their obvious differences, these two shows composed by Kurt Weill, one of the preeminent collaborative dramatists of the century, have more in common than a first glance might suggest. In their time, the two musicals were experimental in both form and subject matter; and in both shows, to a greater degree than in other popular German and American works of their respective eras, music and meaning coalesced in exciting new ways. For the composer, each show entailed high risks. At the same time that he was in the process of transforming his own musical identity, he had to adjust his style to the needs of widely dissimilar cowriters and audiences. The jazzlike rhythms and seductive melodies of *Die Dreigroschenoper* continued a radical break, begun the year before, from Weill's earlier reputation as a classically trained composer whose work was steeped in avantgarde atonality—the show inaugurated a debate about his supposed defection from high to low culture that endures to the present.

The shift from classicist to populist that Weill successfully negotiated in 1928 was in some ways easier than the challenge he faced in New York in 1941, when he had more at stake and more to prove. Could he pass in the only role the occasion could accommodate, that of a Broadway composer able to handle a homegrown idiom? Since his arrival in America six years earlier, the busy émigré composer, a Jew in flight from fascist Germany, had had three shows in New York and contributed the score to a pageant at the 1939 New York World's Fair. But none had achieved hit status in a theatrical culture, then as now, addicted to success. As of January 23, 1941, Weill, who lingered in the precincts of the merely "interesting," was still the new guy in town, an as-yet-unproven commodity in a commodity-oriented marketplace. The jury was out. Yet to survive on Broadway, as he wanted to, Kurt Weill this time needed nothing less than a smash hit, and opening night at the Alvin Theatre, as he was only too well aware, might have been his last chance to grab the brass ring. *Lady in the Dark,* happily, proved to be a critical and commercial bonanza. At the end of a speedy, six-year apprenticeship he had become a full-fledged Broadway citizen, an "American" composer who had performed a kind of double self-erasure: he had managed to camouflage both his European roots and his classical training in a way that has continued ever since to cause delight and puzzlement.

In his native Germany, Weill, born at the turn of the century, on March 2, 1900, had also risen rapidly. An unprepossessing, scholarly-looking young man with large, owlish eyes and a sly, ironic grin that could be interpreted as either shyness or arrogance and in truth contained a bit of both, Weill worked with many of the major theatrical figures of the Weimar Republic. His most famous (as well as most fractious) collaboration was with the renegade poet and dramatist Bertolt Brecht; in addition to *Die Dreigroschenoper* their portfolio includes *Mahagonny-Songspiel* (1927) and *Aufstieg und Fall der Stadt Mahagonny* (*The Rise and Fall of the City of Mahagonny,* 1930); *Happy End* (1929); and *Die sieben Todsünden* (*The Seven Deadly Sins,* 1933). With Georg Kaiser, the preeminent expressionist playwright, Weill wrote two one-act operas, *Der Protagonist* (1926) and *Der Zar lässt sich photographieren* (*The Czar Has His Photograph Taken,* 1927), as well as a full-length play with music, *Der Silbersee* (*The Silver Lake,* 1933). With Ivan Goll, a prominent surrealist poet, Weill wrote a one-act opera, *Royal Palace* (1926), and a cantata, *Der neue Orpheus* (*The New Orpheus,* 1925). With Caspar Neher, Germany's leading scenic designer, he cowrote his longest and most solemn opera, *Die Bürgschaft* (*The Pledge,* 1932).

By the time he was forced to flee for his life in March 1933, Kurt Weill was renowned as Germany's leading composer for the theatre, a firebrand who had narrowed the divide between the formalities of opera and more popular kinds of musical performance such as revue and cabaret. Avoiding a rigid concept of the "operatic," Weill conducted his entire career in the light of the liberating belief that opera is whatever its creators choose to place on an opera-house stage. Like many artistic rebels in Weimar Germany, Weill was fascinated by American jazz and dance music—and by the vibrant popular culture they came from. Years before a historical catastrophe sent him to the real place, "Amerika" and American sounds, freely interpreted, appeared recurrently in his work. Once he was in America, Weill was determined to match the kind of success he had enjoyed in Germany. At home, opera was the major form of music theatre; in the New World, the Broadway musical was the only place for a theatre composer who expected to earn a living wage. And rather than regretting the fact that Broadway was where he would have to hang his hat, Weill was enticed by its possibilities.

Because his German reputation remained in Germany (only a small but impassioned cadre of musical-theatre aficionados were familiar with his work through recordings of songs from *Die Dreigroschenoper, Happy End,* and *Mahagonny*), Weill had to rebuild his career virtually from ground zero. And remarkably, in New York, as in Berlin, he managed to work exclusively with theatrical royalty. The writers, performers, directors, choreographers, designers, and producers he collaborated with comprise a who's who of the American theatre in one of its most vital phases. In his

5

fifteen-year Broadway career Weill's associates included Gertrude Lawrence, Mary Martin, Danny Kaye, Moss Hart, Maxwell Anderson, Burgess Meredith, Helen Hayes, Walter Huston, Elia Kazan, Rouben Mamoulian, Agnes de Mille, Alan Jay Lerner, Harold Clurman, Cheryl Crawford, Langston Hughes, Ogden Nash, S. J. Perelman, Ira Gershwin, Nanette Fabray, Michael Kidd, and Anne Jeffreys. Setting up shop against homegrown talents like George Gershwin, Cole Porter, Richard Rodgers, and Irving Berlin, Weill compiled a résumé of distinguished American musicals that, in addition to *Lady in the Dark,* includes *Johnny Johnson* (1936), *Knickerbocker Holiday* (1938), *One Touch of Venus* (1943), *Street Scene* (1947), *Love Life* (1948), and *Lost in the Stars* (1949). No other Broadway composer except Stephen Sondheim has been to so deep and true a degree a collaborative dramatist, and no other Broadway composer except Leonard Bernstein (with a leaner catalogue) has so successfully closed the distance between the concert hall and the musical theatre.

Unlike many other prominent German-Jewish intellectuals forced to seek refuge in America, Weill adapted quickly. Far from grumbling about cultural displacement, or, like fellow émigrés such as Hannah Arendt, Theodor Adorno, Arnold Schoenberg, and Brecht, bewailing the customs of a new country, Weill was both grateful and intensely patriotic—right from the start he was eager to play his role in an American pageant. For him, as for few others of his stature who had to contend with interrupted lives, America in person proved to be as appealing as the mythic Amerika of jazz babies, bobby-soxers, gangsters, and skyscrapers that had become part of the discourse of Weimar popular culture. Is it possible he succeeded so readily because he didn't have to change in any fundamental way? On Broadway, as in Berlin, he continued to be a practical man of the theatre who held firm to his artistic principles. Nonetheless, as a hero of the German-Jewish diaspora, Kurt Weill was in many ways an unlikely and richly contradictory figure. He was a classically trained composer who earned a lasting fame with bewitchingly melodic songs. A genuine intellectual, he became a hard-nosed businessman who examined the fine print in all his contracts. In the heat of production he was famously unflappable, but offstage he often boiled with anger and resentment; beautifully calm on the surface, he was a tightly wound man with high blood pressure who drove himself to an early death. Tucked beneath his modest veneer were a hefty ego (he always knew just how good he was), a deep-seated competitive spirit, and a fierce ambition. An artist with a lifelong commitment to reforming the musical theatre, he was at the same time a Sammy Glick from Dessau, Germany, with his eye on the box office and the main chance.

Kurt Weill prospered in his adopted country, and yet there was a price to be paid for achieving the money and the fame that came with popular acceptance. Igor Stravinsky and Richard Rodgers, who were both at the opening night of *Lady in the Dark,* came backstage to congratulate Weill, in a moment that may have seemed to promise a reconciliation between the composer's European roots and his newfound American voice. But the harmony was only a momentary illusion. Ever since, critically speaking, Weill has been at war with himself, with defenders and naysayers lining up on either side of his Great Migration. "I belong to the generation of Otto Klemperer who regard Weill's American career as a letdown," said Eric Bentley, Brecht's first English translator and most skillful interpreter.[1] "I actually prefer Weill's American to his European work," Harold Prince, the most honored director in the history of Broadway, said.[2] Those who "regret" the American Weill tend to argue that to win his share of New World riches he had to forsake or at least compromise aspects of his imperial Teutonic heritage. Defenders of the American work contend that writing for Broadway encouraged the composer's strong melodic gift and allowed him to continue to develop exactly the kinds of formal experiments he had begun in Berlin.

Of course there are differences between the European and the American branches of Weill's career—and let it be said at once that Weill's collaborations with Brecht yielded work of a quality not matched by any other show the composer wrote in Europe or America. But long before he hit the Broadway big time, Weill had already established what would be his career-long commitment to change. Self-renewal, creative rerouting, marked shifts in style and idiom were an engrained part of his signature in Germany as they continued to be in America. In the face of the evidence, the myth that there are two Kurt Weills is easily exploded: there are, in fact, many more than two creative masks for a composer addicted to exploration. The persistent legend of two monolithic Kurt Weills confronting each other across vast cultural and geographical distances needs to be adjusted to include the many other Weills clamoring for recognition. In Germany, Weill wrote a symphony, a violin concerto, a children's pantomime, radio cantatas, short and full-length operas of varying modes and difficulty, songspiels, lieder, oratorios, and musical plays of an indeterminate genre that share many familial resemblances to American musical comedy. In exile, first in Paris, then briefly in London, and finally in New

York and Los Angeles, he wrote chansons, a *ballet chanté,* a second symphony, operettas, pageants, musical comedies, Broadway "operas," a musical tragedy, a folk opera, and film scores. Frequently, thriving on collage and on assaulting generic boundaries, he mixed musical idioms within the same work. But if there are indeed many more than two strings to Kurt Weill's bow, they all belong to a single composer with a commanding theatrical intelligence.

One of the unfortunate legacies of the long-standing fiction of the two Kurt Weills is that it seems to require a choice. And the vote seems to be colored by political, nationalistic, even moral implications. Preferring the European Weill implies that you are casting your net with highbrows and imperialists; favoring the American Weill can mark you as a light-minded Broadway baby. But faced with the portfolio of a composer for whom no two shows are exactly alike, why have to choose? Why not, instead, savor Weill's craftsmanship, his irony and wit, his succulent, insinuating melodies, the deft and often surprising ways in which his music interacts with dialogue and dramatic context, wherever they are found, on either side of his migration? Looked at fairly, Weill's career reveals a remarkable continuity of interests and quality. In America, as in Germany, he delighted in confounding rigid categories as he set up a dialogue between elitist and popular musical forms.

And on Broadway, as in Berlin—as *Die Dreigroschenoper* and *Lady in the Dark* demonstrate—Weill continued to rethink and expand the formal and thematic possibilities of musical theatre. For their place and time, both shows were mavericks with an unusual subject matter and use of music. *Die Dreigroschenoper* is a jaunty musical about underworld scoundrels; the tormented heroine of *Lady in the Dark* is in analysis. In both shows Weill's songs intersect the spoken drama at odd tangents. Musical numbers in *Die Dreigroschenoper* are often intended to stop the show; music in *Lady in the Dark* is segregated in a series of mini-operas, musical scenes that upend the standard Broadway syntax of the time. The shows are not equal in quality, to be sure—the former is one of the great theatre works of the twentieth century, the latter has slipped into a historical limbo from which it is likely never to emerge. But at the time they opened, each made a significant contribution to the vocabulary of the musical theatre.

TWO

Enter BB

Apistol shot rings out. Six actors in straw hats scramble beneath the ropes of a boxing ring. And as they were meant to do, the audience at this July 17, 1927, performance at the Deutsches Kammermusikfest in Baden-Baden lets out an audible gasp. The jazz orchestra, prominently featuring a trombone and an alto sax, breaks into an assertive rhythm—somewhere between a fox-trot and a march—as the male performers, two tenors and two basses, lurch into a song with naughty German lyrics. The men (there are no individual characters in this termite piece of music theatre) are off on a journey to a new city, Mahagonny, where "the air is clean and fresh," where there's "booze and poker tables," "good whores and good horseflesh." With "no bureaucracy" in this beckoning free city, there's the promise of "fresh meat for sale on every street."[1]

The next "number," called "Alabama-Song," is sung in a delightfully semicoherent pidgin English by a contingent of female pilgrims—a gaggle of whores—also on their way to the new city. While the men have invoked "the green and glowing moon of Alabama" to light their way, the women now say goodbye to the same "moon of Alabama." Just where is this Mahagonny? the audience in Baden-Baden may well have wondered.

Rehearsal for the finale of the *Mahagonny-Songspiel,* the show that will shock the audience at the New Music Festival in Baden-Baden in the summer of 1927. The audacious boxing-ring set and placards were designed by Caspar Neher. Weill, hands in pockets, is at the far left; Lenya, far right onstage, carries a placard that reads "Für Weill!"

In the number's three-part structure, verse followed by refrain, the voyagers ask for the way to (1) "the next whisky-bar," (2) "the next pretty boy," and (3) "the next little dollar," citing the trinity of booze, sex, and money on which the new city will rise and fall. Half of the time, the haunting melody is carried by a woman with a face that could have been drawn by an expressionist and a voice that stands out from those of her operatically trained costars.

So concludes part 1, "Off to Mahagonny." Part 2, "Life in Mahagonny," sketches the disappointment that overtakes the inhabitants of the new city. Drinking and whoring and time on your hands have grown dull; lethargy has become their lot. The monotony of the "sweet life" is reflected in the verbal and musical repetitions—in the languor of the sinuous cadences issuing from the orchestra. All used up, the citizens want to go to a new

place, an anti-Mahagonny. "Let's go to Benares / Where the sun is shining," they sing. Their collective dream is smashed when Benares "is said
to have been perished in an earthquake!" "Oh! Where shall we go?" the
stranded pilgrims wonder, to the lonely whine of a trombone that seems to
express deep sexual yearning. In the finale, on a gray morning when the
inhabitants are feeling their whiskey, God appears in Mahagonny. As the
deity poses insulting questions, and accuses the citizens of drunkenness
and murder, they answer complacently. But the music rumbles with sinister undercurrents; increasingly threatening chords signify the fate of a people facing their dark Day of Judgment. When God orders them to hell, the
people protest with a collective "No!," maintaining that they are in hell
already. The citizens hold up placards with contradictory slogans as the
city sputters to its end. In a brief coda, Mahagonny is revealed as an imaginary place, a bit of theatrical sleight-of-hand, which had to be invented
"because the world is so rotten."

At the end of this strange twenty-five-minute piece, the last item in a
quadruple bill of short operas that had included Paul Hindemith's *Hin und
zurück,* Darius Milhaud's *L'enlèvement d'Europe,* and Ernst Toch's *Die
Prinzessin auf der Erbse,* the audience erupted. The cultivated viewers knew
that the work they had just seen, the *Mahagonny-Songspiel,* by Bertolt
Brecht and Kurt Weill, had thumbed its nose at opera-house decorum, and
hisses and boos were interspersed with equally fervent cries of "Bravo!
Bravo!" Prepared for such a reaction, the cast blew whistles, a deliberately
insolent gesture that prolonged the uproar. The two young upstarts,
Brecht with his salty, profane poetry and his mockery of religious piety,
and Weill with his sour and sexy melodies and his jazzlike orchestrations,
had in a stroke smashed the barricades that had divided opera from popular entertainment. The straw hats the actors wore, the drawings by Caspar
Neher projected on a screen behind the actors, the boxing-ring set that
separated the performers from the audience as well as from the orchestra—
in all theatrical departments the "songspiel" had been a cheeky assault on
propriety. The show reveled in its bad taste and had had the effrontery to
ask the audience to join in. And even though it had been commissioned by
a music festival dedicated to daring new works, this *Mahagonny,* to many,
trespassed acceptable boundaries of literary, musical, and theatrical
decency.

The sophisticated audiences who supported the new-music festival held
annually in the elegant resort of Baden-Baden would certainly have
expected to encounter the challenges laid down by atonality; they may

even have heard recent experiments in twelve-tone music (the first piece written with a strict twelve-tone technique was Schoenberg's 1924 Suite for Piano). But the modernity of *Mahagonny* seemed something else altogether. Not since the premiere of Igor Stravinsky's *Soldier's Tale* in 1918—which it resembles in its serious use of popular musical forms, its modified jazz band, its montagelike structure, and its musical and verbal economy—had a contemporary work seemed so hard to categorize or so ebulliently of the moment. Responses from critics as well as the audience were extreme. In a review in *Modern Music* for November–December 1927 Aaron Copland snipped that Kurt Weill is "the new *enfant terrible* of Germany. It is not so easy to be an *enfant terrible* as it used to be and nothing is more painful than the spectacle of a composer trying too hard to be revolutionary." Olin Downes, in the August 14, 1927, *New York Times,* called Weill "a bold and bad young man" who earned "the triumph of the festival" with his "witty" music. "The quartet 'numbers' have the character of the coon-song with barber-shop chords gone wrong. The girls parody the lilt and sentimentality of the jazz ditty [that has] a slangy twist and a sardonic sting admirably contrived." Weill's publisher Hans Heinsheimer noted that in the *Mahagonny-Songspiel* his client "cut the last link to the nobly aloof, high-brow tradition of Busoni [the composer's teacher] and presented to an unprepared, shocked world the real Kurt Weill."[2]

Lotte Lenya, the performer with the unusual voice, recalled that in the party after the show the atmosphere was thick with tension. She and the other cast members were worried about how they would be received. "We thought, you know, maybe a spectator, very angry at the show, would attack us." When somebody tapped her on the shoulder, she jumped. "Is here no telephone?" the man asked in a bantering tone, repeating one of the lyrics. The question, posed by Otto Klemperer, recently appointed to head the avant-garde Krolloper, put Lenya at ease: clearly, the great conductor had enjoyed their show. "Klemperer was as aggressive as Brecht and Weill were," Lenya recalled. "Also he was, like them, always slightly making fun of those longhaired composers, which gabble in a music festival like Baden-Baden. They all said, you know, 'That's holy atmosphere,' and here we came in with boxing and straw hats, not 'holy' at all. But Klemperer, you see, got it. He recognized the fresh air coming from Brecht and Weill's direction."[3]

Dressed, in effect, for the scandalous success he had expected, Brecht wore his customary leather jacket, twisted leather tie, and visored cap; a blackish cigar hanging carelessly from his lips completed the outlaw masquerade. Weill's persona—self-effacing, bemused, and professorial—offered a sharp contrast. But he was every bit as confident as his partner. At twenty-seven, he was already the composer of a successful one-act opera and had collaborated with two important writers. He and BB had already begun to think of themselves as music-theatre reformers, and their *Mahagonny-Songspiel* was but the first round in the cultural war they planned to wage against opera-house elitism and insularity.

Kurt Weill's rise to theatrical prominence in Weimar Germany had been remarkably swift. Leaving his family home in provincial Dessau, where his father was cantor of the synagogue, eighteen-year-old Kurt had first come to Berlin in April 1918 to study at the Berlin Hochschule für Musik with Engelbert Humperdinck, the famous composer of the opera *Hansel und Gretel*. Dissatisfied with his studies, Weill returned to Dessau the following January and over the next eighteen months, as he worked first at the local Friedrichstheater and later as music director at the city theatre in Lüdenscheid, two hundred miles west of Dessau, he resolved on a career in the theatre. In September 1920 he returned to Berlin to study with another renowned teacher, the legendary composer, pianist, and theoreti-

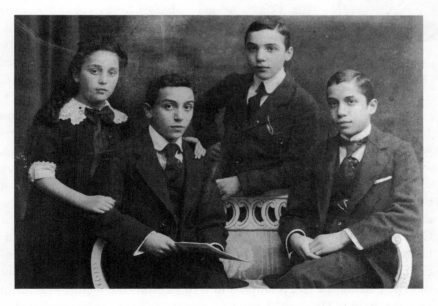

The Weill children, in Dessau, Germany, in 1910. From left, Ruth, Nathan, Kurt (standing and looking preternaturally intent), and Hanns

An ambitious music student from the provinces:
Kurt Weill at eighteen, new to Berlin

cian Ferruccio Busoni. A neo-classicist who spurned Wagnerian music drama and the late-romantic and expressionist traditions, Busoni (in class) advocated a return to abstract music, "pure music," disentangled from literary reference and symbolism. (Busoni's own stage works, however, are highly "literary." His best-known orchestral works are either derived from his operas or, as in the case of the Piano Concerto, linked to a text.)

During the three years he studied with Busoni, Weill composed at a prolific rate. His portfolio included a Divertimento for Small Orchestra with Men's Chorus (1922); *Zaubernacht,* a ballet-pantomime commissioned by the Russische Kindertheater and performed in Berlin on November 18, 1922; the String Quartet no. 1, op. 8 (1923), performed on June 24, 1923, in Frankfurt; *Quodlibet,* a suite based on music from *Zaubernacht,* performed in Dessau at the Friedrichstheater, with Albert Bing, Weill's first mentor, conducting, on June 13, 1923; *Frauentanz* (1923), a song cycle with chamber accompaniment, performed in January 1924 at the Akademie der Künste in Berlin, with Fritz Stiedry conducting; *Recordare* (1923), for four-part mixed chorus and two-part boys' chorus; and the Concerto for Violin and Wind Orchestra, op. 12 (1924). It is an astonishing output for so young a composer. And equally remarkable was the number of high-profile performances Weill secured. Busoni's admiration for the 1923 string quartet prompted him to recommend Weill to Dr. Emil Hertzka, head of Universal Edition, the eminent music publisher based in Vienna, and by the end of 1923 Dr. Hertzka had offered Weill a contract.

Weill, seated left, and "disciples" from the master class, Walther Geiser, Luc Balmer, and Wladimir Vogel, surrounding their teacher, Ferruccio Busoni. Notice Weill's rapt gaze.

An ambitious young man in a hurry, Kurt Weill was very much in the right place at the right time. No longer the somnolent provincial capital of Prussia, Berlin in the 1920s was a vital cultural mecca as well as the epicenter of a brand-new German Republic. Before the Great War, in the last vestiges of the Hohenzollern empire, Wilhelmine Germany had been locked in a bubble, almost completely isolated from foreign music, literature, and theatre. Paradoxically, military defeat, the end of the imperial age, and the demands of postwar recuperation opened Germany to cultural currents from abroad, and a period of cultural famine was followed by a rapturous reception of cultural imports, particularly American but also French, English, and Russian. The so-called Golden Twenties, however, when economic and political stability claimed a fragile victory, lasted only from 1925 to 1928. Crisis, in fact, was the usual order of the day, and the nearly crushing challenges faced by the new Germany—inflation, unemployment, factionalism among splinter parties of all political persuasions, a resurgent nationalist spirit with alarming premonitions, and a steadily

The young composer at work, in Berlin in the early 1920s

simmering anti-Semitism—created a context in which art not only could, but in a sense *had* to, flourish.

The turbulent zeitgeist was the fertile ground against which a swelling number of artistic firebrands played their work. To these creators a new society demanded new ways of making, teaching, and talking about art. In 1918, a group of expressionist painters and sculptors founded the Novembergruppe, naming themselves in honor of the revolution that signaled Germany's abrupt turn from monarchy to (a very uncertain) democracy. By 1921, the membership included playwrights, architects, and musicians dedicated to liberating their work from academic traditions. Shredding the elitist aura of cultural offerings in the Wilhelmine period, and determined to make their work socially useful as well as entertaining, the Novembergruppe artists consciously addressed a broad popular audience. In 1919 the group established Workers' Councils for Art and sponsored new-music concerts, public art exhibits, and film screenings, usually framed by lectures and discussions.

At the time the Novembergruppe was formed, Weill was a budding elitist under the influence of a high-art sensibility; but in 1921, when fellow Busoni student Philipp Jarnach invited him to join the Novembergruppe democrats, Weill readily agreed. Membership conferred immediate entrée into the Weimar avant-garde. Painters Max Pechstein and César Klein, the original cofounders, invited Emil Nolde, Max Beckmann, Wassily Kandinsky, and Paul Klee to join. Walter Gropius, the founder in 1919 of the Bauhaus, and expressionist Erich Mendelsohn, led the architect-members. Ernst Toller headed a group of young radical playwrights. As a new musician-member Weill entered a group that included, in addition to Jarnach, Alban Berg, Paul Hindemith, George Antheil, Stefan Wolpe, Hanns Eisler, and H. H. Stuckenschmidt. Although Weill's period of active membership was brief, in the Novembergruppe he was indoctrinated into ideas about socially useful art that remained a part of his work for the rest of his life.

The Novembergruppe radicals represented only a fragment of Berlin's cultural ferment. Ranging in size from minuscule to grandiose, there were over eighty legitimate theatres. Leading directors included Max Reinhardt, master of all theatrical forms, who was also a pioneer in the new genre of political cabaret. Sets with steeply raked steps dominated Leopold Jessner's bold reinterpretations of classic works. Incorporating film clips, posters, and placards in documentary-style dramas that were to have a decisive impact on the formation of Brecht and Weill's epic theatre, Erwin Piscator was the leader of the political stage. Served by an active native film industry—Robert Wiene, F. W. Murnau, G. W. Pabst, and Fritz Lang were among the most renowned directors—Berlin boasted over two hundred movie houses. After 1923 a flood of American films, with settings, characters, and pacing that delighted many Berliners, was finally released.

Although Germany had long had a distinguished classical music tradition, in the Weimar Republic it thrived as never before. After the war, at a cost of nearly three million marks, the Staatsoper on Unter den Linden was rebuilt. The city also established its own opera house, the Städtische Oper in Charlottenburg. In 1927 the Staatsoper formed an independent company, popularly known as the Krolloper, and from 1927 until 1931, under the inspired if erratic direction of the high-strung Otto Klemperer, it was arguably the most progressive opera house in the world. Throughout the dizzying cycles of economic boom and bust, the Prussian state provided substantial subsidies so that Berliners could continue to attend operas and concerts on a regular basis.

Besieged Berliners, as always, listened to music of the past, to the works of Beethoven, Bach, and Mozart, in particular. But in increasing numbers they were also receptive to new kinds of music—to the free tonality of

Schoenberg and his disciples, and to an American import called jazz that seemed enticingly exotic to many Germans only recently liberated from a prolonged cultural exile. "We all went to hear Paul Whiteman at the Grosses Schauspielhaus in 1926," Weill's friend and contemporary the writer Felix Jackson recalled. "We heard Gershwin's *Rhapsody in Blue*— thrilling, a terrific experience, because nobody had ever heard this kind of thing: a symphony using jazz. Kurt was there, and fascinated."[4] "We went to nightclubs where some American jazz bands—negroes, colored people—played something we had never heard; it was like somebody in America hearing a tune from the Eskimos," according to Hans Heinsheimer.[5]

The jazz that Berliners most often heard, however, was at least two steps removed from the real thing. Paul Whiteman's sound was a smoother, commercial marketing of the New Orleans original, while the homegrown jazz bands that began to appear in Berlin cabarets played an even more corrupted version. But it hardly mattered. However inaccurately translated, "jazz" quickly became an emblem of the openness and modernity of Weimar culture. And the hot new style from Germany's conquerors began to infiltrate all kinds of musical performances, from revue and cabaret to the concert hall and the opera house. As such jazz-based elements as syncopation, improvisation, a greater use of wind instruments, and a driving percussive beat mixed with native expressionist and atonal idioms, a fusion was born that was to prepare the way for Kurt Weill's music-theatre hybrids.

Weill first incorporated hints of the new sound in *Royal Palace,* a one-act opera he finished early in 1926, but a 1927 work by Ernst Krenek called *Jonny spielt auf (Johnny Strikes Up),* which ended with a black musician (played by a white actor in blackface) leading his jazz band on top of a spinning globe, was the first major "jazz opera." The title character, however, has only a supporting role, and "jazz" in fact claims only a modest portion of Krenek's musical program. But the composer's stabs at a shimmy, a Charleston, and a blues song had an intoxicating impact—in rhythm and melody Krenek's sporadic pop numbers were unprecedented on the German operatic stage. "It is *not* a jazz opera," Krenek observed, many years after its astonishing contemporary success. "That's really just a catch phrase. I wrote under a 'foreign' influence, it is true, but it was primarily French rather than American composers. In Paris earlier in the twenties I had met Milhaud, Poulenc, Honegger, and found their music more easygoing and not so ponderous and introspective as the music of the

German composers. I used a little 'jazz,' if you will, but the Paul Whiteman kind, not the real New Orleans kind. From our perspective, 'jazz' represented a new musical outlook, it was what in Germany was later called Gebrauchsmusik—music for use, not for the library. Music as entertainment, for easy reception. It expressed a new atmosphere and a New World, of which, frankly, we didn't know anything."[6] But Krenek's appropriations of an American sound he didn't know much about earned for his essentially romantic opera a success that now seems almost unimaginable. Following the 1927 premiere, there were scores of performances throughout Germany. The work's reception was a sign not only of how German audiences yearned to hear popular American sounds, even when they were embedded in a resistant medium, but also of how opera was a potentially big business.

"Jazz" exploded at full force in Weill's work for the first time in the *Mahagonny-Songspiel;* and although there were fleeting glimpses in earlier pieces, his first four theatre compositions, a children's pantomime and three one-act operas, had quite different musical roots. The pantomime, *Zaubernacht (Magic Night),* was Weill's first theatre score, commissioned and composed in the summer of 1922 and produced at the fashionable Theater am Kurfürstendamm the following November on a double bill with Stravinsky's *Petrushka.* As reconstructed by David Drew, Wladimir Boritsch's scenario is a charming dream play in which, as a boy and girl fall asleep, their toys and storybook characters leap to life and a fairy's magic spell transports the dreamers to a land of enchantment. Writing music for a dream danced by children, Weill, from the first a collaborative dramatist taking his cues from a text, adopted a lighter, more free-flowing style than the dense idiom in which he was composing absolute music at the time. Looking back in 1930, Weill himself described *Zaubernacht* as "the first work in which the simple style can be recognized."[7] Felix Jackson, who saw the production, noted that Weill "had to write simplified harmonies and pleasant melodies to adjust to his little audience," and recalled that "the enthusiastic response of the children had a great effect on Kurt. Here for the first time he experienced a spontaneous, happy reaction to his work instead of the respectful analytical approval in which his previous efforts had been received by his esoteric peers. It was the first cue for him to think in terms of creating on a broader basis."[8]

Performed at matinees only, *Zaubernacht* received scant critical notice. But the show caught the attention of Georg Kaiser, "the Eugene O'Neill of Germany."[9] Learning that Kaiser had enjoyed the pantomime, Weill, as

Kaiser's wife, Margarethe, recalled, "wrote, saying he had read and admired Kaiser's works and wished to make his acquaintance, perhaps even the possibility of a collaboration. Kaiser had an open heart for young artists, and when he met Kurt he took to him at once. He liked Kurt's humor, that little grin he had, and they were full of jokes."[10] Weill persuaded Kaiser that *Der Protagonist,* a one-act play Kaiser had written in 1920, would make a promising libretto for a short opera. Set in Elizabethan England, Kaiser's play is about a troupe of strolling players whose tyrannical director, the Protagonist, has an incestuous attachment to his sister. The Protagonist rehearses his company in a bawdy commedia dell' arte pantomime he expects to perform for a duke and his court. However, when he is informed that a bishop is to be an unexpected guest of the duke, he must quickly rework the piece, and he transforms the farce into a tragedy about a deceived husband. In rehearsal, at the height of a transforming passion, when his sister presents him to her lover, the actor momentarily confuses life and art and stabs his sister to death. He then asks to be allowed to finish his performance before he is arrested.

Weill worked with Kaiser from the summer of 1924 through the following April to transform the short, intense play into an opera. On his first visit to Kaiser's isolated country house in Grünheide, southeast of the city, located on one of the small lakes that form an unbroken chain around the outskirts of Berlin, the playwright's au pair was dispatched to meet Weill at the train station and to row him across the lake. The young woman, Lotte Lenya, with a crooked grin and coarse features, exuded an electric sensuality. Lenya remembered herself as a child asking her mother if she would ever be pretty. "No, but you will always be attractive to men," her wise mother answered.[11] On the ride across the lake, as Lenya enjoyed recounting, she sensed the composer's strong interest in her. And on her side, she liked Kurt's sly smile, his air of confidence, and his intellect. Despite the steep differences in their backgrounds—the beautifully educated composer came from a cultivated middle-class Jewish family; Lenya was a poorly educated gentile who had been raised in crushing poverty in a Viennese slum—she sensed at once that they spoke a common language.

With fatherly interest, Kaiser watched the growing attraction between the two young people who had become an intimate part of his daily life. In May 1925, he offered Kurt the use of his small Berlin apartment. Lenya moved in, although she also spent time with the Kaisers in their house by the lake. To still the gossip of neighbors, or so Lenya liked to claim, she and Kurt decided, after six months of living together, that they really

RIGHT: Lenya in 1925, shortly before her marriage to Kurt, striking a dancerlike pose
BELOW: Lenya and Weill on their wedding day, January 28, 1926. In the paper bag that Kurt is carrying is the couple's wedding dinner, herring and jelly.

ought to marry, which they did in a civil ceremony in Charlottenburg on January 28, 1926. But Weill by then was so preoccupied with plans for the premiere of his and Kaiser's opera that the newlyweds were unable to take a honeymoon until June.

Der Protagonist opened on March 27, 1926, at the magnificently appointed Dresden State Opera. Weill attended with his wife (to whom he dedicated the opera) and with Felix Jackson. "Lenya and I sat there scared stiff—Lenya was actually shaking," Jackson recalled. "Every German opera house is conservative, and we didn't know how the audience would respond. A breeze of surprise went through the audience as they realized they were confronted with an atonal work. The harmonies were unfamiliar, the musical lines short and not immediately recognizable. There were no ingratiating triads. But there was theatrical impact, the clarity and transparency of the instrumentation reminiscent of Richard Strauss. In spite of the atonal structure, one could recognize themes and passages based on an idiom of folk music, already containing the germ of Kurt Weill's future development. But the impatience of the listeners was growing."[12]

Weill disputed the "atonal" designation ("atonal is nothing but a word; you don't put a key [signature] ahead of your notes, that's all. The only important thing is that you have something to say"),[13] but nonetheless cleverly implanted a textual "correction" to the work's dissonant, harmonically unresolved quality. At the finale, eight musicians moved to the front of the stage to perform a fanfare in D major, and as Jackson witnessed, the audience, "relieved they could hear 'real'—what they considered 'real'—music were tremendously relieved. And the impact of their relief brought them to their feet. The audience hadn't heard a major chord for three-quarters of an hour. Everything else was forgotten. This was theatre! What a cunning guy Kurt was!"[14]

"It was a tremendous success," Lenya said. "Forty curtain calls, and Kurt disappeared. 'Where's the composer? Where's the composer?' they yelled. He was down in the orchestra, saying his thanks. Hertzka, the publisher from Vienna, shrewd, shrewd as hell, invited us for lunch the next day."[15]

"It really is exciting to become a world celebrity overnight," Kurt wrote to his parents on April 1. "My telephone won't stop for a minute. And always the same honest enthusiasm. Who would have thought of that!" "There has never been such a successful first opera by a twenty-five-year-old," Weill wrote to his publisher on April 29.

Reflecting the Protagonist's struggle to subdue his inner volcano, Weill

had composed a score of extraordinary intensity. The part of the Protagonist, scored for heldentenor, makes heroic acting and vocal demands.
Weill's dense, difficult, thickly textured writing, with none of the melodic
seductions that would begin to surface in his theatre work within a
year, nonetheless bristles with an acute theatrical intelligence: his contrasting treatments of two pantomimes—the first comic, the second tragic—
demonstrates his already ripened skill in creating character and story
through music. "The music does not illustrate the action: it *is* the action,"
as the conductor Maurice Abravanel wrote in a contemporary review. "The
text conveys the external, visible drama. On a more profound plane, the
music explains the psychological action, which is inaccessible through language."[16]

Before his first opera had had its premiere, Weill with characteristic speed
had already begun to collaborate with another prominent literary figure,
the French-German surrealist poet and playwright Ivan Goll. At the end
of 1924, when Goll traveled to Berlin to attend the opening of his play
Methusalem, he met Weill at the Kaisers', where he and his wife were
guests. "The two men liked each other right away," Claire Goll remembered, and Weill, who wanted to compose a musical setting for Goll's
poem "Der neue Orpheus," "urged Ivan to work with him."[17] Pleased with
the results, a sixteen-minute cantata, Weill asked Goll to write an opera
libretto, and this time the writer rather than the composer suggested the
subject. Inspired by the lakeside setting of a hotel in which he and Claire
had spent a vacation in Italy in 1925, Goll wrote a libretto, *Royal Palace,*
about romantic entanglements in a hotel overlooking a lake. The enchant-
ingly named heroine, Dejanira, resists three suitors—her husband, yesterday's lover, and tomorrow's lover—who attempt to woo her with fantasies
and dreams. But the lake holds more allure for the bewitched heroine than
any of her flesh-and-blood courtiers, and at the end she drowns herself.
Subtitled "a tragic revue," *Royal Palace* is an opera with a vaudeville structure, "a stylistic free-for-all"[18] in thirty-eight scenes that includes a ballet,
a pantomime, acted drama, and film. For the first time Weill injects some
jazz into his writing, but only in fragments and transfigured into bold harmonic settings. As in *Der Protagonist,* the score offers a heavy melange of
compositional techniques, here leavened by his use of more extended (and
more graspable) forms. For example, Dejanira is introduced by a phantas-
magoric ballet that has the clear rhythmic profile of a tarantella. In another
passage, to accompany the suitors' fetishistic caress of the separate sylla-

bles of the heroine's name, Weill spins a series of Berg-like rhythmic variations on a fox-trot. Here he might have achieved a relaxed, jazzy depiction of Dejanira's character—his fox-trot tune is stylish. But Weill wrenches it around harmonically and traps it beneath chromatically complex vocal lines. The poor fox-trot barely survives. Throughout, there are similarly fleeting intimations of Weill's later, more confident populist style. *Royal Palace* is a cautious step in his gradual release from a densely contrapuntal style steeped in expressionist dissonance.

On March 2, 1927, the composer's twenty-seventh birthday, *Royal Palace* opened at the Berlin Staatsoper on a triple bill with *Der neue Orpheus* and Falla's *Master Peter's Puppet Show.* "The impact is extraordinary and interest is constantly rising," Weill wrote to Universal Edition on March 23, adopting the postopening cheerleader tone he typically used in correspondence with his publisher. "[It has been] heralded as a great success in most of the provincial papers and especially in the foreign press (America!) . . . I think it would be important for tactical reasons if you began an effective publicity campaign." Weill's ebullience was short-lived, for after its initial seven performances in Berlin *Royal Palace* was to be staged only once more in his lifetime, for two performances in Essen in 1929, after which the score was lost.

Weill's third and final opera in his early difficult style was another collaboration with Georg Kaiser. *Der Zar lässt sich photographieren (The Czar Has His Photograph Taken),* which Weill started to work on in March 1927, was an opera buffa on a slight theme, a kind of proto–*Roman Holiday* in which the title character travels incognito in Paris in order to savor nonroyal freedom. As part of his madcap jaunt, the Czar arranges to have his photograph taken at the fashionable salon of Madame Angèle. But terrorists on the Czar's trail break into the studio before his arrival, slip a revolver into the camera, and replace the true Angèle with an impostor, for whom the Czar quickly develops an attraction. What follows—the false Angèle tries to maneuver the amorous Czar into sitting for his "photograph"—is in effect a coitus interruptus, a comic courtship danced on the rim of death. After the Czar's bodyguards announce that assassins may be in the building, the terrorists flee, the true Angèle returns to her post, and the Czar, who knows nothing, finally accomplishes what the title promises: he does indeed have his photograph taken.

Set in Paris in 1914, on the eve of a war that was to change forever the status of royalty, Kaiser's droll, brisk, carefree libretto sidesteps politics. The revolutionaries are as silly as the randy Czar and his retainers, and the

ABOVE: Weill on the set of *Der Zar lässt sich photographieren,* with Ilse Koegel (Angèle), left, and Maria Janowska (False Angèle), and an important prop, the camera that will shoot the Czar

BELOW: The full set for *Der Zar lässt sich photographieren* and a chorus of white-bearded gentlemen standing in the orchestra pit, the composer's "Brechtian" touch two years before he began collaborating with Brecht

false Angèle is not essentially different from the original. At times Weill's often overwrought score crashes intentionally against Kaiser's light, farcical scenario. But overall, as Weill wrote in a May 15, 1927, letter to his parents, his work was "getting to be much freer, looser, and simpler," a fact he attrributed to living with Lenya. Weill's harmonic language this time is more nearly tonal than in *Der Protagonist* or *Royal Palace,* and his sparing but persuasive use of jazz and dance rhythms introduces a few bright accents. There are enticing traces throughout of the populist composer almost, but not quite, ready to emerge. But near the finale, there's an astonishing passage that reveals Weill as a full-fledged melody maker. The Czar and his would-be conquest dance to a "Tango Angèle" played on a gramophone that sets the number in a frame of its own. The tango itself is lovely. Sultry and impetuous, it begins and ends in A minor, with frequent digressions to distant keys like E-flat minor. In its central section, Weill takes it to A major and has the soprano float long high B's over it. The effect is stunning: simultaneously heavenly and corny, ecstatic and meretricious— perfect for this scene of sexual allure and deception. And, brilliantly, the only musical accompaniment comes from a scratchy gramophone. Like Weill's use of film in *Royal Palace,* the gramophone represents a new technology that underscores the composer's own "modern" touch. But the theatrical inspiration for the scene is essentially Mozartean. The characters sing to a piece of popular music that is presented as if it existed outside the world of the opera, a device that recalls the act 2 banquet scene in *Don Giovanni,* in which Giovanni and Leporello, accompanied by an onstage band, sing over and around popular operatic tunes of Mozart's day, including one of his own. And in Weill's score, just as in Mozart's, the action of the scene continues as the onstage music develops: The police knock on the door; the conspirators emerge from their hiding places; the lovers must decide whether to flee or stay. All begin to sing their individual thoughts, which will soon force them apart, and yet all are momentarily held together in the sensual spell of the tango. A perfect melding of music to scenario, the moment is breathtaking, a genuine coup de théâtre.

The premiere took place at the Leipzig Opera on February 18, 1928, seven months after the *Mahagonny-Songspiel* had presented the "new" Kurt Weill and almost a year after the composer had begun working with a new collaborator.

Although there are differing accounts of how Brecht and Weill met, it is generally agreed that their active collaboration did not begin until early in the spring of 1927, when Weill needed a libretto for a one-act opera he had been commissioned to write for the German Chamber Music Festival in Baden-Baden that summer. Continuing his already established pattern of seeking out writers, he was eager to meet Brecht. In a weekly theatre column he wrote for *Der deutsche Rundfunk* he had hailed Brecht's *Mann ist Mann* as "perhaps the most novel and powerful theatrical work of our time,"[19] and he also admired the dry, astringent, scurrilous flavor of Brecht's *Die Hauspostille (Domestic Breviary),* a book of poems in the form of ironic hymns, prayers, and sermons. Weill was especially interested in five 1922 poems about a mythical city called Mahagonny, located in a fancifully conceived America. (The name of Brecht's imaginary city may have

come from a 1922 popular song, "Komm nach Mahagonne," composed by Leopold Krauss-Elka with lyrics by O. A. Roberts.)

In his first meeting with Brecht, Weill, who like many Berliners shared the playwright's fascination with America, the great new world power, expressed his keen interest in musicalizing the Mahagonny poems. The idea also to use the poems for the one-act opera for Baden-Baden was almost an afterthought, and at any rate a detour from their ultimate goal, which was to use the poems as the basis of a full-length opera written in a new style that would challenge opera-house decorum. For the short work, Weill decided to set the poems in song form—he and Brecht used the English word "song" to

BB in his standard leather costume, with his omnipresent cigar and his characteristically challenging gaze denote a popular, cabaret, or jazz kind of melodic structure as opposed to an art song or lied.

"Up to that time Weill had written relatively complicated music of a mainly psychological sort, and when he agreed to set a series of more or less banal song texts he was making a courageous break with a prejudice which the solid bulk of serious composers stubbornly held," Brecht observed. "The success of this attempt to apply modern music to the *song* was significant."[20] Despite its title, however, the *Mahagonny-Songspiel* is not simply a collection of discrete songs; rather, Weill supplies a continuous musical fabric in which (mostly tonal) songs alternate with (mostly atonal or polytonal) instrumental interludes leading up to the climactic appearance of the God-figure and the concluding Judgment Day fortissimos. The work is remarkably integrated and provides coherence to a text that has no dialogue, no individual characters, and only the barest hints of a story line. It was the fact that songs had been embedded in a sophisticated musical texture with distinct high-cultural overtones that was to cause either delight or outrage on July 17 in Baden-Baden.

Weill's electrifying synthesis of "high" and "low" musical forms is nowhere more evident than in the "Alabama-Song." Its construction is rough-hewn: verse, chorus, repeat. The verses ("Oh, show us the way. . . .") are built around an utterly simple three-note melody that is musically answered by a second, equivalent three-note melody ("Oh, don't ask why. . . ."). Weill uses these six notes to set the text in a defiantly primitive way: The vocal rhythm is monotonous, absurd; the notes, repeated over and over, seem to weave back and forth in their confined space, to stumble drunkenly over each other. The band accompanies this with an unvarying oompah. Yet, overall, these verses have an unforgettable sound because of Weill's harmony, which alternates between two great chordal blocks, C minor and C-sharp minor, that shift in lockstep with the two three-note melodies. As the verse progresses, the two harmonic "blocks" begin to seesaw more urgently, there is a staccato punctuation, a brief transitional riff, and then we are launched headlong into the tune of the chorus ("Oh, moon of Alabama . . ."), expansive, heartfelt, musically conventional—everything the verse tune was not. This chorus won't let us go. Weill leads us through it once more, manipulating the end (as is conventional in song forms) to provide a full cadence. Then there is one more rhythmic punctuation, one more full stop, and we are back without warning in the dark world of the verse. And so it goes, a journey through bars, dollars, and boys. Weill's orchestration recalls the contemporary sound of Berlin dance bands while also suggesting a debt to Stravinsky. The scoring itself—with its emphasis on woodwinds and brass, the sparing use of the piano to supply bright accents and ostinatos, or simply stride-type song accompaniments, and percussion to simulate the American jazz drummers—evokes Stravinsky's orchestration in *A Soldier's Tale.* Moreover, the blocklike harmonic construction—the "jump cuts" from key to key, song verse to song chorus, instrumental phrase to instrumental phrase—shows a rejection of the old Germanic ideals of development, modulation, and counterpoint in favor of a bright, lean, Stravinskian aesthetic.

To underscore their assault on operatic tradition, Weill and Brecht wanted to cast their "antiopera" with operatic voices. It was only after an opera singer who had been engaged as one of the prostitutes became indisposed that Weill thought of casting Lenya. In a story she liked to tell long after the fact, Lenya, who could not read music ("Don't learn," Kurt told her; "I'm so happy to have married a girl who can't"),[21] maintained that she had to audition for Brecht. Weill invited Brecht to their Luisenplatz pied-à-terre so that Lenya could perform the "Alabama-Song" for him. Before he arrived, Weill was extremely nervous—rarely anxious on his own account, he was always to be agitated when something was at stake for Lenya—and began pacing back and forth between the cramped bedroom and the slightly larger living room dominated by a grand piano and pitch-black wooden furniture. "Brecht came in, exactly at five, very cordial, very gentle, very patient, as he always was with women and actors," Lenya recalled. Lenya had surely met Brecht before, but this was her first sustained encounter with him, and her memories of it remained vivid for the rest of her life. "When he arrived, I thought he had the frailness of tough herring. He had small white feminine hands that, on that occasion and always after, were grimy, with short black fingernails. His shoulders were a little stooped, and he had a stringy neck. His dull brown hair was cropped Russian proletarian style. His dark brown eyes, set very close together, deeply sunk in, were never still, constantly blinking, always registering his reaction to whatever was being said." A cigar dangling from his mouth, he had "wretched teeth, many of them black stumps." His Bavarian accent lent "a softening lilt" to his speech. Despite his evident "mania for filth," he had "a baffling way of looking almost neat." Clearly even then "a towering egotist," he had already cultivated a style, "the Brecht style," that was to be imitated by all the "male disciples under his persuasion"—a group that Weill was never to join. Immediately, "back of all his maneuvers, back of all the charm," Lenya sensed "a gnawing concern for his own myth" and a compulsion to assess others for "what they could contribute to him. He invariably got what he was after."[22]

Lenya began to sing the "Alabama-Song," moving responsively to its strong percussive rhythm, looking vaguely in the general direction of an imaginary audience. When she reached the soaring refrain, "Oh, moon of Alabama," she stood still, her hands folded behind her. Brecht interrupted. "Now, let's really work on it," he said. Brecht directed her to "take in the whole audience, asking them to help her find the next whiskey bar." And when she got to the refrain, he told her to do exactly the opposite of what she had done, to forget the audience and "pour out her sorrow to the moon," raising her right hand in a sweeping gesture. "Kurt relaxed the moment we set to work. I could see he had confidence in me and in Brecht, in the way Brecht was understanding the music. Afterwards, we all went to dinner at Schlichter's, and were very happy."[23]

With only one performance (for a distinguished international audience), Brecht and Weill's incendiary mock-opera created a ruckus. "The sensational success in Baden-Baden has resulted in an abundance of excellent reviews which I'll be sending you since you plan to begin a major publicity campaign for the work," Weill wrote Universal Edition on August 4. "Perhaps you could have the 'Alabama-Song,' which you wanted to publish separately, arranged by one of your popular music specialists for voice, piano and violin and then sent to me for inspection." Ten days later, he informed his publisher that he had "an opportunity to promote the piece as a pop-song in America." Commercial producers approached Weill with an offer of incorporating the *Mahagonny-Songspiel* into a larger revue. "This would be excellent preparation for the opera," he wrote Universal Edition on October 16. "You can easily see the possibilities for musical sales (the 'Alabama-Song!!') with such a revue performance." But the *Mahagonny-Songspiel* did not get tucked into a splashy big revue, and after its single famous performance it was neither published nor promoted. (It was, however, performed again, in expanded form, in Paris in 1932 and in London and Rome in 1933, primarily as a showcase for Lenya.)

Although the "Alabama-Song" achieved some renown, there were no other immediate dividends from the show. Weill returned to work on *Der Zar* with Kaiser while continuing to plan the full-length *Mahagonny* with Brecht, a project that was to engage them on and off for the next two years. In September 1927, working on his own, Weill wrote a brooding, primarily nontonal musical setting for "Vom Tod im Wald" ("A Death in the Forest"), another poem from Brecht's *Hauspostille*. With flowing lines and only

A happy collaboration—at the time: Weill, Lenya, and Brecht in 1927,
working on the *Mahagonny-Songspiel*

scattered suggestions of melody, the ten-minute ballad for solo bass and
ten wind instruments, which had its premiere performance at the Berlin
Philharmonic Hall on November 23, 1927, indicated that the young maverick of the summer was not ready to make a clean break from his earlier
commitments.

The real payoff for the *Mahagonny-Songspiel* was to come nearly a year
later.

THREE

Night Sounds

Ernst Josef Aufricht, a former actor, was determined to present a new show on his birthday, August 31, at a theatre he had just bought. But as of March 1928, he had not yet booked an opening attraction. When an acquaintance at Schlichter's introduced him to Brecht, semifamous as a renegade author of plays such as *Baal* and *In the Jungle of Cities*, both of which simmer with homoerotic undertones, and as half of the team that had caused a stir at last summer's new-music festival, Aufricht asked if he had a suitable script. Brecht mentioned an adaptation of *The Beggar's Opera*, a 1728 show that had recently had a successful revival in London. Aufricht smelled a hit—or so, at any rate, he was to claim in his memoirs. The next morning, in a driving rain, he sent a messenger to fetch what was no more than an unfinished translation of *The Beggar's Opera* that Brecht's assistant, Elisabeth Hauptmann, had prepared. After looking it over, Aufricht decided that this bawdy show spiced with contemporary satiric jabs was exactly what he was looking for.

The London revival had used the original score, a potpourri of popular songs of the time arranged by Dr. Johann Christoph Pepusch, but Brecht suggested that his new collaborator, Kurt Weill, could furnish a new score. Aufricht was skeptical. "My husband, who wanted the original music, referred to Weill negatively as a very Neutöner [one who invents new sounds]," as Margot Aufricht recalled.[1] To his credit, Brecht, infamous for betraying colleagues, was firm about including Weill on the project, and reluctantly Aufricht agreed to allow the *Neutöner* to compose a few songs—in other words, to audition.

Before a select audience that included Aufricht and his wife, Brecht, Lenya, Robert Vambery (the new theatre's dramaturg), and Theo Mackeben (who would conduct whichever score was to be chosen), Weill sang a few of his songs, accompanying himself on a piano that had been rolled onto a bare stage. "Oh my, he was really a bad player, and his voice, he really couldn't sing either," Madame Aufricht said. "But he had something very special. It came over, and Vambery went to my husband and whispered, 'The music has at least such a chance for success as the text.' And so, that was the audition. And then Lenya said, 'My husband will write a song for me, too.'"[2]

Because Aufricht was determined to open on his birthday, Weill and Brecht had to work quickly. By June they had finished a first draft, and in July they traveled to Le Lavandou on the French Riviera to work on revisions. With them was Elisabeth Hauptmann, a key player in Brecht's usual entourage of female companions. It was Hauptmann—who, unlike Brecht, spoke and read English fluently and kept abreast of theatrical offerings in London and New York—who had suggested *The Beggar's Opera* to her boss. As Margot Aufricht observed, "Elisabeth Hauptmann did everything for Brecht, a charming woman, and she's never really mentioned."[3] (Determining how much Brecht there is in *Die Dreigroschenoper* and in most of the other plays has become a cottage industry among Brecht scholars—John Fuegi's accusations in *Brecht & Co.* [1994] sparked an international debate.[4]) Certainly Brecht depended on Hauptmann's skill in English and her knowledge of an age and culture—eighteenth-century London—he knew little about. But his adaptation, with Weill's fresh score, is an essentially new work that turns the world of John Gay's London into a doppelgänger for late-Weimar Berlin.

The Beggar's Opera was an ill-mannered box-office smash. Impishly calling itself a "Newgate Pastoral"—Newgate was a festering prison—John Gay's musical fable was conceived as a challenge to the Handelian opera that was all the rage in 1720s London. Interspersed throughout Gay's satiric portrait of underworld characters who ape the manner of the gentry are sixty-nine airs based on favorite songs of the time, mostly English but also Irish, Scottish, Italian, and French. Selected by Gay, who wrote new lyrics, and Dr. Pepusch, who provided new arrangements, the popular melodies included folk songs ("Greensleeves" would be the most familiar today), barroom ballads, dances, and borrowings from Handel and Henry Purcell. Gay's ballad opera was designed as a counter-opera, the 1728 equivalent of a rowdy musical comedy. (Ballad operas, which continued to hold the stage in England through the nineteenth century, are cognate with French opéra comique and German singspiel, a form Brecht and Weill had reinvented in their little *Mahagonny*.) Gay replaced recitative with spoken dialogue. Sometimes the songs carry the narrative forward; more often they stop the show with wry or saucy asides about sex and money. Brecht and Weill wisely retained the number-opera structure and general tone of their prototype, similarly intending their beggar's opera as a kick in the pants to grand opera as well as a template for a new kind of music theatre. If Handelian opera was the paradigm against which Gay had written in 1728, the Wagnerian Gesamtkunstwerk was Weill's anti-text two hundred years later. Like his teacher Ferruccio Busoni, Weill was convinced that the Wagnerian operatic model, with its continuous musical fabric, had to be discarded and that to renew itself opera had to alternate musical numbers with passages of dialogue. "What we were setting out to create was the earliest form of opera," Weill said. "This return to a primitive operatic form entailed a drastic simplification of musical language. It meant writing a kind of music that would be singable by actors, in other words by musical amateurs. . . . Nothing but the introduction of approachable, catchy tunes made possible [the show's] real achievement: the creation of a new type of musical theatre. . . . Like nearly all worthwhile operatic experiments of recent years, [*Die Dreigroschenoper*] was written as a destructive work, [an attack on opera's] splendid isolation."[5]

Brecht and Weill kept the main characters and general outline of Gay's libretto. Gay's lowlife characters are a ribald, scrappy gaggle of double-dealers. Macheath, his rakish, cunning antihero, is an infamous highwayman with the bearing of a gentleman. Jonathan Peachum, an entrepreneur of the new capitalism, runs a thriving business outfitting false beggars in order to extract money from gullible Christians. After the highwayman marries Peachum's daughter, Polly (as deeply bourgeois as Macheath), Peachum in league with the prison warden Lockit (police chief Tiger Brown in Brecht's adaptation), whose daughter Lucy is also involved with Macheath, conspires to have his upstart son-in-law arrested and then executed—poached for a price. Twice Macheath escapes from prison; twice he is betrayed by one of his whores. Only at the last minute, with a deus ex machina that celebrates its own improbability, is he reprieved.

Theatre historians have noted the topical nature of much of Gay's satire: the excesses of the then-popular Italian opera; the contemporary infatuation with criminals; the misbehavior of political figures such as Sir Robert Walpole, Britain's head of state famed for bribery, wenching, drinking, and general vulgarity; the rivalry between two of Handel's sopranos, the elegant Faustina and the rotund Cuzzoni, who the year before had attacked each other onstage. But the play can be savored with little or no knowledge of the actual world and persons of Gay's London; rising above the topical targets are the timeless sins of greed and lust which Gay's Rabelaisian characters commit with zest. In distinctive ways, the collaborators updated and localized their source. Brecht replaced Gay's orotund, eighteenth-century declamation with a profane, no-frills Berlin bite; using one of the original airs to begin the first act, Weill substituted the sounds of modern Berlin-style jazz for the rest of the score. The dry, detached, contemporary tone which they shrewdly grafted onto their urtext was, at least in a general sense, part of a larger movement called *Neue Sachlichkeit,* or New Objectivity, that had come to replace expressionism as the principal lingua franca of artistic experiment in Weimar Germany. In earlier work, Weill in his one-act operas and Brecht in visionary plays such as *Baal* and *Drums in the Night* had certainly used elements of expressionist intensity and distortion; but the new factual style appealed to them. Their cool, "scientific" musical shared the clarity and rationality prized by such other contemporary postexpressionist works as objective paintings and realistic street films.

As Weill and Brecht and his entourage were working on last-minute alterations on the Riviera, completing their transformation of *The Beggar's Opera* into a Berlin musical in a new style, their producer assembled his creative team. In addition to Theo Mackeben, a close friend who had been hired first, Aufricht appointed Erich Engel as director and Brecht's childhood friend Caspar Neher as designer. "They liked it very much when they heard who was hired," Margot Aufricht recalled.[6] Following the coauthors' instructions, Aufricht and Engel cast singing actors rather than performers whose primary strength was singing. ("The show is in a very light, singable style, since it is to be performed by actors," Weill had written his publisher on June 4.) There wasn't an operatic trace in the voices of any of the actors. The lead, Harald Paulsen, with a standard operetta tenor, probably had the smoothest, prettiest voice in the company. But like Lenya, cast in the small but vivid role of a prostitute who betrays Macheath, all the performers could talk-sing the songs in the style that was to become an indelible part of Weill's Berlin signature. For Weill as well as Brecht, it was crucial that every word be heard clearly above the music. The parlando style, a rude refutation of operatic bel canto, was a key part of their mock-operatic intentions.

The initial euphoria evaporated once rehearsals started at the end of July. Brecht and Weill, who wanted to follow the example set by Gay of having the songs interrupt the show, clashed with Erich Engel, who, favoring a more conventional approach, wanted the music to be tucked smoothly into the action. As Margot Aufricht remembered, "Engel wanted to give up the directing, because Bertolt Brecht insisted on this very good thing where every time there was a song there came three lamps and the other light went out. Only in this light the songs were sung. And when the songs were finished, these lamps went up again and the normal light came on. Engel said no, he wasn't used to something like that—it should all, the whole show, be one. 'The songs have to be cut out completely,' he said in anger at one point. Of course, nobody agreed with this one."[7]

Although he had not yet formulated any of the so-called alienation theories that have clung like burrs to his work, Brecht knew he wanted the performers to sing with emotional detachment and in a space distinctly marked off from the dialogue scenes. "When an actor sings he undergoes a change of function," Brecht was to write later, theorizing a practical solution he had insisted on during the rehearsals. "Nothing is more revolting than when the actor pretends not to notice that he has left the level of plain speech and started to sing. . . . The actor must not only sing but show a man singing. His aim is not so much to bring out the emotional content of the song (has one the right to offer others a dish that one has already eaten oneself?) but to show gestures that are so to speak the habits and usage of the body. . . . As for the melody, he must not follow it blindly: there is a kind of speaking-against-the-music which can have strong effects, the result of a stubborn, incorruptible sobriety which is independent of music and rhythm. . . . When the actor drops into the melody, it must be an event."[8] Weill worked along with Brecht to ensure that his music was kept in its place. "I had before me a realistic plot and this forced me to make the music work against it if I was to prevent it from making a realistic impact.

Accordingly, the plot was either interrupted, making way for music, or else deliberately brought to a point where there was no alternative but to sing,"[9] he observed, looking back a few years after the show had opened.

As a further way of "demystifying" the songs, Brecht wanted the musicians visible throughout the show and asked Caspar Neher to create a space upstage for the jazz band. Neher placed the band on the steps of a large fairground organ, and on each side of the organ were large screens on which the title of each song was projected in bold letters. Announcements of the content of upcoming scenes and drawings that commented on and enlarged the play's social context also appeared on the screens. "Whatever it was, the style was completely different, the way Brecht wanted the music performed," Margot Aufricht said. "It startled the actors, who felt strange during the rehearsals."[10]

Although Erich Engel had been Brecht's "official" director, this time he became a strong-willed and often unsympathetic opponent. Engel was interested in motivation and psychology; Brecht and Weill were evolving their idea of what came to be called "gestic" acting and music. Marta Feuchtwanger, who with her husband, the writer Lion Feuchtwanger, attended numerous rehearsals, offered a clear eyewitness account of the "gestus": "It was Brecht's principle to show first a gesture before he lets the actors speak. He showed them what to do. It came from the chest. From the gesture came the role. The style of movement was primitive, but so new really, so poetical. Even with the best translation, you cannot give out how it was. . . . And that was also how Kurt Weill worked, also with the gesture and with the pauses, when he makes an interruption in the music."[11] Although it eludes precise translation, the gestus was part of the collaborators' attempts to create distance between actors and their roles by stressing external social relations over the inner psychological values Engel wanted to explore. Where Brecht interfered, Weill knew his place. Playing good cop to his partner's combative rogue cop, Weill whispered suggestions off to the side as Brecht barked commands. But in their vision of the kind of show they wanted *Die Dreigroschenoper* to be, they were as one.

Rehearsals rang with the complaints of the director and the actors about the style Brecht and Weill were asking for. With little confidence in the material, or in their ability to perform it in a strange new style, a number of the actors threatened to quit. Only Lenya felt secure. The most perplexed actor was Harald Paulsen, playing, or trying to play, Macheath. "I don't know what I'm doing," Paulsen complained to Felix Jackson, who attended rehearsals regularly. "I have no idea what the whole thing is about. I don't understand how to sing the music. I get different words every day. They're all maniacs. All I know is that it's a disaster."[12] Paulsen agreed to remain only if he could be allowed to wear a blue bow tie, which he felt gave him the key to playing Macheath as a bourgeois gentleman who just happened to make his living as a highwayman. But as opening night loomed, Paulsen developed other grievances. Having trouble performing a climactic number in act 3, "Ruf aus der Gruft" ("Call from the Grave"), which Weill had written to be sung at a staccato clip, Paulsen balked: Could Weill slow it down for him? "Do it as he wants," Weill told the conductor, Theo Mackeben.[13] Still feeling shaky, Paulsen asked Weill to write an opening number that would give Macheath a star entrance. Weill appreciated the theatrical wisdom of the actor's request and quickly composed "Moritat vom Mackie Messer" ("The Ballad of Mack the Knife").

After finishing the song, however, Brecht and Weill decided that it should be sung not by Macheath but by a street singer who would be telling a story in song, a Moritat, about Macheath. (The Moritat is a type of folk song, an account of a violent death, that Brecht had heard at fairs in his native Bavaria.) Paulsen was enraged. "His" number had been given to Kurt Gerron, who, according to Felix Jackson, "had no voice." The actor accused Brecht and Weill of being "double-crossing sons of bitches."[14] But Paulsen remained, and because he was a live wire on stage the writers wanted him to. "He was everything you could ask for," according to Viennese producer Norbert Gingold, who also attended many rehearsals. "Oh, he was an acrobatic Tänzer; he jumped out of a high cage. He would jump higher and higher, and then over the fence. But he used chemicals to keep it up—I saw him injecting drugs in his dressing room."[15] "By the time opening night came, Paulsen had it," as Lenya said. "Brecht and Weill's way of doing things, what they wanted from their actors, was pounded into him, and finally he understood."[16]

Unlike Paulsen, the female lead, Carola Neher, who was also a Berlin star, did not last until opening night. A few days before, for purely personal reasons (her husband, the poet who had taken the pen name of Klabund, was dying in Zurich), she departed. Cabaret performer Roma Bahn, able to learn "this strange music in four days," as Margot Aufricht said,[17] stepped into the role of Polly at the eleventh hour.

Adding to the swelling chaos was the late-in-the-day departure of yet another cast member. Helene Weigel, the future Mrs. Bertolt Brecht, withdrew suddenly when she contracted appendicitis. As strong-willed as

Brecht, and attuned to the style he was in the process of refining, Weigel had been creatively embroidering her one-scene part as a brothel madam; just before she left, she had decided that her character was legless. "Thank god she got sick," Margot Aufricht said. "She was getting stranger and stranger during rehearsals. The scene [which was cut] would have been gross."[18] Another cabaret star, Rosa Valetti, playing Mrs. Peachum, hurled another last-minute grenade when she refused to sing "Ballade von der sexuellen Hörigkeit" ("The Ballad of Sexual Dependency") because of the raw lyrics. And her husband, who was also her agent, had so little confidence in the play's success that, as Margot Aufricht recalled, "he made another contract for her, because he said the show wouldn't go two days."[19]

As tempers erupted, and surrounded by a growing number of naysayers, Brecht and Weill remained remarkably unfazed. "They felt they had the feeling for it and that it would be something, period," according to Margot Aufricht.[20] At this point, the competitiveness that would ultimately destroy their partnership was kept at a low simmer. At least publicly, they quarreled only once, during the rushed composition of the opening number. Marta Feuchtwanger, who was present at one of the sessions during which they hammered out the Moritat, remembered an atmosphere edged with resentment. "Brecht, who was never satisfied with Weill's compositions, said to Weill, who was improvising at an upright piano, 'I'll sing you now what I think this should sound like—how I think this should be the melody.' And he sang. Brecht had no real voice, but it was very impressive. Weill played what Brecht was shouting, or whatever you call his singing. Weill took pieces of old folk songs, but Brecht turned them around, changed them."[21] "Brecht was definite in suggesting authorship of 'Mack the Knife,' " according to Eric Bentley. "But then Brecht always liked to suggest that he invented the melodies."[22] The Moritat was a genre with which Brecht was more familiar than Weill, and he may well have suggested melodic and rhythmic ideas. But the Moritat that has become an enduring popular melody around the world must be credited ultimately to the show's composer.

The dress rehearsal lasted until four a.m., with everyone's nerves at or beyond the fraying point. "For sure, we didn't know then that it would be the greatest success of the century," Margot Aufricht noted dryly.[23] The next morning, when programs arrived at the last minute, Lotte Lenya's name was omitted, and as Lenya enjoyed recalling for the rest of her life, her levelheaded husband exploded in public for the first time. With everyone but Brecht and Weill expecting a colossal failure, the curtain went up at the Theater am Schiffbauerdamm as scheduled on August 31, 1928, the producer's birthday. "At first the audience was icy," Margot Aufricht said.[24] "The first song [the mighty Moritat that had caused such a fracas] fell like a stone in water," according to first-nighter Hans Heinsheimer, who had come from Vienna. "And the second song too, and again the third song. And then [after other songs] came 'Kanonen-Song' [the "Cannon Song"]. And an actor, Kurt Gerron [also the Street Singer], a wonderful actor, fat, strong, sang it [with Harald Paulsen]. And the applause was deafening."[25] And after this song, as the audience realized that it was watching the birth of a hit show, a kind of euphoria settled over the elegant, baroque eight-hundred-seat theatre. At the end, there was a prolonged ovation.

As first-nighter Robert "Robbie" Lantz, a prominent agent in New York for decades, remembered over seventy years later, "No one knew what to expect. It was simply another opening night. People had heard of Brecht more than of Weill, but really, I don't think anyone was that excited. My parents didn't even want to go, and so they gave their tickets to my grandmother and me. When we got on the bus, there was only one other person, an old woman, a character actress who had been Lady Bracknell [in Oscar Wilde's *Importance of Being Earnest*] in a production my father had produced in the Middle Ages. It was amazing to see her on that bus: it was like meeting Bette Davis in a subway. She was an omen of what was to come."

The beautifully appointed Theater am Schiffbauerdamm, on the wrong side of the Spree River and located far from Berlin's fashionable rialto, the Kurfürstendamm, was "far from sold out," according to Lantz. "It was quiet at first—people were a little puzzled, but then, after the fifth or sixth number," Weill's score began to exert "its heady seductions. It was a sound one hadn't heard before. It was not, as many think, based on a cabaret sound, nor was it like Krenek's recent jazz opera [*Jonny spielt auf*]. One had seen and heard other *Singspiele,* but this was something entirely new and fresh, a wholly original sound, utterly contemporary. Weill had produced a sound through which he seemed to express everything about Berlin in 1928." Part of the "new" sound was the fact, as Lantz suggested, that the actors were "not good singers. But oh, they had other qualities. Lenya, for instance, was interesting beyond belief. *Nobody* else had her particular quality and sound. The 'not good' singing was delightful, the entire production was strictly first-class: major avant-garde theatre. The impact cannot be overstated."[26]

An ironic setting for a beggar's opera: the baroque elegance of the Theater am Schiffbauerdamm in Berlin, where *Die Dreigroschenoper* opened on August 31, 1928. The
interior remains unchanged.

Like many other Berliners of his generation, for Robbie Lantz *Die
Dreigroschenoper* was "more than a terrifically good show: it epitomized the
era." In 1970, in his first and, to date, only return to the city of his birth
since 1933—when he had fled Hitler's Nazi battalions—Lantz made a
sentimental pilgrimage to the theatre where he had attended the historic
opening night. On August 31, 1970, forty-two years to the day after the
premiere, Lantz asked at the box office if he could "take a peek" at the theatre. When he was told no in a brusque tone, he was "reminded of what
one loves so much about Berlin." Deciding to be explicit about why he
wanted to see the theatre (which since 1956 had been the home of Brecht's
Berliner Ensemble), he mentioned that he had been at the opening night

Berlin jazz: the seven-member Lewis Ruth Band, led by Theo Mackeben,
seated at the keyboard, was placed at the back of the stage throughout
the performance of *Die Dreigroschenoper.*

of *Die Dreigroschenoper.* "The tune immediately changed: if I had had a letter from God I would not have had better treatment. I was indeed allowed
to see the theatre, smaller than I had remembered, but it immediately
brought a flood of memories of the greatest of all opening nights"[27]—a
symbol of Weimar Berlin before the Nazi hordes descended.

The popular musical languages Weill was inspired by—American jazz
and dance music and homegrown idioms from the *Moritaten* of street fairs
to folk melodies to the kind of music that could be heard in nightclubs,
variety theatres, and coffeehouses—were common currency in late-
Weimar Berlin. "[Composer] Edward Rudini explained to me the peculiar
charm of [Weill's score]—'It rendered utterly convincingly the Jewish
underworld of Berlin,' " Virgil Thomson said. "He was most specific about
it being a *Jewish* underworld. . . . Anyway it had something international
about it and maybe the Jewishness was what was so goddamned international."[28] Weill was again influenced by Stravinsky's *Soldier's Tale,* which
he had seen in its German premiere in Frankfurt in June 1923. "What

Stravinsky attempts in *Soldier's Tale* can count as the mixed genre most assured of a future . . . perhaps it can form the basis of a certain type of new opera," Weill wrote in an essay in 1926,[29] two years before he wrote that new opera. No matter how many echoes Weill's score might have struck, however, Berlin audiences had never before heard music quite like this from the stage of a theatre. The qualities that Weill added to familiar sources made audiences react as if they were hearing the sounds of the Berlin night in a fresh new guise.

In the Lewis Ruth Band (note the Americanized name) there were only seven musicians. Like Theo Mackeben, who conducted as he played piano and harmonium, each musician performed on a number of instruments. The man on the alto saxophone, for instance, also played baritone saxophone, clarinet, and flute. The tenor saxophonist also played soprano saxophone, bassoon, and clarinet. The percussionist doubled on the second trumpet. The guitarist served on the banjo, the bandoneon, and the

Epic-theatre insignia, with banners announcing narrative events, overhanging lamps, and a wire for the Brechtian half-curtain, are evident in Caspar Neher's stage design for *Die Dreigroschenoper.*

cello.[30] Except for the rarely used cello, the Lewis Ruth Band was a no-strings jazz combo that produced (as contemporary recordings reveal) a muted, low-key, smooth and smoky nightclub sound. Weill's unusual choice of banjo, guitar, and bandoneon, however, would have added an exotic touch for Berliners. There was certainly nothing remotely akin to opera, grand or otherwise, in the lean, spiky textures—American jazz laced with Berlin-Jewish motifs—that emerged from the Schiffbauerdamm stage.

The assault on operatic good manners began at once, in Weill's overture, written in 3/4 time but asymmetrically phrased and with unpredictable, seemingly inept voice-leading within its repeated chords. Brief contrasting sections presented a snippet of a jazz tune and a fugue that appeared to fail utterly and be quickly abandoned. Pitted with twisted harmonies and wrong notes, the whole effect of the overture was of a weird piece of baroque music terribly played. It lasted only a minute. Then, to a repetitive, amateurish accompaniment, the Street Singer (Kurt Gerron) appeared to perform—really to hiss—"Moritat vom Mackie Messer."

> See the shark with teeth like razors.
> All can read his open face.
> And Macheath has got a knife, but
> Not in such an obvious place.[31]

Brecht's caustic gutter poetry, with its taunting images of death and dismemberment, braided with Weill's simple, insistent, inevitable melodic whine, immediately declared war on any music-theatre format the 1928 Berlin audience—or any other audience, for that matter—would have been familiar with. Unaware that they were listening to what would become one of the most familiar and celebrated opening numbers in the world literature of musical theatre in the twentieth century, the first-night audience sat encased in silence.

The show's second number also did nothing to put the audience at ease. With a harmonium accompaniment, Mr. Peachum sang "Morgenchoral" ("Morning Hymn") to a melody that is Weill's single borrowing from the 1728 score. In "The Ballad of Mack the Knife," music and lyrics were fused; in Peachum's hymn the musical setting (sweet) clashed with the text (sour) to produce a sardonic ripple that announced Brecht and Weill as a couple of daredevil sneaks working in cahoots to upend bourgeois values. Peachum's blasphemous invocation,

You ramshackle Christian, awake!
Get on with your sinful employment
Show what a good crook you could make,

lanced the straightforward Christian piety of the melody. In the third number, the Peachums, on a very high horse, stepped before a half-curtain—a small, soiled piece of calico running on metal wires that in time would become known as the "Brecht curtain"—to perform "Anstatt-dass-Song" ("The 'No They Can't' Song"), which expressed their dismay over their daughter Polly's poor judgment in marrying the highwayman Macheath. The in-one staging (in which the performers appeared in front of the curtain) marked the song as a performance given its own playing space apart from the book scenes, and was a key way in which Brecht and Weill put their separation-of-elements theory into practice. Performed apart from the book scenes, the number was a comment from the mercenary, bourgeois Peachums. Sharing the verses, always beginning with a little motive ("Anstatt dass") that was pompously classical-sounding (and thus perfect for this grasping, self-important couple), the Peachums expounded:

Where's the old 'wherever you go I shall be with you, honey'?
When you're no more in love, and you're in the shit?

Their realistic philosophy sardonically evoked the *Neue Sachlichkeit,* and Weill's stabbing melody matched the snap of Brecht's lewd lyrics.

Macheath and Polly, who get married in a stable, were serenaded by four members of Macheath's gang, who sang, a capella and off-key, a "Hochzeitslied" ("Wedding Song for the Less Well-Off"), surely the most insulting wedding music ever written. In a sour, ironic melody (with catcalls specified in the score) the oafish singers paid tribute to the new bride and groom by recalling the thoughts of other newlyweds:

He was thinking 'Whose wedding dress was this?'
While his name was one thing she'd rather like to know.

The "hooray!" that concludes their cryptic ditty seemed more a slap in the face than a tribute. If Peachum's "Morgenchoral" was blasphemous, this wedding song was funereal.

Sung by the bride, the second wedding song, "Seeräuberjenny" ("Pirate Jenny"), was also wickedly inappropriate. If, as one of the guests complained, the first song had "no gusto, no fire, and so on," Polly's "little song . . . an imitation of a girl I saw once in some twopenny-halfpenny dive in Soho," hardly improved the mood. Instead of conjuring visions of bliss, Polly warbled a bitter song in which a scrubwoman named Jenny, with the help of pirates who arrive on a ship with eight sails and fifty guns, destroys a town in which she has been poorly treated.

> *In that noonday heat there'll be a hush round the harbour*
> *As they ask which has got to die.*
> *And you'll hear me as I softly answer: the lot!*
> *And as the first head rolls I'll say: hoppla!*

Here, Weill and Brecht give an ingenious modern reinterpretation to that old operatic chestnut, the revenge aria. The passage above is the climax of the entire number, when the singer finally gets her revenge, and in a conventional opera the composer might have brought the orchestra crashing in and sent the soprano spinning through endless histrionic roulades to denote her triumphant retribution. But Weill, showing great dramatic intuition and respect for his actor collaborators, left Jenny's "soft answer" to be spoken without musical accompaniment. It's as if she has been deadened by life, so that when her moment finally comes, she can barely react; her "hoppla" is as bland as today's "whatever." The effect is terrifying. Throughout its extended length "Seeräuberjenny," with its sudden, lurching shifts of tempo and melody from verse to refrain, is more complex than any of the earlier songs. Long verse stanzas build a mounting tension released in the short, haunting refrain "And a ship with eight sails," a chilling cry from the heart, set as a quasi-recitative over a simple progression of chords that opens to the dominant. The expected release of the tonic chord never comes, leaving Jenny, at the last, to board the ship and sail away not in triumph but in uncertainty.

Roma Bahn's performance of a song that would be indelibly associated with Lenya after she performed it in the 1931 film of *Die Dreigroschenoper* did not succeed in melting the still-frosty audience. The following number, however, changed the coauthors' fortunes. Macheath and one of the wedding guests, police chief Tiger Brown, decide to reminisce about their long-ago military exploits. Like "Seeräuberjenny," which was not about the character who sang it, "Kanonen-Song" was also not about its performers, but about John and Jim and Georgie, who presumably served with Macheath and Tiger Brown in India:

> *The troops live under*
> *The cannon's thunder*
> *From the Cape to Cooch Behar,*

they boast, citing the kind of faraway places that enticed Brecht and Weill. Roiling with images of violence and desecration—

> *When they come face to face*
> *With a different breed of fellow*
> *Whose skin is black or yellow*
> *They quick as winking chop him into beefsteak tartare*

—the number was a fitting addition to the wedding-in-a-stable's musical menu. Unlike "Seeräuberjenny," steeped in foreboding harmonies, "Kanonen-Song" was an exuberant trot, bursting with ragtime rhythms and orchestrated in a shipshape commercial style gone slightly askew. The rousing music clashed with the racism exposed in the lyrics—a prime example of Brecht-Weill irony. As a final touch, Weill held in reserve the Hawaiian slack-key guitar, and when it entered on the tune in the last verse, propelling the song into a whopping vaudevillian kickstep finale, the audience erupted with prolonged cheers that necessitated an encore. Suddenly, the audience seemed to realize what the show was up to and began to savor its many ironies and the off-kilter ways in which music skidded across the libretto.

Finally, at the end of the wedding scene, there was a love duet. Macheath and Polly's "Liebeslied" ("Love Song") began as a melodrama, with the actors speaking against Weill's beautifully offhanded wisp of a melody, carried by the Lewis Ruth Band. The song's harmonic and tonal uncertainties ended on a lyric infused with Brechtian insouciance, the equivalent of a metaphysical shrug:

> *For love will endure or not endure*
> *Regardless of where we are.*

In scene 3, as a title projected on one of Caspar Neher's overhead screens explained, "In a little song Polly gives her parents to understand that she has married the bandit Macheath." Although Polly sang in the first person, here was another number with an implied gap between singer and lyrics—indeed, the song is called the "Barbara Song." In this song of sexual realism, the singer explained how she rejected clean, well-behaved suitors but couldn't refuse an unkempt rascal. Weill's melody had all the inevitability of a folk ballad, but his minor-key harmonizations made it purr with sexual palpitation. In writing a straightforward paean to an irresistible roustabout, Brecht, an unshaven, cigar-chomping conquistador, was iconizing himself. (The number was reassigned to Lucy until Carola Neher returned to the cast.)

For the first of the show's three finales, Polly joined her parents to sing "Was ich möchte, ist es viel?" ("Concerning the Insecurity of the Human Condition"), which, like many of the numbers, offered a general observation about man's estate. The news was not good. Though Polly wished only for happiness with her new husband, her worldly-wise parents assured her that fate had something else afoot. Weill's strict, propulsive, hard-hitting rhythmic accents led unavoidably to the song's philosophic conclusion:

> *Of course that's all there is to it*
> *The world is poor, and man's a shit.*

The Peachum family concluded the act with a direct address to the now-tickled audience:

> *That's what you're all ignoring*
> *That's what's so bloody boring.*
> *That's why He's got us in a trap.*
> *And why it's all a load of crap.*

Following a "Melodrama" performed by Macheath and "Polly's Lied," Mrs. Peachum, the show's diehard antiromantic, was to have stepped in front of the half-curtain to sing a diatribe against sexual enslavement. But when Rosa Valetti refused at the last moment to perform the salty number, it was cut. It was seemingly out of character for Brecht and Weill to have agreed to an autocratic demand from a performer, but they liked how Valetti was playing the role. And they knew that the next song in the show, "Zuhälterballade" ("The Pimp's Ballad") (also known as "The Ballad of Immoral Earnings" and "The Tango Ballad"), another shocker, was an ace in the hole. In one of the show's most delicious two-steps, Weill's sinuous tango melody tingled against Macheath and Jenny's no-holds-barred reminiscence of their sadomasochistic affair.

48

Rivals for the affection of a scoundrel: Lenya, left, who had switched from
her original role of Jenny, as Lucy, and Hilde Körber, who had succeeded
Roma Bahn, as Polly, in *Die Dreigroschenoper* in the spring of 1929

That time's long past, but what would I not give
To see that whorehouse where we used to live?,

Macheath sighed. Equally misty-eyed, Jenny recalled the time, "now very
far away," when "he was so sweet and bashed me where it hurt." Alienation
was inscribed not only in the gap between the music's romantic murmur
and the sexual realism of the lyrics, but in the way the ex-lovers referred to
each other in the third person: "He'd lash out and knock me headlong
down the stairs," Jenny sang. "I told you she was generally booked up,"
Macheath reported. "In the end we flushed it down the sewer," the former
lovers recalled, referring to Jenny's abortion.

Betrayed for the first time by Jenny, Macheath in prison then sang "Ballade vom angenehmen Leben" ("The Ballad of Good Living"), in effect his
theme song. Performed by a prisoner anticipating a quick release, the song
was an ode to what money can buy as well as an *apologia pro vita sua*. It was
a wry pep song in which Macheath's rapscallion grace was enfolded in
Weill's jaunty melody and reinforced by jazzy piano solos in fast dotted
rhythms. There followed "Eifersuchts Duett" ("The Jealousy Duet")

49

between Polly and Lucy, in which Macheath's two wives jabbed at each other in three different ways: with a disingenuous Franz Lehár–type tune; with a parody of grand-opera coloratura; and, finally, with a mock-romantic refrain of "Mackie and I, see how we bill and coo." This was another of Weill's takeoffs on opera (and an echo of the rivalry between two contemporary divas that had been one of Gay's satiric targets). In the second finale, "Denn wovon lebt der Mensch?" ("What Keeps a Man Alive?"), Macheath and Mrs. Peachum stepped before the half-curtain to offer another gloomy report on human nature. And again Weill slyly wrapped Brecht's mordant observations in a joyous, strutting rhythm. Food first, morality and preaching later, the singers informed, before asking and then answering the title's global question:

> For once you must try not to shirk the facts
> Mankind is kept alive by bestial acts.

Keeping pace with Brecht's litany of catastrophes, "the fact that millions/Are daily tortured, stifled, punished, silenced, oppressed," Weill's music surged unstoppably to a crescendo worthy of a finale. But this time did the two young radicals overshoot their mark, grafting onto their Rabelaisian fable a perception of human inadequacy a touch too dark for their high-stepping show?

The first two numbers in act 3 were designed as authorial interruptions. "Man is never sharp enough," "never bad enough," "never undemanding enough," Mr. Peachum recited in "Lied von der Unzulänglichkeit menschlichen Strebens" ("The Song of Insufficiency"), a catalogue of universal human failings wrapped in a characteristically dynamic Weillian beat. Jenny's "Salomon-Song" ("Solomon Song") (originally to have been sung by Polly) was to have been performed in front of the half-curtain to a harmonium (portable organ) accompaniment, but was cut late in rehearsals. Its sentiments echoed those in Peachum's preceding number—in each of three stanzas the song cited how a historic figure who possessed (1) wisdom, (2) beauty, and (3) courage was "better off without"—and it may have seemed to Brecht and Weill that another ironic list song might at this point have been one too many. Besides, Weill had carefully controlled his orchestrations in order to wring the most variety out of his small ensemble—two solo accompaniments in a row would have jarred.

The remainder of the score was in a notably different mode. For two numbers sung by Macheath, imprisoned again and awaiting execution,

Weill's palette darkened and virtually all traces of musical irony were erased. Sung softly and at a fast tempo, "Ruf aus der Gruft" ("Call from the Grave") was exactly that, the defeated rake's cry for help, phrased in the third person:

> *Hark to the voice that's calling you to weep . . .*
> *But do stand by him while it's not too late.*

The following number, "Grabschrift" ("Ballad in Which Macheath Begs All Men for Forgiveness"), was the one song with an operatic intensity, although Weill did not score the vocal part operatically. Instead, the character's psychology was illuminated in the orchestra. The accompaniment began with a slow, deadened chiming in octaves of a simple motive. Once stated, this motive would then never be far from the surface of the orchestral texture. Macheath's tortured ambivalence—his anger and fear, his disgust with the whores and pimps he's spent his time with, mixed with his plea for forgiveness—emerged in an unrelieved stream of steady quarter-notes. Meanwhile, the orchestra ascended relentlessly in volume and pitch, always insisting on its own musical motive. Finally, this motive, stripped to its barest form, became the music to take Macheath to the gallows. Weill's scoring contained not a single comic vibration or musical jest.

Where the finales for the two previous acts were decorative, the third finale resolved the narrative: a messenger from the Queen arrived with a pardon for Macheath. And as a consequence, here, and only here, was there full-blown opera in *Die Dreigroschenoper.* In true operatic-finale form, Weill used a musical mosaic in which solos alternated with choral figures and dialogue was dressed in recitative.

As the opening-night audience recognized, they had just seen a defiant, naughty, entirely new kind of music theatre—a terrific show. The impact was immediate. *Threepenny* fever raged. There was wallpaper based on scenes from the show. Songs were played in bars and hotel lounges throughout the city, hummed and whistled on the street and on public transportation. "In the early 1920s a young man dreamed of being Count Danilo in *The Merry Widow,* but after *Die Dreigroschenoper* the ideal young man dreamed to look like a pimp. And the girl looked like a little floozy," John Oser, the sound engineer for the 1931 film, maintained.[32] The prosperous bourgeoisie satirized in the show flocked to the Schiffbauer-damm, responding with laughter and affection. Audiences were delighted by the show's sheer modern stylishness—by Weill's witty pastiche score and Brecht's vernacular tang, and by the deft interplay between music and text.

Some of Brecht's disciples—and later, Brecht himself—wished to read into the show a definite Marxist thrust. But in truth, at the time he was working on the show, he had not yet become an orthodox Marxist convert, and as audiences intuitively grasped, *Die Dreigroschenoper* was simply too much fun to be read as any kind of serious ideological tract. A vibrant, once-over-lightly satire of universal human excess, the show regaled audiences with the collegiate perceptions that capitalism fosters greed; love doesn't last; and betrayal and double-dealing are the way of the world. The show's antiromantic sting barely conceals a really quite youthful romantic spirit, an indwelling optimism that in exposing misbehavior, satire can also correct it. And the fake happy ending is merely a cover for the young coauthors' implicit belief in the possibility of a genuine happy ending for the kind of society mirrored in their play.

Die Dreigroschenoper, then, is neither, on the one hand, a call to arms, a primer for the founding of a new, enlightened Marxist society, nor, on the other, a prediction of the barbaric political ideology that was to overcome the German nation in only a few short years. It is as much a misreading of its creators' intentions to interpret the play's lower-depths milieu as a portent of fascism as it is to twist their swipes at capitalism into a proto-Marxist pamphlet. Nonetheless, because of when it appeared, the show has become, despite its nominal setting of Victorian London, a key icon of 1920s Berlin as a jittery jazz-age bawdy house overrun with sharks, pimps, and tarts, a city perched on the edge of doom. The musical does not condemn its sinners as much as it subversively celebrates their unexpungeable life force, the primal energy that radiates from their misconduct. Rather than reading back into the show a preview of the coming nightmare, it is historically more accurate to place it as an emblem of the last good times in Weimar Germany. Brecht and Weill proved that in 1928 it was still possible to write a satire of contemporary ill manners—and have a big hit. In a few years, as they were to discover, they would no longer be able to.

Theatrically, however, if not politically, *Die Dreigroschenoper,* a transgressive mock-opera that in a stroke confounded boundaries between high and low forms of musical theatre, was indeed revolutionary. In the fall of 1928 Weill luxuriated in his new status as the composer of a hit show. "The impact grows from day to day," he reported to his publisher on September 10. "It seems that the work will lead to a complete revolution of the entire operetta 'industry.' " The next day Hans Heinsheimer, agreeing with his client, called the show "the herald of a really extraordinary development" and asked Weill to write an essay on the new style for the October issue of *Anbruch*. At first Weill demurred. "I don't know whether it would be tactically wise if I myself attempted to give a theoretical foundation to this movement, of which so far I am the only exponent," he wrote on October 2. But he relented, and wrote an impassioned defense of his new populist style as a rebuke to "opera's splendid isolation."

"Every day I hear from all sides that these pieces ["Moritat vom Mackie Messer," "Kanonen-Song," "Zuhälterballade," "Ballade vom angenehmen Leben"] have a popular appeal unlike any music in years," Weill wrote to Universal Edition on October 25. "Everyone assures me that with the five or so pieces of this genre I have written to date one could easily make a small fortune. . . . If my gift for writing a completely new kind of popular melody [that is] unrivaled today . . . were promoted ingeniously on a large scale there is no doubt my popular compositions could take the place of American jazz which is already somewhat passé." Berating Universal Edition for not doing enough promotion and concluding that "musical sales here in Berlin don't work at all," Weill suggested that "we consider giving the best numbers from *Die Dreigroschenoper* to a popular music publisher in America."

That fall, Otto Klemperer, a great fan of the show, asked Weill to arrange a *Kleine Dreigroschenmusik*. "I heard the [music] (I have avoided the word suite) at the rehearsal yesterday and am very satisfied with it," Weill wrote to Universal Edition on February 5, 1929. "There are eight numbers in an entirely new concert arrangement, including some new interludes and completely new instrumentation. . . . I believe the work can be played very often since it is exactly what the conductors are looking for: a rousing final number. What do you say about a potpourri from the show for a salon orchestra?" By the spring of 1929, Weill would confide in an undated letter to Maurice Abravanel, "I'm getting sick and tired of this fame of mine. . . . All at once I have gotten the kind of things I had expected to achieve, at the earliest perhaps in another ten years or so. Of course this offers lots of advantages, not only of the material kind, but also because of my name (which right now is worth a lot of money!). I can assure you I'll be taking full advantage of all possibilities."

Suddenly rich, the Weills remained prudent. Lenya, who was never to forget her impoverished childhood, now as ever closely supervised the household budget. It wasn't until 1931 that, as a birthday present for her, Weill purchased a comfortable but hardly extravagant house in suburban

Kleinmachnow. The Weills lived well within, and probably beneath, their considerable means, as they were to do again in America after Kurt had a big Broadway success with *Lady in the Dark.*

Before *Die Dreigroschenoper,* Weill had enjoyed a modest renown as a *Neutöner.* Busoni's favorite student, he was the composer of neotonal operas and absolute music, an ambitious young man working in a tradition sanctioned by Weimar Germany's musical mandarins. The jazz motifs that had infiltrated into the *Mahagonny-Songspiel,* however, raised doubts among highbrows that *Die Dreigroschenoper* only deepened. "Serious musicians thought he was a traitor," Maurice Abravanel observed. "He was not recognized by operetta composers because he wrote wrong notes, and he was given up by the avant-garde because he wrote successful things."[33] Refusing to honor a clean separation between musical hierarchies, Weill professed to scorn elitists. But his great popular success sat a little uneasily, and with one exception the remainder of his career in Germany can be seen as attempts to reclaim his position in the upper reaches of Weimar musical culture.

FOUR

The Second Time Around

W eill continued to contest his new status as the toast of Berlin's commercial theatre by next writing two short, severe works for radio. In the fall of 1928, working again without Brecht, Weill composed *Das Berliner Requiem,* a cantata based on poems Brecht had written some years before that evoke the feelings of the urban populace on the subject of death. Weill's spare writing—he limits his instrumentation to wind band, guitar, banjo, and percussion harmonium or organ—matches Brecht's dark, cryptic poetry. (The work was performed on Radio Frankfurt on May 22, 1929.) At the time they had been working on the *Mahagonny-Songspiel,* Weill and Brecht, like millions of other Germans, were fascinated by Charles Lindbergh's May 21, 1927, transatlantic flight, and they had discussed the possibility of writing a music-theatre piece about the historic event. Weill's second commission from Radio Frankfurt seemed an appropriate occasion to realize that project. The work would premiere, however, at the Baden-Baden new-music festival in July, and although it was his commission Weill agreed to share the score with Paul Hindemith. Weill would write seven and a half sections, Hindemith five and a half. Brecht wrote a first draft quickly, and by April Weill began to compose his share of the score.

For a number of reasons *Der Lindberghflug (The Lindbergh Flight)* is an anomaly in the Brecht-Weill canon, not only because in its original version it was "corrupted" by the presence of a third creative voice, but also because the collaborators wrote the piece as advocates rather than what was for them the more creatively stimulating role of prosecutors or interrogators. Their often dry, brittle, unlyrical tone—*Neue Sachlichkeit* with a vengeance—cannot disguise what is at heart a tribute to a hero, the kind of Nietzschean *Übermensch* for whom, more than once, Germany has displayed a fatal attraction. (Early in 1950 Brecht changed the work's title to *Ozeanflug [The Ocean Flight]* to erase the name of the flier, who had been revealed to be a Nazi sympathizer.)

For the July 27 premiere, Brecht was determined to present the work in the spirit of a *Lehrstück,* a didactic cantata cut to the measure of his new Marxist politics. "*Der Lindberghflug* is valueless unless learned from," he contended; and to induce in the spectator the kind of detachment he felt was "necessary to learning,"[1] he directed the piece to ensure a separation of elements. He wanted the Listener, taking the role of the Flier, to stand apart from the orchestra and chorus, while images illustrating and commenting on the flight were projected onto a screen behind the platform. And to prevent the actor playing the Listener from identifying with his role, Brecht coached him to speak in the spirit of an exercise, in a flat tone and with pauses at the end of each line. To complement Brecht's sober approach, Weill devised a new hieratic style, bare yet forceful, for the orchestral music of the opening section. Simple modal lines are repeated time and again in unharmonized string octaves, while the chorus declaims in clipped outbursts: "Here is the pilot's plane. Step in! Step in!" But at points Weill's tone departs from the New Objectivity. There is a strange and touching number that the aviator sings to the motor of his plane, which Weill sets as a soft, quasi-pentatonic tune answered by only two chords in the bassoon and alto sax. When trying to resist sleep (a jazzy, seductive clarinet) Weill's Lindbergh shows a serene self-discipline that is quite moving—and may have marred Brecht's attempt to place the Flier as a remote and prosaic figure. The supporting cast, observers and challengers of the flight, include the City of New York (baritone solo); a ship, the *Empress of Scotland* (choir); the fog (choir); a snowstorm (choir); and the American press (baritone solo). In the first version, some of these were set by Hindemith.

Privately, Weill expressed a low opinion of Hindemith's contribution, and hindsight shows him to have been correct. Hindemith's florid vocal lines are overwrought; his writing for the saxophones utterly ignores the jazz idiom; and the sections he composed convey little of either character or setting. Even before the Baden-Baden premiere Weill had plans to write the entire score himself.

But first, he and Brecht were tempted by a return to the rialto, when Ernst Aufricht approached them with another request for a show, to launch his second season at the Theater am Schiffbauerdamm. Pushing his luck, the producer wanted to open on August 31, 1929, one year to the day after the premiere of *Die Dreigroschenoper.* Because both Weill and Brecht had become troubled by the distinctly middlebrow success of that show, they declined. Brecht felt that their show's acceptance indicated that he had been guilty of telling too many people what they wanted to hear. Weill did not want at this point to be accused of exploiting his songwriting skills, and the prospect of returning to a form he had already mastered did not appeal to him. Setting out to repeat his *Threepenny* style, which is what Aufricht was asking him to do, countered Weill's interest in theatrical experiment and in changing his style for each new work. But Aufricht persisted, holding out the promise of the money and fame another hit would bring. Brecht-Weill protested, but eventually they caved in. They were to regret their decision.

Faced with creating a commercial play on demand, Brecht turned once again to the indispensable Elisabeth Hauptmann. "He told me to write a play," Hauptmann recalled. Hauptmann cited as source material a story by Dorothy Lane that had appeared in an American magazine, *The J. & L. Weekly* of Saint Louis. "I made up the magazine and the author," Hauptmann admitted many years later. "There is no 'Dorothy Lane'; there was no magazine story."[2] Hauptmann herself was "Dorothy Lane," the story she fabricated, about the relations between a Salvation Army lieutenant and a gangster, was drawn from her knowledge of American crime movies and from two plays, George Bernard Shaw's *Major Barbara* and Edward Sheldon's 1905 *Salvation Nell.* (Characters and milieu bear a striking resemblance to *Guys and Dolls,* the 1950 musical by Frank Loesser, Abe Burrows, and Jo Swerling based on a story by Damon Runyon, "The Idyll of Miss Sarah Brown," which was not published until 1932, three years after Hauptmann's show had come and gone.)

Nobody wanted to claim authorship of the play Hauptmann wrote. On the opening-night program Hauptmann was credited only for the German adaptation of a magazine story by Dorothy Lane. Margot Aufricht, as closely involved in the rehearsals of the new show, called, in English,

The master and his devoted disciple: Brecht and his indispensable collaborator Elisabeth Hauptmann, in the late 1920s. Did she write more than Brecht was willing to admit?

Happy End, as she had been in those for *Die Dreigroschenoper,* claimed, however, that Brecht "wrote the play, of course. But he thought it wasn't good enough, so he said it isn't his. But it *was* by him."[3] How much Brecht there is in the *Happy End* book can probably never be determined. What is certain is that for the rest of his life Brecht refused to acknowledge any contribution to *Happy End* other than the lyrics. If Brecht denied his authorship, why at the time did Hauptmann? Was her hiding behind the fictitious Dorothy Lane a gesture undertaken at Brecht's request, to confine her to her public role as his assistant? Or did Brecht's marriage to Helene Weigel in April 1929 plunge the lovelorn Hauptmann into a depressed state in which an accurate writing credit seemed only a mockery?

In structure and tone the play that nobody wanted to take credit for writing was just what Aufricht had asked for—a romp in the *Threepenny* style. Once again, two seemingly dissimilar groups—in this case, the Salvation Army and a gang of thieves—are found to share common traits and to discover in the "happy end" that it makes good sense for them to join forces against a common enemy. For Brecht, the evolving hard-core Marxist, despite its hints of class struggle the play's premise was irredeemably slight, and its universal happy end a betrayal of the way he wanted his work to subtend his deepening political convictions. In the fall of 1929, at the twilight of the so-called Golden Twenties, from Brecht's point of view the only possible happy end for Germany would be a revolution of the masses against their capitalist exploiters. This was a thrust the play could not support, even though at the eleventh hour Brecht would try to brush it with a few quick Marxist strokes. *Happy End,* Brecht's unclaimed stepchild, would be of use to him only as the starting point for a complex play, *Saint Joan of the Stockyards* (1932), in which, in full Marxist cry, he charts his own sneaky dialectical course toward the call for a new world order.

Like Brecht, Weill was aware of the thinness of the material but saw its musical possibilities. The book, pivoting on cinematic crosscutting between two groups of characters, offered him the challenge of writing two kinds of songs: raffish numbers for the underworld figures, clustered in Bill Cracker's saloon; and hymns and marches for the Christian soldiers. With characteristic speed and self-assurance, he got down to work as Brecht, who throughout writing and preproduction made no secret of his distaste for the project, fumed. Nonetheless, Brecht tried to run interference from the sidelines. Weill's June 25, 1929, letter to Universal Edition set the stage for the frustrations he was to encounter with Brecht for the next three months. Once again, the partners had decided to go to Le Lavandou in the south of France, where the previous summer they had worked productively on *Die Dreigroschenoper.* "Brecht, who came along in his car, had a car accident near Fulda, where we had arranged to have lunch, and I had to have him taken back to Berlin with a fractured kneecap," Weill reported. "This has meant my plans having to be postponed, as we had intended coming here together to work. We wanted to write the lyrics for the songs to *Happy End* and work out some new plans."

"I haven't sent 'The Bilbao Song' on purpose because it still isn't certain whether it will be included," Weill wrote on July 22. "You already have two songs for *Happy End* to be getting on with in any case. There will be around seven songs in all, three–four of which will be able to be used as hits." Only seven songs? *Die Dreigroschenoper* had twenty numbers, along with other musical scenes and three finales. Brecht may have been uninspired by the material, but under his hectoring supervision *Happy End* was evolving as a comedy with musical interludes. Although they are not theatre works per se, after writing through-composed scores for *Das Berliner Requiem* and *Der Lindberghflug* Weill may have felt he was being sent back to the starting gate. His terse letters to his publisher contained none of the usual drum beating or the claims for staking out new territory that had become customary when he began work on a new project. The composer's "color" seemed to have returned by August 4, however, when he wrote to Universal Edition that he was working on a "big tango which seems to me to have the greatest commercial potential of all the things I have done." Weill's mood had improved, but when the show went into rehearsal on August 7 the script was not finished. "Brecht made only two acts, and even after my husband applied all the pressure he didn't bring the third act forth," said Margot Aufricht. "My husband had the theatre booked, and he felt it wasn't finished and that even what he had was just no good. He was a perfectionist, and he was in despair."[4]

Over the summer, before he had seen the script but confident of success, Aufricht had managed to recruit the same creative team as for *Die Dreigroschenoper.* Reluctantly, Erich Engel signed on as director. Caspar Neher was the designer, and Theo Mackeben would once again be conducting the Lewis Ruth Band. Aufricht's cast was even stronger than for the earlier show. Carola Neher was cast as Lilian Holiday (a.k.a. Hallelujah Lil), a spunky Salvation Army lieutenant who subdues a criminal and his gang. Neher, one of Brecht's favorite performers, exuded the kind of sex appeal her role required. As Bill Cracker, the street-smart hoodlum she seduces, Oscar Homolka (later to win fame in Hollywood as a character actor) had just the right, glowering bulldog looks and guttural voice. Brecht's intensely homely new wife, Helene Weigel, had the harsh edge for the gang boss, the mysterious Lady in Grey. Soon to be launched with his chilling performance as the child murderer in Fritz Lang's 1931 film *M,* Peter Lorre was cast as one of the gang members, Dr. Nakamura. Notably missing from the ensemble was Lotte Lenya. It would have been a stretch for her vocally to play Lilian, not really her "type," but she could have done it (as indeed she did on a historic 1960 recording), and she would have been a splendid Lady in Grey. But at the time she was appearing for another theatrical management in a production of *Danton's Death.*

Although neither he nor Elisabeth Hauptmann ever quite finished the third act, Brecht appeared regularly at rehearsals, and, to Aufricht's mounting anxiety, began to take an active interest in the production. After many clashes with the playwright, who was spending his time directing rather than writing or rewriting (Brecht consistently refused to cut passages of rambling dialogue), Erich Engel withdrew. With its projections, placards, and songs that interrupted the story, *Happy End* was certainly beginning to look and sound like a Brecht play even if, as Brecht would insist, it was not. By opening night—September 2 rather than August 31—Brecht and Weill thought they might have another hit.

This time the first-nighters did not need to get warmed up. They were Brecht-Weill fans and they were eager to have a good time. Laughter and applause were generous right from the beginning; Lenya recollected that during the intermission following act 2, Weill called her backstage at her theatre, his voice vibrating with excitement, to announce another hit. But that was before the unfinished, and soon-to-be-infamous, act

A preview, two decades earlier, of Broadway's *Guys and Dolls*: Carola Neher as Hallelujah Lil in *Happy End,* 1929

3 had been performed. At the end of the show, Helene Weigel as the Lady in Grey delivered a ringing Communist manifesto. Did Weigel improvise her harangue on the spot? Did she read explosive passages from a Communist Party pamphlet calling for revolution? As a gesture of solidarity with his new fellow travelers, had Brecht secretly embellished the speech during the intermission following act 2? All have been claimed, and each is conceivable. Aufricht recalled that during rehearsals "a deputation of communists came to Brecht, complaining that, ideologically, the play was too feeble. This gave Brecht an idea, a bad idea, and suddenly the weak third act became even weaker. . . . Helene Weigel suddenly drew out a sheet Brecht had written during the intermission and began to read a communist pamphlet. A scandal broke loose; our failure was sealed."[5]

"Robbing a bank's no crime compared to owning one! The world belongs to all of us—let's march together and make it our own!"[6] Weigel, a fierce-looking firebrand, declared, introducing a political slant that was out of phase with the essentially good-natured and sentimental play. Her comments, and her challenging stance, angered Aufricht's well-heeled audience. "Hosiannah Rockefeller" ("Hosanna Rockefeller"), a coda in the form of a mock hymn to Saint Henry Ford, Saint John D. Rockefeller, and Saint J. P. Morgan—caricatures of the American millionaires appeared on giant stained-glass windows—further enflamed the crowd. In this single sustained piece of musical irony in the show, the writers attacked money and religion, sacred ground for the bourgeois spectators. At the curtain call a barrage of jeers greeted the startled actors.

Although the score was well received, the play and the production were derided. Not for the first time, Alfred Kerr, the dean of Berlin critics and a staunch anti-Brechtian, accused the playwright of plagiarism. Even Herbert Ihering, Brecht's great advocate among Berlin critics, was negative. (Although identified on the program only as the lyricist, Brecht was assumed to be the librettist as well.) Poor reviews as well as fear of riots spelled silence at the Schiffbauerdamm box office. Two days later, Aufricht closed the show, which disappeared immediately from Brecht's résumé and was never to be produced again during the lifetimes of its cocreators.

Is *Happy End,* the biggest financial and critical failure in Weill's career, that bad? By all means no. In effect, the show was Weill's second musical comedy, and like many others of its genre it suffered from book problems that were never solved. Writing on demand, Brecht-Weill delivered just what their producer had asked for, a brash piece of light entertainment. As an affectionate comic portrait of puritans and lowlife types, it isn't as sturdy as *Guys and Dolls,* but it has likable characters in a colorful setting. It is filled with Brechtian types—a sexy rogue hero, a resourcefully defiant heroine, personable criminals, and snippy moralists—that may be developed in more socially meaningful ways in other plays; but for this piece, in which all the characters participate in a happy end, the thin characterizations are all that is required. To the continuing dismay of many diehard Brecht-Weill devotees, who would wish to place the team securely in the realm of high art and high social consciousness, in *Happy End* there is nothing to "get" but a good time.

For a show that apparently neither writer believed in, they produced a collection of cunning songs. Brecht never denied that the lyrics were his— in their racy, colloquial verve they could hardly have been anyone else's.

"Hosianna Rockefeller," an anticapitalist number in *Happy End* that enraged the opening-night audience at the Theater am Schiffbauerdamm

And contrary to popular belief, the musical numbers are not merely decorative asides thrown in to stop a show nobody cared about. Numbers intersect in several ways. There are songs with a crucial narrative purpose, songs that help to define characters, and songs performed by minor characters that supply rich local color. Although their score certainly has a *Threepenny* sound, in repeating the separation-of-elements of their earlier hit Brecht and Weill came up with some creative twists.

Not surprisingly, the devil has the best lines, and the Brecht-Weill songs for the "sinners," or at any rate the naughty numbers, are the real showpieces. Indeed, "Bilbao-Song," "Surabaya-Johnny," "Matrosen-Tango" ("The Sailors' Tango"), and "Der Song von Mandelay" ("Mandalay Song") are among Weill's most indelible creations. But the Salvation Army hymns and marches also have energy and grit. Lil's first number, "Der kleine Leutnant des lieben Gottes" ("Lieutenants of the Lord"), has all the formal density and biting sound of a classic Weill song. Her second number, "Matrosen-Tango," brilliantly sways between the profane and the sacred. Clearly, to Brecht and Weill the Salvation Army, although puppets of big business, also represented a potentially dynamic force for social change, not just a bastion of primness and inhibition (which it was to be, more or less, in *Guys and Dolls;* Sister Sarah's "If I Were a Bell," it should be noted, has some of the same function as Lilian's sexy numbers). Except for a few stray passages, the Salvation Army songs refrain from the sort of irony that might be expected of Weill, the non-religious Jew, and Brecht, the Communist. The happy end promised by the title is thus prepared for through Weill's musical magnanimity: the gangsters may have the best and most sustained numbers, but the army to which they are ultimately to be joined are snappy performers too.

The star, Hallelujah Lil, the Christian foot soldier who falls for and seeks to reform a gangster, is a musical switch hitter, which places her securely as the show's mediator. Her two showstoppers, "Matrosen-Tango" at the end of act 1, and "Surabaya-Johnny" in act 3, are both deeply integrated. She sings the former to attract skeptical underworld characters, proving to them that salvation can be preached through profane as well as sacred songs. (Is there embedded in this pop song, which seduces an unsophisticated audience, a metaphor for Weill's own agenda in using lively, simple music to win the favor of the crowd?) The song's sailors are a lazy, pleasure-loving group, indifferent to God. They live unexamined lives. But when they face death in a storm, they experience an existential crisis: "You may have been bragging a lifetime or so / But now, when it matters, you're shitting!"[7] Weill builds the number in a series of long verses that reach toward a brief refrain, "Ah, the sea is blue, so blue," whose sweetly languorous rhythm and lilt capture first the sailors' carefree attitude and later their dying regrets. Far from being a detachable item, the long number provides the pivot for the rest of the story: overheard by a shocked officer, Lilian is fired.

In the equally purposeful "Surabaya-Johnny," Lilian resolves the show's romantic conflict. Singing, to the resistant Bill Cracker, of a hard-hearted bloke who seduces and abandons, she succeeds in getting her man. "Surabaya-Johnny" recalls the ironic "Barbara Song"—it's another Brecht ode to a magnetic scoundrel, but framed this time as a torch song of consuming desire. While it expresses potent emotions (and so undercuts the persistent myth that Brecht-Weill were invariably a couple of smart-aleck cynics), the song is glazed with a touch of indirectness the coauthors were both drawn to. Lilian is singing to Bill a song about another man, and although she sings in the first person ("Johnny, how could you do this to me?") the "I" of the song is not necessarily the singer herself. Yet the sexual hunger that ripples through the melody is unmistakable. In its strong but heartbroken attitude, "Surabaya-Johnny" would later become a favorite of cabaret singers. And it hits its target in the show: tough guy Bill Cracker cries when he hears it, then tries to replace his social mask in singing a macho countersong, "Das Lied von der harten Nuss" ("The Song of the Hard Nut") ("If you want to be a big shot / Start by learning to be tough").

Even such numbers as "Bilbao Song," which are introduced by pretexts so feeble the show seems to be mocking its own casualness, are written in the grain of the show's mise-en-scène. "Bilbao Song" is a tribute to Bill's Beer Hall, a dump where "the stools at the bar were damp with rye," "grass grew high on the dance floor, and the moon shone green through the roof."[8] On its surface, the song drips with boozy nostalgia and the memory of good times. Beneath the surface, it is a testament to the power of music to evoke time and place. The beer hall is long gone, but it can be summoned up by remembering the song that used to be played there. And of course, this isn't so easy: "I can't remember the words!" the singer wails, time and again. Throughout the number, Weill brilliantly composes the underlying meaning into the music itself. The introduction of the song is a bare quarter-note beat, played back and forth on the tom-toms—a fragment of memory. The verse begins with the singer taking up this two-note fragment, this nonmelody; it is all he has ("Bill's beer hall in Bilbao . . ."). As his memories surface, the song begins to coalesce: the instrumental lines gradually take on character; the vocal phrases start to spin. Weill carefully controls the harmony here, keeps it dry and unpromising, full of diminished chords. Then he suddenly warms it up with a thrilling C-minor seventh and a burst of melody in the saxes ("The stools at the bar were damp with rye . . ."), before memory evanesces once more. Weill maintains the tension until the entrance of the song's famous chorus saluting "that old Bilbao moon." Even here, memory is imperfect: the piano seems to have caught the tune, while the other instruments hang back with a little dotted-note accompaniment, and the singer keeps forgetting the words. Only in the last verse and coda is the remembered song presented in a full-blown orchestration. In a great performance, this flood of memory can take one's breath away.

In "Bilbao Song," Weill used all his skill and subtlety as a composer to create a small masterpiece of music theatre. Listening to it, one knows exactly why that moon continues to haunt the singer, why indeed it was "fantastic beyond belief." If the last verse regrets the fact that the beer hall has been cleaned up "with potted palms and ice cream," the place remembered remains alive forever in the song.

"Mandalay Song," also ushered in on a dime (in effect, both this song and "Bilbao Song" are request numbers, performed because members of the gang ask for them), is another lament for a good-time place that has disappeared. Performed by a minor character, Sam, a gangster dressed in drag, the song may be the only one in the score that is merely decorative: but who would dream of complaining? Brecht-Weill at their naughtiest, "Mandalay Song," like "Bilbao Song," celebrates the bawdy life. Like the late beer hall, Mother Goddam's brothel, a dive in Mandalay, was a place where you could have some fun for a price. In *Mahagonny,* the world of love for sale would be seen through moralist's spectacles; here, quick, impersonal sex, conveyed in the tripping staccato of Brecht's lyrics and Weill's beat, is the occasion of a dirty joke, nothing more.

> *Goddam, go tell that girl to get her ass in gear*
> *There's fifteen guys already lined up along the pier.*

The fifteen guys keep braying for everyone to go "faster, faster!" Like its impatient paramours lined up on the pier, the song quite properly favors speed and vigor over deeper satisfactions. (Could the lyrics of this unabashedly salty number have contributed, as much as Weigel's Communist manifesto, to the displeasure of the opening-night audience? Is there, in the song's celebration of no-longer-available whoring, an intuition of an end to an era of good times?)

Regardless of their level of integration, all the songs are presented within a specific performance framework, with characters enacting songs for other characters. Brecht instructed the actors to mark their segue from speech to song; before they started to sing, they were either to stride to center stage or to stand rigidly in place, where they would be framed in a spotlight. Writing songs that were designed as performances within the show, Weill gives his score a vibrant vaudevillian shuffle, the energy and uplift of the American jazz he admired. His wonderfully life-affirming score ensures that *Happy End* can be properly played only as a foot-tapping musical comedy, an entertainment set up to celebrate itself.

In *Happy End,* one can hear that the basic elements of Weill's popular-song style are in place. From now on there will be a signature sound, a collection of hallmarks that identify his songs as being unmistakably his own. One of these pop signatures is the three-note pickup phrase (often taken out of tempo, to create a moment of rhythmic suspension) that will introduce a new melody. An example is the beginning of the bridge section of "Bilbao Song" ("I don't know if it would have brought you joy or grief . . ."). This characteristic rhythmic idea, derived from tango, can be traced back to *The Czar Has His Photograph Taken,* through *Threepenny's* "Cannon Song" and "Barbara Song," and forward to "September Song." Another hallmark is Weill's habitual harmonic turn from major or minor to a mournful half-diminished chord. One can hear this formula very clearly in the chorus of "Bilbao Song," where he uses it for the transition of the lyric from "That old Bilbao moon" to the following phrase, "Down where we used to go." In "The Sailors' Tango" the same progression keeps plunging the music into melancholy. And in "Surabaya-Johnny" virtually the entire chorus is defined by this plaintive harmonic turn. A contemporary observer, Weill's friend Felix Jackson, dismissed *Happy End* as "of transitory importance," at the same time admitting that it proved one fact conclusively: Weill "was the only German composer of the twenties who absorbed the American expression and made it his own. From here on in the American rhythm and the American song were an integral part of his music."[9]

After the show's quick demise, Weill returned to completing the all-Weill *Lindberghflug,* which was to receive a prestigious concert performance at the Krolloper on December 5, 1929, with Otto Klemperer conducting. For the recently scorched composer, the performance of the willfully sober new work was to be proof that he had not forsaken his commitment to serious music—or, at any rate, to a form of musical expression that, unlike his songs for *Die Dreigroschenoper* and *Happy End,* could be described in no other way. Indeed, as a November 1 letter to Universal Edition revealed, Weill at this point felt he had to protect himself against his talent to amuse. It is "very important for me to have the *Lindberghflug* performed as often as possible this winter since before *Mahagonny* I absolutely must have a serious work of this kind as a contrast to my song works. I am also working on a concert performance of the *Berliner Requiem* in Berlin for the same reasons." Weill felt *Der Lindberghflug* offered another opportunity as well. "I have given interviews to three major American papers," Weill wrote Universal Edition on November 10, "who all agreed that it should have a sensational effect in America. . . . Consider an English translation," Weill urged, adding that there are "pending negotiations to have the performance broadcast by American radio stations." (Leopold Stokowski was to conduct the American premiere with the Philadelphia Orchestra on April 4, 1931.)

Three years after the *Happy End* fiasco, Weill attempted to salvage his music. "I plan to shorten the work in such a way that the musical numbers, which include some of my best and most popular songs, would build the framework for the whole," Weill wrote Universal Edition on June 3, 1932. He planned to present a song cycle from the show as a vehicle for Lenya in her native Vienna just after she had had a success there in *Mahagonny*. Envisioning the revised piece as a songspiel along the lines of the first *Mahagonny,* with just enough of a narrative frame to anchor the songs, Weill believed at the time that "Brecht and Miss Hauptmann have worked out a final unpolitical version." Hans Heinsheimer at Universal Edition, however, did not approve of the material, nor did he feel it would be tactically "smart" for Weill to appear "with another such Songspiel." "I cannot see anything in this plot, setting or even in its moral purpose, which has any life, effectiveness or artistic justification. Nor can I find anything in the figures . . . which is anything more than a feeble copy of the Brecht types," Heinsheimer wrote on June 10. By June 15 the plans for reviving *Happy End* were over. "Brecht and Miss Hauptmann had left the work *entirely unchanged,*" Weill, apparently surprised, reported to Heinsheimer. "I only took up the whole *Happy End* complex again . . . with the clear understanding the work would have to undergo a thorough revision. . . . the plot so concentrated it would only be a framework for the songs. . . . the best I have written in this form. I never really expected much from *Happy End,* but in combination with a simple, comprehensible and unpretentious book the music could have carried the work across a number of stages." Agreeing with Heinsheimer that *Happy End* should not, in any form, be produced in Vienna, Weill concluded, "I don't want to put my success and popularity there in jeopardy because of something so unimportant."

F I V E

Slouching Toward Armageddon

From his first meeting with Brecht in the spring of 1927 until he completed the scoring in the fall of 1929, Weill regarded the full-length *Mahagonny* as the work that would provide a decisive new direction for opera. "The piece we are going to create won't exploit topical themes, which will be dated in a year, but rather will reflect the tenor of our times," Weill had written to Universal Edition on September 25, 1927, two months after the *Mahagonny-Songspiel* had had its solitary landmark performance. "For that reason, it will have an impact far beyond its own age." In October the partners began to work "every day on the libretto, which is being shaped according to my instructions," Weill reported. "This kind of collaboration, in which a libretto is actually formed according to purely musical considerations, opens up entirely new prospects."[1]

By early December 1927, fleshing out the skeletal framework of the *Mahagonny-Songspiel,* they had worked out a scenario that was to remain essentially intact throughout the prolonged creative process. In act 1 three hucksters on the run decide, when their getaway car breaks down, to found a new city, a "paradise" to which to lure wayfarers bruised by city life elsewhere. They will create a city of profitable snares. But they do it badly; the place becomes comfortably bourgeois; people leave ("All great enterprises have their crises," a placard proclaims). One newcomer, Johann Ackermann, bored by the city's aimless pursuits and resenting a growing list of prohibitions, plans a new utopia. As a typhoon approaches, he envisions rededicating the city to the principle of complete permissiveness. In act 2, eating, sex, drinking, and prizefighting are pursued in the new city without restraint, with often fatal consequences. When Johann is unable to pay his bar bill, he is jailed. In act 3, he is executed. God visits, banishing the sinful citizens to hell, a place they claim already to be in. The city collapses into a state of terminal anarchy. In depicting an anti-utopia, the cowriters intended their work, a morality tale like that of the biblical Sodom and Gomorrah, to stimulate postperformance discussion about what a true utopia might be like.

The work's fragmented, episodic structure is a remnant of the original songspiel in which five poems had been spliced together. For Weill, the crucial point about the play's chronicle or "epic" form, "nothing other than a sequence of situations," was that it enabled "an *organization according to purely musical precepts.*"[2] The new song style he had used for the short work, however, could not sustain the full-length version, conceived from the first as conforming to at least some of the musical requirements and expectations of an opera. To achieve a through-composed texture Weill linked separate numbers—songs in a simple balladlike style—with a dense pattern of harmonic, rhythmic, and melodic cross-references; as songs engage dialectically with larger forms, Weill forces opera and music hall to commingle with often daring promiscuity. Although some of the songs, as Weill fully expected and indeed wanted them to, escaped from their theatrical webbing to become independent hit tunes, they bear strong family similarities—the work is designed as a massive musical echo chamber in which the same musical cells continually cross-pollinate. From a purely compositional point of view, Weill does a masterly job of incorporating the music of the songspiel into this much larger form. Certain motifs are scattered throughout the opera; some are extended to the point that they control huge spans of music; other passages are incorporated unaltered from the earlier work; a few are quietly improved; and, of course, much of the opera's music is brand-new. Weill manages to hold all this material together by creating a consistent, if wildly eclectic, world of sound.

The dialogue between music and words is more varied in *Mahagonny* than in any other Brecht-Weill collaboration. Sometimes, as in *Die Dreigroschenoper,* Weill will wrap one of his lush melodies around the pebbles tossed up by Brecht's coruscating ironies. Elsewhere, music and words merge with a liquid flow, as Weill's matter-of-fact musical phrases match Brecht's casual cynicism.

The opera manages to be heroic (as all operas must be) and still to deflate the very idea of heroism. A soaring, "heroic" anthem, used recurrently in climactic moments, succinctly sums it up:

> *As you make your bed, so you lie on it*
> *The bed can be old or brand-new;*
> *So if someone must kick, why that's my part*
> *And another gets kicked, that part's for you!*[3]

We are put on notice that everything will be inverted in Mahagonny; no pieties—social, musical, sexual—will remain beyond assault. At the end of act 1, when a typhoon threatens to destroy the city, the orchestra concentrates its crucial minor-scale motive from the overture and starts to rise to great Verdian intensities. But deflation comes quickly, this time through a narrative announcement that the typhoon passed harmlessly around the city. In this opera, even a storm becomes an antistorm. Throughout the show, lyrically as well as musically, terrible events—a psychotic breakdown; death in an unequal boxing match—are handled in cryptic, unconventional ways. When a glutton kills himself by overeating, he does so to eerily genteel background music supplied by a solo zither. "Lovers, make haste / Lovers, don't waste," sings a group of men waiting impatiently in line for prostitutes. Here, Weill revisits Brecht's text to "The Mandalay Song," but this time he composes against the coarse grain of the scene, adding an onstage band that plays an enchanting tango melody, impeccably arranged and integrated into the score.

"I think I will eat my old felt hat / The flavors, at least, will be new," the antihero, Johann Ackermann, sings in a moment of terminal existential boredom. He has just been forced to listen to his pals intone a hushed (and very lovely) a cappella setting of some wonderfully absurd bourgeois bromides ("How miraculous the onset of evening," they have sung). The manipulation of layers of irony is so skillful throughout the opera that the listener may have been seduced by a beautiful melody like this one, only to laugh a moment later when it is derisively undermined.

Like Brecht, Weill wanted to be sure that the performers (and therefore the audience as well) remained aware that they were singing, and so he built a presentational performing style into his musical fabric. The ghastliness of the paradise city in which all is permitted for a price is, in effect, put on display as a series of numbered "turns" introduced by a chorus.

> *One means to eat all you are able;*
> *Two, to change your loves about;*
> *Three means the ring and gaming table;*
> *Four, to drink until you pass out.*

Throughout the opera, solos, arias, duets, and chorales with intoxicating melodies rise out of the often harsh, dry scrub of Weill's underscoring and recitative. When they appear, sometimes climactically, like "Denn wie man sich bettet, so liegt man" ("As You Make Your Bed"), or sometimes, like the "Alabama-Song" and the "Benares Song," descending without warning, they too are written as performance pieces, to be presented in an antipsychological style as part of a show rather than as emotional substance.

But in this richly problematic work pickled with contradictions, the this-is-theatre style is sometimes challenged or interrupted. For the aria at the beginning of act 3, as Johann Ackermann lies in irons waiting to be executed (in narrative context Weill quotes Florestan's famous prison aria from Beethoven's *Fidelio*), the composer abandons a detached style. Like another Brecht-Weill antihero, Macheath in the last act of *Die Dreigroschenoper,* confronting his death, Johann becomes a character in a dramatic rather than an ironic opera. There is poetry and pathos in what he sings:

> *Let the dark*
> *Last forever*
> *Day must not*
> *Break at all.*

Throughout the number he succumbs to a feral rage that breaks through the conventional bounds of the aria.

Weill also drops the character's performing mask in a duet with Jenny in one of the brothel scenes, which is psychologically acute, and touching in a way that only Brecht-Weill could be. Johann has chosen Jenny from among the prostitutes; they find themselves alone in her room. It is obvious that they like each other, and yet circumstances dictate that they get on with the business at hand. And so, in simple parlando phrases she asks him if he likes her hair up or down; and should she wear lingerie or not? A solo guitar plays steady eighth-note arpeggios, providing tenderness and also a sense of routine. Then an alto sax enters with a heartbreaking wisp of a tune written in the whole-tone scale: sultry, yet anonymous. Johann and Jenny conclude their negotiations without ever voicing their true feelings. The music provides everything that they cannot express.

Still, Weill was always a pragmatist, and he readily satisfied his publisher's request for a more conventional love duet to replace part of a brothel scene in act 2 that a number of opera managers objected to. Using a poem Brecht had written for an earlier collection, he composed the exquisite "Kraniche-Duett" ("Crane Duet"), in which Johann and Jenny express a tenderness untainted by the city of snares. In both melody and lyric ("See there two cranes veer by one with another / The clouds they pierce have been their lot together") the song, summoning an aura of post-coital satisfaction, a brief period of bliss before the cranes will "veer asunder," is altogether free of the Mahagonny sting. In an elegant, neobaroque composition, cool and detached, a contrast to the propulsive dynamics that dominate the score, Weill's long musical lines seem to weave and flow with the grace of the cranes and clouds they celebrate. (Unfortunately, the duet is often eliminated in performances.)

As with virtually every other component of *Mahagonny,* Weill's orchestrations were filled with controversial surprises. Was his notably under-nourished string section, as David Drew suggested, intended to protect the work from "the perils and seductions of 'romanticism' "?[4] The string section, nonetheless, is used well, notably in the off-the-string accents when the hurricane approaches, and in the surly sixteenth-note lines that accompany the city founders as they bemoan the failure of the first Mahagonny. Weill's other orchestrational choices are characteristically unusual, yet apt for an opera in a new, revue-style format. Harmonium, banjo, zither, bass guitar and Hawaiian guitar, bandoneon, cymbals, gongs, and tom-toms are treated with a generosity and respect unprecedented at the time within an opera-house setting. And his use of alto, tenor, and soprano saxophones is wonderfully sensuous. Like the performers of this immensely challenging work, the instruments are expected to jump through hoops, called on to provide simple solo accompaniment, dry ironic comment, and symphonic counterpoint. The *Mahagonny* orchestra must oscillate between "high" and "low" sounds, from epiphanic declamation to down-and-dirty ditties, from a swelling symphonic plenitude to a smooth-as-silk dance-band sonority. It is in the sheer range of sounds that

Weill demanded from orchestra and performers that the "impossibility" of *Mahagonny* can be measured: *Mahagonny*, after all, is an opera that contains the "Alabama-Song," which became a hit song for the Doors in 1967.

In composing *Mahagonny* Weill deliberately constructed an intricate musical web that does far more than merely support or illustrate Brecht's text. As he had intended from the beginning, and as Brecht only gradually seemed to realize, in *Mahagonny* music is the First Cause, the inescapable primum mobile. "The dramatic conduct of the singers, the movement of the chorus, as well as the entire performance style of this opera, are principally defined by the style of the music," Weill said. "At no time is this music illustrative. It endeavors to concretize the behavior of people in the various situations that the rise and fall of the city bring about. This behavior of people is already so determined in the music that a simple, natural interpretation of the music indicates the style of performance. Therefore, the performer can also restrict himself to the simplest and most natural gestures."[5] Indeed, music shapes the theme, defines the social behavior of the characters, and dictates the performing style. It is no wonder that it was over *Mahagonny* that the Brecht-Weill partnership was to crack.

But if ultimately the opera was to divide librettist from composer, during the work's long gestation the collaborators pursued the same goal, to create a prototype for a new kind of didactic opera, a *Lehrstück* with a theatrical punch. As Brecht wrote, "*Mahagonny* is a piece of fun. . . . It furthers pleasure even where it requires, or promotes, a certain degree of education."[6] To help in fulfilling their intentions, they patterned the work according to their evolving ideas about "epic opera," elements of which they were to employ in varying ways in interim works such as *Die Dreigroschenoper* and *Happy End*. (As often with Brecht, the theory was concretized only after the work had been completed—and the work itself often needs to be rescued from the theory.) In epic (as opposed to dramatic) opera, the music "communicates," "sets forth the text," "takes the text for granted," "takes up a position," "gives the attitude"—in other words, behaves in a cool, rational fashion to achieve a didactic thrust. In dramatic opera, on the other hand, the music, according to Brecht, behaves incorrectly because it "dishes up," "heightens," "proclaims," "illustrates," "depicts the psychological situation."[7] As both partners agreed, epic opera was antipsychological; the characters who found Mahagonny as well as the ones who are enticed by and who ultimately succumb to it are meant only as representative figures, just as "all the songs of this opera," as Weill indicated, "are an expression of the masses, even where they are performed by the individual as spokesman of the masses. . . . The city itself is the main figure of the play."[8]

For both Brecht and Weill, epic opera was a prescription for defying the Wagnerian *Gesamtkunstwerk,* the integrated work of art. "So long as the arts are supposed to be 'fused' together, the various elements will all be equally degraded and each will act as a mere 'feed' to the rest," Brecht wrote. In a vivid passage of phrase mongering, Brecht described fusion as a process in which the spectator too "gets thrown into the melting pot," to become "a passive part of the total work of art. Witchcraft of this sort must of course be fought against. Whatever is intended to produce hypnosis, or is likely to induce improper intoxication, or creates fog, has got to be given up." As cure he proposed "a radical separation of elements . . . *words, music, setting must become more independent of one another.*"[9] And as a result, the spectator, saved from hypnosis, would be receptive to critical thinking— available to the work of learning.

In separating music, did Brecht wish also to alienate it from its primal sources? Ignored in his program for a gestic, ideologically useful kind of music is the fact that no matter how estranged from its usual functions, music still exerts an atavistic power to enchant. No matter how cerebral its setting, musical declaration will always compete with, perhaps even steal from, the words to which it is attached. And Weill, the most strong-willed of any of Brecht's collaborators, entered the arena with his eyes wide open, confident from the beginning that his music would prevail over his part-ner's libretto. Answering early objections from his publisher, who in a December 16, 1927, letter expressed "disappointment" in a libretto that was "just a series of scenes," Weill countered on December 27 that music in *Mahagonny* "has a much more fundamental role than in the purely sto-ryline opera, since I am replacing the earlier bravura aria with a new kind of popular song. As a result I can completely allay any fears you may have that this work is somehow derived from a spoken play. . . . With great dif-ficulty I have succeeded in getting Brecht to the point that he was actually challenged by the task of writing a text to suit musical requirements and I have examined every word with an eye to the demands of the opera stage. It is the first libretto in years that is fully dependent upon music, indeed upon *my music* [author's emphasis]."

In his notorious post-facto notes to *Mahagonny* (cowritten with Peter Suhrkamp) Brecht allowed that within the inevitably "narrow limitation" imposed by operatic form—i.e., by the imposition of music—it was still possible to introduce "an element of instruction." But ultimately he dismissed *Mahagonny* as merely "culinary," unable to resist the pull of music *away* from thought. "It is culinary through and through," he snorted, concluding that *Mahagonny* "is nothing more or less than an opera."[10] In that sentence Brecht revealed both his disdain for opera and his defeat. Indeed, *Mahagonny is* an opera, after all, a piece of theatrical "witchcraft" of the sort Brecht professed to scorn, scored by a composer who, despite Brecht's best attempts, achieved the status of a full-fledged cowriter and who in fact ended up stealing the show.

By the fall of 1929, when the cocreators felt their epic opera was ready, the composer knew that the work's theatrical as well as narrative impact was shaped by its musical ideas. Although Brecht's full recognition of that fact was to be delayed until the opera was finally in rehearsal, he nonetheless distanced himself from all preproduction skirmishes, allowing his collaborator to represent the work on his own. And with characteristic drive, Weill took an active part in a process that was to be as protracted, and as difficult, as having cowritten the opera. Weill hoped *Mahagonny* would open at the theatre it seemed to have been written for, the self-consciously progressive Krolloper. Negotiations with the Krolloper had actually begun the preceding spring, after Brecht and Weill had put what they thought at the time were the finishing touches on a work that would prove to be virtually unfinishable; but from the beginning there were obstacles. Otto Klemperer expressed admiration for the piece but was also deeply troubled by it: the act 2 bordello scene offended him, but beyond that he was unsettled by Weill's fusion of popular with symphonic motifs. Ironically, to the impresario of Berlin's ultraprogressive opera house, Brecht and Weill's opera seemed too progressive. Klemperer hedged, alternately tempted and repelled by a problematic work he could never quite classify. Over the spring, as he contemplated a possible production for the fall, Klemperer suggested directors Weill thought were ill suited to the project. "The only possibility [for director] is BB, who is prepared to do so but doesn't want to be listed on the playbill because he never is," Weill wrote Universal Edition on May 5, at a point where Klemperer seemed ready to commit. But as Klemperer continued to waver, Weill became increasingly impatient. He began to think the Krolloper might not be the right venue, not only because of Klemperer but also because of the theatre's lackluster approach to promotion. Weill was eager to attract the *Dreigroschenoper* audience ("which, for the most part, has never set foot in an opera house") as well as the Krolloper's usual clientele, and to that end he wanted an aggressive public-relations campaign. "It is essential to have the same kind of outdoor posters and newspaper notices that for the private theatres have long since proven decisive for success," he wrote Universal Edition on May 25, but feared that with the Krolloper's track record, "even with a sensational hit not even a cat would come."

In July negotiations with the Krolloper came to a boil. After Weill played the third act for Klemperer and several assistants, one of Klemperer's advisers, Ernst Legal, "urged immediate categorical acceptance," Weill wrote in a July 13 letter to Elisabeth Hauptmann. But Klemperer had remained silent. Weill returned home. Two hours later Klemperer came to Weill's apartment "in a state of absolute despair and declared with tears in his eyes that he had now spent two hours wrestling with himself, but that it was impossible, he acknowledged the importance of the whole thing, he recognized the musical beauties, but the whole thing was foreign to him and incomprehensible," Weill informed Hauptmann. But still hanging fire, Klemperer offered two possibilities: if he could see the work fully staged at a provincial opera house he might change his mind; or perhaps *Mahagonny* could be staged at the Kroll after all, but with another conductor. In a July 16 letter to Universal Edition, Weill suggested "the young [Maurice] Abravanel [who has] incredible enthusiasm and would have neither moral misgivings nor any kind of illusions of stardom [unlike Klemperer]." But in a July 20 response, Hans Heinsheimer at Universal rejected outright any thought of presenting *Mahagonny* at the Kroll ("at present both externally and internally a Klemperer Opera") without Klemperer.

After the collapse of other attempts to place the work in a Berlin house, Heinsheimer offered it to the Leipzig Opera, a major regional theatre. The theatre's director, Gustav Brecher, accepted, and *Mahagonny* would have its world premiere in Leipzig on March 9, 1930 — but only if the authors agreed to changes. Brecher, along with managers at other regional houses where the work was to open simultaneously on March 12, voiced the same kind of objection as Klemperer to the now-notorious brothel scene. Working quickly, Brecht and Weill devised a new approach to the scene. "Completely novel and very successful," Weill wrote to Heinsheimer on October 1. "We have intentionally fashioned it into the opposite of the previous version" by turning the "scandalous" segment into a "scientific" report of Mahagonny's thriving sexual marketplace. "One can say and perform the most daring things if one gives them a scientific character," Weill noted dryly. They also added the lyrical new "Kraniche-Duett." Heinsheimer in an October 10 letter to Weill expressed "joyous shock" on hearing the new scene. "Radical and startling," he wrote, and professed to divine in it "the [Weill] sound of the coming years . . . created out of a new romanticism, a new longing, a new search for the 'unattainable,' in short, an emotional sphere which must fully embrace the *neue Sachlichkeit* in order to overcome it." Heinsheimer welcomed the new scene as a "mark of artistic responsibility on a truly high plane"—and as a rejection of the song style, which "in the long run can serve only as a springboard for you to find your way back to more profound and substantial musical creations." In ringing tones, Heinsheimer urged his client to "free [himself] once and for all from the kind of commercialized artistic activities practiced in Berlin" in order "to adhere to the grand path, which I have always perceived in your works."

"By far the greater part of *Mahagonny* is already entirely independent from the song style and reveals this new style, which in seriousness, 'stature,' and expressive power surpasses everything I have written to date," Weill fired back on October 14. "Almost everything added to the Baden-Baden version [of *Mahagonny*] is written in a completely pure, thoroughly responsible style. My song style has not stood still *for one moment*," Weill argued. Refusing to trivialize "what was achieved through *Die Dreigroschenoper*," he cited *Happy End* as a clear progression. "The music [for *Happy End*] as a whole represents a formal, instrumental and melodic development so far beyond *Die Dreigroschenoper* that only helpless ignoramuses like the German critics could miss it." Disputing Heinsheimer's contention that he has lapsed in his commitment to serious music, Weill claimed to be "the only creative musician who has worked consistently and uncompromisingly in the face of opposition from the snobs and aesthetes toward the creation of fundamental forms of a new, simple popular music theatre."

Heinsheimer's admonition to his client to avoid a popular style and Weill's spirited defense of it reveal the high-culture prejudices Weill had to confront, within himself as well as in his battles with elitists. Their volatile exchange underlined for Weill what was at stake in the upcoming production: *Mahagonny* would be his answer to "the snobs and aesthetes" who charged him with forsaking his "artistic responsibilities." Is it surprising that, as the March 9 opening approached, Weill's anxiety mounted?

Nonetheless, in early 1930, as they were preparing for the Leipzig premiere, Weill collaborated with Brecht for the last time on native ground. At the invitation of the organizers of the 1930 New Music Festival in

Berlin, scheduled for the summer, the partners agreed to write a school opera—an opera for students. Once again, the choice of subject seems to have come from Elisabeth Hauptmann, who at Brecht's insistence had been reading English translations of Japanese Noh plays. Working from an English version by Arthur Waley, Hauptmann prepared for Brecht a translation of a fourteenth-century Noh drama called *Taniko.* Brecht titled the work *Der Jasager (The Yes-Sayer).* In order to visit a renowned scholar, a teacher is to lead a group of students on a dangerous mountain trek. Seeking medicine for his sick mother, another and younger student asks to be allowed to accompany them on their journey. Warning the boy of the risks, the teacher tells of an ancient custom they must obey, which mandates that anyone unable to complete the journey must be hurled into the valley. In the original drama the boy is saved by the spirit of mercy; in Brecht's interpretation, the boy, who cannot keep up and so endangers the group's progress, consents to be hurled into the valley. Agreeing to his elimination, the boy behaves according to the belief that the individual must be willing to sacrifice himself for the good of the community. Is the boy's agreement, his yes-saying, a correct action?

Their work on the school opera was interrupted by the *Mahagonny* premiere. Both Brecht and Weill fully expected that the full-length opera would repeat the incendiary reception the songspiel had elicited in Baden-Baden in the summer of 1927. Indeed, provoking spectators was part of the work's intention, part of the authors' self-appointed roles as cultural renegades. What they hadn't reckoned on was that this time their offense would be regarded as political rather than artistic.

Opening night in Leipzig, Weill and Lenya had to walk through massed groups of brownshirts carrying banners denouncing the show and its creators. Clearly, more was at stake than the fate of an avant-garde opera by a team of professional bad boys. Before the show started, the theatre was thick with a tension that surpassed the usual electricity of first nights. No more than a few seconds after the first scene began, a perceptible low rumble started to form in the audience. As Heinsheimer, who had traveled from Vienna for the occasion, recalled, the faint stirrings soon erupted into "noise, shouts, at last screams and roars of protest. Some of the actors stepped out of their parts, rushed to the apron of the stage, shouted back. The performance ended in violence. It was a purely political demonstration, carefully planned as a test of power and, as such, a great success."[11] Another eyewitness, critic Alfred Polgar, recalled "belligerent shouts, hand-to-hand fighting in some places, hissing, applauding that sounded

ABOVE: The alienation effect in practice: banners and placards, and
Caspar Neher's oversize drawing, enfold the action with comments from
the show's creators in the final scene of *Aufstieg und Fall der Stadt
Mahagonny* at the Leipzig premiere, March 9, 1930.
BELOW: The typhoon scene in the original opera-house production of
Aufstieg und Fall der Stadt Mahagonny in Leipzig

grimly as if the hissing people had been symbolically slapped in the face, enthusiastic fury mixed with furious enthusiasm. Finally, a demonstration en masse by the complainers crushed by a hail of applause." Out of this rabble, Polgar singled out "a dignified gentleman with a lobster-red face [who] had drawn a bunch of keys and was battling piercingly against the epic theatre." Using one of the keys as a whistle, the exacerbated spectator "dispatch[ed] air streams of the highest vibration frequency. . . . There was something merciless in the sound of this instrument, something that cut into your stomach. . . . His wife didn't desert him at the moment of truth. A very large, all-around Valkyrie-type, her hair done up in a bun, dressed in a blue sheet with yellow fillings. With her eyes shut, her cheeks blown up and two fat fingers in her mouth, she out screeched [her husband's fierce whistling]. A dreadful, sordid sight."[12]

The Leipzig first night, which the Nazis used as an opportunity to stage-manage a display of their mounting political strength, was an appalling spectacle, but Weill refused to capitulate or to confront its implications. Seizing on the fact that the response was divided, that cheers were mixed in with the hisses, Weill interpreted the evening not as an emanation from the dark unconscious of the German *Geist* but rather as support for his and Brecht's artistic principles. "I am firmly convinced that this ninth of March has finally led to a clear cut parting of the ways [between philistines and true aesthetes] which will set the tone for the musical life of the next few years," he wrote Heinsheimer from Berlin on March 14. "The path I've chosen is correct and . . . it is out of the question to give up this path just because its beginnings happen to run into a strand of the fiercest cultural reaction. . . . All great innovations encounter violent opposition," he concluded, having chosen to define the eruption on purely cultural grounds. In Berlin, which fancied itself relatively untainted by the bad habits of the rest of Germany, he assured his Viennese publisher in a March 21 letter that the hullabaloo in Leipzig was being regarded as a social comedy, "a real disgrace." "The only way to make a success out of the work is to present it as a sensational theatre event of historic proportions."

"It isn't a political work since there have been positive reviews from papers of all political persuasions," Weill argued speciously. Furthermore, to ensure the work's political virginity, he reported that he had worked with Brecht on "a clarification of events" in the third act. "We now have a version to which even the pope can't object. It is now absolutely clear that the closing demonstration [in the play] is not at all communistic, but . . .

Mahagonny perishes because of the crimes of its inhabitants, the wantonness and the general chaos." "Brecht was very responsive to my suggestions," he added (is there a note of surprise here?), "and I am extremely happy to have so quickly drafted a version that is very nearly beyond reproach. We show clearly that anarchy leads to crime and crime to ruin. You can't get more moral."

Despite Weill's claims, *Mahagonny* was to continue to have a bedeviled history. At the second performance in Leipzig, a few days after the premiere, house lights were turned on, police were placed prominently at the entrance and throughout the auditorium, and from beginning to end the audience was encased in a stony silence. The remaining performances were for invited audiences only. On March 12, as scheduled, the opera opened in Braunschweig, but because of riots staged by hordes of brownshirts it was performed only twice. In Kassel (with Maurice Abravanel conducting), it ran for seven undisrupted performances. But the respite was short-lived. Unnerved managers of the opera houses in Essen, Dortmund, and Oldenburg hesitated, then canceled their contracts.

After the furor over *Mahagonny* subsided, the collaborators returned to work on their school opera, which was to have its premiere at the New Music Festival in Berlin in June. Also for the festival, Brecht was working with Hanns Eisler on a short Marxist play, *Die Massnahme (The Measures Taken)*, which also chronicled the death of an individual whose interest collided with that of a group. When the festival board rejected the play, in protest Brecht and Weill withdrew *Der Jasager,* which instead had its premiere on Radio Berlin on June 23. The next day the school opera was given its stage premiere at the Central Institute for Education and Schooling. Codirected by Brecht and Weill themselves, with designs by Caspar Neher, the production was performed by students from the State Academy for Church and School Music and other local schools. It was conducted by Kurt Drabek, eighteen at the time.

"We had some discussion during rehearsals," Drabek recalled. "Was it sensible that that boy sacrificed himself and let himself be thrown down?"[13] When audiences seemed to feel that the answer was yes, the boy's sacrifice was necessary, Brecht and Weill were startled. And indeed, if their school opera gave ideological support to the death of the boy, what kind of lesson was it imparting? Read with hindsight, it could even be argued that if this was the authors' intention, then the gestalt they were advocating was akin to the one that was rapidly overtaking Germany. If the boy's agreement is accepted as proper, it could be interpreted as a prelude to the catastrophic "agreement" the German nation was to accord the architects of the Final Solution. Brecht had intended a dialectical reading in which performers and audiences would examine and argue with rather than automatically acquiesce to the concept of *Einverständnis* (agreement) as it is articulated within the parable. In the autumn of 1930, after listening to the confused responses of students at the Karl Marx School, who performed in a production he supervised, Brecht made several minor revisions. But when he saw that students were still puzzled, or misguided in their interpretation, he decided to write a companion text, *Der Neinsager (The Naysayer)*, which repeats *Der Jasager* up to the climactic moment in which the boy is asked if he agrees to his own liquidation. This time, the boy refuses to consent to the old custom and argues that each situation should be examined on its own. Speaking up for independence of thought, he succeeds in convincing the others to terminate their journey and carry him home. Uncharacteristically, Brecht was doing the work the audience was supposed to have done for itself. (Near the end of 1930, Brecht published both short works, and suggested in a note that they be presented on the same bill.)

Already at work with Caspar Neher on a long opera, Weill did not write a score for *Der Neinsager*. But he may well have been reluctant to write a score for a "counter" play because he knew he had accomplished what he wanted in the first place; on more than one occasion he was to call this thirty-five-minute piece the best and most important of his German compositions. As David Drew noted, "If *Der Jasager* is studied and performed with true understanding, the original text requires no 'corrections' beyond those which the music itself so eloquently supplies."[14] Part of this eloquence stems from Weill's own understanding of his performing forces. The music is ingeniously written at a technical level that can be reached by talented students. To this aim, Weill revives the hieratic style of *Der Lindberghflug*, but here carries it even further. He simplifies his block harmonies, slows his harmonic rhythm, gives the singers simple but well-crafted diatonic melodies, and provides rhythmically vibrant (but not technically difficult) accompaniments. Even the pentatonic scale (that trite signifier of all things Eastern) is deployed in a sparing and tasteful way. And in this piece Weill's tribute to Bach is perfectly integrated. When the teacher, the mother, and the boy sing a fuguelike trio, we hear something astonishing: Bach made new, Bach concentrated to a primitive universal essence, appropriate to a German schoolroom or to a Japanese mountain pass.

Weill's musical language provides the key to this simple but highly ambiguous play. The strict, authoritarian beat of the chorus that frames the play, announcing the apparent thesis that "above all, it is important to learn to acquiesce,"[15] provides a key thematic clue. The severe music, summoning an aura of grimness rather than triumph, invites the spectator to read against or beneath the words. Is acquiescence important "above all," or, as Weill's musical structure suggests, are other qualities more important still? The insistent, unstoppable march of the choral summation may override the humane melodies Weill assigns to the mother and the teacher; yet the solo melodies—the music of human individuality—suggest that there are ways to combat tyranny. Weill's composition is always firm—he never resorts to full melodic generosity—but in sounding softer notes the solo passages contain a promise of resistance. *Der Jasager* is music with a subtext, music that must be listened to dialectically if the lessons of this *Schuloper* are to be properly apprehended.

For all its musical cues, as Brecht and Weill discovered, it was still possible for the piece to be read as a stern moral lesson in favor of the sacrifices the individual must be prepared to make in order to serve the welfare of the group. Indeed, *Der Jasager* required from its student participants and listeners a sophisticated, nuanced reading that may have been unrealistically demanding. Although it was sometimes misread, *Der Jasager* achieved a remarkable performance record in a country rapidly drifting to the radical right. The short work clearly touched a contemporary nerve, and next to *Die Dreigroschenoper* was Brecht and Weill's most popular offering. It was performed in over three hundred German schools; many of the later productions were interpreted according to the writers' intentions. In an October 27, 1930, letter to Weill, Heinsheimer felt the work's extraordinary success was, in fact, a sign of resistance to the amassing power of the National Socialists. "We really need steady nerves now. . . . We are quite convinced that now, right after the election and after their unfortunate debut in Berlin, the Nazis will be distinguishing themselves everywhere and that it won't last long. . . . In the meantime you can take solace from *Der Jasager,* whose moral success really cannot be overestimated."[16]

As *Der Jasager* began to be presented in schools throughout the country, Weill's focus shifted back to *Mahagonny,* which the Frankfurt Opera, with extreme misgivings, staged on October 16, 1930. After the director expressed concern that the arrival of God in the last scene would be certain to offend his conventional audience, Weill and Brecht agreed to having the scene cut. By this time, even Weill was becoming uneasy. Glazed with apprehension, he and Lenya traveled to Frankfurt for the opening night. As soon as the show started, a low rumble rose from the auditorium, building in steady increments until there was more noise in the house than on the stage. Then, as Weill reported to his publisher on October 21, "the resistance, which was artificially fanned, completely disappeared, and there was frequent applause, with an open curtain, after the first act twelve, at the end twenty-three curtain calls." "It has been absolutely proven (namely with the most stolid, old-fashioned opera audience in Germany) that in the present version *Mahagonny* has extraordinary potential for success." The second performance in Frankfurt, however, was disrupted by a Nazi demonstration. "Naturally [this] was a real stroke of bad luck [but] . . . this scandal was naturally not in any way directed against the work," Weill argued, determined not to capitulate. But in a letter four days later Weill for the first time seemed to recognize the real and immediate danger posed by the radical right's expanding power. "It becomes apparent what kind of people (butchers and train robbers) will now decide the fate of art works in Germany."

Although demoralized, Weill hoped for vindication in Berlin, and began to make plans for a commercial production. In the course of his prolonged negotiations, which began in the spring of 1930, he courted all of Weimar's most prominent theatrical impresarios, expertly playing off one against the other with seemingly little awareness that all the while he was dancing on the edge of a volcano. Ernst Aufricht, Weill's original mentor in the commercial theatre, took an option but had trouble raising money. Without telling Aufricht, Weill approached Erik Charell, a producer of sumptuous revues—the Berlin Florenz Ziegfeld, in effect—who "would like to do it as soon as May in the large Schauspielhaus (3500 seats!)," as Weill reported on March 18. When the plans for presenting *Mahagonny* as an extravaganza collapsed, Weill then explored the possibility of turning the opera into a Max Reinhardt superproduction—a pageant play on the order of Reinhardt's *Miracle*. "It would be better to produce *Mahagonny* in a large representative theatre than with Aufricht. . . . Reinhardt would be both: representative and commercially advantageous," Weill wrote his publisher on March 25. "In any event it will be necessary for reasons of protocol that you *yourself* tell Aufricht that his option expired long ago . . . and that he cannot count on *Mahagonny* the way he apparently assumes."

"The news hit like a bomb today," Weill boasted to Universal Edition in an April 3 letter after Reinhardt's office announced *Mahagonny* as a future production. "They are already negotiating with Marlene Dietrich. . . . The Reinhardt acceptance is for me the best and most convincing proof that I am on the right track with my work." Weill urged his publisher to "clearly use the designation, Kurt Weill's opera, text by Brecht, since otherwise one might find it stated somewhere that the work will now be done as a play."

By the fall, however, negotiations were seriously tarnished. On October 30 Weill wrote to his publisher about rumors that Reinhardt was intimidated by the opera's controversial reputation and was "beginning to peddle [it]." Early in the new year, Reinhardt withdrew. "I heard it in confidence from a well-informed source, that Reinhardt received money from heavy industry circles in the Rhineland . . . on the condition that he not perform *Mahagonny* and Zuckmayer's *Captain from Köpenick*," Weill reported on January 3. Within a month Weill succeeded in attracting the interest of Robert Klein, a commercial producer who offered much less prestige than Reinhardt but who had a lot of money and a taste for taking risks. Once Klein began to suggest changes in the opera, however, the honeymoon was over. "We must absolutely insist on my right of co-determination [in all artistic matters]," Weill wrote to Universal Edition on February 10. "Otherwise we will one day be confronted with a work we won't recognize, an operetta!" By early spring, Klein too withdrew, and having exhausted all the major prospects for a commercially produced *Mahagonny* in Berlin, Weill finally returned to Aufricht, whom he had been stalling all along.

After working over the summer to raise money, Aufricht by the fall was still underfinanced. On October 7, Heinsheimer notified Weill that "we have just received news that the bank on which Aufricht gave us a guarantee has collapsed. A fine mess." According to Margot Aufricht, the cabaret star Trude Hesterberg rescued the harried producer. "She came to my husband to say the role of Begbick [one of the founders of the city of Mahagonny] was just up her alley. My husband said, 'This is very expensive—I don't know if I can afford it. There are thirty-one orchestra members.' Then she said, 'I'll bring you a man who finances it.' Her boyfriend was a banker. So it came to pass."[17]

"*Mahagonny* is an opera, an opera for singers," Weill had written in a February 2, 1930, letter to Maurice Abravanel, just before Abravanel was to conduct the Kassel performances. "Casting it with actors is as good as impossible." Yet for the commercial Berlin production, Weill returned to the practice he and Brecht had established with *Die Dreigroschenoper* and

Happy End of casting a few singing actors. Most of the performers were opera and operetta people, and there were no non-singers in the company. Lotte Lenya was to play Jenny the prostitute; the hero, Johann Ackermann (in later productions Jimmy Mahoney) from Alaska, was Harald Paulsen, the original Macheath; and Trude Hesterberg got the part she wanted, as Begbick, city founder. To accommodate his actors—Paulsen was an operetta tenor and Hesterberg was a chanteuse—Weill rescored extensively. And for Lenya, now a more prominent player than she had been two years earlier, he prepared a revised setting for the "Havanna-Lied" ("Havana Song"). Cutting and simplifying, he nudged the Berlin *Mahagonny* in a popular direction, while at the same time maintaining the highest musical values.

As the opening drew near, Weill was concerned that the upcoming production might affect the reception of his "pure" opera, *Die Bürgschaft,* scheduled for later the same season at the Staatsoper Unter den Linden. Although he pretended indifference toward the critical brickbats he had received as a composer straddling (at least) two musical cultures, he feared the overlapping premieres would only invite further skepti-

Hesto Hesterberg's drawing of Lenya as Jenny in the revised version of *Aufstieg und Fall der Stadt Mahagonny,* which opened for a commercial run in Berlin at the Theater am Kurfürstendamm on December 21, 1931

cism. "We are extremely surprised by your remarks that you have always had mixed feelings about this *Mahagonny* performance," Heinsheimer wrote Weill on November 24, responding to the composer's concern. "Director Hertzka was always firmly against it, while I was and am absolutely in favor and thought that you were completely on my side. . . . This news amazed me. . . . *Mahagonny* at the Theater am Kurfürstendamm and *Die Bürgschaft* do not affect each other," Heinsheimer hastened to assure his anxious client.

Weill's hesitations about a nonoperatic *Mahagonny* were only momentary, however, and within a week he had returned to his usual role of eager team player. "Should it be a great success we must have parts for café and dance bands ready very quickly," he cautioned his publishers in a December 1 letter. "Concentrate on one number and give it a big build up. The best one for that (text and music) would be 'Wie man sich bettet' . . . [which] could be made into an easy-to-play number by a first-class arranger (who would only have to simplify the introduction somewhat)."

It was during the rehearsals for *Mahagonny* that the long-simmering resentments between the collaborators flared into open warfare. Weill and Lenya had the greatest esteem for Brecht as both a writer and a director but had taken a marked personal dislike to him from early on. They bitterly resented Brecht's financial shenanigans over the *Dreigroschenoper* contract: Brecht had required Weill to accept only 25 percent of the royalties while reserving 75 percent for himself. The discreet and fastidious composer was also offended by BB's disheveled appearance, his slovenly personal habits, and his compulsive womanizing. And Lenya, always attentive to her husband's interests, chafed at Brecht's increasing efforts to claim priority for his texts over Weill's music. As a kind of self-protection Weill cultivated a pleasant, equable veneer; like Lenya, he trusted or accepted very few

Veterans of *Die Dreigroschenoper,* Lenya (as Jenny) and Harald Paulsen (as Johann Ackermann), in the Berlin production of *Aufstieg und Fall der Stadt Mahagonny*

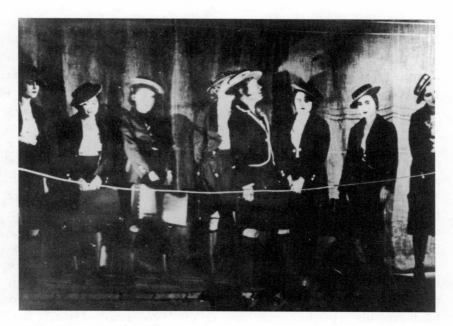

The "Alabama-Song": Lenya as Jenny, middle, and the prostitutes on their way to the
new city, in the Berlin *Mahagonny*

people, but he was better than his wife, who could be prickly and openly
contentious, in concealing his numerous grievances. But working with a
particularly obstreperous Brecht on the Berlin *Mahagonny,* Weill's mask
crumbled.

Because the original director, Walther Brügmann, had asked for more
money than Aufricht could afford, Caspar Neher, the show's designer, had
been appointed in his place. Although Weill had just finished working on
an opera with him, Neher remained under Brecht's influence, and since
Brecht as always was an intrusive presence at rehearsals, in effect he was
directing the show. He wanted this version to be more text-oriented than
the original Leipzig production and demanded changes in the libretto that
Weill had to accommodate musically. To defend his interests Weill knew
he had to have a strong conductor; Gustav Brecher, the original conductor,
had also asked for a larger salary than Aufricht could handle. Weill's first
choice was Maurice Abravanel. "Kurt was grateful to me that at the time
things looked so black, after the Leipzig *Mahagonny,* that the Kassel production which I conducted was a big success," Abravanel recalled. "But
my Intendant refused because by that time things were getting very dan-

gerous in Germany, and he did not want me to be mixed up with Brecht, a known Marxist by then."[18] Weill forbade Theo Mackeben, who had conducted *Die Dreigroschenoper* and *Happy End,* and insisted on Alexander von Zemlinsky, Schoenberg's brother-in-law and teacher, a strong-willed opera conductor whom Weill knew he could count on to guarantee the work's musical values as well as to stand up to Brecht. (Mackeben was essentially a dance-band conductor without any opera-house experience.)

As the arguments over music vs. words escalated, Brecht at one point called Weill "a phony Richard Strauss" and threatened to push him down a flight of stairs.[19] To distract Brecht, Aufricht and his dramaturg Robert Vambery promised to produce *The Mother,* a Communist agitprop play of his own that Brecht was eager to stage. They gave Brecht rehearsal space in the basement of the theatre where *Mahagonny* was rehearsing. In his "lair," his attention focused on his new play, in which he was directing Helene Weigel, Brecht, as they had hoped, became a less meddlesome presence upstairs. "It was the only way to get *Mahagonny* on," Aufricht said.[20] But contrary to the producer's claims, Brecht did not suddenly disappear. Gerhard Henschke, a production assistant on *The Mother,* reported that, in fact, Brecht was frequently summoned upstairs, where his opinion continued to be sought and to be listened to. "Brecht was up and down the stairs many times a day," Henschke recalled.[21] And when he appeared the tension between the collaborators was palpable. "I was with Weill upstairs when Brecht comes up from rehearsal in the basement, sees us, and turns in the opposite direction," Felix Jackson remembered. "The move looked primitive, ridiculous. 'I didn't start it,' Kurt said in a petulant voice. He sounded like a child. 'Brecht's getting everything his way,' Kurt said, and added, 'He always does.' "[22]

Despite the backstage contretemps, the feuding partners expected the show to be a critical hit that would open without political disturbance, since even in late 1931 Berliners by and large still liked to think themselves immune from the stench of Nazism. On opening night December 21, a battalion of brownshirts in full regalia, a not uncommon sight in the winter of 1931–32, marched down the Kurfürstendamm in front of the theatre, shouting the words of the "Horst Wessel Lied" in a threatening military staccato. Whistling, stomping, and barking, the storm troopers passed by the opening-night crowd waiting for admission to the theatre. "It's a terrible melody," Weill pronounced. "Only a Nazi could write it."[23] The mixed audience—precisely the kind that Weill was eager to attract—was dressed in a polyglot fashion: women in minks and sables and men in black tie moved in and out of crowds of students and bohemians dressed in crewneck sweaters and ready-mades. The air crackled with anticipation: Was it for the new Brecht-Weill, or for the possibility of a Nazi countershow, or a perverse desire for a mixture of the two spectacles? But the excitement that night came from the stage rather than the auditorium. "There was no outcry in Berlin," Margot Aufricht said. "The Berliners are no Nazis. They were all imported."[24]

"The press surpasses all expectation, especially in the big boulevard papers," Weill wrote Universal Edition on December 27. But, as even Weill had to admit, there were some problems. "The score is much stronger with the public than with the specialists, who would gladly deny or suppress it because they find it annoying when any musician finds an understanding outside a circle of twenty. The completely uncomprehending review by Alfred Einstein in the *Tageblatt*, read precisely by those circles that ought to see *Mahagonny*, is a serious blow for the success. Aufricht is mounting a major publicity campaign, and he would like the two popular numbers played in all the hotels and bars." The production received an important boost from Theodor Adorno, rigorous musicologist and social critic. "*Mahagonny* has improved [over the opera-house productions]," Adorno reported with a note of surprise, "becoming clearer both in content and surrealistic form, more tightly-knit, in a representation where finally the music gains real presence. No denying that here the conducting of Zemlinsky is crucial. . . . He has freed this music from uncomprehending association with élan, jazz, and infernal entertainment, and shown us what it is; with its mouldering, shrill, then deathly sad, faded background, with a careful sharpness, which sets in relief the leaps and swerving of which the public who loves the 'song' would rather not be aware."[25] Adorno concluded, however, that *Mahagonny* belongs in the opera house.

"The right wing press has proven very loyal to me, basically much more decent than the 'Jewish press,' " Weill noted in his December 27 letter. "The National Socialist *Deutsche Zeitung* writes of the 'great talent of one who has gone astray' and in the nationalistic *Der Tag* Hans Joachim Moser writes with genuine understanding about my music. I therefore believe less than ever in the fairy tale that it is only the nationalistic or anti-Semitic movement which stands in the way of modern theatre endeavors. The noncommitted and apprehensive attitude of liberalism is at least as much at fault." Weill accurately assessed the muted voice of the liberal critics, reticent in the face of a reactionary stampede; but once again he misjudged the enemy.

For Lenya, the opening was an unqualified triumph. The Berlin *Mahagonny* provided a frame in which her magnetic, untrained voice could claim the spotlight, and at the premiere her new song received a tumultuous reception. But the production was far from the commercial success Weill and Brecht had hoped for. It ran for fifty far-from-sold-out performances—an outstanding run for an opera, but disappointing for a commercial venture. Although Weill and Brecht may have momentarily believed that their nonoperatic version might yield another commercial hit, they were of course deluded. *Mahagonny* is too abrasive, too demanding both musically and structurally, ever to become a popular favorite. Rather than providing the kind of critical vindication Weill needed and fervently wanted, the December 21, 1931, opening of his and Brecht's great work heralded the beginning of the end of their careers in a country becoming rapidly submerged in the sickening swell of National Socialism.

SIX

Last Rites

O ver their years together Brecht had insulted Kurt right and left, saying that he, Brecht, had composed the 'Alabama-Song,' for instance, which is of course a damned lie," Maurice Abravanel recalled. "By 1930 Kurt was furious and fed up, he wanted to prove he could have a success without Brecht, and so he decided to team with another partner."[1] In choosing Caspar Neher as his colibrettist for a new opera, however, Weill remained well within Brecht's orbit. Although married (Weill, in fact, was having an open affair with Neher's wife, Erika), Neher was a homosexual long infatuated with Brecht, his best friend since boyhood. But Weill composed and cowrote the libretto of *Die Bürgschaft (The Pledge)* not only to prove that he could have a success "without Brecht," but also to demonstrate his renewed commitment to opera in an unadulterated form. His longest work, *Die Bürgschaft* was Weill's one more or less orthodox three-act German opera, an answer to elitist critics who had accused him of stooping to conquer. According to Lenya, it was the work "he *had* to write. He told me, 'I have now written for singing actors, *Die Dreigroschenoper* and *Happy End. Der Jasager* was for students, for untrained voices. Now this is the time when I have to let go. I have to. Otherwise I'll burst.' "[2]

Based on *Der afrikanische Rechtsspruch (The African Judgment)* by Johann Gottfried von Herder, *Die Bürgschaft,* like *Mahagonny,* is a dark allegory about a society plunging toward doom. The prologue and act 1 are set in the land of Urb during precolonial times; acts 2 and 3 take place after an invasion by a Great Power. The story of a ruined friendship occupies the foreground. In the prologue, David Orth, a corn dealer, rescues Johann Mattes, a cattle dealer who gambles compulsively. At the conclusion of act 3, set six years after the political change, to save his own life Orth offers Mattes as a sacrifice to a mob. A transformed Orth at the climax proclaims his belief in Money and Power. Like the characters in *Mahagonny,* Mattes and Orth are embodiments of general social tendencies; their shifting behavior represents the fault lines of a culture overtaken by a maleficent new regime. Although it may have been artistically less troublesome than *Mahagonny,* in subject matter the new opera was to prove equally explosive.

Part political broadside and part fairy tale, *Die Bürgschaft* may lack BB's earthy, profane lyricism, his aphoristic wit, and his love of paradox, but it is a powerful work nonetheless. It is also not a forbidding one. Indeed, quite the opposite: it is a number opera filled with the composer's by-now-characteristic program of placing popular idioms—here, marches and a variety of dance music, including tangos, waltzes, and fox-trots—in acerbic contexts. Songs or songlike forms appear throughout. Weill quotes from Bach and Handel chorales, oratorios, and passion plays, but refashions his sources, and filling his opera with action and incident he avoids the stasis of traditional oratorio. There is no question that, as the dominant partner in the collaboration with Caspar Neher, Weill seized the chance to write the entire show with music; and indeed his score, by turns double-edged, detached, surging with passion or indignation, carries the opera's story and theme.

At once seductive and meaningful, the music sometimes tells the audience what the words cannot or do not. "Man does not change. It is circumstances that change his behavior,"[3] the chorus intones throughout; but as in *Der Jasager,* Weill's music plays against a banal, declarative text and alerts the audience to be wary of the false message the chorus bears. (Weill's use of two choruses that move in and out of the action offering comment and advice is one of the opera's numerous epic-theatre touches.) The way the music, a lush, overwritten, Bach-like chorale, rubs against the clunky language provides musical underlining for what the action reveals, that in fact men *do* change. The composer's musical and theatrical instincts dovetail in his use of a Gang of Three—a tenor, a baritone, and a bass—

who appear in different guises throughout. First, they are creditors who are after Mattes; later, they are highwaymen, blackmailers, bailiffs, and agents. Always subservient to the twin gods of Money and Power, they are shape shifters who for their own advancement use and subvert whatever political system is in force at the moment. For these three wily lords of misrule Weill has composed a variety of ironic numbers, including an old-fashioned choral glee, a mild fugato episode, and a nifty little tango. Without the Gang of Three the opera would be almost unrelievedly grim, a march toward damnation; with them, ideology is wrapped in the seductions of entertainment. Intermittently, Weill forsakes irony and achieves a genuine pathos. He gives to Anna, Mattes's long-suffering wife, and the most sympathetic character, music of heartrending emotional directness. Her aria, "Oh, meine Tochte, warum kommst du nicht zurück?" ("Oh, my daughter, why aren't you coming back?"), which expresses her grief for her daughter's descent into a life of prostitution, is exquisitely beautiful and shorn of any Brechtian curves. Weill uses an unadorned two-part form of strophe, bridge, and returning strophe, this last not sung but played by two cornets in duet. The bridge section is a conventional eight bars that uses the cycles of fifths—that most standard of harmonic progressions, and one he had previously avoided in his song forms. The result is simple, inevitable, and gorgeous.

Because Weill was especially proud of *Die Bürgschaft*—even in his American career, when he disavowed almost all his German catalogue, it would remain for him, and for Lenya, an example of the kind of work he always maintained he wanted to return to—he was eager to secure a prestigious Berlin opening. And in Berlin in 1931, despite the double strike against him of being Jewish and an artistic renegade, it was still possible for him to aspire to the leading opera houses. In the summer and fall of that year his correspondence glistened with his usual confidence; as Germany's leading theatrical composer *of course* the best theatres would be vying for his important new work. He signed a contract with the Städtische Oper for a production that Fritz Stiedry would conduct, Carl Ebert would direct, and Caspar Neher would design. When the long-delayed Berlin production of *Mahagonny* at the end of 1931 threatened to overlap with the planned premiere of *Die Bürgschaft* in early 1932, Weill with customary verve became embroiled in a round of cultural politics. "Ebert just called and expressed serious misgivings about *Mahagonny*," Hans Heinsheimer wrote Weill on October 17, 1931. "He thinks a success would detract attention from *Die Bürgschaft*, a failure or scandal would make his

The double chorus oversees the tragic finale in the 1957 Berlin revival of *Die Bürgschaft,* a work that angered Nazi censors during its original productions in 1932.

production more difficult." "I have always had mixed feelings about this *Mahagonny* performance," Weill responded on November 19, but added that "I really don't see that a scandal could prove any threat for *Die Bürgschaft* which as a work and as a production proceeds from an entirely different set of assumptions. . . . It ought to be stressed in various places with absolute clarity that *Mahagonny* represents the end of a creative period which began with the Baden-Baden version and which I have already superseded, while *Die Bürgschaft* is the first major product of a new style which began with *Der Lindberghflug* and above all *Der Jasager.* I would be very pleased if you could expand upon these thoughts in some sort of public forum in the weeks before the *Mahagonny* premiere."

Die Bürgschaft opened at the Städtische Oper on March 10, 1932. Within the week, Weill attended provincial openings in Wiesbaden and Düsseldorf. Given the lateness of the hour, the work was surprisingly well received in Berlin; as Weill had hoped, the opera was judged primarily on artistic grounds, with critics noting how the composer had moved beyond the song form of his popular works. Whatever doubt remained about *Mahagonny* did not seem to tarnish the critics' responses to Weill's more well-behaved opera. Nonetheless, managers throughout Germany were reluctant to present the work. Faced with a growing number of rejections, Weill wrote directly to Walter Bruno Iltz, the intendant at Düsseldorf, who had had the courage to stage the opera despite right-wing intimidation. Applauding Iltz for standing up to the threats, Weill asked him to write a letter of support that he could then distribute to other managers. "The directors of almost all the German theatres are more than positive about *Die Bürgschaft*," Weill wrote on May 16, "and are convinced of its artistic importance, and most are also in favor of performing it. But they don't dare. No one forbids them. But hints are enough to undermine their resolve. I therefore ask you to be so kind as to describe in a few sentences the events preceding the premiere." On May 25, Iltz declined: "I have decided not to fulfill your very understandable wish." Weill bristled, calling Iltz's "a cowardly retreat." "I have already had a number of meetings for mounting a campaign against the cowardice and lack of standards of the so-called leaders of German culture. I meet with great resistance almost everywhere," Weill informed Heinsheimer in a May 29 letter.

Throughout the spring of 1932 Universal Edition had only bad news for Weill. "Intendant Hartmann, from Breslau, wrote to say a member of his administrative advisory committee exclaimed he left after the second act because the work seemed too gloomy. This letter is really quite idiotic," Heinsheimer fulminated in a May 12 letter, "and it is absolutely outrageous for a theatre director not to perform a work because an advisor finds it too sad. When the politics of the theatres begin to depend on such things, it is no wonder everything is going to the devil." On May 14 Heinsheimer received a rejection from Coburg in which the intendant explained that, "considering the special constellation of the audience I will scarcely be able to do [the work]. As you know, the entire right-wing press has made a particularly solid front against the work and it would be senseless to try to force the work on a city like Coburg." "I have not been permitted [to do the opera]," the intendant at Hamburg informed Heinsheimer on May 15. "Since, as you know, we have to reckon with certain influences at present, I simply have to bow to pressures." Teetering under a wave of cancellations, from Zurich and Prague as well as from Stuttgart and Karlsruhe—only Konigsberg was going forward—by June 15 Heinsheimer had to acknowledge that "the *Bürgschaft* matter is getting much more difficult than I suspected just a while ago." His glum conclusion: "In purely financial terms your prospects for the coming years are anything but rosy," he wrote Weill.

In the late summer of 1932, the Nazis lost ground in the general elections, and for what was to prove an agonizingly brief interlude it became possible to imagine a Nazi-free Germany. "I hope that the serious political defeat dealt the Nazis in the last weeks will also work to our advantage," a revitalized Heinsheimer wrote to Weill on September 7. "I hope that at least a couple of theatre directors will come out of the mousehole they've crawled into. . . . If we have four–five stages this season, we'll be out of the woods with *Die Bürgschaft*." Weill, once again allowing his wishes to cloud his judgment, wrote on September 10 that "everywhere where they were already openly following Nazi policies in deference to the anticipated dawning of the Third Reich they are now quite plainly and openly dissociating themselves from Hitler. . . . Even the theatres must have heard by now that Hitler is done for." But after visiting several provincial theatres Heinsheimer was forced to topple his composer's reverie, concluding in his October 4 letter that although "there is a relaxation of political tensions," nevertheless "it isn't easy with *Die Bürgschaft*."

Indeed it wasn't. History interceded, ensuring that the work was noted at the time more for the censorship it provoked than for its composer's renewed commitment to traditional opera. In the darkening political climate of Germany in 1932, Weill at last was forced to admit that his opportunities in the state-supported opera houses had become severely limited. But he refused to be defeated, and began to explore possibilities in the commercial theatre in Germany and abroad. Although he was to be unsuccessful, once again he courted a number of prominent commercial producers in Berlin. Nonetheless, despite the odds against him in all theatrical sectors, and in the face of his awareness that his days in Germany were growing short, Weill managed to produce one final work—under the circumstances, an act of great courage.

After working with Caspar Neher, an inexperienced librettist (Weill was always to be dissatisfied with act 2 of their opera), he felt he needed a stronger literary foundation on which to rest a score and so turned once again to Georg Kaiser. Between the older writer and his young collaborator there had never been the same competitive edge as between Brecht and Weill—and that Weill did not feel threatened by Kaiser accounts for the curious musical form of their new work. Weill realized that if he had any chance at all to get the work produced, his musical contributions would have to be limited—it would have to be a play with music rather than an

opera. But the approximately hour and a quarter of music he was to contribute to Kaiser's three-hour play was an unusually modest portion of the
whole and represented a balance of power he would have been unlikely to
concede to Brecht under any circumstances. If the form of the new work
reflected political and historical pressures, so did its content. Weill and
Kaiser called their play with music "a winter's tale" and hoped to sheathe
their social critique in a world of fantasy—a stage world even further
removed from contemporary Germany than the city of nets in *Mahagonny*
or the mythical land of Urb in *Die Bürgschaft*. But always alert to attacks,
no matter how veiled, the Nazis were not to be fooled.

"Kaiser has come up with a very nice, truly Kaiserian idea," Weill wrote
Universal Edition on July 29. "It isn't to be an opera," Weill explained,
"but a work between genres. It remains up to me whether it is a 'play with
music,' that is, with simple songs sung by plain actors, or whether I want
to make greater musical demands and write music of the length and difficulty of, say, an Offenbach Musiquette." Weill admitted that he was "more
attracted to the latter because I could go beyond the genre I created in *Die
Dreigroschenoper.*" He decided against "simple songs sung by plain actors,"
favoring instead music of a "length and difficulty" that would provide further ammunition against austere critics who had labeled him a songwriter.
In an August 2 letter to Heinsheimer Weill described the new work, now
called *Der Silbersee: Ein Wintermärchen (The Silver Lake: A Winter's Tale),* as
"a kind of modern fairy tale with well-mounted musical numbers, somewhat in the manner of a *Singspiel.*" Once again, Weill hoped that Max
Reinhardt would direct. "Reinhardt has been wanting to do something
with Kaiser for a long time and will certainly be especially wild about this
play, which offers a stage director the greatest possibilities," Weill wrote.
"Naturally in Berlin and Vienna, it would be a great advantage in terms of
audience and commercial potential if Reinhardt were to do it." For the
proposed production at the maestro's Deutsches Theater Emil Jannings
and Luise Rainer were rumored to star, but Weill wanted Lenya to play the
female lead in Vienna and held out the possibility that she would also play
the role in Berlin. But casting any of these performers contradicted Weill's
own claim that this time he had written music for trained singers rather
than actors with a seductive *Sprechstimme* or a ripping Berlin bark.

Once again, negotiations with Reinhardt collapsed. On the last day of
1932, Reinhardt's production team withdrew, claiming to be unable to
mount a work with chorus and orchestra. "It just proves how right we all
were in our mistrust of the Deutsches Theater," Weill sniffed in a January 2

letter to Universal Edition. Having in fact anticipated Reinhardt's defection, a few weeks earlier Weill had begun talks with the Altes Theater in Leipzig, where *Mahagonny* had had its premiere in 1930, and was able to report in the same January 2 letter that *Der Silbersee,* amazingly enough, would have its premiere there on February 18. "My goal," he announced, was to have "as many stages as possible for the eighteenth of February, then the first Berlin performance in the Volksbühne."

Once Weill had secured Leipzig, he was able to arrange for two other productions, and on February 18, 1933, *Der Silbersee* would open at three theatres, the Stadttheater Magdeburg and the Stadttheater Erfurt in addition to the main production in Leipzig. As he had for *Mahagonny* three years earlier, Gustav Brecher would conduct. The director was Detlef Sierck, who was to immigrate to Hollywood, where, as Douglas Sirk, he would have a major career.

As Weill, along with Kaiser and Caspar Neher, who was designing, attended rehearsals in Leipzig, the world around them was heading toward conflagration. On January 30 a senile, doddering Colonel Hindenburg made the fateful decision to appoint Adolf Hitler chancellor of Germany. On February 27, Nazis set fire to the Reichstag, then as an alibi for instituting a massive repression of civil rights claimed the fire had been a Communist plot. In the press of history that surrounded it, it is not possible to see *Der Silbersee* as other than a report from the front lines disguised as a fairy tale. A winter's tale indeed, for one of the worst winters in German history, the beginning of the crimes Hitler's regime was to pursue until its defeat in 1945, *Der Silbersee* depicts a society devastated by unemployment, hunger, and social chaos.

Like *Die Bürgschaft, Der Silbersee* is about a relationship between two men. In the former, a bond between the two protagonists is broken; in the latter, a bond is formed between two former enemies, a police officer, Olim, and an unemployed worker, Severin, who steals a pineapple, for him a symbol of a world of unattainable luxury. Olim shoots the thief, but begins to view the crime from the thief's point of view. When he wins a lottery, Olim buys a castle and, hiding his identity, takes Severin to live with him. Unaware of who his benefactor is, Severin, now an embittered invalid, rages against the policeman who shot him. When he discovers who Olim is, at first he is consumed with hatred, which gradually is transformed into a kind of love. At the end, the former enemies walk together into the mists of the silver lake. The core of the drama, distinctly unlike the epic-theatre pieces Weill composed with Brecht, is in the characters' complex psychology, the great changes of feeling that push the story forward.

Beneath the fairy-tale settings—a castle, a forest, a lake that magically freezes over—the work has an unmissable contemporary pulse. All the admirable characters have unusual foreign names—Olim (Nordic), Severin (French), Fennimore (American, the writer James Fenimore Cooper)—while the villains, dispossessed former aristocrats who succeed in taking over the castle, are the Teutonically named Frau von Luber and Baron Laur. (Fennimore is Baron Laur's impoverished niece, brought to the castle to act as companion to Frau von Luber, Olim's housekeeper, who has been forced to sell her ancestral home to the newly rich Olim.) The real Nazis, amassing their strength in the winter of 1932–33, did not misread the import of this winter's tale and reacted in the only way they knew how, by silencing the authors.

Although Weill's score covered only approximately one-third of Kaiser's overlong tale, it exhibits a remarkable diversity that in many ways

Masochism in Weill and Georg Kaiser's *Der Silbersee (The Silver Lake),* another incendiary music-theatre work: Ernst Busch as Severin in a Saint Sebastian pose in the 1933 Magdeburg production

Olim's castle, as seen in the 1933 Leipzig production of *Der Silbersee,* Weill's last work produced in Germany. The tyrants' seizure of the castle at the end of the play anticipated the fate that was to befall Germany—the Leipzig premiere took place on February 18, only ten days before the burning of the Reichstag, which marked the end of the Weimar Republic.

comprises a summary of the composer's German period. It begins with an excellent, Rossini-loves-fox-trot overture and continues through a typically wide-ranging variety of musical episodes. The cynicism distilled in the Brecht collaborations is evident in three numbers with dance rhythms. There is a tango for a lottery agent who tells Olim how to expand the money he has won. "Interest! and compound interest!" he hisses, as the strings divide and sway over a habañera rhythm. Frau von Luber and Baron Laur express their creed for seizing power in a scintillating fox-trot. Two shopgirls forced to destroy food that they would rather donate to the unemployed speculate on human greed and the economics of inflation to the strains of a lush waltz; Kaiser's lyrics have an acrid Brechtian undertow that chafes against Weill's lilting melody. The balladlike "Cäsars Tod" ("Caesar's Death"), which recounts a tyrant's rise and fall and was aimed clearly as a warning to the tyrant outside the theatre, was also the only number Weill had intended for export beyond the show. It is one of his great narrative ballads, a polemical "Barbara Song." A stirring Mahlerian march ushers in each verse and returns for each refrain. In between, there is brilliantly light orchestration, with a harp used as a rhythm section, and a rich musical word painting of the conspirators' plot—all soft snare-drum rolls and low clarinet flourishes. A comment song bristling with political disapproval, and sung by Fennimore, ostensibly as an after-dinner entertainment, "Cäsars Tod" kindles Severin's rage against his unknown attacker.

Elsewhere, Weill forsakes irony and indirectness as he marries his music forthrightly to the sentiments expressed in Kaiser's words. In Fennimore's song about the fate of being a poor relation with no real home or place of her own, the character's touchingly clear-eyed text is sympathetically matched by Weill's melody. Singing along with her are two flutes, scored in flowing parallel fifths—a leitmotif associated with Fennimore throughout the show. Her lament, which exacts greater vocal demands than the ironic numbers, attains the complexities of an arietta. For Severin, Weill wrote a revenge aria of Verdian passion. Three stanzas concluding with a repeated refrain—"It will not be forgiven or forgotten: an eye for an eye!," ". . . a tooth for a tooth!," ". . . blood for blood!"—build toward a torrential climax: ". . . a life for a life!"[4] The orchestra seethes and roars along with Severin. There is no question that only a trained opera singer, rather than a singing actor, could do justice to the aria's musical magnitude. And yet, *Der Silbersee* also requires this same performer to act in lengthy dialogue scenes. Later, Severin will have an equally feverish aria about the reasons for having himself restrained so that in his rage he cannot kill his former assailant, now his comrade. He compares himself with Odysseus, tied to the mast of his ship to resist the Sirens' fatal song: "I am condemned to listen to the siren voice of my anger," Severin wails, words and music evoking the character's psychic tumult.

> *Everything presses upwards in a burning stream.*
> *When will this feverish flood subside?*
> *When will the wild raging be calmed?*

The rage, the fever, the flood, are given a galvanic musical expression, a key example of how Weill's musical intensities fuse with Kaiser's language of extreme emotion.

An act 1 duet for Severin and Fennimore, in which the two characters never sing together and are accompanied differently—he by strings, she by woodwinds—is a charming trope of their disagreement, Severin's skepticism brushing against Fennimore's mystical belief. Scenes 5 and 14 are melodramas, with scoring beneath dialogue, and elsewhere there are purely instrumental passages (including a fox-trot that Weill will reuse in *The Seven Deadly Sins*) in which the action is carried forward by the music alone. Also on hand is a commenting chorus that oversees and seems mystically to guide the characters' last-act transformations:

> *Error still envelops you,*
> *As this fall of snow bars your way.*
> *When no more flakes swirl,*
> *The view will be clear to you.*

There is a moving moment in the final scene when the sentimental, Mahlerian choral writing that has predominated suddenly transforms into an orderly Bach fugato, with the chorus singing:

> *Where there was tempest and darkness,*
> *There shall be stillness and light.*
> *And the turbulent waters*
> *Turn to a path at your feet.*

This, the last musical passage Weill was to write in Germany, achieves a transcendent note, an almost palpable longing for a comprehensible existence in a chaotic world.

At the opening night in Leipzig on February 18 the tension was unmistakable. Laura McCann, who as Gert Riederer performed a small role that night, recalled that "a fellow actor had to go out to quiet the audience down. Remember, the show was done less than a month after Hitler had been appointed chancellor, and so it took a lot of courage to do it at all. This was the last time Weill was to be performed in Germany before the Nazis were to be completely in charge, and people seemed to know it, or to sense it somehow. The audience that night knew it was a historic occasion, the end of something. Prominent people from all over the country had come to Leipzig to see the show. The director, Sirk, did not close the show that night, though he certainly had provocation; but Sirk was not a coward."[5]

"It was a tough play of criticism, ten times tougher than any Brecht play," Douglas Sirk recalled.

> One of the Nazis, a man called Hauptmann—who wasn't one of the worst of them—asked me to drop the play. Otherwise, he told me, something would happen. So I got together with Kaiser, Weill, and Neher . . . but we decided to go ahead, feeling the play to be artistically as well as politically very important. On the morning of the opening Dr. Goerdeler [the intendant] called me up and advised me it would be best for me to fall ill and postpone the opening a couple of weeks. . . . I told him that I thought it was a time when it would be disastrous not to stand by one's opinion and give in. . . . But I went ahead, and the play was a huge success. The SA filled a fairly large part of the theatre . . . and there was a vast crowd of Nazi Party people outside with banners and God knows what, yelling and all the rest of it. But the majority of the public loved the play, in spite of all the racket the Nazis made. . . . I ran it for about thirty performances [*sic*] in Leipzig, all completely sold out, and we had SA in there every night barracking and rampaging around. . . . It was a good production, and probably my most mature effort in the theatre—a kind of milestone in theatrical history . . . or rather the end of a chapter. Hans Rothe, the famous translator of Shakespeare, later wrote that this was the occasion when the curtain rang down on the German stage. The Nazis did make a lot of trouble. They turned up and staged scandals. But you could go ahead with a play, and the audience was such that they couldn't stop it being a success. And so I thought at first, well, things are going to be tough but perhaps it isn't impossible to overcome. Of course, things turned out to be not like that at all. No play, no song could stop this gruesome trend towards inhumanity.[6]

Despite staged protests both outside and inside the theatre, scheduled performances in Leipzig were not canceled. Demonstrations in Magdeburg were far more threatening, however, and, as Heinsheimer predicted in a February 24 letter to Weill, "These protests will naturally be dragged through all the papers and I doubt very much whether there are many intendants willing to subject themselves to the kinds of things Götz [the intendant at Magdeburg] has experienced . . . people will naturally pay more attention to the screams from Magdeburg than the applause from

LEFT: Weill with his mistress, Erika Neher, the wife of his collaborator Caspar Neher, 1932. As his survival in a country being overtaken by Nazis grew increasingly precarious, Weill, on January 29, 1933, wrote to Erika that "without you I could never have survived all this but would have perished by now."

BELOW: Lenya (as Jenny) with her new lover, Otto Pasetti (as Jim Mahoney), in the Vienna production of *Mahagonny,* April 1932

Leipzig. . . . We don't need to kid ourselves: as nice as the Leipzig success was, the situation is just as grave as we have felt all along." Because reviews were startlingly positive, Weill, for the last time, was able to delude himself. "I am really amazed how favorable almost all the press was, even in the German national camp," he wrote to Universal Edition on February 26. "No one believes that things can go on much longer as they are," he predicted, little realizing how almost unimaginably worse they were about to become.

On March 4, Nazi officials closed down all three *Silbersee* productions. The next day Weill was warned that he should leave Berlin until the outcome of the Enabling Act (the single law providing the constitutional foundation for Hitler's dictatorship, enacted on March 24) had been decided. With Lenya and a friend, photographer Louise Hartung, who had hurriedly packed for him, Weill drove to Munich. On March 14, aware by now that he would have to leave Germany, he returned to Berlin to arrange his affairs. On March 21, after being warned by a well-informed friend that he risked imminent arrest, Weill drove with Caspar and Erika Neher to the French border. The next day he left the country that his ancestors had lived in for seven centuries, never to return. His wife was not with him, although in her ritualistic retelling of their departure she would place herself in the getaway car. But by March 1933 husband and wife had become estranged. Weill was having an affair with Erika Neher; and Lenya, having left Weill in Munich, was in Vienna with her own lover, Otto Pasetti, a handsome blond tenor she had been living with since April 1932, when they had appeared in the Vienna production of *Mahagonny*. Despite the sexual break, the deep emotional bond between Weill and Lenya endured. Living apart, they continued to feel closer to each other than to anyone else, and each of them fully expected their professional and personal lives would continue to be entwined. Kurt Weill left Germany not with his wife but with his mistress and her homosexual husband. In a letter in 1953 Lenya asked Caspar Neher, "What happened after Munich? Did Kurt return to the house in Kleinmachnow? When did he decide to leave Germany? Were you with him? What did he take along?"[7]

SEVEN

In Transit

O n March 22, 1933, Kurt Weill, alone, with five hundred marks, entered France carrying a small suitcase. His exile was sudden and enforced, the decision to leave having been made for him at the eleventh hour by concerned gentile friends. Did the small suitcase suggest the hope of a short stay or the exigencies of a hasty departure?

Despite the appearance of vulnerability, however, Weill was by no means unprotected. In Paris only four months earlier, on December 1, 1932, in a program at the Salle Gaveau that had been sponsored by Marie-Laure de Noailles, prominent socialite and arts patron, a Weill double bill (conducted by Maurice Abravanel) of *Der Jasager* and the *Mahagonny-Songspiel* (in which Lenya re-created her original role) had been a triumph. "It took the town by storm," as Abravanel recalled. "I mean, the greatest night since the Ballets Russes. Stravinsky came to me, spent one hour to convince me he knew we were going to be asked to go on the road, it was a perfect piece to go with his *L'histoire du soldat*. 'It's like the *St. Matthew Passion*,' he said."[1] Savoring the reception yet little suspecting that he would be returning soon as a refugee from Germany, Weill with his usual skill sought collaborators and projects. Princesse Edmond de Polignac commissioned what would be his three-movement Symphony no. 2. With

Marie-Laure de Noailles and her husband, Charles, he launched tentative plans for a Weill season the following spring.

When he arrived in Paris on March 23, with the memory of the evening at the Salle Gaveau still potent, and with friends in high places, Weill was confident that he could sustain his career at a lustrous level. He checked into the Hotel Jacob and Splendide, but soon moved to the home of his patron, the Vicomtesse de Noailles. Stravinsky, Cocteau, Picasso, Honegger, Gide, and Auric had attended the Salle Gaveau evening, but for Weill the most important spectator was Edward James, a wealthy Englishman who was to underwrite the first season of Les Ballets 1933, a new company founded by George Balanchine and Boris Kochno, defectors from the Ballets Russes de Monte Carlo after Balanchine had been dismissed. James's sole proviso was that Balanchine would create a new ballet for Tilly Losch, James's wife. Weill had not been in Paris for more than a week when Kochno approached him with an offer. "I was very reserved since I wasn't quite convinced of the whole affair," Weill informed Universal Edition on April 3. "Now yesterday an English financier, Mr. James, husband of Tilly Losch, wants to finance on condition that I write something. . . . Artistically, I have requested collaboration with a poet of equal stature. I have a plan for which I need good texts, since under no circumstances do I want to write the kind of ballet others do." Weill's choice of a collaborator was Jean Cocteau, who declined. It was only then, and only because James insisted, that Weill very reluctantly asked Brecht to write the libretto. It was also James who urged Weill to cast Lenya. James had admired her in the *Mahagonny-Songspiel* but also noted her resemblance to his wife, which had sparked an idea for a ballet scenario. (In later years, incorrectly, Lenya would maintain that Weill conceived the role in what was to be *The Seven Deadly Sins* for her. "That one was for me. Weill had nobody else in mind. It's my favorite part.")[2]

Brecht and Weill had not spoken since the opening of the Berlin *Mahagonny* fifteen months earlier. Another problem from Weill's point of view was that by the time Brecht was asked to participate, Weill had already collaborated with James, Kochno, and Balanchine on a concept for the ballet; Brecht, in effect, would be a hired hand, a combustible circumstance, as Weill well knew. Like Weill, Brecht had also fled from Germany in March. With his wife, Helene Weigel, and their young son, Stefan, he had gone first to Vienna and then on his own traveled to Lugano, Switzerland, where Weill contacted him. Weill "asked him out of pure pity," according to Maurice Abravanel, who would conduct the ballet. "Brecht had really been abominable to him. It had gotten around that Brecht had been mocking Weill's work, and now Kurt was offering that scoundrel a helping hand."[3]

In their sudden exiles both Brecht and Weill faced serious financial problems. But in Paris, as later in New York, Weill, quite unlike his erstwhile partner, proved to be a shrewd businessman able to adjust quickly to the customs of whatever country he was in. Brecht was disdainful of the project but could not afford to turn it down. When he arrived in Paris, his sour mood was not helped by the fact that he and Weill had unequal positions. Weill at this point was a high-culture hero while Brecht, as Abravanel observed, "was totally unknown in Paris and was totally out of his element. He didn't speak a word of French and was lost there. He was a nobody."[4]

Lovers and costars: Tilly Losch, left, as Anna II, Lenya as Anna I, playing two sides of the same personality, in *Die sieben Todsünden (The Seven Deadly Sins),* "a spectacle in nine scenes," which opened at the Théâtre des Champs-Elysées on June 7, 1933

As Weill had expected, Brecht caused trouble. First, he demanded revisions of the Freudian scenario that had already been sketched: Working from James's perception of Lenya's resemblance to Tilly Losch, the team had formulated a variation on the Freudian theme of the split personality. In what they were calling a *ballet chanté,* Lenya would sing and Losch would dance two aspects of the same personality, designated Anna I and Anna II, respectively. Weill convinced Brecht that the psychological focus of the piece, called

The Seven Deadly Sins, could be reworked as a Marxist critique of capitalism. (And indeed, Brecht's title for the piece became *The Seven Deadly Sins of the Petite Bourgeoisie.*) Anna's split personality is induced by economics—having to survive under capitalism forces her to transform her innate decency into a hard-edged practicality. Over the course of a seven-year sojourn in which the two Annas wander from city to city earning money to build a house for their family back home in Louisiana, Anna I must continually check, conceal, and condemn the goodness of Anna II. In Brecht's sardonic rewriting of the seven sins, Anna II is "sinful" because her charity, kindness, honesty, and commitment to art interfere with Anna I's goal of making money. After seven years traversing a mythic Amerika filled with cities like Memphis, Los Angeles, Philadelphia, Boston, Baltimore, and San Francisco that the cowriters clearly had never seen, the moneymaking wanderers return home, Anna I vindicated, Anna II dispirited.

The *ballet chanté* had a painful genesis. As Weill had foreseen, Brecht, who stayed for only ten days, after which Weill composed the entire score quickly, missed no opportunity to act up. In an April 18 letter to his mistress, Erika Neher, in Berlin, Weill wrote that, "after having worked with Brecht for a week I am more than ever of the opinion that he is one of the most repulsive, unpleasant characters on the face of the earth. But"—and it is this "but" that enabled him, in Paris as earlier in Berlin, to collaborate—"I am able to separate this completely from his work." Brecht worked efficiently but belittled the project. Caspar Neher, uncharacteristically, also caused problems. Initially he had turned down the assignment on the curious grounds that he didn't like the text. "Just imagine, this is the same Cas who never dared to say anything against Brecht, who kept quiet whenever there was a complaint, who left me completely in the lurch in my battles against Brecht during the Berlin *Mahagonny,* who always got together with him even after Brecht and I had become enemies," Weill wrote to Erika in early May when her husband declined to design the production. "I'm in one hell of a situation," the composer grumbled. "I have to find another designer, right when I'm working day and night on the full score—to say nothing of my problems with the divorce lawyer and problems with the Dresden bank, problems with the ballet rehearsals, and the continuing aftereffects of the serious dizzy spells I suffered on Sunday afternoon. But I should not close this letter without telling you that, despite everything, the thought of you makes me quiet and happy, and my thoughts of you are sad but very beautiful." Chastising his mistress for siding with her husband, Weill tried to convince her of the project's merit.

I had so wished that in this matter you would take an attitude which would have made it possible for me to sort out the whole affair with Caspar alone—and be able to write you a very sweet love letter. But you quite unequivocally take Caspar's part, and what in Caspar's letter is there only between the lines, you spell out directly: a deep contempt for me for composing this "literary rubbish." . . . I too don't believe it is immortal poetry. . . . The worst thing is the fact that neither of you (how terrible that I have to include you both in this) has any confidence whatsoever in me; otherwise you'd realize that every text I've set looks entirely different once it's been swept through my music. . . . [*The Seven Deadly Sins*] contains several elements which really suit my music (and that should be decisive for me and really should be for you as well); it displays an intellectual attitude completely in control (all Frenchmen who read it—and they really aren't all idiots—compare it to *Candide* by Voltaire), it contains—as always [with Brecht]—formulations of great individual beauty and phrases of a simple human expressiveness, which you recognize only when you hear the music I have come up with for it. . . . Everyone to whom I have shown it was totally speechless about what I have created here.

Finally, to Weill's relief, Neher relented. When Lenya arrived to begin rehearsals, some of the *Dreigroschenoper* team was reunited; their lives and personal relationships, however, had changed radically since 1928. The former colleagues were now an uneasy group festering with ancient as well as fresh grievances. Except for Neher, who would return to Germany and remain there throughout the Nazi years, the others had become displaced persons. Surely the ballet they were working on, a story of a journey in a faraway country, had bittersweet autobiographical references for each of them, just then at the beginning of their own uncertain hegiras. The only easy relationship was the one between Weill and Abravanel. Lenya, who had asked Weill for a divorce, was accompanied by her lover, Otto Pasetti, cast in the production as part of a male quartet. Weill, still deeply devoted to Lenya, did not hesitate in casting Pasetti (or in paying some of the sizable gambling debts Pasetti and Lenya had accrued). During rehearsals Lenya, according to rumor, also began an affair with her look-alike costar, Tilly Losch, estranged from Edward James. Although primarily homosexual, James offered his wife the gift of *The Seven Deadly Sins* in order to win back her affections (but to no avail: Losch was to divorce him within a year).

Brecht had departed cavalierly as soon as the libretto had been finished: *The Seven Deadly Sins* was only a ballet, after all, and as such even lower than opera in Brecht's ranking of "culinary" entertainments. He may also have felt that it was his ideological duty to leave; the show was to open at an elegant theatre, the splendid art-deco Théâtre des Champs-Elysées, before a wealthy audience. In creating a ballet for rich people, Brecht, by now a fully committed Marxist, knew he was consorting with the enemy. The least he could do was to take the money and run, hoping that his anti-bourgeois libretto would bring some necessary enlightenment to the haute-bourgeois audience.

Rehearsals, even without Brecht, were fraught with tension engendered not only by the knot of entangled offstage relations among the creators, but also by the problematic nature of the work itself. Once again Brecht and Weill had written one of their in-between pieces—in both musical and narrative terms their work defied ballet conventions. "A small clique has developed among the devotees of the old Russian ballet, for whom our ballet isn't 'ballet' enough, not enough 'pure choreography,' " Weill, in the thick of rehearsals, informed Brecht in a June 1, 1933, letter. "Because of that there were tremendous fights during the last few days and I succeeded in getting one man 'put on ice.' Though Balanchine is swaying between two factions, he has worked excellently and he has found a performance style, which is very 'balletistic' but still sufficiently realistic. . . . The rest depends on whether Balanchine will overcome his innate laziness—which is even fomented by the other faction—and whether he will work on the precision of the dances or not." Another major problem during rehearsals was Brecht's cryptic libretto, which teemed with vintage cynicism and paradox as it upended the ethics of capitalism and the Bible, but which provided few details about setting or action and almost no connections between episodes. With so few clues to work with, Balanchine and his dancers were frustrated. Weill and the on-site collaborators had to supply the missing pieces—Edward James and Boris Kochno devised a not-always-clear scenario for the dancers, and the composer's leitmotifs and refrains created an illusion of continuity.

That Weill had written a ballet in Paris was significant, for despite the deeply Germanic nature of the piece, Weill was working within a civic tradition. In Paris, dance had a cachet it had never claimed in Weimar Berlin. At least since 1909, when Diaghilev's Russian troupe made a sensational debut, ballet had occupied a place of honor in the Parisian avant-garde. In 1912, Nijinsky's orgiastic movements at the end of his *L'Après-midi d'un faune* caused a cultural scandal of the sort Parisians clearly relished. The premiere program of Les Ballets 1933 consisted of *Les Songes,* with music by Darius Milhaud and décor by André Derain; *Mozartiana,* danced to Tchaikovsky's Mozart-inspired Fourth Orchestra Suite and designed by Christian Bérard, at the time the most chic of Parisian couturiers; and what promised to be a strange new work by a trio of Germans—all three ballets sharing an English patron and a Russian choreographer. Would the new, rule-breaking ballet cause the kind of stir by which the Parisian avant-garde anointed its heroes? Probably many in the fashionable audience on June 7, 1933, hoped so. It had been a momentous week for dance. Two nights earlier, Serge Lifar, the head of the Paris Opéra Ballet, had presented, to acclaim, a new work at the Salle Garnier. At the Théâtre du Châtelet, Leonide Massine, who had replaced Balanchine as ballet master of Colonel de Basil's Ballets Russes de Monte Carlo, was presenting his choreographed version of Tchaikovsky's Fifth Symphony, at a time when the "symphonic ballet" was a novel dance concept.

Weill was optimistic that *The Seven Deadly Sins* had the formal daring that had customarily pleased Parisians in the know. He anticipated a warm reception and generously sent Brecht one thousand francs so that he could attend the premiere. Because he wanted to pursue potential film contracts, Brecht accepted. But it was not a happy occasion for him or for Weill. "The ballet was pretty enough, though it wasn't all that significant," Brecht reported to Helene Weigel from Paris on June 10; the playwright's indifference echoed that of the critics and the public. (It must be remembered, however, that the piece was sung in German and was therefore incomprehensible to most of the audience.)

"Weill's ballet has been a disappointment to most people here," Count Harry Kessler, the town crier of the Weimar Republic, reported in his June 15 diary entry.[5] On June 17 Kessler wrote, "It has had a bad reception both from the Press and the public, despite Weill's popularity here. I thought the music attractive and individualistic, though not much different from *Die Dreigroschenoper.* Lotte Lenya, whose voice has only small range but considerable appeal, sang (in German) Brecht's ballads. . . . Obviously too much has been expected of Weill, snobbery dictating that he should be put right away on the same level as Wagner and Strauss."[6] Weill's score seemed at the time to satisfy no one. Ballet traditionalists scoffed that the music was not properly or sufficiently dancelike, while vocally it was an in-between, neither operatic enough nor popular enough to appeal to purists of either persuasion. Although Lenya brought her incomparable irony and razor-sharp diction, she was not, in fact, the ideal singer for the difficult work, and it may have been for this reason, rather than their strained relationship, that Weill had not in the first place thought of her for the role. In her renowned 1956 recording she lowered the key to accommodate a voice grown pebbled and raspy with age (and in this way made the work available to chanteuses and cabaret singers with a strictly popular range). But the original high key ideally demanded a trained voice with a security of tone and pitch not in Lenya's arsenal.

As planned, following the engagement in Paris, the company traveled to London, where the *ballet chanté,* now called *Anna-Anna,* opened at the Savoy Theatre on June 28. For the opening night, the performance was in German; for the rest of the run, in a hasty, last-minute translation by Edward James and Lenya, it was performed in English. London reviews were as unappreciative as those in Paris; and by July 15, Les Ballets 1933 had disbanded.

Despite its initial failure, *The Seven Deadly Sins* has become one of the most frequently performed, and most highly regarded, of Weill's works. In this first piece written in exile, Weill was in a notably Stravinskian mode—perhaps he was conscious of Stravinsky's string of successes with Diaghilev's Ballets Russes. There are passages of delicious Weillian melodies, but there are no pop-tune hits, no individual numbers that can be extracted for salon orchestra or jazz-band renditions. Instead, there are lightning-fast transitions and quick, brilliant evocations of numerous popular forms, all held together by a crisp, expert orchestration. Weill's characteristic reliance on dance rhythms comes framed in often balletlike and symphonic musical settings. His music for prologue and epilogue and seven scenes strictly observes Brecht's scenic divisions; yet in a purer and more restrained way the musical content fulfills the "separation of elements" Brecht posited as a key component of epic theatre. The music does not imitate or illustrate, and one listens in vain to discover a musical comment on, or depiction of, any of the seven sins. The only sustained mimetic touch is a recurrent note of world-weariness that registers Anna II's existential defeat, her resignation to a life of money gathering. Rather than supporting in a literal way what Anna I sings or Anna II dances, the score is faithful only to its own inner voice as it provides an independent, parallel commentary. And in each section there are passages, as dances take over from text, in which the music exists entirely on its own. Perhaps because he wasn't there for rehearsals, perhaps because this was only a ballet and so not "very significant," Brecht did not insist on his words saturating every moment of the score. To a greater degree than in any of their earlier work Weill has been given room for passages of purely instrumental writing, in a few of which he approaches climaxes of *Mahagonny*-like power. Once again, Brecht's orthodoxy is qualified by Weill's liberalism; without ever descending to sentiment, or a cloying, facile lyricism, Weill throughout injects humanist undertones that soften Brecht's attacks on the sins of the bourgeoisie. Weill's score both challenges and deepens Brecht's caustic text. "The great thing about Kurt is that he could take any text and by the time it was set to music, the dogma was forgotten, no matter how Marxist Brecht became," the work's conductor, Maurice Abravanel, observed. "In *The Seven Deadly Sins* you see the fruits of Brecht's Marxist studies. But with Weill it becomes about human beings."[7]

The signature Brecht-Weill irony was displayed for the final time in a mock chorus, a male quartet representing the Family and consisting of a father, two brothers, and a mother (sung by a basso in drag). Reversing gender roles, the Family has sent the women into the world to do a man's work as the menfolk remain at home, offering admonition and thanksgiving, and intoning religious pieties as they wait hungrily for money from the two Annas. They are useless, heartless capitalist consumers, bottom feeders who hide behind religious slogans and who, in Brecht's lexicon, are even more contemptible than capitalist producers. The Family inspires a gallery's worth of Weill's musical ironies. In close four-part harmonies the Family express their worship of money in a variety of mock-religious styles that, in turn, evoke a Bach chorale, a *Singverein* (German glee club) style with guitar accompaniment, and an a capella barbershop quartet.

In a work lasting only thirty-five minutes Weill employed his remarkably wide-ranging musical vocabulary as a sort of summing-up of his German career. In fact, this may account for the piece's enduring popularity—if you seek the quintessence of the Weill of Brecht-Weill, you will find it here. A waltz, a shimmy, a march, a fox-trot, a tarantella are all here, tucked within shimmering Stravinskian orchestrations. Everything is handled with great professionalism and aplomb, yet nothing seems as if for the first time. Written in exile, this last "German" composition, the finale to Weill's short collaboration with the most truculent and most talented of his coworkers, displays Weill the confident pragmatist at work: forced from his cultural home, he will show the world what he has done and what he can do.

Broadway, April 1933: the American premiere of *The 3-Penny Opera*. The production, directed by Francesco von Mendelssohn, failed, but the set design by Cleon Throckmorton, "after the designs by Caspar Neher," looks authentic.

. . .

As Weill was in the midst of anxious preparations for *The Seven Deadly Sins,* on April 13, 1933, *The 3-Penny Opera* (as it was billed) had its American premiere at the Empire Theatre on Broadway. "You can well imagine the eagerness with which I await the news from America," Weill wrote from Paris to his publisher on April 3. Hans Heinsheimer reported on April 22 that the music "seems to have done quite well, while the play seems to have met with general rejection. It is impossible to tell from here how much that will affect the success." Two days later, Heinsheimer relayed "an especially sad and catastrophic piece of news": In a mangled adaptation by Gifford Cochran and Jerrold Krimsky, and a production greeted with general puzzlement, *The 3-Penny Opera* had closed after a run of only ten days.

Other major losses followed. On September 18 Weill's divorce from Lenya was finalized. On November 19, because of the complete collapse of the German market for his work, his contract with Universal Edition was formally canceled. (Universal would not publish his new works but would keep the old catalogue.) A week later, on November 26, three songs from *Der Silbersee* were performed in French by soprano Madeleine Grey at the Salle Pleyel in Paris. The numbers were received enthusiastically, and there were requests for an encore. But amid the cheers, a group led by Florent Schmitt, the composer and music critic of *Le Temps,* stood up and shouted, "Vive Hitler!" Abravanel, an eyewitness, reported that Weill was "stunned. It was the worst thing that could happen to Kurt, because up to there, the public at large was still with him. It was only in music circles that people were furious that a foreigner came in. That reaction put in the open the envy, the jealousy, of French artists," Abravanel said.[8] It also "put in the open" a swelling tide of virulent pan-European anti-Semitism.

Even during this difficult transition, Weill labored tirelessly. After working with Les Ballets 1933, he won a commission from Radio Paris for a ballad, now largely missing, about Fantômas, a pulp-fiction underworld antihero embraced by the surrealists, which was performed on November 3, 1933, in a production directed by theatrical visionary Antonin Artaud. And, as in Berlin, he continued to seek collaborators for music-theatre projects. Once he was in America, Weill would shun any link to his German past, but in Paris in 1933 he could not afford to close off any possibilities; and when another Berlin émigré, Robert Vambery, Aufricht's chief dramaturg at the Theater am Schiffbauerdamm from 1928 to 1932, came to him with an idea for a musical, he listened. Vambery "has a charming subject from the old English theatre for some sort of folk play with music; I believe it's what I need at this moment,"[9] Weill wrote Lenya, then in San Remo with Pasetti.

When Weill grew disenchanted with the material, Vambery came up with an idea for a comic opera on a political subject. In *Der Kuhhandel (Cow Trading),* two adjoining nations coexist peacefully on a Caribbean island until a zealous American salesman incites them into an armaments race. In the foreground is a story of rural young lovers disrupted by rumors of war. The source of their livelihood, a cow, having been taken from them as a war tax, Juan and Juanita are forced to go to town to earn money to replace it. Juan becomes a soldier, Juanita a prostitute. When the munitions sold by the American prove defective, the new dictator cancels the war, and peace returns to the island. With enough money now to buy a cow, the lovers join in the universal well-being.

With Offenbach his avowed model, Weill composed an operetta score stocked with romantic and comic duets, arias, ariettas, ensembles, choral passages, and two extended, highly elaborated finales. Along with the chance to launch an attack against events in Germany, another country suffering from the ministrations of warmongers, the subject provided Weill with many ready-made opportunities for his brand of musical satire. His score includes burlesques of military marches, a national anthem performed by drunks in a whorehouse, and a lullaby sung by a dictator. The setting also demanded some Caribbean flavoring, a welcome challenge for the composer. Weill also pauses for pure schmaltz. The lovers' duet, "Auf Wiedersehn," is as high in calories as any comparable number in a regulation operetta by Franz Lehár or Emmerich Kálmán. By turns syrupy and sprightly, *Der Kuhhandel* marked a distinctly post-Germanic turn in Weill's work.

As he was completing *Der Kuhhandel,* Weill also started on two other projects. In December 1933, Max Reinhardt, another artist-in-exile, offered, and Weill accepted, the job of composing the score to a biblical pageant, *Der Weg der Verheissung (The Road of Promise),* to be produced in New York. And early in 1934 Jacques Deval, "the season's most in-demand and most frequently performed French playwright," as Weill described him in a January 25 letter to Lenya in San Remo, asked him to write songs for a new play. "We want to dramatize his most successful novel, *Marie Galante,* [in which] a French peasant girl runs off with a man and ends up somewhere in Panama, but once there she wishes only to go home again; she earns money in a whorehouse, and when she has saved up enough and has already bought her steamship ticket, she dies. . . . An excellent, *serious* subject. . . . If at all possible, the play is supposed to open as soon as May at the most beautiful theatre in Paris, the Theatre Marigny, and then in the fall in London and New York. It looks as if this might be the big international opportunity I've been waiting for."[10]

Weill was undaunted by juggling scores in different states of preparation. But the extreme diversity of the shows reflected his uncertain new status as a composer-in-exile, a man without a country or a secure cultural base. With its Offenbachian overtones, *Der Kuhhandel* is Parisian operetta. Evoking the demimonde of the Parisian chanteuse, *Marie Galante* is written in the idiom of the French music hall and cabaret. *Der Weg* required a re-examination of the composer's religious roots. From February to June Weill was occupied primarily with *Der Kuhhandel.* In little more than a month, from late August to the end of September, he composed the music for *Marie Galante.* On both projects he had to cope with diffident collaborators. Vambery was slow and stubborn. Deval spent his $25,000 advance and refused to do any more work. "He is the worst yet of the literary swine I've met, and that's a bunch. . . . Even Brecht could still learn something from Deval!" Weill wrote Lenya on April 6.[11] Intermittently, from August to early November, he began sketches for Reinhardt's pageant while also conferring with the librettist, Franz Werfel, who was to prove an even more irritating collaborator than Deval. On August 26, in a letter to Lenya in Zurich, Weill outlined a routine that, by necessity, had become habitual. "I'm working nonstop today. . . . I did two songs for *Marie Galante:* a lullaby she sings to the old Negro and the song she sings before she dies; she's shot before the last words. For the Bible thing I already have two excellent numbers and all kinds of preparatory work. I'm diligently studying the original liturgical music that my father sent me."[12]

If the operetta style he adopted for *Der Kuhhandel* represented a departure, so, in a radically different way, did his cabaret score for *Marie Galante.* In a remarkable masquerade, Weill's songs for the show bear the stride and sentiment of the kind of chanson popularized by self-flagellating singers like Edith Piaf. Nonetheless, despite the French glaze, Weill, as David Drew noted, "as if to cover the break with his past which [*Marie Galante*] represented . . . drew on some of his music for *Happy End.*"[13] Embedded in the Gallic patina are reminiscences of "In der Jugend goldnem Schimmer," "Das Lied von der harten Nuss," and "Das Lied vom Branntweinhändler," reworked, and gleaming anew with a different national stamp. Perhaps because of his indolent partner, Weill was left to work out the musical spots on his own. And to a degree unmatched elsewhere in the canon, Weill's music, including a march for the Panamanian army, a tango for a dance-hall scene, a few songs for bordello scenes, and a gospel-like number performed by a quartet of black singers, is merely decorative or incidental. Because Deval, in effect, refused to collaborate, Weill was forced to work on his own, and so there is no revelatory dialogue between book and score, no audacious music-theatre concepts. Far removed from the social and political satire in which Weill had carved his distinctive musical niche, *Marie Galante* was strictly boulevard fare. Yet the motif of returning home, sounded with increasing insistence throughout the play, struck a sympathetic chord in the newly dispossessed composer and may have induced him to declare this canned bill of goods a "*serious* subject."

"Le Roi d'Aquitaine," a fantasy of a market girl who imagines herself chosen by the King ("Tough luck for the Queen"), is both sly and stirring, a celebration of a loser's bravado that in an unforced folksong style echoes the sentiments expressed in "Pirate Jenny." "Le train du ciel," sung at the death of an old black man the good-hearted Marie has spent her savings to care for, mimics the rhythm of a train picking up speed, and in a decidedly Gallic interpretation uses elements of blues and gospel music. For the dance-hall scene Weill composed another of his deliciously sultry tangos (published in 1935 as "Youkali / Tango Habanera"). The only number that carries more than a decorative charge is "J'attends un navire," Weill's perfect-pitch homage to a French music-hall style, in which the homesick heroine sings from the heart about her determination to return to France.

> *I'm waiting for a ship that will come,*
> *Driven by the beating of my sighing heart,*
> *By the welling of my tears.*
> *And if the sea wants to destroy*
> *My ship*
> *As it comes in,*
> *I'll carry it away*
> *In my arms as far as Bordeaux!*[14]

(With its aura of fervent resolve, "J'attends un navire" was to be adopted as an anthem of the French Resistance.) Terrific show music for a show that never had a chance of working, these are among the richest, most sweeping melodies Weill ever wrote.

With its galvanizing score awkwardly positioned in Deval's melodrama, *Marie Galante* opened at the Théâtre de Paris on December 22, 1934, and expired in less than three weeks. Smarting from the abrupt closing, Weill was desperate for the vindication he believed *Der Kuhhandel* would offer. When he failed to find a producer in France, he decided to pursue contacts in London. "It won't be easy," he predicted to Maurice Abravanel in a December 29 letter, "because the whole thing is on a very high level, a true comic opera, with two big, colorful, well constructed finales. If I should succeed in bringing out this work, which I believe to be my very best work, I would be over the worst." "Right away everyone asks for an English translation of the libretto,"[15] he wrote Lenya on January 24, 1935, after he had only just arrived in London; and as Weill realized, translating Vambery's operetta would require making musical adjustments as well. Weill was willing to "write British" if it would ensure a production, but Vambery became paralyzed. "His laziness is simply driving me to despair," Weill reported to Lenya. "It's now becoming obvious that the play is too long, something I've been telling him for half a year. He was supposed to cut it for the translation, so it would be easier to read, but he hasn't lifted a finger. Enough to make you throw up."[16] "After two months of tremendous efforts I've succeeded in getting a brilliant deal [with Charles Cochran, a major commercial producer in the West End]," Weill informed Heugel, his new French publisher, on March 15. "I think I have thought of everything that should go into the contract. . . . We are working with people who for a number of years now have financed the finest productions in London, and who want to continue this collaboration with me."

Commissioning an English translation from Reginald Arkell (book) and Desmond Carter (lyrics), Cochran demanded changes. He wanted the political satire softened, the addition of some British music-hall songs to ensure the comfort of his audience, and, of course, a new title: the untranslatable *Kuhhandel* was now to be called *A Kingdom for a Cow*. Always thrifty, Weill worked in fragments of songs from *Marie Galante* into the six new songs he wrote at Cochran's request. One in particular, a music-hall strut for the arms dealer, called "A Jones Is a Jones," displayed Weill in full British drag. Other numbers evoke the trot of a Gilbert and Sullivan patter song. During rehearsals Weill made further revisions to disguise his and Vambery's foreign origins. In a twenty-minute excerpt broadcast on the BBC on June 8 a few weeks before the show was to open, Weill's abbreviated score was performed and orchestrated in a stock British style. Beneath the clipped diction and swift pacing—Vambery's Caribbean warmongers sounded like British fuddy-duddies, and the music contained echoes of scores by Ivor Novello and Vivian Ellis, the two reigning practitioners of bread-and-butter West End operetta—little remained of the caustic German original. Lacking a personal voice, the work reeked of the kind of compromises Weill was forced to make.

Nonetheless, in the weeks prior to the opening Weill remained convinced that the show would give him a prominent place on the new cultural map fascism had drawn. His optimism was bolstered when Lenya joined him for the premiere on June 28 at the elegant Savoy Theatre. After eighteen months, Lenya had broken with Pasetti, who had run off with some of her money and who was never to be heard from again. At the time, Weill and Lenya had no plans to get back together as a married couple, but their mutual regard remained as firm as ever. Lenya wanted to be with Kurt for his important opening night, and during this uncertain period he welcomed his former wife's common sense and her clarity. Lenya did not remain in London, and when Weill vacationed in Italy later in the summer she was not with him; but it may have been when she joined him for the opening of *A Kingdom for a Cow* that Weill realized the bond between them would always survive sexual infidelity.

A Kingdom for a Cow did not break Weill's losing streak. Both the revamped book and Weill's score were coolly received. "The music comes out of a familiar stockpot, a recognizable and tolerably respectable pedigree, from Offenbach and Johann Strauss through the café-concert and the modern revue," wrote the critic in the *Daily Telegraph*. The *Times* called the political satire the best part of the show and noted that Weill's music was "less morbid than *Anna-Anna* and is satiric like *Die Dreigroschenoper*, but as with those works which are all we have had of his music here, it leaves an unpleasant taste behind." The review ended on an appallingly flippant note: "It is not stated whether his recent departure from Germany was occasioned by his partiality for politically tendentious satirical texts like this one or for the kind of music he writes, but the music would be the German authorities' most valid justification."

A Kingdom for a Cow lasted for two weeks only, and for the transplanted composer this second musical-theatre flop was more painful than the one in Paris six months earlier. Weill withdrew *A Kingdom for a Cow*, and although the original (and unfinished) *Der Kuhhandel* did not receive a performance until sixty-five years after Weill had first composed it, he would raid it for material for a number of his American projects. During his six months in London, Weill had continued to work on "the Bible thing" that would take him to America. Now, with his calendar cleared of other commitments, he turned his full attention to a project that may have presented the greatest challenge of his career. On vacation in Italy (disturbing because of its "warlike atmosphere," Weill noted) and still recovering from his London ordeal, Weill wrote to Lenya from Venice on July 23: "I would be so happy to be able to do something big again, something right—without having to think about those dull-witted audiences of Europe's big cities. Maybe it'll be possible to build up something in America so that I can write my kind of operas again. But that Reinhardt thing—it's full of peril, and also very difficult."[17]

EIGHT

The Road to America

T*he Eternal Road,* as the project "full of peril" would eventually be called, had the longest and most tortuous genesis of any of Weill's shows. At first, it was only a concept in the mind of Meyer Weisgal, an American Zionist smitten with theatre after he had produced a pageant, *The Romance of a People,* at the 1932 Chicago World's Fair. Weisgal's idea was a dramatization of the history of the Jews framed as "our answer to Hitler." ("We did not dream then of the coming unbelievable horror, or I would not have used such language, which in retrospect sounds almost flippant," Weisgal wrote.)[1] When he learned that Max Reinhardt had been forced to leave Germany, Weisgal was determined to hire him to direct. In November 1933, he visited Reinhardt in Paris, where the exiled maestro was working on a production of *Die Fledermaus.* "My father was sympathetic to Weisgal's personality," but not to the project, Gottfried Reinhardt recalled.[2] But once set on a course of action, Meyer Weisgal, an impassioned advocate who was to found the Chaim Weizmann Institute in Israel, was not an easy man to refuse. "He had a big personality," Weisgal's son, actor Michael Wager, said. "He screamed, he never edited his speech, he was a great charmer and raconteur, and perhaps above all he was

Librettist Franz Werfel, left, director Max Reinhardt, composer
Kurt Weill: the embattled creators of *The Eternal Road,* looking off
in three different directions, in Salzburg, August 1934

unafraid of people. He was completely unintimidated by the powerful. He
was a remarkable man—but it wasn't much fun being his son."[3]

When he finally relented, Reinhardt claimed he was "act[ing] against
his instincts."[4] Worried, like other émigrés, about his future financial
prospects, Reinhardt was tempted by Weisgal's generous terms. Weisgal
also allowed Reinhardt complete freedom in selecting his creative team.
The director chose Weill, Franz Werfel, and, to design the show, Norman
Bel Geddes, with whom he had worked on his famous production of *The
Miracle* in 1921. It seemed to Weisgal that Reinhardt had selected an
unlikely group for a pageant of Jewish exile, oppression, and endurance.
"Unlike me, Kurt had shaken himself free of Jewish life," noted Weisgal,
who like Weill was a cantor's son and descended from a long line of rabbis.
"He did not appear to me the most suitable choice of composer for the
score of a Biblical pageant."[5] About Werfel, Weisgal observed that he
"never consciously came to terms with his Jewishness. The mystic strain in
him which might have identified with Chassidism he transferred to the

Catholic Church, but the advent of Hitler kept him from formalizing his conversions."[6] Weisgal recalled "spend[ing] a whole night walking with Werfel in the garden and explaining to him, as well as I could, that this was a *Jewish* play—that and nothing else. It was our history, the history of his and my people, that had to be portrayed—not some alien or abstract concept. Remote as he was from Judaism, there was enough of the poet in Werfel to grasp at the idea even through my barbarous German." Weisgal remarked dryly about the one gentile in the group, the pinch-faced anti-Semite Bel Geddes, that "even genius has its limitations, and the truth was that the spiritual content of the play left him cold; he had as little feeling for the great historic tragedy of Jewish life as for the contemporaneous tragedy that was developing visibly in Europe."[7]

When the ill-matched team, festering with personal animosities and colliding egos, convened for the first time, in Salzburg in August 1934 at Max Reinhardt's baroque Schloss Leopoldskron, set in a large park with its own lake and eerily within sight of Hitler's summer residence, the stage seemed set for a disaster. Scorched by his experiences with Reinhardt in Berlin, Weill retained an elemental distrust for the director he sarcastically referred to as "the magician." "Everything is so tedious with these jerks,"[8] he steamed in a letter to Lenya. Himself trim and fastidious, Weill was personally offended by Franz Werfel's obesity, social clumsiness, and infamous table manners, and both he and Lenya despised Werfel's pretentious, anti-Semitic wife, Alma. The collaborators had differing ideas about what kind of music theatre piece they were about to start work on. Like Brecht, Franz Werfel was a writer jealous of his words, and from the first he thought the music should provide no more than an incidental support for his text. Weill, on the other hand, regarded the project's musical demands as approaching those of an opera or oratorio. And for the director, the contributions of both of his writers were the scaffolding on which he intended to construct one of his monumental spectacles. To this uneasy mix—*Der Weg der Verheissung* as lyric poem, as opera, and as extravaganza—must be added the ardent Zionism of the producer, Meyer Weisgal, who wanted his Jewish pageant to be a fund-raiser for victims of fascism.

After the initial meeting, which had been fraught with ill omens, Werfel returned to Vienna, Weill to his house outside Paris in Louveciennes, their relationship cordial on the surface. But a September 15 letter from Werfel to Weill suggested openings for future battles. Where Weill was contemplating a through-composed score, Werfel was resolved to limit the amount of music as well as to assign to himself a crucial role in defining its character. "Think in terms of melody, melody, melody, which makes me happy," Werfel counseled, and pointed out that the scene of the consecration of the temple would be a spot for "a genuine hit number (pardon this profane word) with a tremendous *Stretta*-effect. . . . I am afraid of one thing. If all of the rabbi's recitations are to be sung, can and will there not in the long run be a torturous liturgical monotony? There are moments where music under speech seems right and necessary," he conceded—as long as the underscoring is limited to these "moments. . . . Please always remember that we don't have singers at our disposal and that unattractive singing *will* certainly scare off an audience which is used to opera and bel canto."

By early October, Werfel sent to Weill all four parts of the libretto he had been working on since early 1934. Pointedly calling *Der Weg der Verheissung* "a drama in four acts," Werfel had devised a meter of his own (in which lines have four major accents while the number of syllables shifts) that suggested a chant or incantation. With a minimum of assistance from the score, he wanted his words to maintain the drama's rhythmic pulse. Werfel set his play in a synagogue in an unnamed city in which a community of Jews, victims of a pogrom, awaits news of their possible exile. During the long night the rabbi reads passages from the Bible that commemorate episodes of persecution, oppression, and salvation in Jewish history. As he reads, biblical events are dramatized upstage. When the focus returns to the present, the congregation wavers between faith and despair as they await their fate. Act 1, "The Patriarchs," tells highlights of the stories of Abraham, Sarah, and Isaac; of Jacob and Rachel; and of Joseph in Egypt. Act 2 dramatizes events from the story of Moses in Egypt: the tribal wanderings in the wilderness; the defection of the Jews to pagan rituals, as symbolized by the dance of the Golden Calf; and Moses' death in sight of the Promised Land. The story of Ruth, David's triumph over Goliath and his seduction by Bathsheba, and Solomon's building of the temple are the subjects of act 3. In act 4, the true prophet, Jeremiah, battles with Hananiah, the false prophet, as King Zedekiah capitulates to Babylonian invaders. The play concludes with the exodus of the congregation, forced to leave their country and so to begin a new chapter in the Jewish diaspora.

After Weill read the text Werfel sent, battle lines were clearly drawn. "Now that I am aware of the entire libretto, the more it seems a puzzle to me how Werfel can think of this piece as 'spoken drama,' " Weill wrote to Reinhardt (in Hollywood), on October 6, 1934. "It would be unplayable as spoken drama even in smaller theatres since it contains hardly a single page which does not implicitly scream for music." Werfel, in an obvious ploy to limit his rival's influence, urged Reinhardt to cast actors with limited vocal ability. Weill was careful to assure his director that he was not writing an opera (although he maintained that opera singers would naturally perform in the required "elevated" style rather than realistically), that he was thinking in terms of separate musical numbers, and that he was "mov[ing] melodic lines into the foreground. That way I am only sparingly making use of original Jewish motifs, i.e., only when there is a connection to the liturgy. The Jewish liturgy is actually rather poor in 'melodies'—it consists mostly of mere melodic turns and short motifs."[9] But Weill eagerly endorsed Reinhardt's proposal of casting opera star Feodor Chaliapin.

Throughout the fall, with very little communication with his collaborator, Weill continued to work on the score. On the first day of 1935, in a letter to Maurice Abravanel, he called *Der Weg der Verheissung* "opera—the best one I've done up to now," and claimed to have resolved "problems of form" by writing "large ensembles, not à la Bach, but rather entirely catering to melody with the broadest audience impact." But from March, when Reinhardt informed him that the production had been postponed, until August, when the collaborators convened once again at Reinhardt's castle, Weill did no further work on the score.

Reporting to Salzburg after his vacation in Italy, Weill was still wounded from the London failure of *A Kingdom for a Cow* and in no mood to deal with the Werfels. After the second day of a projected ten-day collaboration, the conflict between composer and librettist that had been simmering for over a year erupted. "Werfel is about the most obnoxious and slimiest literati pig I've ever met," Weill fumed in an August 11 letter to Lenya in London, speaking in the brutal tone they reserved for writing to each other about the many people they found offensive. But unlike the obtuse Werfel, Weill was a cunning strategist who knew how to get what he wanted from coworkers. "[Werfel] is easy game because he's a coward and immediately gives in, as long as one remains firm," Weill informed Lenya. And his case was strengthened because he had enlisted Reinhardt, as "crazy about the music as he is about me," as his ally. "Max behaves nobly, is very outspoken and unequivocally on my side, deciding all discussions in favor of the music. He understands completely what I want. . . . Of course, he really does realize what he's got in me. . . . I hope that this Werfel beast will leave on Tuesday; then I still want to work alone with Max for one or two days."[10] As Weill was waging a cunning contest of wills with his librettist, Weisgal on a daily basis was cabling Reinhardt from New York about problems in securing a theatre. Expecting the show to be mounted that winter, Reinhardt alerted Weill to be ready to leave for New York by early September, when casting would begin.

For some time before the August meeting, Weill had been confident that at least one part—Moses' sister, Miriam—was already cast: Lenya would play the role. By July he and Lenya had agreed they would go to America together at the start of rehearsals. "I'll write out the 'Miriam Lied' ('Miriam's Song') for you in English so you can begin studying it already," he had written Lenya in July. "I'm really looking forward to this trip to America. You too? I hope it'll all work out."[11] Now, in Salzburg in August, Lenya's casting seemed to be unexpectedly endangered. Rudolf Kommer, Reinhardt's ubiquitous assistant, "who's really repulsive," seemed to be "raising a stink about [your] getting a part," Weill wrote on August 14 to Lenya, still in London. Attributing Kommer's resistance to the machinations of Lenya's ex-lover Tilly Losch, Weill assured her that he would "push it through via Max, once I have him to myself."[12]

Two weeks later, in a characteristically abrupt about-face, Weill turned against the director. "Max is opposing it [the theatre Weisgal had engaged, which Reinhardt protested wasn't big enough] because he's lazy and evidently doesn't smell enough money (for quite a while now his veneration of money has made me feel like puking). He's also trying to talk us into giving this thing up altogether. . . . I'm thoroughly disgusted with this tired king of the castle,"[13] he grumbled to Lenya on August 26. Nevertheless, despite his growing resentment, Weill was still planning to sail to America on the *Majestic,* a luxury liner, on September 4, and still hoping that, although she had still not been officially cast, Lenya would be with him. "It'll all work out for Miriam," he assured her in his August 26 letter. (And indeed it did: ever since he had seen her in *Die Dreigroschenoper,* Reinhardt had been a Lenya fan.) "Naturally, it would be great if we could sail together, and I've reserved a double cabin, just in case. But the *Majestic* is a very expensive ship, and your trip comes out of our own pocket."

On September 4 Weill and Lenya embarked on the *Majestic.* On September 10, the former Mr. and Mrs. Kurt Weill set foot on American soil for the first time. When they checked into the elegant St. Moritz Hotel on Central Park South, Weill expected to stay for only three months of casting and rehearsals; Lenya planned to remain only for the run of the show. After they were finished with their commitments to "the Bible thing," they expected to return to Paris.

. . .

It became apparent to Weill almost at once, however, that the show, now called *The Eternal Road,* could never be mounted in the three months that had been projected. The obstacle was not Werfel or Reinhardt, and certainly not the speed-king composer himself, but Norman Bel Geddes, a designer with aspirations as grandiose as Reinhardt's. Originally, Reinhardt had proposed staging the pageant in a vast tent set up in Central Park, a plan Bel Geddes vetoed. Bel Geddes suggested the Manhattan Opera House, a theatre that had been built in 1905 to house the folly of another producer with visionary plans. Oscar Hammerstein, grandfather of the famed librettist and lyricist, built the house to launch the impossible challenge of breaking the Metropolitan's monopolistic control of opera. Long abandoned, the theatre in 1935 was in serious disrepair, had poor sight lines from the balcony, and an inconvenient location on West Thirty-fourth Street, outside the Broadway theatre district. But to the inexperienced Weisgal, *any* theatre, no matter how shabby or how awkwardly located, was preferable to staging the show in a tent.

Once Weisgal had secured the Manhattan Opera House, the designer realized that he would have to make changes in order to accommodate the five-tiered set he had in mind. "Bel Geddes embarked on 'structural alterations' of the Manhattan Opera House akin to God's alteration of the universe during the six days of creation, except that God's was cheaper and faster," Meyer Weisgal recalled. "It soon became clear that no time table could be set."[14] Bel Geddes's architectural rearrangements were to have an unexpected impact on Weill's score. In October, after originally omitting the synagogue altogether from his design, Bel Geddes decided to place the synagogue scenes in the orchestra pit and gave Weill the surprising news that it would now be impossible to have an acoustically acceptable place for an orchestra.

As extensive reconstruction of the Manhattan Opera House continued, Weill faced a two-pronged battle. On the one hand, he had to determine how to prerecord the score; on the other, he had to defend his work against Werfel, who in asking for many passages to be declaimed rather than sung was attempting to demote much of the music to underscoring. After Werfel demanded that Moses' farewell song be cut and Reinhardt for technical reasons decided to eliminate the scene of Solomon's temple building, for which Weill had composed musical passages he was particularly proud of, the composer exploded. "From the first day of our collaboration on I have— as you know—always stuck to my point of view that I did not have to write incidental music, but rather a kind of music in which singing, a new kind of 'loosened up' singing, should play a prominent part," Weill wrote in a November 27 letter to Reinhardt in Hollywood. "You know—and you have often confirmed this to me—how simple and easy it is to collaborate with me," Weill asserted. "I have adapted myself to yours and Werfel's wishes to a degree I have never done before. Of everything I had originally composed, one-third has been cut already and large sections I had composed to be sung are now being treated as *Sprechgesang*." Reinhardt, on the defensive, responded the next day. "Do I really have to remind you that from the beginning until today I

Reaching for the angels: a sketch by Harry Horner of Norman Bel Geddes's visionary, five-level set for *The Eternal Road*. In placing the synagogue scenes in the orchestra pit, the designer created unique problems for the composer.

have stood up passionately against all opposition in favor of complete musical continuity throughout the entire work, and in the manner of new forms you have developed?" Despite his protestations, Reinhardt's ultimate loyalty was to neither his composer nor his librettist but to his own epic vision, and once rehearsals finally began, in early January 1936, it was clear that the director regarded *The Eternal Road* as a Reinhardt spectacle for which Franz Werfel's poem and Kurt Weill's score were accessories.

"Mr. Reinhardt is working full steam ahead," Weill reported to his French publisher, Heugel, on January 10, 1936. "The music sounds very good and the rehearsals prove it to be effective. . . . The reconstruction of the theatre is going much slower than expected," he added. The crew excavating the orchestra pit where the synagogue scenes were to be played "hit rock, and then water, like Moses," recalled Meyer Weisgal, who was forced to suspend rehearsals at the end of January.[15] And it was at this point that Weisgal, according to Michael Wager, became "totally obsessed with *The Eternal Road.* He was not going to allow this setback to deter him, even though it meant he had to go back to his original sponsors with hat in hand. To continue, he had to find many other backers as well. Really, at that point, our lives were changed. Before that, we had been relatively normal. Desperate now for money, my father approached every rich Jew. He literally bankrupted the family. It was madness of a certain kind. This show, not *The Eternal Road* so much as *The Eternal Load,* dominated my childhood. We had to move out of a nice apartment to the Oxford, a fleabag hotel. My father wasn't taking a salary as he scrambled to get the show back up. Kurt complained when he wasn't paid—but did Kurt have to live with cockroaches, as we did?"[16]

Lenya and Weill pose for a formal portrait by Louise Dahl-Wolfe shortly after their arrival in America.

With the show on hold for an indefinite period, the company, as Weisgal recalled, "dispersed to the four winds."[17] Reinhardt returned to Hollywood, Werfel to Vienna. Weill and Lenya, who had remarried on January 19, decided to remain in New York, moving out of the expensive St. Moritz and into a modest hotel on Riverside Drive. Like many other Weimar Berliners, the Weills had been seduced by an imaginary, Hollywood-bred America of gangsters, flappers, and jazz babies—a sleek, capitalistic fairground dotted with speakeasies and skyscrapers. What delighted both Weill and Lenya was that the "real" America, at least as embodied in the metropolitan energy of New York, seemed so closely to match the myth of Amerika they had absorbed in Berlin. They were both determined to make America their new home, despite their awareness that re-establishing their careers would not be easy.

Once *The Eternal Road* was on hiatus, Weill shifted into high gear exploring other opportunities. But except for a small group of aficionados familiar with recordings of *Die Dreigroschenoper* and those who had seen the failed Broadway production in 1933, Weill in America in 1936 was an all-but-unknown composer whose European reputation had remained in Europe. Although at first he spoke with a thick and unmistakably Germanic accent—not at the time an asset in the Jewish-dominated world of the New York theatre—Weill was adept in the kind of networking he would now have to do. He was hard to get to know in an intimate way—even Lenya wondered how deeply she had ever really known him—but socially he had an engaging manner people took to at once. His wry smile and pleasant demeanor, which passed for warmth of a kind, effectively concealed his often harshly critical reactions to others. And in a remarkably short time his English became fluent as well as delightfully accented.

"I now have a little time to occupy myself with new theatre projects, through my American friends," Weill wrote to Heugel on January 31, just after *The Eternal Road* had been put on hold. "There is a very good chance to have another show. I'm in discussion with [Ben] Hecht and [Charles] MacArthur, the famous authors of *Jumbo,* New York's biggest theatre success. They want to do a musical with me and we're in the process of finding a subject matter. I'm also having discussions with The Group Theatre, the youngest and most modern theatre of New York. They are also very interested in me. Finally I'm having discussions with two motion picture companies in Hollywood (MGM and Paramount)." It was Weill's contacts with the Group Theatre that were to ripen into his first show for Broadway.

. . .

From the time he had arrived in New York, Weill went regularly to musicals on Broadway and to operas at the Met, and it did not take him long to recognize that the show that brought him to America, written, directed, and produced by outsiders to American show business, would not earn him the kind of acclaim he needed to pursue an American career. Indeed, his association with *The Eternal Road* would mark him as a European composer, when his goal now was to be accepted as a composer for Broadway. Weill deplored the rigor-mortis staging that was standard operating procedure at the Met at that time and felt that it was on Broadway, rather than at the Met, where opportunities for living composers were dwindling, that he had a real chance of continuing what he had been able to do in Berlin, make a living as a composer. By the time Weill was on the spot and ready to compete, the American musical theatre had already assembled a world-class track record. It had a legacy of great performers, including Al Jolson, Marilyn Miller, Ethel Merman, Fred and Adele Astaire, Gertrude Lawrence, Beatrice Lillie, George M. Cohan, the Marx Brothers, Lillian Russell, Helen Morgan, Fanny Brice, among many others; and a pantheon of composers, including Sigmund Romberg, Victor Herbert, Jerome Kern, Rudolf Friml, George Gershwin, Cole Porter, Irving Berlin, and Richard Rodgers, whose work brimmed with melody, rhythm, and wit. In Germany Weill had tailored his work for a broad audience, and the prospect now of catering to the popular tastes of another culture posed no aesthetic or ethical quagmires for him. Having dedicated his career so far to kicking opera out of its splendid isolation, and to writing for a wide audience, he was not repelled by the New York theatre's commercial motor.

Weill's desire to leave behind a heritage that had become braided with the pain of his enforced exodus was probably greater than that of any other distinguished émigré from fascism. From 1933 on, as events in Germany and Austria spiraled toward the Final Solution, America received a cavalcade of eminent expatriates, among them film directors Fritz Lang, Billy Wilder, Otto Preminger, Douglas Sirk, and Robert Siodmak, composers Arnold Schoenberg, Franz Waxman, Ernst Křenek, Hans Eisler, Erich Korngold, and writers Thomas Mann, Hannah Arendt, and Theodor Adorno, each of whom had to confront a baptismal period of adjustment. To achieve the kind of prominence they had enjoyed at home, a certain amount of compromise and realignment were unavoidable, especially for the directors in Hollywood and Weill on Broadway, seeking acceptance in popular media. Lang and Weill, whose American careers were to intersect in 1938, faced a parallel challenge, of conforming to the American grain while holding on to the distinctive styles that had won them acclaim in Berlin.

Like Lang and the other Teutonic directors making their way in Hollywood, Weill in choosing Broadway was setting up shop in an American industry with its own codes and house styles. But Weill sensed that the institution he wished to join had some give. He surmised that the Broadway theatre he had studied closely would not be resistant to his kinds of experiments. Providentially, one of the first musicals Weill saw was *Porgy and Bess,* a landmark show that challenged the traditional split between opera and the popular musical stage. For the rest of his life *Porgy and Bess* remained for Weill at once a model of the kind of American opera he wanted to create and a reminder of the Broadway musical's flexible boundaries. Weill appreciated the variety of the Great White Way, the fact that many different kinds of shows were folded within "the Broadway musical." There were the European-based operettas of Romberg and Friml, with their regulation musical menu of waltzes, romantic ballads, comic and novelty numbers, and military marches. And there were the jazz-age musicals (George and Ira Gershwin wrote the best of them) with contemporary settings and sounds. In both the Ruritanian romances and the modern fables, musical numbers were introduced in an often free-form, casual, but seldom merely haphazard way. Book shows comprised only one branch of the American musical theatre, however. Revue, extravaganza, vaudeville, burlesque, and minstrelsy had formats of their own in which comedy sketches, dances, songs, specialty acts, and production numbers were shuffled with varying degrees of cohesiveness. Advertised by the brand names of their producers, the Ziegfeld *Follies,* the Shuberts' copycat *Passing Shows*, George White's *Scandals,* J. J. Shubert's *Artists and Models,* Irving Berlin's *Music Box Revue*s, Earl Carroll's *Vanities,* and John Murray Anderson's *Greenwich Village Follies* were the most renowned of the revues, often presented in annual editions. Each show plied its own specialty. Ex-hoofer George White featured more dancing than the shows of the senior revue meisters such as Ziegfeld and the Shuberts. Irving Berlin's revues boosted the work of new songwriters. Ziegfeld's *Follies,* with eccentrically costumed showgirls on steep stairways and settings noted for color coordination, set the pace for sheer opulence. *Artists and Models* bested the competition in risqué costumes. By 1935, a victim of the Depression and of changing tastes, revues had passed their heyday. But the form in all its versions had bequeathed to the musical theatre a vibrant performing style.

With Broadway his target, *The Eternal Road* could only be a detour; Weill's ticket to the American fame and fortune he eagerly sought would have to come from a show conceived and developed on native soil. As if in answer to his need—and an example of extraordinary beginner's luck—at a party in the winter of 1935, just before *The Eternal Road* was to be postponed, he met Harold Clurman.

In 1931, with Lee Strasberg and Cheryl Crawford, Clurman had cofounded the Group Theatre, one of the most influential organizations in the history of the American theatre. Since the late 1920s Clurman and his cofounders had been working in minor posts for the prestigious Theatre Guild. Although it professed to be a true repertory company dedicated to the production of plays of literary value—the kind of plays strictly commercial producers were likely to be wary of—the Guild in fact had become a showcase for the husband-and-wife team of Alfred Lunt and Lynn Fontanne, its most famous members. The Guild's pledge of no-star ensemble performances was shattered by its evident worship of its two stars-in-residence. And while by and large the Guild kept its word about presenting quality material, the quality it believed in bore a distinctly European stamp. To correct what he considered the Guild's misplaced priorities, Clurman in a series of midnight lectures throughout 1930 spoke to groups of young people of his vision of a true theatrical ensemble dedicated to presenting new American plays that examined the rips and tears of America in the grip of the Depression.

Clurman wanted not only to inspire a group of socially conscious American plays of literary merit but also to instruct a cadre of specially selected young actors to perform them. In envisioning a program of actor training Clurman was offering a correction to the many acting schools that adhered to antiquated nineteenth-century notions or followed no firmly grounded technique of any kind. For guidance in how to achieve a performing mode of psychological truth—realism lit with a palpitant inner life—Clurman turned to the example of Konstantin Stanislavsky, the great Russian director and acting theorist. Along with Lee Strasberg, Clurman had profoundly admired the performances of Stanislavsky's Moscow Art Theatre he had seen during the company's visit to New York in 1923. Both he and Strasberg later studied the Stanislavsky system, a series of exercises to stimulate an actor's creativity, with Richard Boleslavski, a Stanislavsky disciple, at the American Laboratory Theatre.

Like Brecht and Weill, Harold Clurman was a scholar of the theatre as well as a practitioner, an enflamed theorist as well as an eager day laborer.

But above all he was an artist of the monologue-as-harangue, and the sheer intensity of his oratory was the Group's First Cause. His handpicked band of native players, trained in a common style for the purpose of presenting American plays of literary and social significance, was a true repertory company which, on Broadway, endured from 1931 to 1941: a Broadway record both unprecedented and virtually certain to remain unmatched.

At the time Kurt Weill met Clurman, the Group Theatre had already weathered the best and the worst of times. After four frustrating years, the Group in 1935 discovered a playwright, Clifford Odets, one of their own, who was equal to the scale of Clurman's vision. That year, the Group's annus mirabilis, productions of Odets's *Waiting for Lefty* and *Awake and Sing!* fulfilled the company's original manifesto. But, as if by some demonic law of balance, 1936 began with the Group's perennial problem, a larder bare of appropriate plays. Another issue—rivalry and resentment among its three high-strung, complex cofounders—added to the developing crisis. Each cofounder nursed a set of grievances against the other two and wanted a change of role within the company's structure. Clurman, the Group spokesperson, chief administrator, final arbiter in literary matters, and principal director, wanted less responsibility in day-to-day management. Lee Strasberg, self-appointed Group guru passionately engaged by acting problems, wanted complete control in all matters of actor training. Crawford, fund-raiser and principal caretaker, yearned for greater creative leverage.

Always on the prowl for new material, and eager for the Group to develop an original musical, Clurman, a fervent admirer of *The Threepenny Opera,* invited Weill to explore ideas. Weill's presence, in turn, provided Cheryl Crawford, a musical-theatre enthusiast, with exactly the creative opportunity she had been seeking. But to Strasberg, the prospect of developing a musical seemed both threat and distraction. Of what possible use to his priestly quest of psychological truth in acting could performing a musical be?

The Group's agenda of illuminating the American moment coincided precisely with Weill's readiness to bury his European past, and over the spring he explored with Cheryl Crawford possible subjects for a 100-percent made-in-America musical. As collaborator, Crawford suggested Paul Green, "the most American playwright I could think of . . . [who] also wrote poetry, a not unimportant consideration."[18] (As their opening production in 1931, the Group had presented Green's *House of Connelly,* a drama of the Old South.) "The material that seemed most promising was on the subject of World War One, in which Paul had served, believing with Woodrow Wilson . . . that it would be the war to end all wars," Crawford recalled.[19] Once the Great War had been selected as the ground against which to set Weill's music, the three collaborators began to pore over newspapers and books about the period. Although determined that he would not write anything even remotely resembling a German musical, Weill nonetheless mentioned German works such as *The Good Soldier Schweik, Woyzeck,* and *The Captain from Köpenick*—stories about embattled Everymen. Gradually, with these pieces as models, the seeds of what was to become *Johnny Johnson* were planted.

Significantly, at the time that he was preparing his first American musical, Weill dissolved his contract with his French publisher, Heugel. "I am trying to create a position for myself in American theatrical life," he wrote on June 4. "That will be very difficult and I will need all my patience and energy. . . . But once I have found this position over here I will be able to return to the kind of work analogous to my talent and ambition, and that would be the time to offer you operatic works of international calibre." (Is Weill merely appeasing Heugel, or at the time did he mean what he wrote? Placing Mammon before Art, he seemed to be identifying America—the Broadway theatre—with the former, Europe with the latter: a position he would often publicly disown, but traces of which he may have continued to hold in private. The truth was, he wrote Broadway musicals for the money *and* the art, and in time, with increasing bravado, attempted to combine Broadway with opera.)

By the end of April Clurman had decided that *Johnny Johnson* would be the Group's fall production. To get the script in shape for rehearsals, which would begin in the summer, Weill went to Paul Green's house in Chapel Hill, North Carolina, in early May. "America's oldest university is here," Weill wrote Lenya. "You see only young people here and you realize for the first time what America is really like and how unimportant New York is for this country. . . . Paul Green makes a very good impression: refreshing, young, easygoing."[20] Only three days after his first letter to Lenya from Chapel Hill, Weill's feelings about his collaborator became more complicated. "He's a strange fellow, and I'm not quite sure whether he's able to handle this project. But Cherill [*sic*] is terrific, and it's astonishing how much she understands. Anyway, it's interesting for me, and I think it's not impossible for something worthwhile to come out of this."[21]

With hefty contributions from Weill and Cheryl Crawford, the episodic script that Paul Green finalized in April and May follows the misadventures of a simpleton who joins the army because he believes Woodrow Wilson's pledge that the Great War will ensure a permanent peace. Johnny Johnson is "a sort of innocent Sunday school guy who believes wholeheartedly in the greatness of America, her mission in the world as a leader of peace and democracy . . . a balmy softy, but with a queer childlike and instinctive wisdom about practical matters," Paul Green wrote.[22] Going to war, he is tossed into a chaotic world he cannot understand. He befriends a German sniper he has been sent to kill and decides to let his enemy go free instead. After he tries to stop the war by administering laughing gas to top-level officers, he is arrested and sent to a sanitarium, where he conducts a mock League of Nations forum, instructing other inmates in brotherhood. Released into a world gearing up for another war, he sings a peace song to a world unable to hear it.

With abrupt shifts in tone (the satire of act 1 is followed by the tragedy of act 2) and flat, cartoonlike characterizations (Johnny's girl, Minny Belle, is "fed on the schoolbook romanticism of war"; his rival, Anguish Howington, with his "eye [always] to the main chance, represents business"),[23] the play is a sentimental American vaudeville, and distinctly unlike Brecht. And its well-intentioned, self-congratulatory antiwar thesis, in light of contemporary events in Germany, was curiously mistimed. "We were all for the Spanish War at the time," as Phoebe Brand, who played Minny Belle, recalled, "yet we also felt we had to do an antiwar play. There was a great antiwar feeling at the time, though, of course, by the time America entered World War II we knew we had to go to war to stop Hitler."[24] "This play deals with the last war, not the next," Weill said. "If we were dealing with the conflict that is to come, an entirely new play would have to be written. The last war didn't really save the world for democracy; the next one will."[25]

The show's revuelike format demanded an eclectic score, and despite its faults *Johnny Johnson: The Biography of a Common Man* provided a splendid platform for Weill. Musical satire, echoing the Weill of Brecht-Weill, abounds, but there are plentiful examples of pathos as well. Numbers with a surreal quality, and ones in which there is a marked incongruity between song and context, recall elements of Weill's Germanic style. ("Kurt was trying for an American style," Phoebe Brand said. "He loved jazz and the musical influence of blacks. But even so the score was half-German." Indeed, the overture recycles "Lied der Bramweinhändler" from *Happy End*.)[26] Some numbers are conventionally integrated; others seem like casual interjections. Some songs are fully developed, others exist as entic-

The stars of the Group Theatre's *Johnny Johnson*, 1936, Weill's
first Broadway musical: Phoebe Brand as Minny Belle and
Russell Collins in the title role

ing fragments. A few songs are half-sung against orchestral accompaniments; others are simply declaimed, while still others are spoken first and
then sung. Occasional filmlike underscoring helps to make transitions
between scenes and provides emotional cues for the audience.

The show opens with a choice example of Weillian irony. To the same
melody, the people in Johnny's small southern town sing first about their
belief in peace, then, after receiving news that war has been declared, pro-
claim their commitment to fighting. (Weill's anthemic tune and unusual
harmony may have been in Leonard Bernstein's ear two decades later when
he wrote "Tonight" for *West Side Story*.) In the repetitive rhythm of
"Aggie's Song," performed at her sewing machine by Minny Belle's wid-
owed, overworked mother, a foolish woman who chooses the wrong man

for her daughter, Weill captures the flavor of the character's drab, monotonous life. A musical aside that provides no more than a thematic grace note, the song is a potent example of the composer's conciseness. Minny Belle's "Oh Heart of Love," sung to Johnny before he leaves for battle, is another deft character number, this time in the garb of an old-fashioned Victor Herbert–like waltz. Minny Belle is so enamored of experiencing the pain of loss that she can't wait for Johnny to enlist so she can begin to pine for him. Weill's melody and Green's lyrics parody the silly heroine's romantic excesses; but "Oh Heart of Love," apart from its ironic placement in the show, can also pass as the real thing, a robust Broadway ballad from an earlier epoch, in which Weill pays sly homage to his Broadway forebears. "Captain Valentine's Song" also derives its punch from narrative context. On the job in a recruiting office, the self-infatuated Captain Valentine reads movie magazines and daydreams—the obvious inappropriateness of the song's lyrics and of its insinuating tango rhythm is exactly the point. The "Army Interlude" is one of the orchestral numbers that mixes various kinds of martial music (the "Marseillaise," "You're in the Army Now") into a polytonal stew. This can seem trite now, but it is important to remember that it was Weill and his generation of European-trained classical composers (such as the film composer Max Steiner) who introduced this sophisticated sound into American commercial music.

Against melancholy orchestral strains Johnny, speaking rather than singing, addresses the Statue of Liberty, a prelude to one of the show's musically surreal interludes. "The Song of the Goddess" is a solo with operatic texture for a mezzo-soprano in which the Statue performs a bitter ode about how she has been used to send young men to their deaths. In the equally surreal "Song of the Guns," cannons come to musical life to serenade soldiers with a lullaby. And the lullaby they sing is extraordinary: Weill arranges the heartbreaking melody of Schubert's "Ständchen" for a gorgeously tranquil Hawaiian slack-key guitar. For Weill, the singing cannons were the nucleus of the show, an index of the off-center, enlivening ways in which music and text intersect throughout. "Instead of doing what most composers would do—make the music grim and stark, with timpani and such devices—I wanted it to be seducing, as if sung by prostitutes," Weill said. "For cannons are like prostitutes: their metal could have been used for better purposes, and moreover they do anybody's bidding, right or wrong. They say to the soldiers, 'You sleep, we do the work for you.' "[27]

For the moving scene which follows, between Johnny Johnson and Johann, the German sniper he has been sent to kill, Weill wrote grave,

Musical surrealism in *Johnny Johnson*: in "Song of the Guns," cannons (voiced by a men's chorus) serenade the sleeping soldiers. Setting by Donald Oenslager

symphonic underscoring called the "Music of the Stricken Redeemer." An astonishing change of pace is provided by "Oh the Rio Grande (Cowboy Song)," a novelty item for company member Tony Kraber. In one of his most virtuoso feats of musical ventriloquism, Weill composed a country-and-western song that's a dead ringer for the kind of number Roy Rogers or Gene Autry might have performed. "That song has nothing do with anything in the show," Phoebe Brand said, "but Kurt was dying to write some American songs of all kinds, including folk songs of the type that Tony would sing for us. Kurt especially liked that song, and so did we."[28] Celebrating the open, rolling American land and the he-man's place within it, "Oh the Rio Grande" evokes galloping horses on the prairie and the sound of the wind on the plains.

"Mon Ami, My Friend," a saucy ditty sung by a French nurse trying to cheer up wounded soldiers, finds Weill in convincing French drag. For two comic scenes that follow, Weill supplies instrumental music only. He treats the meeting of the Allied High Command as a Gilbert and Sulli-vanesque musical parody and underscores the scene of the Laughing Generals (Johnny has plied them with laughing gas) with a lurching, accelerating atonal introduction that leads into a witty Charleston. The mood changes once again for "In Times of War and Tumults," as on either side of the stage an American and a German priest pray to God to protect their men. The American priest's voice slides from declamation to singing, pitched at operatic intensity.

For Johnny's fellow inmates in the asylum Weill wrote two songs, the "Asylum Chorus," a salute to their fellowship, and an a capella fugue, "Hymn to Peace," both gently brushed with irony and pathos. For the former, Weill arranged a version of an old Methodist hymn, "Blest Be the Tie That Binds," which Paul Green suggested, while the latter is a vivid composition in Appalachian shape-note style—the numbers indicate the composer's fascination with the indigenous music of his new home. There follows a purely comic piece of vaudevillian shtick sung by a nutty psychiatrist, "The Psychiatry Song," which burlesques past and present methods of treating insanity and is Weill's first, and triumphant, version of an American show-business tradition, the rousing eleven o'clock number.

"Maybe [there should be] a scene at the end [in which Johnny] is with a hand organ grinding out a tune . . . he enters with an organ, people passing, a penny dropped here and there," Paul Green suggested.[29] Taking Green's cue, Weill wrote an American Moritat, the haunting "Johnny's Song," heard in snatches throughout but sung by the hero only at the finale. As Minny Belle goes off with Anguish and her son to a Preparedness Parade, Johnny sings his song, which expresses his belief that "we'll never lose our faith and hope and trust in all mankind." "The last song is a heartbreaker, I cry every time I hear it," Phoebe Brand said.[30] For this key song in his first Broadway show Weill refashioned the refrain of his "J'attends un navire" and created a "heartbreaker" indeed, simple and unabashedly sentimental. The song, in this instance, failed to become a hit, but the structural idea underlying it—that a song adumbrated throughout a show would finally be sung fully and simply in the final scene—was to soon find more successful expression in "My Ship" in *Lady in the Dark*. (And interestingly, that song, too, shows the influence of "J'attends.")

Like the musical numbers, Weill's orchestrations had both surprising range and the delight of novelty. A Hammond organ was used prominently in several numbers, including the invocation of the two priests and the inmates' hymn to brotherly love. A banjo accompaniment to parts of "Johnny's Song" and the "Cowboy Song" added a homespun western twang. In one orchestral interlude, trumpet blended with organ to create a spectral, otherworldly effect. One of the composer's favorite instruments, the alto sax, provided a jazzlike accompaniment to "Captain Valentine's Song" and "The Psychiatry Song." The score, which Weill completed in early July before rehearsals began, was on many counts extraordinary—in the many ingenious ways that music ducked in and out of the action there really was no precedent in the American musical theatre.

Each summer of its ten-year life the Group retreated to a camp, usually in Connecticut, where the performers would "sing for their supper" as they worked on acting exercises and began rehearsing plays they would be presenting in New York in the fall. In the summer of 1936 the Group was based in Nichols, Connecticut, where Weill and Lenya joined the troupe in mid-July. Because the Group had never before performed a musical, and because many of the actors were not vocally trained, Weill eagerly took on the job of vocal coach, instructing them in how to sing or, in places, talk-sing his material. "He knew exactly what he wanted," Phoebe Brand recalled. "To get his style, he showed us the film of *Threepenny Opera* and played the German records. How we all loved that music! He taught us the half-talking, half-singing style he wanted us to use. To him—and he stressed this over and over—the action and the acting were more impor-tant than the singing. Your attitude, your character—these were what he had us examine. He suited the songs to our abilities. His music has a satir-ical quality, but also a very tender and sad, romantic kind of quality, too." Accompanying the actors as they stood by a piano, Weill would often demonstrate an intonation or how he wanted a phrase to be sung. "He was not a singer, not at all," Phoebe Brand recalled, "but he would sing with us very often, showing us precisely how the song should be *acted. Johnny John-son* isn't exactly a musical: it's a musical play. It was realism, and as in all the other shows we worked on, it was the acting that was all-important. To achieve that, Kurt worked with us very, very closely and so patiently."[31]

Weill, who enjoyed working with the mostly untrained singers, told the Group that he had begun writing for the theatre because opera houses in Germany were "museums" stuffed with performers who were merely "voice acrobats."[32] He urged the actors to approach lyrics as they had been trained to work with dialogue. "How should the actor sing?" he asked. "Not like an opera singer," he answered. "Opera singing is sensual; opera teachers take away the personal character of the voice and make standard singing." In contrast, Weill wanted the actors to retain their own voices. "Talk on the note," he urged. "Pay attention to the phrasing of the word, not the melodic line."[33]

Curiously, Lenya, who was with Weill in Nichols for the remainder of

the summer and who knew more about how to perform her husband's theatre songs than anybody else in the world, "didn't interact with us; she
didn't mingle, Kurt did," as Phoebe Brand remembered. "She didn't help
with the singing. But Kurt wanted us to listen to Lenya on records—she
was made for his style, we knew that. . . . I don't think any of us really
achieved the kind of singing Lenya did, but how we tried!" Adapting less
easily than her husband to their new country, Lenya seemed content to disappear into the sidelines—she was the composer's wife. That summer, she
began an affair with Paul Green, who also remained aloof from the actors.
"We didn't get to know him very well either," Brand said.[34]

Speaking that summer to the eager young actors, then undergoing a
difficult transitional moment in the company's history but still alight with
the idealism Clurman had instilled, Weill could not have found more
responsive or like-minded listeners anywhere in America. His messianic
tone—Weill was a born teacher—made a tight fit with the oracular style
of both Harold Clurman and Lee Strasberg. Weill and the Group had
much in common. Both were dedicated to theatrical reform; both believed
in the social uses of art. But many members of the Group, fiercely critical
of the American moment, were more politically engaged than Weill, who
was grateful to be where he was and who seemed moreover to embrace
wholeheartedly the American system with all its debits. (A number of
Group members joined American Communist organizations and many
years later were to become permanently divided when members such as
Elia Kazan testified against each other before the House Committee on
Un-American Activities. Weill never joined the Party, and so conse-
quently never had to face the problems that would beset some of his Group
colleagues.)

"In a way, at least in the beginning, Kurt was more the director than
Lee was," Phoebe Brand recalled.[35] Skillfully, Strasberg would outline the
play's social and thematic significance, but he stumbled once he started to
put the show on its feet. "The directing was miserable," Group member
Robert Lewis, himself an aspiring director at the time, declared. "How
helpless Strasberg was to find musical staging. The show was heavy with
the kind of realism he was comfortable with. Lee only knew about the text
and about the psychology and its relation to life. But with the music he
was not sure what he was doing. He could not help anybody deal with
rhythm or movement, or things that come out of the score. He didn't
understand the style a musical—*that* musical—needed. And if Lee was the
director you couldn't open your mouth."[36] Favoring text over score, Stras-

berg cut a number of songs. "Lee cut a song, 'Farewell, Goodbye,' that Kurt had written for me," Brand, one of the few trained singers in the company, recalled. "Over the years, whenever we'd meet, Kurt would tell me that Lee had cut the best song in the show."[37]

Because he desperately wanted to be a part of this great American theatre enterprise, and because he and Strasberg did, after all, speak a similar theatre language—Weill wanted his songs to be acted with a realism that paralleled Strasberg's quest for truthful acting—the composer kept the peace. His forbearance was especially evident as he watched the demolition of his delicious French music-hall number, "Mon Ami, My Friend." During rehearsals it was apparent to everyone except Strasberg that Paula Miller (Mrs. Strasberg) was unable to put the number over. That July, as later on stage in New York, Paula Miller performing the song stopped the show in the wrong way. "Not the kind of way you want," as Robert Lewis recalled. As Strasberg staged it, Paula performed the song in one, finishing the number center stage. "No two hands were put together ever in applause," Lewis said. "I would see her kind of creep off, embarrassedly kind of half smiling to the audience. I asked Lee if it would be possible for her to travel with her last four bars. He was so angry. 'This is not a vaudeville show, this is a theatre piece. Don't come around here with your vaudeville tricks.' "[38]

Weill kept his silence because he was shrewd enough to know that he was winning the undeclared war with Strasberg in another way as well. "Kurt was always jovial and sweet to us, and we all adored him," Phoebe Brand recalled, while no one would have voted Strasberg Mr. Congeniality. "We learned a lot from Lee, but we also had to unlearn a lot," Brand observed. "We always had trouble with him."[39]

Throughout the summer, as Paul Green handed in new episodes and Weill made cuts and changes in the score, everyone was agreed about the show having an intimate, homemade quality. *Johnny Johnson* was going to be a different kind of musical, distinguished by its modest scale, by the prominence of acting over singing, and by the casual treatment of some of the numbers, presented as throwaway fragments rather than fully developed routines. "The whole thing was going to be small, the picture of little people being ground out and down by war," Morris Carnovsky, who played the mad psychiatrist, recalled. "And that was the main idea that guided us and kept us interested. Unfortunately, that idea was not carried through."[40]

Back in New York in the fall, the cast began to rehearse *Johnny Johnson*

in a small theatre, where the show seemed "charming: informal, unpretentious, and sweet," as Harold Clurman remembered.[41] But the only theatre
that Cheryl Crawford was able to book was the Shuberts' cavernous Forty-
fourth Street ("Thank goodness it's no longer there," Phoebe Brand said)[42]
with a stage designed for a big Broadway hootenanny. "The orchestra"—of
conventional Broadway size—"was so far away, we couldn't hear it,"
Carnovsky said. The cast also had to contend with the nineteen oversized
sets designed by Donald Oenslager, which, according to Carnovsky,
"dwarfed us. The sets should have been little and delicate, instead they
were expressionistic in a huge way. I had a sinking feeling when I first realized that we were really stumped by these sets." When Carnovsky
expressed his doubts to the director, Strasberg snapped, "Never mind!
Donald knows!" "It was at that moment that I personally lost a little of my
faith in the management of the Group," Carnovsky recalled.[43] "By the
time our show got on the large Forty-fourth stage, it needed opera singers.
If only we had stayed in that little theatre, we would probably have been a
success," Phoebe Brand maintained.[44]

The first preview at the Forty-fourth Street Theatre was a low point in
the Group's history—"one of the most distressing experiences I have ever
gone through in the theatre," said Harold Clurman.[45] The actors were frequently inaudible; the sets looked monstrously oversized; and, in dismay,
Clurman felt that "the performances now looked amateurish." People
began to leave after the first ten minutes, and by the end of the show,
"there were no more than twenty people" in the large theatre.[46] In a post-
mortem dissection, Weill sat calmly and silently as his American colleagues joined in a heated battle that, given the Group's peculiarly
intimate history, had the flavor of sibling rivalry. Strasberg lashed out at
the actors, the playwright, and the composer, making what Clurman characterized as "feverishly irrelevant and disparaging references."[47] For Weill,
who in only a matter of weeks would be facing equally embattled
rehearsals on a reborn *Eternal Road,* the moment was a trial by fire. But
buoyed by his inborn confidence, Weill prevailed. "He knew, no matter
how Lee carried on, that all of us loved his music," Phoebe Brand said.[48]

A number of Group Theatre loyalists urged Clurman not to open the
show, an option he never considered. The company persevered and later
preview audiences began to react favorably. Many in the cast started to
believe what Weill had told them during the summer, that *Johnny Johnson*
contained the seeds of a musical-theatre revolution; they also began to
think that they might even have a hit. "Surprisingly, opening night went

smoothly," Cheryl Crawford remembered. "The three huge cannons pushed out to the audience over the top of the trenches on time, singing sweetly to the sleeping soldiers. The large Statue of Liberty appeared promptly to sing a lovely song to Johnny."[49]

For Weill, if not for the show as a whole, the reviews were thick with praise. The Broadway newcomer was gratified that the major drama critics grasped his style, appreciating his twisted, satiric harmonies, his captivating melodies gurgling with corrosive undercurrents, his imitation of and comment on several kinds of American popular music. Brooks Atkinson in the *New York Times* of November 29 praised Weill's "trenchant and beautifully orchestrated score," which has "a great deal of strength to give *Johnny Johnson* when Paul Green's cartoon composition is weakest." "A delectable and fascinating score by that brilliant German exile," Richard Watts Jr. raved in the *New York Herald Tribune.* "Even to my untrained ear, the new musical is original in the same immediately recognizable way as *The Three-penny Opera,*" Joseph Wood Krutch wrote in the *Nation* of December 5, and added, perceptively, that Weill "seems to employ with equal facility any one of the idioms of popular music. He writes things which sound like military marches, popular ballads or jazz tunes. But what he is really writing is some sort of mordant commentary on each." And Marc Blitzstein, a rival composer not always friendly to Weill's work, wrote in *Modern Music* of November/December 1936 that "for this American *Schwejk,* a folk play . . . Kurt Weill has written some of his best music. . . . The song of the Goddess of Liberty, the one called 'Soldiers, Masters, Men' ["Song of the Guns"], the comic one on psychiatry . . . are all in their own way quite as fine as 'Barbarasong' and 'Surabaya-Johnny.' Weill has practically added a new form to the musical theatre." A number of reviews, commenting on Weill's recent émigré status, detected some foreign notes. *Time*'s November 30 notice referred to the composer's "Europeanized foxtrots," and a review in the November 27 *American Hebrew* observed that Weill has "evidently succeeded in blending his deep understanding of European chaos with the spirit of guileless but awakening America."

In the 1936–37 season, not a bonanza for musicals, there was certainly room for a show like *Johnny Johnson.* The Group's strange new musical play was a healthy antidote to the uncomplicated high spirits of the season's biggest musical hit, *Babes in Arms,* a Richard Rodgers–Lorenz Hart confection about stagestruck kids putting on a show. Strictly commercial and wholly dedicated to fun, *Babes in Arms* was fresh, peppy hometown entertainment by the leading musical-comedy writers of the decade. The season's smartest revue was *The Show Is On,* the Christmas opening at the Winter Garden, for which several major composers, including Vernon Duke, George Gershwin, Hoagy Carmichael, and the busy team of Rodgers and Hart, provided material for a star lineup that included Bert Lahr and Bea Lillie. It was staged, with a vibrant sense of color and movement, by Vincente Minnelli, who would become a major director at MGM. Otherwise, the season was routine. The big fall ticket was *Red, Hot and Blue!,* a regulation star vehicle for three stars, Ethel Merman, Bob Hope, and Jimmy Durante, with an indifferent book by Howard Lindsay and Russel Crouse and, except for two winners, "It's De-Lovely" and "Down in the Depths," a mostly ho-hum score by Cole Porter. European operetta still had a hold in the Broadway market, but three entries—*The White Horse Inn,* an American adaptation of Ralph Benatzky's hit Berlin operetta and a piece of overstuffed schmaltz (there is no evidence that Weill saw it); *Frederika,* a show about Goethe with a score by Franz Lehár; and Sigmund Romberg's *Forbidden Melody,* a potboiler about marital infidelity in Bucharest—did little to attract new audiences to the form.

After *Johnny Johnson* opened, Weill, as in Berlin, pursued promotional angles and berated his publisher for not doing enough. "Maybe it is the difference between the American and European music business which makes the whole thing so difficult to understand," he wrote his American publisher, Max Dreyfus, on December 20. "Here is a musical play running in its fifth week with growing success, after an excellent, partly sensational reception. The audience simply loves the show. There are between eight and twelve curtains every night, and people are humming the music in leaving the theatre (which is, I think, internationally the best test for the success of a music)." For one of the score's most melodious songs, "Oh Heart of Love," Edward Heyman had written what Weill called "a very good commercial lyric," which, "after a long fight," Paul Green agreed to have sung in the show. "There is no doubt, that *Johnny Johnson* has a great chance to run through the whole season, if Chappell would finally start to push this one song [now called "To Love You and to Lose You"]," Weill wrote, and added that "we have a very good chance to sell *Johnny Johnson* to the movies if at least one of the songs would be really plugged by the publishers."

There was no sale to the movies (as a more objective observer than Weill might have foreseen), and the show did not last the season but closed after a disappointing sixty-eight-performance run. *Johnny Johnson* may not have been a hit, but for Weill it accomplished what he had wanted, and what he had needed in order to pursue a career on Broadway. He had proven, in a strange country and in a new language (both verbal and theatrical), that he was a steady collaborator and stalwart soldier in the line of fire.

Robert Lewis, fifty years after *Johnny Johnson* opened, recalled that "the whole score is marvelous, the numbers hold up beautifully. It's a shame it hasn't been revived because of that book, which has to be cut—it's cutesie-pie beyond belief and goes on forever. It has to be strengthened to come up to the strength of the music."[50] Lewis recalled only three moments in the Group's production that measured up to the quality of Weill's score. "In 'The Psychiatry Song,' Morris [Carnovsky] found a kind of heightened way of playing it. The funny makeup, the scenery askew—the scene had a complete stylistic unity most of the rest of the show did not achieve. The scene between Julie [John] Garfield, who played the German sniper, and Russell Collins as Johnny, with only Kurt's instrumental music, was so beautiful and moving—it was all the things the whole show was supposed to be." And like everyone else, Lewis praised Collins, who had a harrowing history of alcoholism but steadied himself for the greatest role of his career. "He was too old for the part; he had to wear a wig because he had no hair at all; but his acting was so moving, he was such a simple actor. The last song was unforgettable: he never moved, the house was absolutely silent as he sang Kurt's beautiful melody."[51]

Always capable of juggling more than one project, Weill did not forget *The Eternal Road* even as he was working intensely with the Group. Indeed, his immersion with a band of American players was to influence his thinking about the Reinhardt show. After he heard from Meyer Weisgal in late July that the pageant would be restarted before the end of the year, Weill wrote Franz Werfel on August 3. "Weisgal did not give up his endeavors to salvage this project (something anybody else would have done in his place)," he acknowledged. But the real reason for writing was to offer his Viennese collaborator the benefit of his nearly year-long experience in having scrutinized the American theatre and its audiences "very carefully." "I think we should do everything possible to develop the action in the synagogue into an overall, unified, gripping one . . . holding the bible scenes closer together than is the case now." From his semi-Americanized perspective, Weill concluded by noting he was "very skeptical about the fate of *The Eternal Road,* even if Weisgal should really succeed in getting all of the money."

"Werfel is not in favor of building up the synagogue scenes," Alma

Werfel answered huffily on her husband's behalf in an August 20 letter. "He thinks this could easily turn into a thriller with musical hits from the Bible. Even if the—probably—Jewish audiences of New York would react positively to a 'thriller,' that kind of action would definitely kill the essence and purpose of the whole: the Bible. Up to now *I* always had the feeling that there were too many Galician-Jewish elements. This synagogue action has to take a back seat so that the real poetry and the music will retain the purity with which they have been conceived." Alma Werfel's letter revealed her palpable distaste for Jewish concerns—a Catholic, she wore a large cross to every production meeting of a show about the Jewish Diaspora—as well as the fact that the show's cowriters remained adversaries. The problems that had plagued the production the first time—Weisgal scrambling for money (though this time, at the request of his backers, he had an experienced commercial producer, Crosby Gaige, as adviser); Bel Geddes literally raising the roof; and Weill and Werfel in a standoff—remained.

Just before rehearsals began, Weill, on November 21, sent a note to Max Reinhardt in Hollywood, urging him to cast Lenya in the role of Ruth, a more prominent part than Miriam. Typically, Weill was looking out for opportunities for Lenya, and also typically, he did not always choose well for her. As a gentile, Lenya may have seemed to her Jewish husband a reasonable choice for Ruth, the outsider who joins her Jewish in-laws; but the role required a sweet-voiced singer who could project an enchanting melodic line, and this was not Lenya's forte, as Reinhardt recognized. "Have enormously high regard for the artistic strength and the uniqueness of Lotte Lenya, but am leaving the role of Ruth uncast," Reinhardt declared in a November 23 telegram. "Deeply convinced that she cannot offer the part or the part her any advantages. One principal part of my life's work has been my casting being successful for both works and artists therefore I feel bound to be totally open with you and hope you will receive this in the same spirit of friendship I hold for both of you."

For Weill, the rejection seemed another lost round in an ongoing battle. Indeed, by the time rehearsals restarted, at the end of November, Weill felt he was fighting to protect his score against the combined onslaughts of his librettist, his director, and his producer, all of whom, for different reasons, had chipped away at his original musical continuity. Each of his collaborators resisted "opera" as a format or a guiding concept. As David Drew noted, for *The Eternal Road* Weill's major influence was "popular oratorio in the nineteenth-century sense [Mendelssohn and Gounod]. Yet it was a twentieth-century work that offered him the closest precedent—the oratorio of *Le roi David* by Arthur Honegger, whose friendship and advice had been important to him during his residence in France."[52] But whatever label was attached to it—and *The Eternal Road* was certainly another of the composer's in-betweens—Weill was determined to safeguard his score from any further interference. He had already pared it down for the recording, made a year earlier; the only changes that could be made now were in the small live stage orchestra that unions had demanded. "The stage orchestra was the only medium available for interpolations, so each interpolation also served to strengthen the stage orchestra's somewhat tenuous raison d'être," according to David Drew, who noted that Weill's changes were not for "musico-structural 'improvements,' " but for matters of immediate production "expediency."[53]

During rehearsals, Weill disguised his frustration. "He spoke not a word," recalled the show's choreographer, Benjamin Zemach. "You were not aware of his presence; he was a very quiet person, and very calm, outwardly." (But Zemach caught a glimpse of another side to the composer, who was "peeved that I hadn't heard about him before he came to this production. I beat my breast, but it's a fact: I had never heard of him. Closeness, I didn't feel any.")[54] Scrupulous as always in observing theatrical decorum, Weill never interfered with the work of his colleagues. He allowed Reinhardt to direct the actors, Zemach to coach the dancers, and musical director Isaac van Grove to work with the singers.

Weill's immediate problem was where to place the small live orchestra. Because Bel Geddes had reserved the orchestra pit as the space for the synagogue, some other area had to be found. "What Weill had to do was to put the live musicians on the top floor, three floors above the stage, with the conductor wearing earphones," Maurice Abravanel said. "You couldn't see the orchestra, you couldn't hear them live . . . early 1937, you can imagine what kind of canned sound came out. It felt like a movie sound track."[55]

Two major sections were cut. During a rehearsal, the set of Solomon's Temple, with columns that stretched across the stage, reached up to the rafters, and required the services of seventy stagehands, collapsed with a tremendous boom. Reinhardt eliminated the entire scene. And though there are conflicting reports about when the decision was made, Reinhardt decided to remove all of act 4, "The Prophets," which featured the brilliant Yiddish Theatre actor Jacob Ben Ami and some of Weill's strongest writing. (Act 4 could not have been performed opening night, as it is some-times claimed, because, for the most part, it was never orchestrated.) Wer-fel, "for whom each line counted—he had adapted most of them from the Bible, anyway—was furious at all the last-minute cuts," Maurice Abra-vanel said. "But Weill was ready to throw overboard the work of months, for the good of the production. He wasn't a purist. He liked what he had done; he knew his music was good. But he had the vision of the interest of the whole. But another reason . . . he knew he could write some more tomorrow."[56] Abravanel's portrait of unshakable Weill may be too rosy, for the substantial cuts robbed the score of its original momentum, as the composer was painfully aware.

Equally troubling were the often lengthy stretches in acts 1 and 2 in which his music had been silenced altogether to allow for sustained pas-sages of entirely unaccompanied dialogue. It had been Weill's intention to create a fluid, diverse, continuous musical support for Werfel's text; as underscoring, melodrama, recitative, chorales, and songs as solos, duets, and arias, the score had been designed as an unbroken conversation between words and music. In banishing Weill's "language" for lengthy periods, Reinhardt changed the function of the music that remained, which became handmaiden to, rather than cocreator of, the narrative.

Even in reduced form, however, Weill's score is considerable. Drawing on and reinterpreting the traditional melodies of the Jewish liturgy that he had learned in childhood from his father, *The Eternal Road* is pre-eminently a score by a Jewish composer. Forced by the circumstances of his emigra-tion to honor his religious heritage, Weill wrote emotionally vibrant music designed to send hearts and pulses racing. A score for a monumen-tal pageant, it is exactly what it needed to be: generous, accessible, and varied as it moves among what even for Weill is a remarkable array of musical structures, from Jewish cantorial forms and oratorio-like recita-tives for the Rabbi, to extended arias for Moses and Bach-inspired choral episodes. For each character and each section, Weill developed a distinct musical personality. The laughter of Sarah has a klezmer shading reminis-cent of the "Barbara Song." David's melody has a jaunty, assertive quality that befits a scrappy hero. For Bathsheba Weill wrote a sensuous, jazzlike motif with a daringly contemporary flavor. Jacob and Rachel sing a duet that recalls the liquid lyricism of the "Crane Duet" from *Mahagonny.* His music for the story of Ruth exudes a sweet-natured generosity that reflects the heroine. For the Voice of the Infinitely Remote, Weill devised a refrain that, almost by omission, evokes the divine: just a lovely melodic strand over a drone bass. In contrast, the pounding beat for his dance of the Golden Calf summons head-on a spirit of pagan revelry.

There are also disappointments. What remains of Weill's treatment of the story of Joseph is melodically and harmonically undernourished. And there are lapses in taste. In a show introduced by a rabbi, it seems odd for the children of Israel to celebrate their triumphs by singing Bach-like motets. The march that recurs in many musical variations throughout— the destiny theme, in effect the anthem of the Jewish Diaspora—often sounds embarrassingly derivative of Mahler and rarely rises to the extraordinary thematic and narrative demands placed on it. As Michael Wager recalled, "The anthem was to represent the triumph as well as the oppression of the Jews. At the end, musically, the effect was to be one of transfiguration, as the characters in the synagogue march upwards to unite with the great figures of Jewish history."[57] Unfortunately, Weill misjudged the effect. His final treatment of the march theme, replete with brass chords and timpani rolls, has inadvertent militaristic and Teutonic undercurrents.

Once again Weill had written an unclassifiable work of music theatre, one that borrowed from oratorio, opera, liturgy, and popular revue. Fusing a variety of "high" and "low" styles, and often integrating Hebraic motifs into a contemporary framework containing echoes of the jazz idiom of *The Threepenny Opera* and *Happy End*, Weill fashioned a score that effectively conceals its complexity. For a spectacle to enthrall multitudes, and for actors with limited vocal technique—there were no Chaliapins in the cast Weill and Reinhardt assembled—the composer employed a direct, melodically rich style.

After two extraordinarily trying rehearsal periods and ten postponements, *The Eternal Road* finally opened on January 7, 1937. "It was to cost between $150,000 and $200,000; it cost more than half a million," Meyer Weisgal recalled. "In all other respects it was faithful to the original terms of the contract, as well as to the conception. It was a musical biblical morality on a grand scale. It was artistically and Jewishly the greatest theatrical production of all time."[58] Given the sacrifices he had made, Weisgal was entitled to his hyperbole. But if it wasn't exactly the Greatest Story Ever Told, it most certainly was a pageant of stupendous size conceived by a quartet of squabbling visionaries. Weill's score, Werfel's text, and Bel Geddes's five-tiered set extending from the bowels of the orchestra pit up to the Stair of Heaven, "the sphere of the angels and of the divine Voice, framed within a gigantic door of rock and removed from the traffic of mortality by mystic veils,"[59] were subordinated to the director's epic vision. First to last, *The Eternal Road* was a Max Reinhardt superproduction.

Meyer Weisgal's overworked press agents promoted the show as a sight and sound spectacle of cosmic magnitude. Large ads promised spectators that "*The Eternal Road* will inaugurate a new era in the history of the drama"; "only America with its unlimited technical and human resources

Max Reinhardt's ancient-world re-creation for *The Eternal Road,* 1937. In the opening musical scene of act 1, Abraham (Thomas Chalmers) makes a covenant with God.

The exodus from the synagogue at the end of *The Eternal Road*

could have dared to do justice to the demands of Reinhardt, Werfel, Weill, Bel Geddes—geniuses of such calibre never before have collaborated in one production"; "the settings for the 91 scenes occupy nearly two-thirds of the auditorium of the new Manhattan Opera House, completely rebuilt and redecorated." Prospective customers were urged to see Max Reinhardt's "greatest miracle of all . . . set in a panorama of unforgettable splendor by Norman Bel Geddes with [in small print] music of sweet and impressive beauty by Kurt Weill and stirring dances created and directed by Benjamin Zemach." Not forgotten was Franz Werfel's play, "already destined to be an immortal classic."

Surprisingly, the Barnumesque hard sell did not stifle the critics. Brooks Atkinson's January 24 review in the *New York Times* was typical. "The ballyhoo has concentrated on size, mechanics of production, finance and the princely personality of Max Reinhardt. What the theatregoer is promised is not a religious fable but a circus . . . yet it is sincerely affecting . . . [and it has] a triumphant score that gives [it] enormous emotional vitality." "The most vivid Biblical pageant ever staged in the United

States and perhaps in the world," trumpeted *Variety*. "During some interludes there is an effect of vastness which seems inspirational." Music critics, on the whole, were less impressed.

Weill at first was thrilled by the reception. "The success of the play is really extraordinary," he wrote to his parents on January 15. "It's wonderful for me, since I now have a fantastic name here and once again I can start at long last to improve my sadly deranged finances." Weill left for Hollywood at the end of January to work on a film; during his absence from New York he received, rather than royalties, reports about the show's financial problems. With fifty-one actors, thirty-six dancers, a massive chorus, scores of supers and stagehands, *The Eternal Road,* according to the January 18 edition of *Variety,* was "the world's most costly show, with a weekly nut of $31,000." Prices ranged from 83 cents for Wednesday matinees to $4.40 for evenings. "One of the insane things about the production was that it lost money even when it sold out," Michael Wager said. "That's because they couldn't sell all of the seats. The way Bel Geddes had designed it, you couldn't see the synagogue from about half of the seats upstairs. And a lot of the seats in the orchestra had been taken out. From the minute it opened, no matter what, it could only lose money week after week."[60] "The whole thing is *deeply* disgusting," Weill wrote Lenya on February 13. "Reinhardt keeps behaving like a big flaming asshole. He's furious because he isn't getting any money, but of course he won't lift a finger . . . to hell with him."[61] "I don't think that ever in the history of the American theatre an author has been treated in the way you treat me," Weill wrote to Louis Nizer, the lawyer for the show, on April 8. "I know you are paying royalties to Reinhardt and Geddes, and I don't see any reason why you should not pay me. You cannot imagine how this whole affair looks from the point of view of a man who has spent two years of his life, who has risked his whole existence, who has used all his talent, his strength, his personal influence, his friends, to bring about this show and who does not get anything out of it."

The Eternal Road closed on May 15. The final performance was a benefit for Meyer Weisgal, who had suffered weekly losses in the attempt to keep his beloved project running for four and a half months. "Those idiots were unable to make use of the gigantic success," Weill wrote his brother Hanns on May 31. "I haven't made a penny. Well, let's forget it." And although Weill raided his score for incidental music he was to provide for other Jewish pageants in the 1940s, the show was indeed forgotten— silenced—for the next sixty years. A work that defied the limitations of live theatre to reach for a visual amplitude probably attainable only in films, *The Eternal Road* was a glorious folly, not only for its obsessed producer but for each of its high-strung creators as well.

Sixty years on, only Weill's score holds up. Werfel's text is limp, stodgy, hopelessly old-fashioned, and shot through with vestiges of anti-Semitism. Reinhardt and Bel Geddes's production seems now less a visionary scheme than a camp attempt to compete with Cecil B. DeMille. But hovering over the misbegotten project is the impulse of a heroic, long-gone theatrical spirit praiseworthy precisely in the overweening scale of its ambitions.

"For me, *The Eternal Road* is still very close to Kurt Weill's whole European background," Lenya said.[62] Indeed, the show that brought Weill to America was not Weill's first American show. Although advertising claimed correctly that the production had American size, in its musical spirit and structure the piece was European, the work of a group of exiles responding to the National Socialists' escalating crimes against humanity.

NINE

How Can You Tell an American?

Surviving two problem-plagued productions, Kurt Weill clearly knew how to cope with the New York theatre. Indeed, many of its rites were familiar from his experiences in Berlin. In Hollywood, America's other entertainment marketplace, he was not to prove as skilled.

It was through his Group Theatre connections that Weill got his first job in films. When the film director Lewis Milestone, one of the angels of *Johnny Johnson,* decided to cast his new project, *Castles in Spain,* a story about the Spanish Civil War written by Clifford Odets, with actors from the Group, he hired Weill as composer. Right after the opening of *The Eternal Road,* Weill went to Hollywood. It seemed almost too good to be true—and, as it happened, it was: the project developed into *Blockade,* a 1938 film directed by William Dieterle which had no appearances by Group Theatre actors, no script by Clifford Odets, and no score by Kurt Weill.

In Santa Monica in March, at a party for André Malraux given by Salka Viertel, Weill met Sam and Bella Spewack, writers who worked successfully on both coasts. They discussed ideas for a Broadway musical. "I absolutely want to do a show for New York, and my position here [in Hollywood] would be totally different if I had a real success with a *'musical'* in

New York," Weill wrote Lenya on April 5.[1] Soon after they met, Weill began to work with the Spewacks and with lyricist E. Y. Harburg on the book of a show tentatively titled *The Opera from Mannheim,* whose subject hummed with autobiographical vibrations. Originally the projected musical was about an opera troupe that leaves Germany in 1933 to try its luck in America; in a later version, the opera company was transformed into a group of Jewish actors who toured Germany in their own musical comedies. Forced to leave Germany quickly, they misplace their music, which they must reconstruct once they arrive in America. The lost music, surely, is Weill's, the work that *he* had to leave in Germany and which he felt he had to deny or repress, or borrow from covertly, in order to build a new career in America. By May 15, although Weill had completed the score, for which he was paid $10,000, the project had fizzled. As David Drew observed, "We are left with the irony that all the music Weill managed to write for an unfinished play about a lost score has itself been lost."[2]

Weill thought his second Hollywood assignment, composing the score for a movie to be directed by Fritz Lang, would give him the chance to create "a new form of musical film," as he wrote Lenya on April 29.[3] But working with Lang ("[He] makes you want to puke ... I completely understand why he is so hated everywhere")[4] and with Sylvia Sidney, the film's deeply (and famously) obnoxious star, was to be another Hollywood misfire. Weill's innovative score was assigned to studio arrangers, who with the director's support proceeded to butcher it. When it was released on June 8, 1938, to mostly negative or puzzled reviews, *You and Me,* set in a department store staffed by former convicts who revert to their old ways before a last-act redemption, contained only three traces of Weill's original concepts. Enticingly, the film opens with "The Song of the Cash Register," performed by an off-screen singer in Weill's patented *Sprechstimme* style to a montage of transactions on the theme "You can't get something for nothing; if you want something you must pay for it." The pro-capitalist lyrics (by Sam Coslow) notwithstanding, in its biting rhythm and didactic impulse the crisp, startling number could have come from *The Threepenny Opera* or *Happy End.* A Hollywood "alien," it's a tease without a follow-up, introducing a fresh radical style the film has no intention of pursuing. In the second Weill interlude, the hero (played by George Raft, a former criminal himself) and heroine (Sidney) go to a nightclub, where a singer performs "The Right Guy for Me," a number in the mold of the "Barbara Song" and "Surabaya-Johnny" that celebrates an unwashed sexual vagabond. Shots of the singer are intercut with stylized images of the "right guy," in silhouette, moving through a waterfront setting pulsing with sexual decadence—a world conjured from popular notions of late-Weimar Germany. In this moody, fragrant sequence, a ripe German expressionist sensibility flares briefly in a made-in-Hollywood product. In the third innovative sequence, planning a robbery of the department store they work for, the felons begin to speak in a kind of rhythmic verse with a percussion underscoring. For a few thrilling beats, before it slides back into the verismo style mandated by Hollywood classicism, the film seems on the verge of flipping into another mode. In the end, despite the Weillian eruptions, *You and Me* is no more than a minor curiosity.

In late May, as Weill was finishing his work with Lang, *Johnny Johnson* was presented in Los Angeles by the Federal Theatre. But the production, which had no connection to the Group Theatre, was in fact much less well received than the original, and did nothing to advance Weill's prospects in Hollywood, which by this point he was desperate to leave. But it earned him two commissions from the Federal Theatre. The first, begun that August, was another collaboration with Paul Green, who served on the Federal Theatre's board of directors. Thinking big and American, Weill proposed a three-part work about "the birth of the Constitution as the drama of an idea," as he wrote to Green on August 19. But when he went to Chapel Hill in early October 1937 to begin working with Green ("hyperhysterical; he has no ideas, no pep, no enthusiasm, no courage"),[5] Weill soon realized he would be adding *The Common Glory* to a growing list of unrealized projects.

As the project languished over the fall, Weill began work on another patriotic subject. Burgess Meredith, who had become a personal friend, suggested musicalizing *The Ballad of Davy Crockett* by H. (Hoffman) R. (Reynolds) Hays, a left-wing writer who had worked for the Living Newspaper and who was later to work with Brecht and Hanns Eisler. Like Johnny Johnson, Hays's Davy Crockett is an idealized American Everyman, a folk hero whose story is told in chronicle form. But unlike Johnny, Crockett thrives, making his way from the backwoods of Appalachia to the halls of Congress to a valiant death defending the Alamo against Mexican attack. Weill had doubts about the content, but was drawn by the chance to experiment with a new theatrical format. "In December 1937, Kurt Weill, Charles Alan, and I formed a corporation, the Ballad Theatre," Burgess Meredith recalled, "which would take the following musical form: a chorus of singers would sing the main story line, and the actors would go into the action only when the mood was prescribed by the chorus. The chorus would be large and varied, and would replace the orchestra. The voices would perform the harmonies and functions of the orchestra. It was essentially Kurt's idea. If any instrument at all was used, it had to be a part of the action, like a flute or drum."[6]

From January to April 1938 Weill completed about forty-five minutes of choral music, but apparently without much regret stopped working on *Davy Crockett* to pursue other projects. "Although [it] has some good moments, Weill was surely right to abandon it," David Drew wrote. "It seems undernourished and lacking in both vitality and conviction. For that, the play must certainly bear part of the blame. Much simpler in style than *Johnny Johnson,* and also more 'American'—or at least, less obviously European, [*Davy Crockett*] was an essential step in Weill's determined project to Americanize his work."[7]

During this time, as Weill steeped himself in the history and music of his new country, moving restlessly among unfinished pieces with a nationalistic spirit, he decided he would seek American citizenship. Meanwhile, events in Germany were becoming increasingly blasphemous. In January 1937, Germany withdrew from the Treaty of Versailles. In September Mussolini visited Hitler in Berlin, a summit that ended with a massive rally at which multitudes cheered the ravings of the two dictators. In October, with Hitler's legions marching to Rome, the two fascists signed the Anti-Comintern Pact. In March 1938 Hitler invaded Austria. Surely Weill's immersion in creating patriotic spectacles that celebrated an American spirit of heroic individualism was a defense against the politics of fascism, a way of holding on to a measure of security in a world gone mad.

In the early spring of 1938 Weill accepted a commission to furnish the score for yet another patriotic pageant. Organized and written by Edward Hungerford, a specialist in the history of the railroad, *Railroads on Parade* would be presented at the 1939 New York World's Fair; the seventy-minute pageant was to be a tribute to American engineering and (implicitly) the capitalist ethic that spawned robber barons. Weill would be collaborating with some veterans of *The Eternal Road,* including conductor Isaac van Grove, designer Harry Horner, and director (and lyricist) Charles Alan, who apparently were undaunted by the prospect of staging another larger-than-life event. If Weill had any ideological qualms about the material, he never voiced them.

As he began to plan the score for this richly indigenous subject, he was interrupted by the chance to work on a Broadway musical with Maxwell

Anderson, one of America's most illustrious playwrights. Weill had been trying to spark Anderson's interest in working on a musical ever since he had met him at a Group Theatre gathering in the fall of 1936. The author of numerous plays, including *Elizabeth the Queen* (1930), *Mary of Scotland* (1933), *Both Your Houses* (winner of the Pulitzer Prize in 1933), *Valley Forge* (1934), and *Winterset* (1935), Anderson was exactly the kind of writer Weill had always sought in Germany—acclaimed, dedicated to serious work, and well connected. Enjoying a contemporary pre-eminence that posterity has not confirmed, Anderson was virtually assured of a Broadway production for anything he wrote. Although he had no experience in the musical theatre, Anderson was interested in Weill's suggestion. A former journalist, Anderson had been working in the theatre steadily since his first hit, *What Price Glory,* cowritten with Laurence Stallings, had been produced on Broadway in 1924; but his keenest interest was in writing poetry. "He always wanted to be a poet, but didn't think he could measure up—his biggest thrill was in getting a poem into *The New Yorker,*" his daughter, Hesper Anderson, recalled.[8] Anderson wrote a number of his plays in blank verse (more than anything else the cause of his current crit-ical and popular disfavor), and the prospect of writing for the musical the-atre seemed another possible forum for experimenting with poetry. "Lyrics to him were a kind of poetry," Hesper Anderson said. "But because they weren't *exactly* poetry, he didn't take the lyrics that seriously, and that freed him."[9]

Despite their obvious differences, Anderson and Weill discovered they had much in common. Both came from religious backgrounds they had rejected (Anderson's father had been a self-ordained Baptist minister), and both transferred to their work a distinctly messianic streak. "My father would have violently dismissed the idea that his plays were religious," Quentin Anderson, the playwright's eldest son, said. "But that there is a religious tone in the work was a factor ingrained from his father. Max felt the theatre had a religious ground, that it represented a kind of popular celebration of the glorious assertion of religious devotion. Many of my father's generation"—including Kurt Weill—"would show this kind of translated piety."[10] Anderson's tone was certainly different from that of the Brecht-Weill pieces; but in his own way Anderson wrote teaching plays—dramas with didactic purpose.

After their initial meeting, Weill continued to court Anderson with possible subjects, but nothing took shape until April 1938. The catalyst was Burgess Meredith, a neighbor of Anderson's in New City, New York,

who had had great success as the lead in three Anderson plays, *Winterset,*
High Tor, and *The Star Wagon.* Anderson, no fool, asked Meredith what he
would like to do next. The actor, who had a remarkable speaking voice,
unique in timbre and resonance, said he would like to do a musical with
Kurt Weill—Meredith had appeared in the small role of Crooked Finger
Jack in the ill-fated Broadway production of *The 3-Penny Opera* in 1933.
Already being wooed by Weill, Anderson may have suspected a conspiracy
but, as Meredith recalled, "liked the idea. So I brought Kurt up to the
country for a talk. I remember the afternoon we three were strolling
through the woods [surrounding Maxwell Anderson's house on South
Mountain Road in New City], when Max brought up the idea of adapting
Washington Irving's *Knickerbocker History of New York* [1809]. He said he
admired Irving and was fascinated by the old Dutch settlers, who had
lived in the very countryside where we were walking. It was during that
walk that the idea of *Knickerbocker Holiday* was born. The next day Kurt
and I bought copies of Washington Irving's work and were intrigued."[11]

Just as he began to work with Anderson on a general outline, Weill was
summoned to Hollywood for dubbing sessions on *You and Me.* On April 17,
on the train to Los Angeles, Weill wrote Anderson a long letter that
revealed not only his relish for their subject but also his instincts as a collaborative dramatist. "In showing our young hero as a man who is physically unable to take orders, you make him one of the fathers of all people
who live in this country because they consider it 'the land of the free,' "
Weill declared. "On the other side you show the rich man as the father of
all crooks who try to make a profit out of this very freedom, and in
between you show [Governor Pieter Stuyvesant] as the father of all ambitious governments who try to help the country but cannot get along
without the help of crooks. . . . You paint a picture of the time which originated today's problems . . . how this country at the very first, primitive
start of its history was faced with the same problems and difficulties [as
today], with the same fight between the great conception of a new world of
individual freedom on the one hand—and the human nature on the other."

Wanting (and needing) a Broadway hit, Weill was showman enough to
realize their history lesson would have to contain a love story: fiction up
front, the weight of history behind. "There are several ways of connecting
this story with our love story," he wrote, offering several banal variations
on a romance that crosses class lines. Then, as if suddenly aware that he
might have been poaching on the terrain of one of America's foremost
dramatists, he apologized. "I don't know, I just wrote [this] down because

you may get some idea from it. . . . I hope you don't mind. But you know how excited I am about this idea and the possibility of doing a musical play with you."

When Weill returned from Hollywood in late May, he was surprised to learn that Anderson had completed a first draft and had already written many lyrics. Weill had looked forward to a closer working relationship; bursting with ideas about how to structure the show, he wanted, in effect, to be colibrettist as well as composer. But what Anderson had done did not, in fact, violate the composer's usual procedure of beginning his own work only after an entire libretto was finished. (Weill's method surely accounts for why there are so few "trunk songs" in his catalogue.) "Max was not a sociable man, and as a writer my father had a habit of doing it by himself," Quentin Anderson observed. "In an earlier famous collaboration, with Laurence Stallings, when they were writing there was alternating handwriting on a single page. And my father may have been wary of collaboration because Stallings, who sold their play to Hollywood, turned out to be a fink."[12] Weill was disappointed by Anderson's solitary methods, but realized there was still much work to be done. And it had to be done quickly, because, on the strength of Anderson's reputation, production plans were moving ahead at dizzying speed. Guthrie McClintic, married to Katharine Cornell and an A-list director, had been signed, and the show was scheduled for fall production. So that he could work with Anderson throughout the summer, Weill, with Lenya, rented a cottage in Suffern, close to Anderson's farmhouse in New City.

As they began to meet regularly, the collaborators developed a genuine affection for each other. "My father didn't have existing good friends—he didn't know quite how to handle people, and made the mistake of doing it with money, and the relationship that formed between him and Kurt was unique," Quentin Anderson said. "I saw them talk with an intimacy that in my father's case was very unusual. Kurt, unlike Max, was uniformly charming. He was an engaging, social man with an amusing and quite charming voice and accent, but even so I suspect that his ease and intimacy with my father were rare for him too. My father would only have been happy writing with Kurt."[13] Anderson held the reins—their show was to be more Anderson than Weill—but the solitary playwright grew to appreciate his colleague's judgment, and his composure. "My father was moody, he had so much melancholy," Hesper Anderson said, "and Kurt was so even-tempered, so gentle and funny. He had a kind of reserve, but he also had a certain authority, and he was much more attractive than you can gauge from photographs. In person, he was virile and compact. My father would give him a lyric and Kurt would come back the next day with four or five melodies. 'Which one do you like, Max?' he would say, with a twinkle. My father used to say that Kurt was picking melodies out of the sky. Kurt was strong-willed, but he would defer to my father's judgment. Whatever tension he felt would emerge in rashes and high blood pressure, but I didn't see it, I don't think anyone saw it, except Lenya. He was this really attractive, sweet man for whom the work came so easily."[14]

Weill may have been deferential to his famous partner, but he was also well aware that in musical theatre Anderson was a novice who needed coaching. "In using music, you can express your philosophy with great bite and irony," Weill wrote to Anderson in a May 14, 1938, letter, skillfully instructing the playwright in the functions of music in the musical theatre. "I have started to work out a style which would give a feeling of the period and yet be a very up-to-date music. This combination of old and new gives great opportunity for humor in music, and my idea is that the

Walter Huston, Jeanne Madden, Maxwell Anderson, and a bemused, owlish Kurt Weill study the score of *Knickerbocker Holiday*.

music in this play should take active part in the humorous as well as in the sentimental parts, because the more we can say in fun the better it is. For instance if we have the fight between the flute and the trumpet I want our audience to laugh as much about the music itself as they'll laugh about the situation and the dialogue." ("The evidence is thin that my father had a sense of humor," Quentin Anderson said. "*Knickerbocker Holiday,* under Kurt's influence, is as much humor as he was open to or capable of. He was a very serious man.")[15] As his youngest son, Alan, recalled, Anderson "loved music and felt it belonged in the theatre, but he did not have a strong sense of musical-theatre structure or of the connections between lyrics and notes. Kurt would ask Dad for phrases—for more song, less poetry."[16]

As the starring role for Burgess Meredith, Anderson created a fictional hero, Brom Broeck, a self-reliant vagabond who can't take orders, who defies tyranny, and who wins the girl. Broeck may have been the hero, but Meredith noted that Broeck's antagonist, the newly arrived, dictatorial governor of Nieuw Amsterdam, Pieter Stuyvesant, seemed to be engaging Anderson's deepest attention. "My father wrote *Knickerbocker Holiday* as an attack on Roosevelt and his New Deal policies, which for him represented a dangerous centralization of power," Quentin Anderson said. "Max scorned political affiliations, and he never voted. About Roosevelt he had almost violent feelings."[17] "My role became less interesting while the part of old Stuyvesant grew bigger and better," Burgess Meredith recalled. Beginning "to feel a chill come over [him]," Meredith bailed out before a star had been cast as the wily new governor. "Guthrie McClintic withdrew for the same reason: he didn't like the way it was headed," Meredith claimed.[18]

The show's new director, Joshua Logan, young, filled with ideas about how to stage musicals, and fresh from a big hit, Rodgers and Hart's *I Married an Angel,* was also troubled by Anderson's treatment of the governor. He felt Stuyvesant was overbearing and too darkly conceived to fit comfortably within a musical-comedy framework. Logan—"marvelous with humor," according to the playwright's son Alan, who was the show's stage manager[19]—urged Anderson to lighten his portrait. Weill, a refugee from Hitler's Germany, for whom Roosevelt's—or Stuyvesant's—brand of authoritarianism was child's play, a mere jest, also helped to temper the playwright's hostility. To his credit, Anderson listened to his colleagues, and in Stuyvesant created one of the richest and most vigorous characters of his long career, a wry comic-opera tyrant with a silver tongue.

After Logan felt that Anderson had transformed a solemn, high-minded history lesson into a smart, audience-friendly Broadway musical on the order of the swiftly paced Rodgers and Hart hit he had just directed, he suggested Walter Huston (the father of the director John Huston and grandfather of Anjelica Huston) as Stuyvesant. Logan flew to Huston's house in Lake Arrowhead, California, to read through the script with the actor. Huston was interested but felt that the character was still too icy, "too one-note, too coolheaded."[20] Even in an unsympathetic role, Huston wanted to be sure that audiences would love him. As Logan recalled, Huston asked for a song in which "for a moment the old son-of-a-bitch [could] be charming. . . . Couldn't this old bastard make love to that pretty young girl [Brom's girlfriend, Tina] a bit . . . she could even consider him for a fraction of a second when she hears his song."[21]

"When Walter Huston was chosen, I didn't know anything about his voice," Weill said. "He told me to listen to him that night on radio, and I heard this odd, almost tuneless but appealing voice [performing 'I Haven't Got the Do Re Mi,' a patter song Huston had made famous during his years in vaudeville] . . . and it came to me, all at once, that that voice singing a sentimental song would be unique."[22] Huston's scratchy, crackling voice, oiled with a roguish wit and a rough charm, was, as both Weill and Anderson recognized at once, the ideal voice for their rascally and now increasingly good-natured tyrant. With remarkable speed, Anderson wrote the lyrics and then just as quickly Weill, borrowing from *Der Kuhhandel,* composed the melody for "September Song"—the moment in the show when the "old son-of-a-bitch" could court the girl and the audience.

Although they managed to coax some uncharacteristic humor out of him, his collaborators were less successful in taming Anderson's long-windedness. "It was full of lengthy speeches. Political speeches. Very dull, of course," Maurice Abravanel, the show's peppery conductor, complained. "Besides, Walter Huston never could memorize them. He was used to vaudeville, with very simple material, or movies, with cue cards. Logan, who said talking to Maxwell Anderson was like being asked to go to the King, knew we would be facing a disaster if we kept the speeches. He had to convince Anderson during rehearsals that it had to be shorter. Not so much talk. It was, by 50% if not 60%, and that helped. But not enough."[23]

Even trimmed and brightened, *Knickerbocker Holiday* was still unmistakably a play by Maxwell Anderson—with seventy minutes of music by Kurt Weill. Songs "speak" to the action in mostly conventional and some-

A charming rogue: Walter Huston as Stuyvesant (with Jeanne Madden
as Tina) in *Knickerbocker Holiday,* 1938

times clunky ways, and occasionally merely repeat points made in the dialogue. But in his first full-fledged Broadway score, Weill demonstrated a
sure command of the genre's two staple tones, darting wit and fearless sentimentality. And many times more than once, a musical number compen-
sates for a dull or protracted patch of dialogue.

The show begins with Washington Irving in his study in 1809 deciding
to write a history of old New York. Irving thus becomes a musical-comedy
master of ceremonies who sets the scene, introduces his characters, provides comment, and in the climax intervenes to prevent an unhappy ending. His sprightly introduction, in which he confides his desire to write a

book that is "both good and amusing" (and so reflects the intentions of his authors), is set as a melodrama, "I'll Sing of a Golden Age." Dialogue and lyric, the spoken word and melodic fragments, intersect in a wonderfully fluent give-and-take that regrettably is not pursued elsewhere in a score comprised only of separable numbers. The first regular number, "Clickety-Clack," misfires. In old New Amsterdam, Tina (the show's dippy heroine) and her female companions are engaged in scrubbing and cleaning as they sing about scrubbing and cleaning. It is a stilted attempt to set the scene (which has already been set!) with some operetta-style charm.

Enter the Council, a corrupt, incompetent bunch of buffoons who speak and sing in a comic Dutch accent of the sort that had been the stock-in-trade of many vaudeville comics. "Hush Hush," their first number, is a peppy disquisition on the delights of hush money. Pivoting back and forth on the insistent rhythm "hush *hush,* hush *hush,*" the rascals strut their stuff. "I need a hero," Irving announces, understandably enough, then chooses a local troublemaker and knife grinder, Brom Broeck. Brom's entrance song shows Weill in a frolicsome, all-American mode. Anderson pitches him some all-purpose declarative lyrics (no Brechtian curve balls here) and Weill swings for the fences. He almost makes it. The song has a catchy hook ("When you're on rock bottom") but an unsatisfying structure—Weill confines his melody, launching it upward only at the end of the title phrase, "There's Nowhere to Go but Up." Still, it is a pleasant song, and its sentiments are sufficiently generalized that they can later be appropriated by Washington Irving (reprise #1) and by the entire company in the finale (reprise #2).

"It Never Was You," Weill's first sterling Broadway ballad, about the reunion of the young lovers, is sung first by Brom to Tina, and then by Tina to Brom, with the two concluding in duet. Anderson's fresh, folksong lyrics reveal a genuine touch of the poet that was often to elude him in work he considered more serious. And Weill's triple-tiered melodic structure matches the plangent simplicity of the lyrics, the eager yearning of young love that they embody:

> *I've been hunting through woods,*
> *I've been fishing over water,*
> *For one certain girl*
> *Who's a certain father's daughter.*
> *I've been following trails,*
> *I've been staring after ships,*

For a certain pair of eyes
And a certain pair of lips.[24]

The host, Washington Irving, joins his hero for a song that, according to musical-theatre historian Miles Kreuger, president of the Institute of the American Musical, "stands as the leitmotif of Weill's years in America."[25] "How Can You Tell an American?" the song inquires. The answer, in Anderson's ringing, impassioned lyrics: "It isn't that he's short or tall. . . . It isn't that he's black or white."

An American . . . hates and eternally despises
The policeman on his beat, and the judge at his assizes,
The sheriff with his warrants and the bureaucratic crew
For the sole and simple reason that they tell him what to do.

Although they were attacking different tyrants—Roosevelt for Anderson, Hitler for Weill—the song's cowriters met on the common ground of their belief in a policy of personal and governmental laissez-faire. Building on their shared feeling, they audaciously subvert the list song (a Broadway staple) with a meaningful political message. The list may be a little long, and the items on it a little wordy—here Anderson betrays his inexperience as a lyricist. Nonetheless, Weill's jaunty rhythm achieves a show-stopping verve. As performed in lockstep by Irving and his rebellious hero, the number exudes an irresistible brio—written as the composer's love letter to his new country, "How Can You Tell an American?" is a near-great Broadway anthem in a not-great Broadway show.

"Will You Remember Me?," the romantic duet that follows, perhaps inevitably, is a letdown. Placed right before the renegade Brom is to be hanged, the song holds up Stuyvesant's too-long-delayed entrance and is unforgivably maudlin. "My love will cling to you / My dust will sing to you," the hero croons. (One can't help thinking that this romantic vow is only slightly less unsavory than if his love did the singing and his dust the clinging.) A blast of trumpets and a beat that wittily mimics Stuyvesant's peg-leg walk announce the arrival of the star. Stuyvesant's first song, "One Touch of Alchemy," performs a sly double function, summing up the character's political philosophy of fooling citizens into giving him total power while also highlighting the alchemy—the magic—wielded by the show's star, Anderson's charming villain. A Weill Gilbert-and-Sullivan-type song written to accommodate Walter Huston's nonexistent range, the number celebrates the "regimented life" of the new governor's reign. "The One Indispensable Man," performed by Stuyvesant with Council chief Tienhoven, is a comic patter song about payola that hearkens back to Weill's Weimar style. Like "One Touch of Alchemy," it lays out Stuyvesant's modus operandi and expresses low policies in high musical spirits.

"Young People Think About Love," an operetta-like waltz number for the whole company, sets up a firm division between generations, with youth and age squared off on opposite sides of the stage. The oldsters bring in the title refrain disparagingly and the youngsters repeat it approvingly. This is skillful dramaturgy: a barrier has been set up between young and old that Stuyvesant will dismantle in "September Song." For now comes the pivotal moment in which he must convince Tina to forsake her strapping young man in order to marry him, a peg-legged tyrant of advanced years. Kurt Weill, the great collaborative dramatist, rises to the narrative challenge, creating an indelible, heartbreaking melody for his star. "September Song" is by now so well known that everything about it seems inevitable. Yet, in some ways, it is profoundly unconventional. The verse eschews standard eight-bar phrasing. Instead, it proceeds by a series of folk song–like phrase extensions, the first in the seventh and eighth measures ("I let the old earth take a couple of whirls") and the second in the eleventh and twelfth measures ("And as time came around she came my way"). This unpredictable, discursive beginning sets a tone of intimacy, of spontaneous revelation. Then the refrain begins in C major, which the verse has artfully avoided. A bittersweet flavor, C half-diminished, is immediately asserted ("long, long while"). (This is the trademark Weillian progression heard so often in *Happy End.*) A moment later, it happens again, as the dominant chord on D collapses into D half-diminished ("When you reach . . ."). Hope and despair, desire and memory are in conflict. Now there follows the strangest part of the song, the seven-bar release. Stuyvesant struggles to express the ineffable:

> *For the days dwindle down*
> *To a precious few*
> *September*
> *November*

And Weill supports Stuyvesant with a progression that hesitates on two unstable chords, as if the character is fearful of continuing. Consolation comes with a harmonically surprising return to that unforgettable refrain.

Once again, Weill masterfully musicalizes a dramatic subtext—Anderson's poignant reflections on time in its flight, on romance and aging, are illuminated in the musical structure. "September Song" is as forceful as the best numbers in Weill's German portfolio. And Walter Huston's performance of the song, his voice lined with pathos and a touching common sense ("I have a little money, and I have a little fame") was a legendary moment in the American musical theatre. Through the combined sorcery of Anderson's lyrics, a great American poem, and Weill's melody, Walter Huston night after night mesmerized Tina and the audience. "When he sang 'September Song' to Tina we didn't know why she didn't just melt right on that stage," recalled actor Carl Nicholas, who toured with the show following the Broadway run. "But she went back to Broeck. Oh, well, that's what the script had her do, but no one could believe it."[26]

Right after this musical high point, Weill wisely did not try to compete with himself. The number that follows, a lively but conventionally scored Dutch clog dance, functions in effect as a way of cooling the onstage temperature. Act 1 concludes with Stuyvesant, musket in hand, forcing the citizens of Nieuw Amsterdam to serenade him with "All Hail the Political Honeymoon," a song of praise lyrically as well as musically insincere. It is a big ensemble number that could have become part of a fully articulated musical scene, an embellished operetta finale of the kind Weill had written for *Die Dreigroschenoper* and *Der Kuhhandel.* That the act ends with a song rather than an extended finale points up a certain caution in Weill's first commercial Broadway venture.

Washington Irving opens act 2, appearing before the curtain to sing the "Ballad of the Robbers." Clearly placed outside the show, the song comments on the upside-down world of Nieuw Amsterdam, in which honest men are put in jail by robbers who take over. A comment song in the Brecht-Weill mode, the ballad has a tinkly tunefulness that is fitted to Anderson's barbed lyrics. Keeping up the Brecht-Weill echoes, Stuyvesant's caustic serenade to Brom, the man he has jailed for daring to voice opposition, assures the prisoner that the best place to think is where he is, behind bars. The song, "Sitting in Jail," reveals Stuyvesant as a tyrant with a wink who relishes a Brechtian love of paradox; like Macheath, the character Anderson was coaxed into writing is a humanized scoundrel. "We Are Cut in Twain," the following number, is a conventional lovers' duet despite the unconventional context—the lovers are to be separated by Brom's upcoming execution. For these regulation musical-comedy juveniles, whose material does little more than pass the time between the appearances of the governor, Weill reined in his customary irony. But the romantic ballads aren't fully the real McCoy either, as, however narrowly, Weill manages to hold at bay the insipidity that often engulfs the form.

Weill reserves musical parody for the march number that follows, in which the parading Nieuw Amsterdam army proclaims, "We don't know what we're fighting for." And there is further irony in the Council's "Our Ancient Liberties," a comic lament about how Stuyvesant has cornered the market in extortion and graft that used to be theirs. Weill's restricted melody and Anderson's lyrics point up the degree to which their "liberties" meant enslavement for everyone else. Bridesmaids for the upcoming nuptials between the governor and Tina are on parade in a vapid ensemble piece, "May and January," which dutifully fulfills the musical comedy mandate that solos and duets should be balanced by ensemble production numbers.

Following Anderson's one undisputed triumph in dialogue—Stuyvesant's proclamation on the rules of proper behavior in a wife—the governor launches into "The Scars," a Gilbert and Sullivan–style patter song in which battle wounds are compared to those inflicted in romantic skirmishes. A surprise Indian attack is also the occasion for a musical surprise from Weill, as the invaders perform a Harlem jazz dance. The musical and racial anomaly carries an aesthetic charge, and Weill's modern orchestration invigorates the show at a flagging moment. A "Dirge for a Soldier" strikes a radically different mood. Supported by a steady drumbeat, the dirge moves in the stately rhythm of a pavane, another seemingly sincere moment for Weill broken by the fact that the presumably dead man rises up and rejoins the action. The one-two movement of music played against action anticipates the turn of the screw that the play holds in reserve for the finale. Fed up, the Council refuses to follow Stuyvesant's orders to hang Brom, their sentiments expressed in the dynamic rhythm of their final group number, "We Want to Make the Laws." Washington Irving interrupts, reminding the characters and the audience who's boss and urging Stuyvesant to consider the opinion of posterity. Realizing that he may qualify as an American too, since after all he doesn't like to take orders himself, Stuyvesant releases his prisoner. (The ending, in which a deus ex machina intervenes to save the hero from hanging, recalls *The Threepenny Opera*.) The governor's first acts as a new democrat are to agree to the political reforms the Council demands and to consent to the marriage of Tina and Brom. Instead of an operetta-like finale ultimo, the company performs a reprise of "There's Nowhere to Go but Up"—a concise ending to an overlong show.

"How Can You Tell an American?" the song asks, and for this deeply homegrown show the composer attempted to disguise his own foreign origins. Does his score for *Knickerbocker Holiday,* a show about the principles on which American democracy rests, pass as a work in the native grain? The verdict of his contemporaries and of historians has been mixed. Maurice Abravanel, fellow refugee, observed that "the ballads are different from anything you heard in the Broadway shows at the time . . . and so no matter how much Weill tried to adapt you can still recognize his own palette."[27] "Much of Kurt Weill's score for Anderson's book and lyrics was not at all traditional Broadway material," theatre historian Gerald Bordman wrote. "[His] score was free in form, shaped within the requirements of the scene and lyrics, but too sprawling to be extracted and given a separate life. [Unlike much of the score] 'September Song' was written in the customary AABA pattern."[28] But to producer Jean Dalrymple, Weill's score was all too American. "I was a little disappointed because it was so American. And nothing like *The Threepenny Opera,* which I had gotten used to and loved. I felt shocked that he Americanized himself so quickly. He wrote a regular musical comedy score with one big smash hit . . . all you need is one big hit in a musical."[29] Miles Kreuger, on the other hand, contrasted the score favorably with the "severe quality, a mordant deliberateness, an insistently pulsating meter, and a melodic economy," that characterized the Weill of Brecht-Weill. "Filled with an airy spaciousness that was quite new to him—'September Song' and 'It Never Was You' in particular possess a delicate gentleness—[the score] reveals that perhaps Weill, a refugee from Nazi tyranny, had begun to feel a sense of peace in America."[30]

Aside from the question of its split musical allegiance, the score firmly reveals that Weill's instincts for the stage survived the crossing. For a star who couldn't sing, he shaped numbers that do indeed recall the "melodic economy" of his Brecht pieces. But, for balance, he also wrote melodically succulent ballads (a few more than necessary, in fact) for the pallid young lovers played by Richard Kollmar and Jeanne Madden, whose meager acting skills were made up for by their Broadway-sturdy vocalizing. And for his Washington Irving, Ray Middleton, who could both sing and act, he wrote an operetta-style opening number, a Brechtian-style satiric number, and the show-stopping "How Can You Tell an American?" To beef up production values—a Broadway rule of thumb was that each act of a musical ought to have a big production number—Weill filled his bill with a variety of dance music, from a Dutch clog to a jazzy Harlem trot.

In September and early October, presented by the Playwrights Producing Company, Inc., which Maxwell Anderson had organized with a group of other Pulitzer Prize–winning dramatists early in 1938, the show had tryout engagements in Boston and Washington. Weill's score was widely praised; Anderson's book met a much cooler reception. "Anderson is occasionally on the grim side for so antic a medium," John K. Hutchens wrote in the *Boston Transcript* on September 28. "But when Mr. Weill's tunes get to skipping, the Anderson verses skip with them. . . . A pleasant and even stirring entertainment when the orchestra pit is busy, a labored one when it isn't." In Washington, occupying the presidential box at the National Theatre, FDR attended and laughed loudly at the antics of a character in the show named Roosevelt, a corrupt Council member, and pretended not to notice the possible resemblances between him and Stuyvesant. (It was only the second time Roosevelt had been able to attend the theatre since he became President; the first had been to see Huston, one of his favorites, in *Dodsworth*.) *Knickerbocker Holiday* opened in New York on October 19, 1938, where once again Anderson rather than Weill was greeted as the Broadway interloper, the outsider in a milieu he did not seem fully to grasp. "If Mr. Weill could find a Gilbert, he would be another Sullivan; Mr. Anderson is no Gilbert," Robert Rice wrote in the *Morning Telegraph* on October 20.

Knickerbocker Holiday was the high point of a busy musical-theatre season. Two shows, *You Never Know* and *Leave It to Me,* had indifferent scores by Cole Porter. In *Leave It to Me,* a wholesome-looking young woman from Texas named Mary Martin sang one song, "My Heart Belongs to Daddy," in her wonderfully clear and unforced soprano, and was on her way to becoming a Broadway star. Other notable productions included *The Boys from Syracuse,* a romp by George Abbott based on Shakespeare's *Comedy of Errors* with yet another sparkling score by Rodgers and Hart; two updated versions of *The Mikado—The Swing Mikado,* produced by the Federal Theatre, and Mike Todd's rival *Hot Mikado; Stars in Your Eyes,* a star vehicle for Ethel Merman and Jimmy Durante, directed by the busy Joshua Logan; a smart revue, *Blackbirds of 1939,* which introduced Lena Horne; and *Hellzapoppin',* the season's surprise runaway hit, a free-for-all toplined by Ole Olsen and Chic Johnson, a couple of low-level vaudevillians from the sticks.

Despite the prestige of its producer and its playwright, the beauty of a production designed by Jo Mielziner, an irresistible star, a hit song, a book with an idea, and Weill's generous, zesty score, *Knickerbocker Holiday* closed after 168 performances without having made a profit. From March 18 to May 20, 1939, the show went on a short tour—with Weill tagging along part of the way because he wanted to sightsee. Carl Nicholas remembered that Weill "really wanted to come on the tour. The producers told him, 'The show is set. I mean, there's nothing for you to do.' He said, 'I want to see America. I want to see this glorious country.' In the Midwest he went to the stockyards, and outside Detroit he went to see Greenfield Village, fascinated because there he felt he could see how America works. He reveled in it. 'No wonder people come to America,' he said."[31]

As Weill traveled across America with the touring *Knickerbocker Holiday,* the news from Europe grew darker. More than ever, he was grateful to be far from the homeland he often vowed he would never visit again. His good spirits were further improved by the fact that over the spring and summer of 1939 he was at work on two challenging projects: making final preparations for *Railroads on Parade* and laying the groundwork for a new musical called *Ulysses Africanus* which Anderson had suggested. Anderson's book was based on a 1919 Civil War novel by Harry Stillwell Edwards in which a plantation master, fearing his property is about to be overrun, entrusts his slave, Ulysses, with the family silver. A simpleton, Ulysses leaves with the silver but soon becomes lost because he has no sense of geography. For eight years, in a journey of Homeric length, he crisscrosses the American South trying to return home to his master and to his wife, Penny. He joins a minstrel show, in which he is presented as a "darky" dancing man, performing "black" for white audiences as white performers imitate him. In order to set up his own minstrel show, he sells his master's silver. But after he has become an impresario, a freeman competing successfully in a white man's game, he has a moment of reckoning in which he realizes that freedom entails manly responsibilities. He recovers the silver and decides to return it to his former master. Ulysses' homecoming restores the antebellum "purity" of plantation life.

Hewing faithfully to a novel he admired, Anderson rests his book on a startlingly reactionary longing for the Old South, a world in which masters and slaves observed their places in a chain of being. In the new South, where enfranchised blacks have become corrupt new masters, the natural is out of balance, a state of affairs corrected by Ulysses' return. In dialogue and theme, this mistaken project rankled with racist condescension. "Reason I wants to raise a little money, Massa, I trying to git to my old home. My old place what's called Beauregard, where old Massa Beau live,"

Ulysses says, speaking in the black-argot equivalent of the Dutch comic accent in *Knickerbocker Holiday.*[32] There's the kernel of a promising concept musical here, with a minstrel show-within-the-show providing ironic comment on the world beyond the stage. The collaborators' treatment of minstrelsy is technically and racially accurate, and it may have been possible to tip the material so that it became a critique of how the dominant culture, and sometimes blacks themselves, exploited "blackness." But that did not seem to be the direction Anderson was heading; rather, his book seemed to affirm the kindly master–loyal slave coupling as a social and racial ideal, the way things ought to be, and to present racial stereotypes not to contest but to reinforce them.

Weill wrote a number of musical sketches, and Anderson completed three lyrics, for songs called "Lost in the Stars," "A Little Gray House," and "Lover Man" (later changed to "Trouble Man"), which were transferred ten years later to *Lost in the Stars,* a better-judged musical about blacks. Weill's keen desire to write his own *Porgy and Bess,* his fascination with minstrelsy, his faith in Anderson, and his distance from the tormented history of race relations in America seem to have blinded him to the project's insensitive glaze. Surprisingly, neither he nor Anderson had second thoughts about moving ahead with the show. Once a first draft and some musical sketches had been completed, in March 1939, Anderson offered the title role to Paul Robeson, who turned it down because of the "innate condescension in the story."[33] The partners persisted, offering the part next to Bill "Bojangles" Robinson, a renowned dancer famous for his costarring film roles with Shirley Temple. When Robinson expressed interest, Anderson and Weill returned to work.

First, however, Weill had to focus on the railroad extravaganza for the World's Fair, to open in Flushing Meadows on April 30. In sixteen scenes, *Railroads on Parade* presented an encapsulated history of transportation in America, from the prerailroad era of the stagecoach and canal boat to a procession of sleek trains of the 1930s. Weill's score—he called the show his "circus opera"—was written to enhance the show's stars, the Iron Horse in its varying, evolving forms. For a show that ran seventy minutes Weill wrote an eclectic forty-five-minute score that included marches played by a brass band, jazzlike orchestrations for scenes set in the present, and numbers for both a female and a black chorus. He merged original music with his own arrangements of traditional folk material—exactly the kind of chameleon-like challenge he was always tempted by. Typical of Weill's inventive patchwork methods was his treatment of the scene of the Golden

Spike at Promontory Point, Utah, 1869, where the first transcontinental railway was completed. A male chorus performing the traditional song "I've Been Working on the Railroad" was followed by an infusion of Weillian surrealism in "What the Engine Said," in which the iron horses became tooting, whistling prima donnas.

Suffused with affection for his new country, his score evoked the movements of the trains as well as the energy, dynamism, and modernity of "The World of Tomorrow," the theme of the fair. Both musically and ideologically, the pageant presented Weill in a new guise as an American booster—as the fair brochure trumpeted, "to do full honor to the American Railroad in more than 100 years of its triumphant success there will be presented each day a huge dramatic spectacle of growth and achievement." To house a cast of 250, fifty horses, and twenty locomotives, old and new, each operating on its own steam, a stage two to three city blocks in width was constructed. Resulting acoustical problems required creative solutions. A chorus of eighteen housed below the stage performed all the talking and singing for the onstage cast, who mimed their roles. In a soundproofed, glassed-in booth the mixed chorus sang into microphones as their voices, piped up though an amplification system, were carried over the roar of the locomotives chugging and strutting across tracks extending from one end to the other of the great prairielike stage. The open-air theatre, housed in the gigantic Railroads Building, which covered seventeen acres of the fairgrounds, had four thousand seats and was almost always sold out for the four daily performances at 2:15, 4:15, 7:15, and 9:15.

After *Railroads on Parade* opened, Weill, this time with Lenya, spent the summer with Maxwell Anderson in Los Angeles, working toward a projected premiere of *Ulysses Africanus* on Broadway in the fall. "Our play is finished, after long fights and lots of work," Kurt wrote his brother Hanns on August 5, 1939. "But now we have great difficulties in getting Bill Robinson, and if we don't get him we might have difficulty getting this play financed because it is very expensive." Although, unlike Paul Robeson, Robinson had taken racially stereotyped roles, he began to have doubts about *Ulysses*. He hesitated, decided to proceed, then withdrew. At that point, Anderson and Weill abandoned the project.

That fall, without a major project in sight, Weill, with Anderson's help, got jobs writing incidental music for two plays by members of the Playwrights Producing Company: *Madam, Will You Walk?* by Sidney Howard, which closed out of town, and *Two on an Island* by Elmer Rice, which opened at the Broadhurst Theatre on January 20, 1940. (Both scores are missing.) In December, for Lenya, Weill composed "Nannas Lied," a song for voice and piano based on a text by Brecht. And to Robert Frost's poem "Stopping by Woods on a Snowy Evening," he wrote a song for voice and piano which he dedicated to Maxwell and Mabel Anderson. In January, working again with Anderson, he wrote a fifteen-minute score for *The Ballad of Magna Carta,* a cantata for tenor and bass soloists, chorus, and orchestra, which was broadcast on CBS radio on February 4, 1940. The piece is a direct attack on tyranny of the kind Anderson had wanted to make in *Knickerbocker Holiday* but had been talked out of. This time, without commercial pressures—and at a time when Germany invaded Poland, and France and Britain declared war on Germany—he said what he wanted.

After just over four years in America, Weill had yet to establish a secure place for himself. Demonstrating an astonishing versatility, *The Eternal Road, Johnny Johnson,* and *Knickerbocker Holiday* had certainly been worthwhile projects, but none had become the kind of box-office success that would have carried Weill to the winners' circle, where he wanted to be. As Weill continued to pursue many contacts, Lenya seemed to have withdrawn from actively pursuing a career. Apart from her run in *The Eternal Road* and a brief cabaret booking at Le Ruban Bleu, a chic East Side nightclub, she had not worked. And challenged and distracted by problems of his own, Weill seemed for the moment to have abandoned his sometime role as his wife's promoter. To date, even after three important productions as well as the railroad pageant, for all of which he had earned praise, Kurt Weill remained a curious, marginal figure—a noteworthy foreign composer who hadn't yet hit his American stride.

TEN

Limelight

Introduced by Walter Huston, Kurt Weill first met Moss Hart at a
party in the fall of 1939. Like Maxwell Anderson, Hart was gold-
plated Broadway royalty, the coauthor with George S. Kaufman of a
series of hit comedies, including *Once in a Lifetime* (1930), a satire of Hollywood, and *You Can't Take It With You* (1936), a warmhearted play about
a lovably eccentric family that had won the Pulitzer Prize. When Weill
met him, Hart wanted to write a play on his own. At the party, the two
men agreed to meet for lunch to discuss possible projects.

Could Moss Hart, a native New Yorker with conventional tastes in theatre, and Weill, a refugee composer with a strong experimental streak,
speak the same theatrical language? When they had lunch at the Haps-
burg, a fabulously expensive Midtown establishment, they found they
shared a similar desire to break new ground in musical theatre. "[We] told
each other vehemently why we would not write a musical comedy," Hart
recalled. "Kurt Weill because he would not write the music for the regulation musical comedy book, and myself because I would not write the book
for the regulation musical comedy music. . . . We were both completely
disinterested in doing a show for the sake of doing a show, in Broadway
parlance, and the tight little formula of the musical comedy stage held no

interest for either of us. We met again the following week and after another luncheon, that lasted well into the evening, we discovered the kind of show we both definitely *did* want to do."[1]

Hart suggested the subject matter—he was writing a play about a fashion-magazine editor undergoing intensive analysis, an idea that grew out of his own daily sessions with Dr. Lawrence S. Kubie, his renowned therapist—but was not sure about the form. Could *I Am Listening,* his rough first draft of the play, be the springboard for the new kind of musical he and Weill had talked about? *I Am Listening* contained a spot for only one (as yet unwritten) song—in her sessions on the couch the tormented heroine recalls the melody but not the lyrics; retrieving the lyrics and thereby completing the song helps her to unlock a childhood trauma and so to overcome her impasse. Although he had conceived *I Am Listening* as a straight play, Hart was open to the possibility of expanding the use of music. "The music could describe the [heroine's] dreams," Weill observed. On a single typewritten page, Weill casually jotted down his own thoughts about dreams, and suggested some musicalized dreams for the show.[2]

By January 1, when Moss Hart called his pal Ira Gershwin in Beverly Hills to offer him the job of writing lyrics, Weill had convinced Hart that *I Am Listening* demanded far more than one song. Virtually in retirement since his brother, George, had died of a brain tumor in 1937, Ira was content living the easy life in the California sun, playing cards, golfing, swimming, reading, and socializing; but when he heard the idea for Hart's play, he accepted on the spot. In March, Hart began rewriting *I Am Listening,* leaving his collaborators free to work out the dream sequences. "I don't think I have any strong lyrics you can be fooling around with—much as I'd like to send you a batch," Ira wrote to Weill on March 18. "In nine cases out of ten I have written to music, or just have given a title or a couple of possible first lines." But citing the "experimental nature" of the show, Ira admitted he would have to alter his routine. Weill kept nudging Ira, but little progress had been made by the time Ira came to New York in mid-May. "Kurt and I worked in my hotel suite at the Essex House for sixteen weeks during the hottest summer I'd ever known, and no air conditioning either," Ira recalled.[3] But at last, with Weill lighting a fire on a daily basis, Ira began to produce.

Hart had written his play as a vehicle for the nonsinging Katharine Cornell, a star of the grand manner on whom he had had a crush since the time he had been a stagestruck youngster from the Bronx. But with the piece now shaping up as some kind of musical, he was placed in the awkward spot of having to fire his diva. "The music went 'round and 'round," he wrote Cornell in an undated letter in the early summer. "I mean by that that the play fairly reeks of music now—if there were great musical stretches before there are veritable 'Traviatas' now. . . . It became more and more apparent that we ought to have someone almost musical comedy to handle it. . . . I was accused of thinking only of my play and not of the music (partly true, I must admit) and I could not dismiss the fact that you would most likely say it was not right for you. I tell you earnestly that the young fellow who stood in the alleyway without an overcoat still wants very much to write a play for you, and damn well will. There's a kind of grim humour in the fact, Kit, that the way this whole bloody thing started was my dream of writing a play for Katharine Cornell."

The "almost musical comedy" performer Hart began to court in June was Gertrude Lawrence, the British-born actress who had been a Broadway star since her American debut in 1924 in *Charlot's Revue*. Before she would sign, however, Lawrence had to consult her astrologer; and Bertha Case,

An ebullient Moss Hart, librettist and codirector, lunches
with Gertrude Lawrence, the star of his upcoming show,
Lady in the Dark, 1941.

183

her hard-as-nails, foghorn-voiced agent stirred up numerous obstacles. Lawrence hadn't been in a musical in a while, and part of her hesitation came from self-doubts: Could she perform what was clearly going to be a challenging score? Her anxiety was fully justified, because Gertrude Lawrence may well have been the poorest singer who ever became a major musical-theatre star. There was no song she didn't have trouble with. Her quavering voice buckled on high notes, she never landed securely on a single note, and her pitch wavered like a palm tree in a hurricane. Her vocal range was as narrow as Walter Huston's. On recordings, which provide ample evidence of technical deficiency, she is painful to listen to. She was a legendarily poor singer—and a great performer who took command of the stage and of her audience. She was a kind of star the stage no longer produces. But as she was the first to realize, in *Lady in the Dark* (which became the show's title on August 14), she would not be able to coast on "quality" or personality. She would face the double challenge of creating in Liza Elliott a brittle character the audience would not warm to easily and singing at least passably the operetta-like score Weill and Gershwin were composing.

Backstage, as everyone knew, Gertie was trouble. But for savvy Kurt Weill, a diva who could barely sing but knew how to sell a song was not too much to handle. And right after Lawrence finally signed a contract, Weill in effect became her confidant and caretaker. "If the two F's at the end of 'My Ship' are too difficult please try the whole song one tone lower (in e flat) and let me know which key is better for you," he wrote to her on August 24, 1940, as she was touring in a play. "The verse of 'One Life to Live,' " he assured her, "is written as a kind of monotone because it is supposed to be done in the style of a soap box orator on Columbus Circle." (In other words, if Lawrence had to sing some high notes in "My Ship," or at least attempt to, she could talk her way through the verse of what was to be her first song in the show.) Outlining her other musical responsibilities, Weill wrote that "in the second dream you'll sing a charming Fairy tale, 'The Princess of Pure Delight,' and a kind of Hollywood song, 'Unforgettable,' as a duet. In the third dream you have a little waltz and a song, 'No matter under what star you're borne [*sic*]' which leads into an 'Habanera' and in the last dream you have a duett 'Our little home in San Fernando Valley.' " Although Lawrence was to perform only two of these numbers, Weill from the start was writing duets and dances as a kind of damage control for his vocally challenged star.

"This tour is long and arduous and I shall be very tired by the end of it,"

Lawrence, from Kansas City on September 14, wrote Weill. "Also I am dreadfully upset over the goings on in England, which makes sleep very difficult, and there is so much to do for War Relief. Frankly I do not feel that it is humanly possible or wise for any woman in normal times to go from one run of one play into another play with music the size of Moss's— and these are not normal times. I do want to do the job well for you, but it's got me very worried." A few weeks later, on October 11, with rehearsals for *Lady in the Dark* scheduled to begin on December 2, Lawrence wrote asking for Weill's help. "I would like someone to come to me for a couple of weeks while I am still on tour, to work on my voice and then go with me to the country to study the score. Do you think Moss would let me hide away at his place in Bucks County? You and I could work together and you could watch my progress—if any."

The three men in Liza Elliott's life were cast with nonsingers. Bert Lytell, president of Actors' Equity, would play Kendall Nesbitt, the owner of *Allure* magazine and Liza's longtime lover; Macdonald Carey, soon to become a leading man in films, would be Charley Johnson, Liza's scrappy coworker and the man she ends up with; and Victor Mature, also on the hinge of Hollywood stardom, would play Randy Curtis, a film star who makes every heart but Liza's flutter. Neither Kendall nor Charley was being written as a singing role. Randy, who would have to sing a little, had been particularly difficult to cast. At a desperate moment, after they had seen a number of actors ("They are either too operatic or they cannot sing," Weill wrote Ira on September 14), Ira recommended the terminally effete Vincent Price as a candidate for the role of the Hollywood hunk. "I've just heard that he can sing—how good I don't know," Ira wrote on September 20, adding in a moment of clarity that Price would look "somewhat more poetic than rugged." The Platonic ideal of Hollywood machismo, Victor Mature was the visual knockout the play needed, but he couldn't sing (and as Mature would later admit, when denied admission to a club that didn't admit actors, he wasn't an actor either and had ample documentary evidence to prove it).

The casting choices certainly seemed to favor Hart's book over Weill and Gershwin's score—when they first started, Hart thought of the show as a play with music, Weill considered it a musical play. But the balance tipped in the latter's favor after Broadway producer Max Gordon urged Moss Hart to see a new performer in a cabaret show at a nightclub called La Martinique. The highlight of the act was a number called "Stanislavsky," a burlesque of the Russian director and theorist of acting in which, in a thick accent oozing with an antic comic spirit, Danny Kaye delivered lyrics in a staccato style that was to become his trademark. Like many others in New York's café society, Hart was delighted by the new performer's timing, wit, and brio. He decided to add Kaye to *Lady in the Dark* and created the role of Russell Paxton, a flamboyant photographer for *Allure* magazine who would also appear in the dream sequences. Hart asked Weill and Gershwin to write a novelty number for Kaye similar to "Stanislavsky." Unlike Gertrude Lawrence, Kaye, with his wonderfully smooth baritone, was a skilled Broadway-style singer, and his timing was as cunning as hers. Once rehearsals began, the star would not be pleased.

Working together throughout the summer, Weill and Gershwin wrote what the composer described as "three one-act operas of about twenty minutes' length each."[4] Except for "My Ship," the song that Liza tries throughout the show to reconstruct, all of the music in *Lady in the Dark* is confined to the dreams Liza recounts to her analyst. From the first these interruptions of the spoken drama were conceived as through-composed scenes packed with recitative, rhythmed dialogue, and dances in addition to regulation songs. Although, as always, Weill wrote individual numbers he hoped would achieve hit status outside the show, the extended musical scenes contained traces of his classical European background—indeed, the show's unusual structure allowed Weill a forum in which he could present himself as a composer rather than a Broadway tunesmith. Weill was faced with finding transitions from book scenes to the music of the dream world, and from patter to song within the dreams. "Aaron Copland said to me, 'It's amazing how quickly Kurt Weill gets from the realistic play scenes [in the psychiatrist's office] to the dreams,' " conductor Maurice Abravanel recalled. " 'What does he use there?' I said, 'Clarinet.' He said, 'Oh, yeah, clarinet and what?' I said, 'Just clarinet.' He said, 'Damn, we slave six months to get a thing like that, and Kurt does that with two notes on the clarinet.' "[5] Although Weill claimed to have created an entirely new form, both he and Ira were drawing on their own earlier work, Weill "raiding" the three operetta finales he had composed for *The Threepenny Opera,* particularly the extended musical scene for act 3 in which for the first time in the show the story is advanced through the music, and Ira borrowing ideas from musical scenes he had written with George for their political satires *Of Thee I Sing* and *Let 'Em Eat Cake.*

In the first one-act opera, Liza imagines herself to be the kind of idealized woman featured in her magazine, a bewitching cosmopolite universally admired, a devotee of high life in need of constant adulation. Liza in

ABOVE: On the couch: psychoanalysis leads to music in *Lady in the Dark.*
Dr. Brooks (Richard Hale) takes notes as Liza (Gertrude Lawrence) speaks.
Set design by Harry Horner

BELOW: Reminiscences of epic theatre staging? Gertrude Lawrence in the "Glamour
Dream" in *Lady in the Dark*

the real world cultivates a severe style, but in the "Glamour Dream" ser-
vants attend to her every whim; messengers from the President come to
paint her portrait for a stamp. She is serenaded ("Oh, Fabulous One in your
Ivory Tower . . .") by a chorus of worshipers and courted by the famous
("Huxley"). In a soapbox oration ("One Life to Live") she celebrates her
philosophy of carpe diem. These opening numbers are written in an elegant, old-fashioned style appropriate to Liza's fantasies of wealth and pam-
pering. As another serenade (this one with a refined rumba beat)
announces, she is indeed the "Girl of the Moment." Such high spirits, of
course, are destined to crash. The music begins a dark trajectory from the
point when Liza examines her new portrait and imagines that it exposes
her. As reality invades her dream world, Weill uses his skills at musical
development to undermine what we have heard. "Girl of the Moment"
recurs in ever-grander choral settings and, climactically, in a complex
rumba arrangement. Intimations of "My Ship" (violin doubled by oboe)
appear. The previously confident accompaniment is now shaken by dissonant passing tones—a technique Weill has employed ever since "The Ballad of Mack the Knife"—and the climax manages to be at once sinister and
triumphant. Finally, the sequence plunges into a musical crash landing
from which Liza wakes screaming.

Those ready to accuse the composer of going soft once he became a
Broadway hitmaker fail to hear the musical mockery that pervades the
entire dream. The musical and lyrical excess of "Oh, Fabulous One," for
instance, clearly sets up the heroine as a legend in her own mind. Broadway sentimentality? A mindless paean to the good, rich life? Hardly.
Would BB have written such a scene? Certainly not. But in the "Glamour
Dream," as in the other two dreams, Weill was exploring a kind of musical-theatre syntax he had begun to chart with Brecht. Of the three music
dreams, this first one gave the collaborators the least trouble.

The "Wedding Dream" isn't as tightly conceived. The opening section,
set in Liza's high school—classmates with differing opinions sing about
her; a chorus performs, and fractures, the school's alma mater—seems like
material from an earlier concept that the creators remained attached to.
But the school anthem presents Weill in high-chameleon mode, imitation
cunningly interwoven with satire. In one of the delicious musical fragments that the through-composed form allowed Weill to play with, a
classmate recalls how Liza charmed the French teacher. The dream comes
into focus once it becomes about Liza's impending marriage. If the "Glamour Dream" demolishes the heroine's jaded fantasies about the high life,

the "Wedding Dream" exposes Liza's aversion to marrying Kendall Nesbitt—the "Wedding Dream" is about a marriage that is not to happen. As in Weill's dual arrangements of "Girl of the Moment" in the first dream, here too he sets up a song only to twist it out of its original, seemingly sentimental context by changing its key signature, its rhythm, and its mood. Performed for the first time, "This Is New" is a clever Broadway entrance number, orchestrated to a suave bolero beat and featuring a second phrase ("I was merely existing") written in the whole-tone scale. Originally, the song was assigned to Randy Curtis, the movie star who hankers for Liza. His bolero version, exciting and slightly louche, of "This Is New" was to have been his siren song, his attempt to interrupt Liza's plans to marry Kendall. But once Weill and Gershwin realized that Victor Mature would not be able to sing the number, even as a duet, they reassigned it as a solo for Liza. It lost its original purpose, but gained another, perhaps more pertinent, one. Now the song was used to present Liza in a dreamy, sentimental mood, in love with love, and therefore set for the fall to come at the end of the sequence. Once Liza's illusions about marrying Kendall start to crumble, the song itself becomes untrustworthy and begins to deconstruct around the singer. But its underlying bolero rhythm courses through the "Wedding Dream" as the rumba did through the "Glamour Dream."

The writers wanted a strong solo for Gertrude Lawrence that would provide a contrast to her upbeat—indeed, close-to-manic—anthem, "One Life to Live," in the first dream. They wrote a delightful story ballad, "The Princess of Pure Delight," laying in a variety of comical accents as a showcase for their star. Weill's repetitive rhythm and unvarying stanza form throw the spotlight on the song's narrative, in which the princess faces a dilemma that echoes Liza's romantic conundrum: three princes vie for her, but she is in love with a quick-witted wandering minstrel who wins her hand by solving a riddle. But it is only the "princess of pure delight" who wins a fairy-tale ending; Liza, not yet ready to choose the right man, slips into a frenzied state mirrored in the increasing complexity of Weill's scoring. For the climax, Liza and the chorus engage in musical collision. The chorus voices thoughts Liza tries to repress; cornered, Liza continues to profess her love for the man she will jilt. "Tell them the truth!" the chorus importunes her.

For all its problems, the "Wedding Dream" was still relatively clear sailing for the collaborators. A "Hollywood Dream" that was never used and the climactic "Circus Dream"—the two musical scenes originally slated for act 2 — sent them into a tailspin. Unlike the other fantasies, evolving from Liza's sessions on the couch, the "Hollywood Dream" occurred after Liza had had two drinks at lunch with Randy Curtis. Convinced that both the musical dreams in act 2 had been licked, and exhausted from almost four months of intensive daily collaboration with his hard-driving composer, Ira returned to Beverly Hills before Moss Hart had even had the chance to look over the material. But following a production meeting in the office of Sam Harris, the show's producer, Kurt wrote Ira the unwelcome news that they would have to revisit both dreams. "Moss suggested to throw both the bar scene and the Hollywood dream out," Weill wrote on September 2, feathers ruffled. "He first talked only about cutting out the Hollywood dream and I refused flatly." Weill, the practical showman, admitted to "certain advantages in cutting out the bar scene. . . . It would mean we would go from the flashback scene directly into the last scene of the play. The balance between music and book would be very good in the second act because we would make the flashback scene a complete music scene . . . and then 'My Ship' will become the big song of the second act. Another advantage would be that with this cut, the show would be 25 to 30 minutes shorter and we save two sets and about 20,000 dollars." Weill tried to salvage some of the "Hollywood Dream" by placing numbers from it in other sequences, but wisely Hart and Sam Harris persuaded him to jettison all the Hollywood material, which was trite and seemed, at any rate, to belong in another show. (This is how Ira Gershwin recalled the "Hollywood Dream": "After Randy has just asked Liza to marry him, she began to visualize her life with him on an enormous ranch in the San Fernando Valley, with butlers galore, a private golf course, Chinese coolies, oil gushers and so forth."[6])

The main problem at this point with the "Circus Dream," which because of its placement had to be the play's musical and theatrical highlight, was in creating an eleven o'clock number in which Liza, put on trial for having deserted Kendall Nesbitt, must justify her romantic indecisiveness. Neither Hart nor Harris felt the piece Weill and Gershwin had written, "The Song of the Zodiac" (which continued the astrological motif that then ran through the "Circus Dream"), fit the bill. "Sam Harris said it was too pessimistic and downbeat, too contemplative," Ira remembered.[7] And, as Weill wrote Ira in his September 2 letter, "Hassard [Short, production supervisor] said he wished [the zodiac song] would have a little more of the sophisticated humor of which you are a master." Weill urged Ira to support him in his campaign to save their astrological theme, prom-

ising him that then there would be no more work "except for the possibility to make the Zodiak [*sic*] couplets musically lighter, more on the line of
a patter."

But Weill's position collapsed when Gertrude Lawrence also voted no
on the song. Because she suspected there was a scene-stealing sneak on the
premises in the person of the newcomer Danny Kaye, she wanted a funnier
song that would be a certain showstopper. Her fears grew when she discovered that Weill and Gershwin had shoehorned a novelty number for
Kaye into the still-amorphous "Circus Dream." (Like many interpolated
numbers in old-fashioned musical comedies, the new song, "Tchaikowsky
(and other Russians)," had no raison d'être apart from providing a spot for
a performer.) "Hassard seemed sure that Gertie will not be still if we don't
give her a material of this kind [a show-stopping song with laugh lines],
and I'm afraid he might be right about that. . . . Hassard's idea was that it
would be a perfect situation for a funny song when the clown jury would
sit on the floor in front of her, with the backs to the audience, and she
would explain them her point-of-view. Let me know the results of your
thinking," Weill concluded, having just handed his lyricist the setup that
would result in "The Saga of Jenny"—exactly the kind of song Lawrence
had asked for.

Reluctantly, Ira was forced to return to New York, where he toiled
with Weill for three weeks completing the "Circus Dream." Once "The
Saga of Jenny" was in place, and, after much haggling, all the zodiac
imagery was slashed, the third and most troublesome of the show's musical scenes was finally ready—or so the collaborators thought. Once
rehearsals began, the star began to complain that the number wasn't good
enough. Despite the haphazard solutions—what, after all, did the prevail-
ing circus metaphor have to do with either Tchaikovsky (Kaye's number)
or a trial by jury (Lawrence's)?—the third opera disclosed tremendous
theatrical cunning. Weill and Gershwin provided singular proof that
entertaining songs easily blot out murky setups. Not only that, they
wisely decided to let the audience in on the joke. Chorus and Ringmaster
(played by Kaye) launch the dream with a march that announces "The
Greatest Show on Earth."

> *The Greatest Show on Earth!*
> *It's Full of Thrills and Mirth!*
> *You Get Your Money's Worth!*
> *Come one, come all!*[8]

Where strings dominate the "Glamour Dream," here assertive brass instruments take charge and trumpets ring with expectation. The song, in its lyrics and its dynamic beat, is a hymn to show-business dazzle and a promise of what's to come. In their opening announcements the Paraders call Liza "The Flower of Womankind / Who Can't Make Up Her Mind / . . . a Feature You Will Always Recall!" and thereby set up Gertrude Lawrence with the kind of make-or-break star platform she demanded.

The high-octane opening ballyhoo segues into the energetic "Dance of the Tumblers," which Weill borrowed from *Die Bürgschaft* and which sounds like a divertissement in a Russian ballet. Then it's down to narrative business in "The Best Years of His Life," in which the chorus levels the charges against Liza. The number is presented in fragments interspersed between passages of recitative and spoken dialogue. Solos alternate with choral comments as Weill introduces scraps of interrupted melodies and abrupt rhythmic shifts. In one brief, virtuoso pastiche, Weill and Ira quote from *The Mikado:* "Our object all sublime / We shall achieve in time / To let the melody fit the rhyme . . ."—to which the Ringmaster responds, "This is all immaterial and irrelevant— / What do you think this is— Gilbert and Sellivant?" Here, as throughout, composer and lyricist cheekily call attention to the tricks of their trade while at the same time reminding the audience of what a good show they are watching. As the Ringmaster boasts,

> *What a show! What a situation! Can you conceive it?*
> *If you saw it on the stage you wouldn't believe it!*

It's precisely that persistently self-deprecating grandiosity that provides the hare's-turn transition to Danny Kaye's number. Responding to the show within the show, the Ringmaster exclaims, "Charming, charming! Who wrote that music?" When the jury informs him, "Tchaikowsky!" (of all composers, it sounds least like Tchaikovsky), he's off and running. "Tchaikowsky! I love Russian composers!" he says, launching into a tongue-twisting recitation of the names of fifty-three Russian composers. This interpolated song contradicts the weblike construction present elsewhere in the musical scenes; but who's complaining? Over the years there have been unsubstantiated rumors that Danny Kaye's wife, Sylvia Fine, wrote the melody, which recalls the one she wrote for "Stanislavsky," but Weill's imitative skills could easily have included writing such a specialty number. Introducing a song that doesn't "fit in" was not, after all, a new

ABOVE: Poised for stardom: Danny Kaye, right, as the Ringmaster in the climatic "Circus Dream" in *Lady in the Dark*. (Gettrude Laurence and Victor Mature are on the opposite side of the stage.)

BELOW: Gertrude Lawrence bumps and grinds in "The Saga of Jenny," refocusing the audience's attention after Danny Kaye's showstopping "Tchaikowsky." Hattie Carnegie designed the star's wardrobe; Irene Sharaff was responsible for all the other costumes.

tack for Weill: in the wedding scene in *The Threepenny Opera,* the guests ask
Polly to entertain them with a song; and in *Happy End,* members of the
gang ask Bill Cracker for the "Bilbao Song."

After his just-for-fun number, the Ringmaster brings the story back
into focus. "Proceed with the trial!" he orders. Now it is Liza's "turn," her
time to glitter in the limelight, with a song about how she cannot make
up her mind. Weill wrote "The Saga of Jenny" as a swing number pulsing
with a Broadway, not a Berlin, jazz beat. He finds in the blues scale an ana-
logue to his beloved harmonic turn from a tonic to a diminished chord,
and he builds his melodic hook on this ("Poor Jenny! Bright as a penny!").
Around it, he creates a simple, swinging minor-key rhythm song as a
frame for Gershwin's sardonic lyrics. The choral coda, turning to the parallel major, swings hard. It nicely incorporates a standard jazz arpeggio figure for the memorable lyric:

> *Jenny and her saga*
> *Prove that you are gaga*
> *If you don't keep sitting on the fence.*

Entirely instrumental in derivation (think saxophones), this arpeggio figure provides a cool, gratifying finish.

Like the other one-act operas, the "Circus Dream" unravels into musical
cacophony, here a dark-toned, sinister reprise of the melody and rhythm of
"The Greatest Show on Earth." The jury begins to hum "My Ship," a
sound that returns the dreamer to reality. "Don't sing that!" she implores.
"You're afraid of that music, aren't you?" Charley Johnson asks. In the final
"Childhood Dream," unlike the others because this time Liza is recalling
an event that actually happened, "My Ship" is the only number. Recovering the lyrics, Liza associates the song with the traumatic moment in
which her father cruelly compared her to her beautiful mother. And as she
now realizes with her analyst's help, the image of her dazzling mother has
continued to brand her in her own mind as a plain woman unworthy of
love. In enticing fragments, the melody of "My Ship" has been distributed
throughout the other dreams and served as a bridge between realistic and
fantasy scenes. Now, it completes her process of self-discovery. Just as
Weill had always wanted, music is enlisted in a crucial narrative responsibility.

Tonally and lyrically, "My Ship," which Liza performs in the guise of
her much younger self, occupies a distinct place in the show's musical pro-

gram. And for the star, who had to sing it in a simple, straightforward manner, it represented a startling change of pace following the theatrical high jinks of "The Saga of Jenny." It once more begins as it has throughout the show, with Liza humming the tune. But this time, her humming is only the introduction. For the harmony begins to form around her in a lovely way, slipping us effortlessly into the song. The melody is defined by an expansion of the motif that Weill first employed in "J'attends un navire" and "Johnny's Song." Beneath the simple, folksong flavor, Weill's detailed harmony is wonderfully poignant, as, for example, in the unexpected turns toward D minor at the cadences ("There's a paradise in the hold"). The bridge is gorgeously unfussed, the ending perfection. Along with "September Song," "My Ship" is one of the loveliest melodies in the literature of the American musical theatre. And one has to be grateful that Weill keeps the arrangement so simple. For all his skill as an orchestrator, he would occasionally clothe his best melodies in garish garb—wordless choruses and turgid strings intrude upon some reprises of "September Song" and "Lost in the Stars." Here, the treatment is as clear and lapidary as a sapphire sky: ravishing.

"I am working eighteen hours a day," Weill informed his conductor, Maurice Abravanel, in a November 8 letter. "I am writing new material with Ira, orchestrating, holding auditions, conferences, etc. I don't know how much longer I can do all this. We haven't found any chorus people yet who satisfy both Hassard Short (for looks) and me (for voices)." Frazzled, Weill was writing to ask Abravanel to obtain a release from his present employer, the Chicago Opera, in order to be available for the start of rehearsals. The Sam Harris office, as Weill noted, is "the only production organization on Broadway which always has their conductor for the full rehearsal time and they say that in the case of my show it is also necessary because it is a difficult score, and it is to a great extent chorus work and we have only three weeks before we go to Boston. . . . You know very well the jam I am in. So it comes down to this: you have to arrange immediately that you can be here from the beginning of rehearsals. . . . I know that means a sacrifice for you . . . but I have made more sacrifices for you than I would do for anybody else." Abravanel, a loyal friend from Berlin who was to remain Weill's conductor of choice throughout his Broadway years, was ready for work on December 2.

When *Lady in the Dark* went into rehearsal, Moss Hart moved into the director's role, more comfortable for him than writing. "Moss had mood swings but never brought private problems into work," said Paula Laurence, who starred in *Junior Miss,* the show Hart was to direct the following fall. "When he was at work on a show, he was ebullient—he was a world-class charmer, just this side of mafiosi in dress, with a gold watch and gold ring, gold clips on his garters, and gold cigarette case. It was when he wasn't working that he got into trouble. He had impeccable theatre deportment, and as a director he was like a divining rod; he had a wonderful way of reaching his actors. He was extremely savvy about the theatre, and was always practical in theatre terms; what he would ask of his actors and collaborators was very reasonable."[9]

Hart's love of putting on a show was tested by the many challenges *Lady* presented. At the top of the list of problems was his star. Lawrence continued to pester him and Weill for more comedy material because she was worried that otherwise this show about a neurotic executive would be too dark for her audience. But like Weill, Hart knew how to handle Gertie. During the second week of rehearsals, Lawrence started a campaign against Danny Kaye, complaining that he was a pallid nightclub performer who would not have the technique to hold the legitimate stage. To no avail, she asked Hart to fire him. As her anxiety mounted, she turned against "The Saga of Jenny." "This is not a song for me," she told her director. "This is for Ethel Merman. And it's not very funny anyway." But Hart told her she had to do the number. "We have a right to hear it. We're going out of town and if it's no good it'll be cut but you have to sing it."[10] Hassard Short shared Lawrence's uncertainty about the number, and before the opening he approached Maurice Abravanel to urge him to cut it. " 'You're the only one who can tell Kurt. It will be a catastrophe. It can kill the whole show. You must tell him.' Of course I didn't tell him," Abravanel recalled.[11]

Another major concern for Hart was the look of the show. Hassard Short favored a heavy design; Hart wanted to keep the production "light, imaginative, and not too expensive," as Ira Gershwin recalled.[12] Hart prevailed. To keep the show moving swiftly, a way had to be found to manage the transitions from the realistic scenes in the doctor's office to the dream sequences. The designer, Harry Horner, recalled that "the script that Moss gave me, was terribly complicated and read like a film, with DISSOLVES and FADE-INS." To avoid cumbersome pauses for scene changes as well as to suggest that Liza's waking self flows seamlessly into her dream projections, Horner "invented a scheme of several turntables (two large ones with two small ones working inside the large ones and another turning device as background, altogether five 'moving-tables'). On this compli-cated mechanical device I was able to create all the variations of a kaleido-scope and it worked."[13] The bookcase in the doctor's office split in the center and slid apart as Horner's turntables moved the dream scene into view, all done in a single cue. Despite Hart's vigilance, costs mounted. And by the time it opened, *Lady in the Dark,* with its complicated scene shifts, cost over $125,000, a near-record for the time.

On the morning of the premiere in Boston on December 30, 1940, a weary team gathered in the dining room of the Ritz-Carlton to share their anxieties. "When Hart asked me how I slept," Abravanel recalled, "I answered, 'Not a wink.' I mean, it's a point of honor not to have slept at all. 'And how 'bout you, Kurt?' Moss, who was always very kind and benevolent, asked. Kurt said, 'I slept fine,' and realizing right away what an insult it was said, 'But I had nightmares.' "[14]

The opening-night audience seemed to accept the show's unusual form and subject, but the clincher would be how they reacted to the "Circus Dream" and to Liza's eleven o'clock number. Danny Kaye had indeed been "pallid" during rehearsals, but now that he had an audience to play off, he exploded. "Tchaikowsky" was his moment, and he tore into the one-minute list song with an electric energy. After he hit the last syllable, the audience erupted with torrential applause. They demanded an encore, and then another. And then, as Kaye (disingenuously) recalled, "I was still bowing and smiling when the awful realization hit me! The great G.L. was onstage waiting to sing. . . . I bowed all right—but I wanted to bow out."[15]

During Kaye's song, the star had been sitting in a swing stage right, a murderous gleam in her eye. With the aroma of the audience's rapturous response to Danny Kaye lingering over the theatre, Lawrence rose up from the swing and walked majestically to center stage. After throwing Kaye a smile, she began to perform the song neither she nor Hassard Short had any faith in. "She sang 'Jenny' as I [had] never heard her sing before," Danny Kaye recalled. "She used every trick known to show business and kept the audience in the palm of her hand."[16] Ira Gershwin, standing at the back of the house, recalled that "she hadn't been singing more than a few lines when I realized an interpretation we'd never seen at rehearsal was materializing. Not only were there new nuances and approaches, but on top of this she 'bumped' it and 'ground' it, to the complete devastation of the audience. . . . 'Tchaikowsky' had shown us the emergence of a new star in Danny Kaye. But 'Jenny' revealed to us that we didn't have to worry about losing our brighter-than-ever star."[17] Rising to the bait Kaye had tossed, Gertie for the first time performed a boogie-woogie version of "The Saga of Jenny" filled with burlesque-house bumps and grinds that showed off her trim, long-legged figure. Tweaking Ira's lyrics with a number of comic voices—baby-doll peekaboo, little-girl lisp, grande-dame hauteur—she laced the song with a bawdy humor she claimed not to be able to locate throughout the rehearsal period. In strictly musical terms, "The Saga of Jenny" isn't groundbreaking, but it was the right song for Gertrude Lawrence at this point in the show—and proof to Broadway insiders that Kurt Weill could play on their terms.

The song, which chronicles Jenny's progress from age three until she "kicked the bucket at seventy-six," is Liza Elliott's defense of why she cannot make up her mind. Look at the havoc Jenny stirred up throughout her life with her mind-made-up approach! The song may poke fun at Jenny, but it is also a celebration of her primal energy, the zest with which she seizes the day.

Opening in Boston the same night as *Battle of Angels,* Tennessee Williams's first produced play, *Lady in the Dark* was praised for its scenic splendors, its fluid pacing, its ambitious collage of drama, spectacle, and music. Weill and Gershwin's score received far more praise than Hart's book, generally considered both overlong and too solemn. As with *Knickerbocker Holiday,* a number of the critics regretted the long waits between musical numbers. And there were some grumbles that Gertrude Lawrence needed to calm down. But with all sixteen performances at the Colonial Theatre sold out, *Lady in the Dark* looked like a winner. By the time the show opened at the Alvin Theatre in New York on January 23, 1941, trimmed and tightened and with its star having relaxed into her role, Broadway had a new hit.

"Bless you Kurt *mon petit choux,* lets stay together for a nice long Weill, Love Liza," Gertrude Lawrence wrote her composer in an opening-night telegram that bubbled with an effusiveness born of the knowledge that they were partners in a successful venture. "Kurt just looked so fulfilled backstage that night," Ann Ronell, a composer who worked with him in Hollywood, recalled. "He felt like a big shot. You better believe it: big shot. Surrounded, he bowed to me very magnificently. Then, later when we had a few moments together, he was Kurtsky and I was Annie. But he took this position. He wanted that position more than anything."[18]

The New York reviews were among the strongest Weill was ever to receive in America. There was one significant pan, however, from a critic from whom approval would have meant a great deal. In his February 23 column in the *New York Herald-Tribune* Virgil Thomson sketched a portrait of "the two Kurt Weills" that endures to the present. He measured the score for *Lady in the Dark* against the composer's "finest creative period, that of his collaboration with the poet Bertolt Brecht . . . characterized by satirical writing both melodically and harmonically. In parodying cheap sentiment to the utmost he achieved a touching humanity. . . . Maybe it was Brecht's poetry that was so touching in *The Threepenny Opera* and *Mahagonny*. . . . Those sentimental days are gone and Mr. Weill seems to have avoided working with major poets as he has avoided all contact with what our leftist friends used to call 'social significance.' His music has suffered on both counts. It is just as banal as before, but its banality expresses nothing." Contradicting other reviewers, Thomson faulted the score for not "follow[ing] the play or . . . aid[ing] it," and cited the "Circus Dream," a clear favorite with audiences, as "little more than numbers, so far as the plot is concerned. . . . They constitute a lengthy *ballet divertissement* in a play already so full of these that the accentuation this one receives (plus the success it has with the public) makes it clear where the producer's confidence and the public's interest lie." Thomson had a kind word only for "The Saga of Jenny," "a ballad about a fabulous character with music of that American folk-melody type chiefly familiar to urban audiences through 'Frankie and Johnny' and 'Casey Jones.' It is the most successful of [Weill's] efforts to write in the local idiom." In a sentence that Weill found particularly galling, Thomson dismissed the rest of the score as "monotonous, heavy, ponderously German. It reminds one of Berlinese jazz from the early 1920s, of reviews [*sic*] called '*Die Schokoladen Kiddies,*' of sentimental ditties called '*Ein kleiner Slow-Fox mit Mary.*' "

"Thomson's violence was all very personal," Weill wrote Ira in a March 8 letter. "His main point was that I am no good any more since I stopped working with Brecht and that I am 'constantly avoiding' collaboration with 'major poets' (a rather bold statement, don't you think so?). Well, I am used to this kind of attacks from the part of jealous composers. In some form or another it happens every time I do a new show." ("Interesting news about Virgil Thomson in Winchell's column: it seems that the FBI has investigated him because of his connections with sailors!" Weill wrote Lenya on April 13, 1942. "Bravi [Abravanel] met him in a party and Virgil started to talk about me after dinner and talked till 5 a.m. He says he would call *Lady* a masterwork if I had not written it, because he always thought the three most important European composers were Debussy,

Weill and Lenya at Brook House, New City, bought with money from
the movie sale of *Lady in the Dark*. Standing at 100 South Mountain Road,
the house today looks exactly as it did during the Weills' residency.
Lenya would remain in the house for the rest of her life.

Satie and Weill. What is really wrong with me is that I have no character
(!!) and I had behaved very badly to him in a personal matter. Well, I must
be pretty good if the great Thomson talks all night about me. It seems to
bother him!"[19] Of course, it bothered Weill also.)

Thomson's devastating notice could not remove the joy Weill felt in
having his first genuine American success—a Broadway smash. Against
the odds, Weill had managed to re-create in his adopted country the kind
of popular success he had won in Berlin in 1928 with *Die Dreigroschenoper*.
Less than a month after *Lady in the Dark* opened, Paramount bought the
film rights for a then record-breaking figure of $285,000; Weill and Ira
each received $42,500, Moss Hart $85,000, Sam Harris $115,000.[20] With
money from the film sale, Weill and Lenya in the summer of 1941 purchased an eighteenth-century farmhouse on bucolic, winding South
Mountain Road in New City, New York, on property adjacent to Maxwell
Anderson's. The Weills' rustic new home, called Brook House, where
Lenya would live until her death forty years later, still sits by the roadside

behind a stone fence and in the back faces a large open field surrounded by woods. At Brook House, their American place in the sun, the newly rich Weills lived comfortably but far from extravagantly.

"It's lots of fun to have a smash hit," Weill wrote to Ira on March 18. "There are between 20 and 100 standees in every performance. I go about twice a week to check on music and lyrics." For his hit show, Weill monitored auxiliary markets with particular zeal. "There are seventeen records of songs from *Lady,*" he crowed to Ira in an April 11 letter. "That's more than twice the number of records any other show in town has got. Max Dreyfus showed me a weekly statement about the sale of sheet music. 'Jenny' was at the top of the list, next was 'My Ship,' then followed 'The Last Time I Saw Paris' and a couple of popular songs, then 'This Is New' and then a song from *Pal Joey.* All the small independent stations are playing 'My Ship' and 'Jenny' all day long and there is no doubt that both songs would be on the Hit Parade when as and if [the radio strike of 1941 is settled]."

Weill's contentment was lanced only by "all kinds of little troubles with our star," as he told Ira in the April 11 letter. "She can be very bitchie, as you know." Worried about the war in England and eager to return home, Gertrude Lawrence insisted on closing the show over the summer for fourteen weeks, and after strenuous negotiations agreed to reopen on September 2. "It's a great pity that we lost all the men [from last season]," he wrote to Ira on August 14. "Danny Kaye behaved like a real pig—especially to Moss who was always extremely nice to him. Well, we still have the show and Gertie." But Gertie was causing a stir again. She had begun to ask Weill for a new song to replace "One Life to Live," "which she still says is only an 'ice breaker' and she doesn't get anything out of it and she would like to have a funny song instead. I dismissed it the first few times she talked about it, but she keeps nagging," Weill wrote Ira on September 19. "I personally don't think she does all these things purposely. She is just moody and temperamental, as women of her age are sometimes, and we have to see how we can get along with her. One rehearsal she got a fit and said, any other actress in her place would just demand a new song. Moss asked me to write you about it. If you could write a free lyric I could set it to music." But to Ira's immense relief, Gertrude Lawrence survived the second season without his having to write her a new song.

Lady in the Dark closed on May 30, 1942, having played a total of 467 performances on Broadway. A tour opened in Philadelphia on September 28, and then the production returned to Broadway the following

February for eighty-three additional performances before going out on the road again. After a twelve-city tour, the show played its final performance in Los Angeles on July 10, 1943—a total of 777 performances. From first to last Gertrude Lawrence was the one and only Lady in the Dark. (On October 19, 1947, in a live radio broadcast from the Boston Opera House, opposite Macdonald Carey, the original Charley Johnson, she played Liza Elliott one final time, in a highly abbreviated version later released as a long-playing record.)

A solemn preface to the published text written by Moss Hart's psychoanalyst, Dr. Lawrence S. Kubie, writing pseudonymously as "Dr. Brooks," his fictional counterpart, made extravagant historical, therapeutic, and literary claims for "this gay and tender play [in which] perhaps for the first time on any stage, the struggle of a vigorous and gifted human spirit to overcome deep-seated, self-destructive forces is portrayed accurately. . . . In its ultimate implications, it is a Song of Songs of Woman, not merely the tale of a particular woman."[21] Sixty years on, however, *Lady in the Dark,* stripped of its musical dream sequences, reads like a strictly conventional period piece. At heart it is an old-fashioned Cinderella romance sprinkled with a dusting of simplistic psychoanalysis. Hart's routine boulevard playmaking, and his starchy dialogue, standard at the time for well-spoken characters in well-made plays, are overshadowed by the musical-theatre ebullience of Weill and Gershwin's three one-act operas. The now-dated treatment of psychoanalysis and the awkward join between the book and its musical interludes may account for the fact that *Lady in the Dark* to date has not been seen again on Broadway or even in a major American production. "If I had a nickel for everybody who wanted to do it, I'd be rich as Croesus," Hart's widow, Kitty Carlisle Hart, said. "But it's a hard show to do, and Liza is a very hard part to cast." Indeed, a career woman with a strychnine personality who speaks in a brittle theatrical diction of yesteryear, Liza is unlikely to find many contemporary takers. But as Mrs. Hart contended, "Liza's problems are current. It's still tough to be a female in business, and women still aren't given enough responsibility. When Moss directed me in a summer-stock production of *Lady in the Dark* in 1952, he had Charley Johnson push me out of the chair at the end. Today the two characters could and should share the same chair."[22] Even with that adjustment, however, Liza remains a career woman who, with the playwright's apparent endorsement, needs the assistance of males who know more than she does—the "superior" Dr. Brooks interprets her problems, while Charley Johnson cuts her down to size. "This ultimate man," as "Dr. Brooks" averred in his preface, "is the one who refuses to play the role either of the subservient parent [like Nesbitt] or of the submissive child [like Randy Curtis], and who, by his outrageous mockery and overt erotic foolery, challenges her right to live in her no-man's land between the sexes."[23]

But in its time, *Lady in the Dark,* a musical play about psychoanalysis in which book and score addressed each other in an unusual way, could claim membership in a small, exclusive club of genuine musical-theatre mavericks. The show became the progenitor of an important subgenre of stage and film musicals about personal discovery in which the protagonist's inner life is dramatically (often fantastically) projected upon the musical-comedy form. Without *Lady in the Dark,* there might not have been such musicals as *On a Clear Day You Can See Forever, All That Jazz, Sunday in the Park with George,* or *Nine.*

For the musical, the 1940–41 season was not a particularly banner year. Besides *Lady in the Dark,* only two other shows seriously challenged Broadway routine. *Cabin in the Sky,* starring Ethel Waters and Todd Duncan (the original Porgy), was a vibrant show about black characters written and composed mostly by whites. Waters's performance of Vernon Duke's "Taking a Chance on Love" became a Broadway legend. "Can you draw sweet water from a foul well?" Brooks Atkinson asked in his December 26 review of *Pal Joey,* a daring Rodgers and Hart musical about a gigolo with the aura of a criminal. In 1940, Atkinson doubted it; by the time of the show's revival in 1952, he thought otherwise. The season had opened on September 11 with the return of a beloved Broadway veteran, Al Jolson, in *Hold On to Your Hats,* a strictly nostalgic item and the great star's Broadway swan song. *Boys and Girls Together,* starring Ed Wynn, and *It Happens on Ice,* starring Joe Cook, were vaudeville-style carnivals cobbled together to showcase the antics of popular Broadway clowns. The season's biggest hit was *Panama Hattie,* a standard musical comedy tailored for the brassy, boisterous Broadway baby Ethel Merman, with another only-serviceable score by Cole Porter. Kurt Weill, new man in town, an outsider in the Broadway "family" of American-born composers, never wrote a merely formulaic show like *Panama Hattie,* and never felt he had to. To a remarkable extent, he gained the keys to the kingdom on his own terms.

ELEVEN

I'm a Stranger Here Myself

A s he worked sixteen-hour days preparing for the opening of what was to be his first American hit, Weill closely monitored news of the escalating war in Europe. Anticipating and hoping for an end to America's isolationism, he was eager to serve his new country in the war against the country he had been forced to leave. But as an alien he realized he could not enlist in the armed forces. "I remember Kurt saying one of the worst things that ever happened to him was he couldn't get drafted," Hesper Anderson recalled.[1] Nonetheless, he was determined to prove his patriotism in other ways.

When Ben Hecht and Charles MacArthur approached him in the summer of 1941 to provide a score for *Fun to Be Free*, a pageant sponsored by Fight for Freedom, Inc., that would urge American participation in the war against Germany, Weill accepted immediately. The pageant was to be staged as a benefit rally at Madison Square Garden on October 5, 1941. Since he had been asked at the eleventh hour for a score intended only to be incidental, Weill made arrangements of traditional melodies and borrowed from some of his own earlier work, including a march theme from *Davy Crockett* and isolated passages of triumphal music from *The Eternal Road*. His sketches and the full score are missing, a surprising gap that

Patriot: Weill, right, as an enemy aircraft spotter during
wartime, serving with his best friend, Maxwell Anderson,
second from left, and two unidentified men

suggests the merely occasional nature of his contribution. *Fun to Be Free,*
part 2 of a massive six-part program representing an all-star Broadway
support for America's taking up arms, was narrated by Burgess Meredith,
Tallulah Bankhead, Melvyn Douglas, and Franchot Tone, with Weill's
music performed by the chorus and orchestra of the International Ladies'
Garment Workers' Union. As Helen Hayes (Mrs. Charles MacArthur)
recalled, "It was an inspiring pageant [which represented] the wish to get
everybody together as an army for freedom. . . . It didn't get everybody
together. But it achieved the wish of being a marvelous rallying call. It
wasn't particularly Jewish. Charlie wouldn't allow that. Nor would
Kurt."[2]

After the attack on Pearl Harbor on December 9, 1941, finally jolted
America into joining the war, Weill became a full-time patriot in both his
private and professional lives. With Maxwell Anderson he served as a civil-

ian plane spotter for Rockland County. In February he contributed incidental music for *Your Navy,* a half-hour radio program by Maxwell Anderson directed by Norman Corwin, with Fredric March and Douglas
Fairbanks Jr. as narrators. From February to April, he wrote such morale-
boosting songs as "Buddy on the Nightshift" (lyrics by Oscar Hammerstein), "Song of the Free" (lyrics by Archibald MacLeish), "Schickelgruber"
(lyrics by Howard Dietz), "The Good Earth" (lyrics by Oscar Hammerstein), "We Don't Feel Like Surrendering Today" (lyrics by Maxwell
Anderson), and "Toughen Up, Buckle Down, Carry On" (lyrics by
Dorothy Fields). In March Helen Hayes commissioned him to provide
musical settings for patriotic poems she would record on RCA Victor for
Fight for Freedom. (For Fight for Freedom, Weill also orchestrated three
Walt Whitman songs, "Oh Captain! My Captain!" "Beat! Beat! Drums!,"
and "Dirge for Two Veterans.") Also in March, when Brecht sent him a
bitter, powerful poem, "Und was bekam des Soldaten Weib?" ("And what
did the soldier's wife receive?"—she received the news that she had
become a widow), Weill composed a musical setting in a coruscating style
spiked by a heavy, premonitory beat. (On April 3, 1943, as part of an anti-
Nazi cabaret, "We Fight Back," coproduced at Hunter College by Ernst
Aufricht, Lenya sang the song with Weill accompanying her on the piano.)

Throughout 1942 Weill produced "The Lunch-Hour Follies," which
provided entertainment for factory workers during lunch breaks. Gigi
Gilpin, who worked closely with Weill on the "Follies," observed that
Kurt "was the most patriotic man I have ever known. He took the 'Follies,'
which were miniature musicals, maybe twenty minutes, very seriously. He
didn't use his songs primarily, although he composed about eight or nine
for the shows, but they didn't sound like Weill. They put a platform up in
the middle of the factory—with six dancers—to present just something
lively and light and fast, to keep the crowds awake as they ate lunch. You
worked around the clock, with about four hours between each show. We'd
go from factory to factory. Kurt was often there, a very humble man, who
never thought of himself as a celebrity."[3] A composer in a gray flannel suit,
Weill produced about fifteen shows.

After months of selfless patriotic endeavor, Weill was itching to get to
work on another Broadway musical. Once again, Maxwell Anderson came
up with a project for him—a show to star the Lunts for which S. N.
Behrman was writing the book. *The Pirate,* as the work-in-progress was
called, had a Caribbean setting. After studying generous samplings of
Spanish and Latin American folk music and revisiting some of his own

Caribbean-flavored score for *Der Kuhhandel,* Weill proposed using a calypso ensemble that would be on stage throughout the show and periodically would interrupt the spoken drama with musical commentary. "What I want to get out of it is to try again something new in the theatre, and to have my name again connected with a big success," Weill on April 21 wrote Lenya (who was on tour with Helen Hayes in *Candle in the Wind,* playing the role of a maid, which Maxwell Anderson had written for her).[4] But within a week Weill discovered that neither the Lunts nor Behrman would support his musical concept. "They [the Lunts] are absolutely awful and she [Lynn Fontanne] is definitely the greatest bitch I've ever seen," Weill wrote Lenya. "He is so dumb and so egocentric! He reminds me of [Otto] Klemperer all the time—the same fake voice and the same stupid chicken-eyes. . . . Life is too short to be bossed around by two old hams— and the results are too meager."[5]

Without Weill's music, the Lunts appeared in *The Pirate* during the 1943–44 season. Had they and Behrman followed Weill's advice, it might have been a better and certainly a more original show, but it would not have been a suitable vehicle for the stars. The first couple of the American theatre may well have been as haughty, as ignorant, and as double-dealing as an enraged Weill claimed. But they knew what worked for them, and the "two old hams" didn't want to take the chance of being upstaged by a troupe of calypso singers and dancers.

As he was ensnared in conflicts over *The Pirate,* Weill received a disturbing proposal from Brecht. Since their departure from Germany in 1933, the erstwhile collaborators had been in touch sporadically, usually at Brecht's initiation. In the summer of 1941, by then in Santa Monica and becoming increasingly frustrated by his inability to establish himself in the American "culture industry," Brecht in an undated letter wrote about a black theatre company headed by Clarence Muse that had expressed interest in doing a production of *The Threepenny Opera* set in Washington during a presidential inauguration. "They want to do their own orchestrations for the band (I hope you don't mind this . . .)," Brecht wrote, well aware that a composer who always insisted on doing his own orchestrations might mind very much indeed. "To me this seems to be the only chance to take advantage of the piece," Brecht ended, and then almost as an afterthought mentioned the real reason for his interest. "It might practically get me settled over here." "I would like to propose to you to take up our collaboration again and to simply liquidate all misunderstanding," Brecht wrote the following February, still trying to obtain Weill's consent.

"So far I really have not lost any of my friends and in our collaboration there always had been so much fun and so much progress"—an assessment that would certainly have surprised Weill and Lenya. The conciliatory tone that Brecht adopted in all the correspondence about the proposed production highlighted the difference between his status and Weill's in the American theatre. Whatever Brecht may have thought of Weill's Broadway shows (and there is no evidence that he ever saw any of them), and however much he may have accused Weill of capitulating in supplying "culinary" entertainment to the American "culture industry," the fact remained that Weill had established himself whereas Brecht was an outsider who needed a job.

"There can't be any doubt that someday we're going to have a first class 'revival' [but not if] we would allow *The Threepenny Opera* to be performed by a group of negroes in California," Weill answered on March 9. It wasn't the "negroes" but the "California" that Weill balked at, "for the simple reason that whatever they did in California just wasn't good enough," he informed Brecht. But Brecht would not relent. To strengthen his case, he enlisted Mrs. Paul Robeson to write Weill a letter of support for the project. Weill began to weaken. On March 31 he wrote to Clarence Muse, impressing on him the "special singing style of *The Threepenny Opera*." "I must appear an awful troublemaker," Weill wrote a week later, concerned that Muse planned to take liberties with the score. "But you don't seem to realize that *The Threepenny Opera* music is one of the best known, most beloved, most sung, most sold, most recorded pieces of music that have been written in the last twenty years . . . [this explains] the great feeling of responsibility which I have in connection with this score." The next day, grumbling, Weill wrote to Brecht giving his consent to a production in California only (which, Weill felt, as far as Broadway was concerned, might as well have been Outer Siberia). "I am doing this only because you seem to expect great things for yourself from this production," Weill concluded. After he informed Lenya that he had given in, Lenya wrote back unleashing her fury at that "swinish" Brecht. "The whole Brecht shit—is just too funny for words. . . . But please Darling insist, that they are not allowed to show it outside Hollywood. Don't give in . . . and this stupid Brecht, this chinese-augsburg Hinterwäldler [backwoods] philo-so-pher. It's too much already that letters from him soil our mailbox."[6]

Once Weill received a copy of the contract, however, the saga was over. "According to this contract, these people can do anything they please with *The Threepenny Opera* and the funniest of all is the 'payment' . . . we would [end up getting] $10 a week," he wrote Brecht on April 20. Weill, playing the diplomat, admitted that he would have been willing to make "all kinds of financial concessions just to help you further along. . . . I too would like by all means to prevent any kind of misunderstanding between us, because I always am reminiscent of our collaboration with great joy and I do so hope we will soon find an opportunity to resume this collaboration."

"Maybe we are a little unjust with him," Weill had written Lenya on April 16. "I just hate to triumph over somebody who is down on the floor, and I don't want anybody to feel that I am cruel or egoistic. I would rather have the reputation of being a sucker than of being greedy or stingy or *'kleinlich'* ["petty"]. He knows now he cannot play ball with me, and I think I can afford to be nice to him. I am inclined to offer him some financial help (something like $50 a month for a few months). What do you think?"[7]

"If it makes you feel better, send Brecht $100 but don't send him anything monthly," Lenya answered from Memphis on April 19. "I don't trust him at all. I never believe, that he ever can change his character, which is a selfish one and always will be. . . . I know Darling how easely [*sic*] you forget things but I do remember everything he ever did to you. And that was plenty."[8]

Still trying to shore up his reputation as a Broadway composer, Weill was not eager to see any of his European work, including *The Threepenny Opera,* produced in America. Of course he recognized the potential appeal of his Berlin blockbuster, but unlike his desperate former partner (Brecht had written in his March 12 letter that he was in an "unsufferable condition") he wanted to wait for a first-class production in New York at the proper time. And as Weill, if not Brecht, realized, 1942 was not the time to present a show so deeply associated with a country America was at war with.

Weill was relieved to be rid of both Brecht and the Lunts because he wanted to concentrate on a new project with Cheryl Crawford, who had become an independent producer since her departure from the Group Theatre. He had enjoyed working with her on *Johnny Johnson* and sensed then that she had the taste to produce the kind of form-breaking musicals he was interested in writing. In the years since, he had talked with her regularly about show ideas. For her revival of *Porgy and Bess* in February 1942 he served as her unofficial adviser, urging her to cut the passages of recitative that he did not like so that George Gershwin's shimmering songs would become more prominent. As his bitter experience with *The Pirate* was drawing to its end, he began to work with Crawford on an idea he had presented to her early in the year. His source material was *The Tinted Venus,* an obscure novella of 1885 written by a British humorist, Thomas Anstey Guthrie (who signed himself "F. Anstey"), which an acquaintance, set designer Aline Bernstein, had given him.

In Anstey's story a statue of Venus comes to life when a hairdresser impulsively slips his fiancée's engagement ring onto the statue's finger. In human form, the goddess of love falls in love with the hairdresser and intervenes in the romantic imbroglios of dim mortals before she returns to her heavenly realm. Weill felt Anstey's slight fantasy might serve as the basis of an elegant, witty opéra comique modeled after the work of one of his favorite composers, Jacques Offenbach. Finally free of other entanglements, Weill began to work full-time with Crawford in June, only to discover that he had exchanged the frying pan for the fire.

To write the lyrics, Weill urged Crawford to hire Ogden Nash, a *New Yorker* humorist who had never before written a musical—a good choice, as it turned out. To write the book, Crawford turned to Sam and Bella Spewack, friends of Aline Bernstein's—a very bad choice. Weill wanted Marlene Dietrich to make her Broadway debut as Venus—the worst choice of all. Over the summer, as the book and lyrics began to be drafted, Weill started his campaign to win over the slippery, self-centered German diva. Weill felt he had an entrée to Dietrich because they had known each other casually in Berlin (he knew she had admired *The Threepenny Opera*) and he had written songs for her in France. His opening shot was a letter to Dietrich on July 24. "The Spewacks will write the book and Ogden Nash who is the foremost light verse writer of America will do the lyrics," he informed her. Expressing interest, Dietrich began a hesitation waltz, both skillful and maddening, that was to last for the next seven months. "As this would be my first appearance on Broadway I must withhold sending formal agreement until I see at least a first draft of the play," Dietrich wrote. "I am positive that with the Spewacks Kurt and Nash writing the material that it would turn out to be grand but at the same time anything can happen in the writing."[9]

But Crawford and Weill were withholding the script because they were having doubts about it. Sam Spewack left early on, and Bella was proceeding on her own at a pace and in a direction Weill found increasingly unnerving. On the sly he sought the assistance of George S. Kaufman, Broadway's premier play doctor, who in an undated letter in the summer of

1942 commented that "this is something I couldn't help much with, Kurt. I would not be at home with it although I like a lot of it, and imagine that with Dietrich you'll have a hit. The lyrics seem superb to me—certainly the comedy might be improved, perhaps made a little *smarter....* Sorry not to be with you, but, as the old saying runs, if you don't *feel* it, you don't *feel* it."

Dissatisfied with Bella's book, Crawford and Weill nonetheless flew to Los Angeles in late September to begin working with Dietrich. After *Lady in the Dark,* it was strictly first-class for Weill, who checked in at the Beverly Hills Hotel while the notoriously frugal Crawford stayed in less imposing digs. In a September 26 letter to Lenya, Weill was all smiles. "Marlene came over from the studio to say hello. . . . She is a swell girl— and she seems very enthusiastic [*sic*] about going to Broadway. Tonight we go to her house to read the play and play the music."[10] "Marlene found out immediately [that Bella had written] all the other parts much better than hers," he wrote Lenya two days later. "She was extremely intelligent about it and put her finger right on all the wrong spots. She also was very constructive with suggestions how to improve the play. I am glad about it because it will break down Bella's stubbornness. . . . Marlene liked the music, but started that old business about the different quality of my music here in America. I cut it short by saying: 'Never mind those old German songs—we are in America now and Broadway is tougher than the Kurfürstendamm.' That stopped her."[11] At Weill's request, Bella Spewack flew to Los Angeles to begin working with Dietrich. "There are still a lot of problems to solve with that show, but Marlene is more and more interested and seems definitely set to do it. Well, we'll see if she signs a contract."[12]

But instead of signing, Dietrich came to New York to study statues of Venus at the Metropolitan Museum. "She would purchase yards of light gray chiffon . . . and drape herself in the style of the latest Venus she had discovered," Cheryl Crawford observed. "She would model her latest dis- covery . . . and ask our opinions."[13] By this point Weill was steaming—at Dietrich's time-wasting self-absorption and Bella's resistance. He insisted that he wanted to hear how Dietrich's voice sounded on a stage. With her then-lover Jean Gabin in tow, Dietrich performed for the composer in a small voice choked with timidity. She failed her audition, but Weill and Crawford were hooked on the idea of her name above the title and per- suaded her to sign a contract before she returned to Los Angeles.

After they got their star they fired their writer. Bella's first draft of what

was then called *One Man's Venus* was copyrighted on October 6, 1942; her
second draft, which incorporated some of the suggestions of her collaborators, was copyrighted on January 26, 1943. After reading this second
draft, Weill, Crawford, and Ogden Nash agreed that Bella would have to
go. When Crawford told her that she was off the project, Bella (as Crawford enjoyed recounting with a mischievous gleam in her eye) fainted
twice, then in unprintable language threatened to sue. She never did (perhaps because she received about $10,000 in "severance pay"), but contin-
ued her threats, bad-mouthed the show to her many show-business friends
after it had opened, and never again spoke to Crawford or (to his relief)
Weill. As he wrote to his parents, now in Palestine, on February 5, 1943,
"The lady who was supposed to write the libretto was a total flop . . . I
have lost all of five months."

Toward the end of 1942, as his collaboration with Bella Spewack had been
dwindling to a deadly standoff, Weill responded affirmatively to another
request from Ben Hecht to provide incidental music for a pageant. "I am
writing the music for a big Jewish rally memorial for Hitler's victims [*We
Will Never Die*, sponsored by the Committee for a Jewish Army of Stateless
and Palestinian Jews]," he wrote his parents in his February 5 letter. "I will
again be using a lot of liturgical music and will end with the Kaddish."
Weill made new arrangements of the Kaddish and "Hatikvah" and borrowed fragments of "Miriam's Song" and the destiny theme from *The Eternal Road* as underscoring and as choral and orchestral solos. Patriotic
songs, including "The Battle Hymn of the Republic," "Over There," "Tip-
perary," and the "Marseillaise," constituted the other category of ready-
made material he used. Accommodating the split between religious and
martial passages in the text, and underlining the thesis that in opposing
the Nazi menace military action acquired a religious purpose, an organ,
bugles, and drums dominated his orchestrations. Weill did not have much
time to devote to the project, and "the score is not in fact a composition,
but a rough-and-ready conglomeration of pre-existing material and new
arrangements," as David Drew wrote.[14]

We Will Never Die, written in white heat by Ben Hecht, had a three-part
structure: a roll call of the Jewish great, from ancient times to the present;
an account of Jewish heroism in the armed forces of many nations and in
the battle of the Warsaw ghetto; and "Remember Us," in which Jewish
martyrs recalled the circumstances of their dying at the hands of Nazis.

Weill composed the incidental score for *We Will Never Die,* "a
memorial dedicated to the Two Million Jewish Dead of Europe,"
presented at Madison Square Garden on March 9, 1943.

"Our memorial service is an attempt to cope with the Jewish situation as it
exists in the befogged and bemused soul of our city," Hecht wrote. "We are
not going to make speeches. We are going instead to sing a *Kaddish* for the
two million dead. . . . What good will it do? Will it save the Jews from
having their four million defenseless heads bashed in, from being burned
in piles like the refuse on Riker's Island? I don't know. Maybe we can
awaken some of the vacationing hearts in our government. And maybe we
can induce a voice to sound somewhere in behalf of human dignity. . . . We
are making only propaganda and our propaganda is a call to sing for the
dead."[15] An advertisement signed by the pageant's creators—Ben Hecht,

Moss Hart, Kurt Weill, and Billy Rose—promised that "any profits made from the Memorial will be used to further the campaign to save the remaining millions of European Jewry by action—not pity."

On March 9, 1943, before a combined audience of forty thousand, the memorial pageant, with twenty cantors, two hundred rabbis, four hundred actors, one hundred musicians, and "the Spirit of the Fighting Jew," was presented at Madison Square Garden for two performances. For the occasion the arena was decorated as a temple with two forty-foot tablets at center stage inscribed with the Ten Commandments. Prominent Jewish actors, including Edward G. Robinson, Luther Adler, and Paul Muni, alight with conviction, declaimed Ben Hecht's memorial service. "Tonight's rally is the key to a door that may remain bolted," Edward G. Robinson declared at the finale. "It is for us to remove the lock from that door and free those who are gasping their last breaths behind it. *But it is not too late.* When you leave Madison Square Garden tonight, there will be 4,000,000 pairs of eyes watching your fading form as it merges with the night. There will be 4,000,000 hearts praying that you return, and that you bring means of escape. They are not yet defeated—for with your help THEY WILL NEVER DIE! 'WE WILL NEVER DIE.' "[16]

A cry to the world to oppose the ongoing genocide of European Jewry, *We Will Never Die* was oratorio, concert reading, religious service, propaganda. Transcending the category of "entertainment," it received press attention but no traditional reviews. In the face of its message, matters of artistic concern were not only irrelevant but impertinent. And so they remain.

"You have probably heard about the great memorial for the two million Jews murdered by Hitler for which I initiated the performances here together with Ben Hecht and Moss Hart before 40,000 people," Weill wrote to his parents on April 17. "It was a gigantic success and has kicked up a lot of dust. Last week we repeated it in Washington for the government and now we're going to do it in several other cities." Unfortunate philosophical and political conflicts among Jewish organizations prevented the massive tour that Weill and Hecht had envisioned, but after the performances in New York the memorial was staged in five cities, concluding with a triumphant presentation at the Hollywood Bowl on July 21, 1943.

That spring Weill moved from the high purpose of *We Will Never Die* to the task of shepherding a commercial musical comedy from concept to production. With Bella at last removed, and still committed to a project that so far had yielded nothing but trouble, the *Venus* team selected a new book writer. Nash proposed a *New Yorker* colleague, humorist (and Broadway novice) S. J. Perelman. Working closely with the two Broadway neophytes, Weill was able to claim a greater control than with earlier and more experienced American colleagues such as Paul Green, Moss Hart, and Maxwell Anderson. "Sid Perelman, Ogden, and I set down to work out an entirely new story line, under complete disregard of Bella's script," he informed Ira Gershwin on April 5. Under Weill's watch, the show was changed from an overstuffed, mock-heroic period operetta to a contemporary, New York–based musical comedy now called *One Touch of Venus.* Weill believed that with a new, more swiftly paced script and his star still in place, the time of his "terrible troubles" with *Venus* was over.

But when the revised script was submitted to Dietrich in the early summer of 1943, she rejected it. "The show is too sexy and profane . . . I will not now exhibit myself in that way . . . I have a daughter who is nineteen years old," the star told Cheryl Crawford, who reported that Weill, enraged, started screaming at Dietrich: "How dare you? Have you lost your sense of values?"[17] "Marlene is out," Weill, in Hollywood to work on the film versions of *Lady in the Dark* and *Knickerbocker Holiday,* wrote to Lenya on July 3. "She is a stupid cow, conceited like all those Germans. I wouldn't want her if she would ask to play it," he thundered.[18] Now, in addition to the problems he was having with film studios (both movies would mangle his scores almost beyond recognition), he and Crawford had to find a new star for their seemingly bedeviled show.

Weill asked Gertrude Lawrence to play Venus, but, reasonably enough, she couldn't see herself in the role. "I auditioned for Venus that summer," Kitty Carlisle Hart recalled. "Kurt was so charming, but the woman they eventually cast was better than I would have been. She got the role, I got Moss Hart, and everybody was happy!"[19] It was Jean Dalrymple, the show's publicist, who found their star. "I went to Westport for the weekend and at the other end of the platform was Mary Martin and her husband [Richard Halliday, who was her manager]. I knew she was free because she had just closed in a show in Boston. . . . She hadn't played in New York since she made a hit [singing 'My Heart Belongs to Daddy'] and people were beginning to say, 'Let's bring her back.' She needed a job badly."[20]

Mary Martin, in fact, did need a job. After her New York splash in 1938, she had gone to Hollywood, where she appeared in a few minor Paramount musicals and discovered that she and movies were not a good match. By the summer of 1943, her brief film career over, she had been unsuccessful in finding another Broadway role. But when Dalrymple called Cheryl Crawford to suggest Mary Martin for Venus, Crawford was not enthusiastic. "That skinny thing with a Texas accent to play Venus?" Yet Dalrymple persisted. "I had raised all the money [*sic*]; I had something to say." As it turned out, Dalrymple also had to convince Mary Martin, who also couldn't see herself as Venus. "I felt, if it's a Marlene Dietrich part, it couldn't be mine," Martin said.[21] Reluctantly, on a hot August night, Mary Martin and her husband went to hear Weill perform some of the songs from the show. "All my life I will remember that man singing Venus' lovely number, 'That's Him.' I longed to sing that song, but I still could not see myself as Venus." Nonetheless, following Dietrich's example, Martin made several visits to the Metropolitan Museum to study Venus statues, "even one who was noticeably broad of beam."[22]

But still she felt the part was not for her—until she arranged to audition for Mainbocher, a prominent fashion designer who had never before worked on Broadway. He agreed that if Martin could convince him that she could be Venus, he would design her wardrobe. She chose to sing "That's Him," because the moment she heard Weill sing it she knew the song expressed "exactly what any woman feels about the man she loves."[23] The performer in her also knew that the song was a splendid piece of musical seduction. With Kurt playing the piano, Martin serenaded Mainbocher in the casual, intimate, endearingly homespun style that was to make her one of the most beloved of Broadway leading ladies. "I sat on [a chair] sideways and sang 'That's Him' right smack into those kind brown eyes," Martin recalled. "When I finished, Mainbocher said, 'I will do your clothes for the show if you will promise me one thing. Promise me you'll always sing the song that way. Take a chair to the footlights, sing across the orchestra to the audience as if it were just one.' "[24] Mary Martin signed on to play Venus, but remained very unsure that she could deliver.

To direct, Crawford chose Elia Kazan, a cohort from the Group Theatre whose subsequent career would clearly indicate musicals were not his forte. To choreograph, Crawford hired feisty Agnes de Mille, fresh from her landmark work on *Oklahoma!* "A good producer chooses a good team, and this was not a good team," said cast member Paula Laurence. "The elements didn't mix; the various components of this salad that Cheryl tossed together were not sympathetic."[25]

Rooted in the Method, Kazan was in alien territory as the director of a musical fantasy. "He didn't know what he was doing," Agnes de Mille recalled. "He had no visual sense. Kazan had no eyes at all. He had a wonderful ear, though, not for music but for speech."[26] Kazan respected Martin, however, a hard worker eager to do well, and helped her to develop what was to be a star-making performance. "Kazan asked me how I 'approached a part,' " Martin recalled. She was untouched by acting theory, but felt she had "to say something . . . [so] I told him I thought in terms of movement, of how I should walk. . . . If I can work out the right walk, the tempo, everything else comes naturally." The untutored performer hit a nerve in the Stanislavsky-trained director, who sensed she had instincts for musical-theatre performance he could learn from. "Your tempo should be legato, slow and graceful," Kazan told his star. The style of movement he worked out with her provided the spine to her characterization.[27] "Kazan had a lot to do with her acting, which was less mannered, less artificial than she'd been as a beguiling, adorable soubrette," Paula Laurence observed.[28]

When not working with Mary Martin, Kazan seemed disengaged. "I never got any direction at all from him," Laurence recalled, and neither did

An early rehearsal for *One Touch of Venus,* 1943. From the left: Kenny Baker, director Elia Kazan, librettist S. J. Perelman, John Boles, Teddy Hart, Weill, Ruth Bond (seated), Paula Laurence, and an unidentified cast member

the other actors, at least two of whom needed help. The film actor John Boles, cast as the wealthy man infatuated with Venus, was handsome but bland and according to Laurence "had no musical intelligence whatsoever. When he couldn't learn the song 'Who Am I?,' which was to open the second act, it had to be dropped." As the hero, the lowly barber pursued by Venus, Kenny Baker was "agreeable but not a good actor" in Laurence's assessment. "I began to wonder how many musicals Kazan had ever seen," Laurence said. "He would let people move on laugh lines. And he was asking me how to get laughs. He'd have me stand in the wings and take notes."[29]

Kazan also seemed stumped by the story. "He despised the book, well, who wouldn't, it was appalling," Agnes de Mille said.[30] Failing to appreciate Perelman's brand of wit and whimsy, Kazan cut large sections, heedless of causing transitional glitches. "He emasculated the book; he kept cutting it until it was only song cues," Paula Laurence maintained.[31]

An insecure leading lady not yet a star; a director almost openly hostile to musical theatre; a company chafing under directorial neglect; wide-

Delighted to discover that they shared common artistic goals, Weill and choreographer Agnes de Mille confer about the ambitious ballet sequences for *One Touch of Venus*. Weill chose de Mille even before her ballets for *Oklahoma!* earlier in 1943 had made her famous.

spread belief among the ranks that the book was silly—*Venus* rehearsals had all the signs of a disaster-in-the-making. Crawford, responsible for hiring the mismatched crew, kept a low profile. Only two people seemed to have confidence in the show: the composer, who had initiated the project, and the choreographer, who thought she knew how to save it.

Of all Weill's Broadway shows *One Touch of Venus* would seem the most conventional and impersonal. And yet Weill had chosen the subject, supervised the rewrites, and persisted through many roadblocks; as Paula Laurence said, "The show would never have gotten sorted out without him. Kurt was the eye of the hurricane. He was always calm, always pleasant, and seemingly oblivious to all the personality conflict. He listened profoundly to you, but kept you at arm's length. He could be scathing, but never cruel. When I read the bitchy letters he wrote to Lenya I was shocked; I never saw that side of him then. He wouldn't permit anybody to see that. The truth is, nobody really knew him."[32] Did Weill perhaps see in the misadventures of Venus on earth an allegory of his own experience as an "alien" in America? "I'm a Stranger Here Myself," one of several meltingly beautiful ballads he wrote with Ogden Nash, finds comedy and melancholy in Venus's sense of estrangement, her inability to interpret local customs accurately. Was her odyssey somehow a submerged autobiography, a reflection of the way he and perhaps Lenya too had felt on their arrival in America in 1935 and perhaps still felt eight years later? But Weill was attracted by the material in strictly professional terms as well. He sensed, correctly, that a story about the goddess of love who defies mortal limits offered a fantasy with particular resonance during wartime, when loss of loved ones overseas was a daily occurrence. And in a more technical sense he was excited by the fantasy's musical challenges—if music in *Lady in the Dark* was equated with dreams, here, for at least part of the score, it would be linked to the realm of the gods.

Buoyed by her success in *Oklahoma!,* in which she introduced a new dance vocabulary to Broadway, Agnes de Mille meticulously prepared two ballets and two production numbers for *Venus.* And because this was a much less organized production than the tight-as-a-drum Rodgers and Hammerstein machine that had oiled *Oklahoma!* she had greater creative leeway. Unlike Elia Kazan, de Mille took *Venus* seriously—she felt challenged by the material and was convinced that her dances would add elements missing in Perelman's book. Weeks before the start of rehearsals, and even before the producers had found their star, de Mille had begun to prepare the climactic act 2 ballet in which the show's major question is resolved: Will Venus keep or discard her human form? On July 11, in New Mexico, de Mille wrote to her composer that "day after tomorrow I shall air mail you a synopsis of the ballet. Let's give it as much time as we possibly can in the show because, by God, it's good."

De Mille composed the ballet in two contrasting sections. The first part, as the choreographer described it in her letter to Weill, is Venus's "vision of her life [in suburban Ozone Heights] with Rodney [the barber who inadvertently brought her to life]. The interior of three houses is revealed more or less alike and all furnished by Bloomingdale's. In all three the housewives are cleaning . . . a rhythmic pantomime . . . Rodney is very affectionate but matter-of-fact and daily in his attitude toward her . . . the epitome of all that's average American." The middle-class idyll is broken by "two nymphs stand[ing] on the lawn calling. Venus grows restive . . . a roll of thunder . . . heat-lightning . . . Venus is listening very strangely not to the thunder but to pipes—and faint drums. The nymphs call again, hauntingly—eerily. . . . There are voices calling Venus from every direction—far and near. She rushes out of the house, dances wildly and starts tearing her clothes off. . . . The stage gradually fills with the Bacchantes . . . a very low drum starts to throb softly . . . the Bacchantes are swaying in an hypnotic and repetitious manner—from here on the dance builds to absolute madness. The drumbeat should never stop . . . the dancers start the true ritual. This is going to be a killer—but very free, built on leaping and running . . . (Did you ever see a Southwestern American Indian ritual?)" At the end, Venus appears, "naked, translucent, Olympian, awful—and walks in wreathings of mist against the stars. The enormous and terrible figures of the Zodiac appear in the heavens." Still breathless with excitement in her letter to Weill two days later, de Mille described the scream that should issue from Venus at the climactic moment when she is to join the Bacchantes. "It should be a long musical wail in descending quarter tones (I once heard a Basque battle-cry from the fifteenth century and my blood hasn't warmed up since) sliding into the melody at the bottom."

For the lead dancer, de Mille on her own hired Sono Osato. "Do you know her?" she asked Weill in a July 22 letter. "Look up her pictures in any old Ballet Russe Program and drop dead with joy. She'll lead the Bacchanale and make history . . . she has the body of a sylph and can play comedy."

De Mille choreographed three other dances. In "Forty Minutes for Lunch" in act 1, as dancer Robert Pagent recalled, Venus "picked Sono out of the crowd [of frantic fast-moving New Yorkers on lunch break] and taught her how to be relaxed and ladylike. I played a French sailor and Sono, having been taught by Venus and now rid of her hysteria, gets the sailor," Pagent said.[33] For the act 1 finale, de Mille choreographed "Dr. Crippen," a story of a crime of passion. De Mille also, she said, "set the movement for all the songs. Singers can't move, as a rule, so you get them to do something expressive on the music that would emphasize what they were singing about."[34]

Six weeks before the rest of the show went into rehearsal de Mille hired the dancers and began to work with them. "Agnes was very demanding. She ran us," Allyn Ann McLerie remembered. "We all had ballet training—that was a requirement for working with Agnes."[35] Robert Pagent agreed. "There was no one in Agnes's shows who could be classified as a Broadway dancer." De Mille dancers also had to act. "Her dancing had character and behavior," Pagent said. "She chose us because she felt we could project character. In all the dances for the show we were furthering the story, just as the dances in *Oklahoma!* had done."[36]

Since de Mille had begun working before Kazan, she was already in charge once the full company convened. On one level Kazan (who "was totally lost; he didn't know how to do a musical," as Allyn Ann McLerie said)[37] was grateful for de Mille's take-charge manner, and fascinated by the way she blended acting with dance. But inevitably, the two strong-willed directors clashed. Even if he was uncertain, Kazan was not likely to have backed off or to have been willing to share control. "The director and choreographer were working toward the same goal, but from different perspectives," Robert Pagent observed. "When Agnes would be giving Sono dramatic gestures, Kazan sat there dumbfounded. 'What the hell is that supposed to mean?' he snapped. He was helpless in being able to direct musical movement. I remember him once telling us to think of ground glass."[38] Many in the company feared and disliked Kazan, recalling him as "an arrogant bully," "common and vulgar with women," who "ruined many lives and careers."[39]

"Agnes would sell her idea no matter who the director was; Weill, on the other hand, was very quiet," Robert Pagent said. "We dancers had no direct contact with him. He was less visible than any of the creative people."[40] "I have a picture of Kurt going by, quickly, as he often did, but not lingering," Allyn Ann McLerie remembered. "We knew who he was, who Lenya was, and we were honored to be working with him."[41]

Weill and Kazan maintained a wary distance. They respected each other but sensed that they were quite different personalities, unlikely to mix: Kazan's hard-boiled, street-tough demeanor and his obsessive womanizing did not play well opposite Weill's European wit and cultivation. Weill and de Mille, on the other hand, had a joyful collaboration. They were theatrical rebels who spoke the same language. Both had a wicked sense of humor, and they made each other laugh, usually by their sharp comments on the follies of others. Weill shared de Mille's intensity, her grand, ecstatic vision about what the show could be—and he was the only one on the team who could help her realize it. "Kurt sat in on most of my rehearsals and was very astute theatrically," de Mille recalled. "He had visual knowledge, visual imagination. He would say, 'It's too long here and I'd cut from there to there and I think you'll get your crisis better.' " De Mille noted that Weill composed "to the exact counts. That is remarkable. He's the only one I knew who ever did. Richard Rodgers did better tunes [than Kurt Weill] but didn't begin to have his musicianship. Kurt was a real musician."[42]

Intoxicated as they may have been, both choreographer and composer were also capable of being ruthlessly objective about their work. During the Boston tryout, they both saw that the ballet on which they had lavished so much time and conviction needed to be trimmed. "It was boring to the audience, and stopped the show," de Mille remembered. And although Weill was proud of his work, he agreed. "He would never say, 'This may not be so successful but it's a gorgeous piece of music and I want to save it,' " de Mille said. "Kurt wanted money . . . he was mad for success. He would cut cut cut if it meant success."[43] Nonetheless, even in a tamed version their ballet was the dramatic as well as musical high point of the show, and a musical-theatre landmark in integrating dance within the needs of storytelling. "The ballet reaffirmed what I'd done in *Oklahoma!* and proved that ballet was a good part of musical entertainment. The big Bacchanale, in fact, was a much better dance composition than anything I had done for *Oklahoma!*" de Mille claimed.[44]

To fulfill de Mille's vision, Weill composed music of a quasi-symphonic sweep and richness. His theme-and-variations format, and his sumptuous orchestrations, transcended the usual parameters of a musical-comedy score. But he did not neglect, or treat with merely casual competence, the standard genre requirements, and his musical program for *One Touch of Venus* is laced with appealing romantic ballads and comedy numbers. The opening number, "New Art Is True Art," performed by the chorus and art patron Whitelaw Savory, gets the show off to a jaunty start with its brisk rhythm and Nash's penchant for interior rhymes. But the song introduces a theme, "New art is true art, / The old masters slew art," that the show is going to disprove. It is "old art," in the form of a classical statue of Venus that Savory dotes on (because it reminds him of a woman he loved and lost), that counts here. Venus's allure, both timeless and timely, is celebrated in the following number, the title song, performed by Paula Laurence as Molly, Savory's sharp-tongued secretary, which Weill treats primarily as a frame for Ogden Nash's sparkling wordplay. "How Much I Love You" is a deft example of Weillian counterpoint—looking at a photo of his fiancée, Gloria, a shrew, Rodney the barber may think he is singing a love song, but the stingy melody and stilted rhythm slyly sound warnings the hero doesn't yet hear.

"I'm a Stranger Here Myself," the first of four delicious numbers Weill wrote for Venus, comes from the vein of minor-key rhythm numbers that he had successfully mined in the recent "Saga of Jenny." Despite the fact that Venus is expressing her puzzlement at the customs of the country in

Molly (Paula Laurence), a saucy secretary, leads the chorus in the title number in *One Touch of Venus*.

which she has been suddenly brought to life, Weill introduces musical clues that this goddess will be perplexed only momentarily. Celestial tones evoke that other world that Venus comes from, but a wailing brass section sliding into jazzlike riffs lets us know that this Venus can swing too. The song is based on little more than a repeating jazz/blues progression and a sense of swing—slow swing, in this case. At one point, against murmuring strings, Venus confidently slips into a trademark Weillian parlando, half singing, half speaking her lyrics. Expressing the character's irritation along with her erotic fizz, the number demands a performer who can be cool, sexy, and regal all at once: a tall order, which only the right kind of star could fulfill.

Passages of "I'm a Stranger Here Myself" are reprised, and rhythmically varied, in the comic ballet, "Forty Minutes for Lunch," that follows. Much of this is a fine urban cityscape instrumental, anticipating some of Aaron Copland's later forays into the genre. A propulsive, relentless percussion rhythm, suggesting frazzled New Yorkers on a quick break, plays against string passages embodying Venus's Olympian grace. To be sure, the show's dramatic conflict between the breathless metropolitan mortals and the elegant, observing goddess is here fully articulated, perhaps to a fault. The characteristic "divine" motive, first used when Venus's statue awakens, is tired and middlebrow—chords sung by a wordless chorus ("Aah, aah") and often accompanied in "otherworldly" fashion by glissando string harmonics right out of Stravinsky's *Firebird*. The obviousness of such musical rhetoric can make the show seem quaint from a present-day perspective. Nonetheless, Weill's purpose was to supply vibrant, Broadway-style instrumental music, and in this he succeeded. He accommodated not only de Mille's exact choreographic beats but also wrote for the talents and limitations of the performers. The difficult passages are reserved for Sono Osato, as the harried office worker Venus rescues, while for the nondancing star he created a musical line calling only for graceful movement.

"Westwind" is a ballad for Whitelaw Savory about the girl who got away. Written to provide Martin's costar John Boles with a solo, the song, more practically, was also intended to cover a scene change. Nonetheless, Weill was not cavalier. "Westwind," a ballad with one of Weill's insinuating melodies, helped to deepen Perelman's sketchy treatment of Savory, and not incidentally was also a potential stand-alone, the kind of exportable number tucked into many Broadway shows of the era. (" 'Westwind' was the song which you all picked out as the hit song when I played the score for you," Weill reminded his publisher Max Dreyfus on December 31, after the show had opened, urging him to plug songs in the show. "It is a straight ballad, a very simple tune and lyric . . . with great possibilities for arrangers and singers.")

For Gloria, the fiancée from hell, and her equally obnoxious mother, Weill composed "Way Out West in New Jersey," a song with a cowboy twang that recalls "Oh the Rio Grande" from *Johnny Johnson*. Garnished with Nash's lyrics addressed to sleek Manhattanites for whom New Jersey is indeed the hinterlands, the number is the sort of disposable item included in musical comedies of the era and was further proof that despite his maverick qualities Weill could also play by the rules. The song injected a dash of vaudevillian verve at a moment when the show needed it.

"Foolish Heart" is a waltz for Venus in which she momentarily questions whether or not she has lost her touch: Is her love for Rodney putting a crimp in her usually casual style? The song demonstrated Weill's mastery of the verse/refrain structure standard on Broadway. (The verse is the introduction or prologue intended to arouse anticipation for the refrain or chorus that carries the main melodic motif.) Weill's verse works hand in hand with Nash's lyric to create a space—to clear the ground—for the melody: Venus asks a series of self-doubting questions ("When did the magic vanish? Have I somehow lost my touch?") echoed by Weill's unresolved chords, which seem to float in midair, as if seeking to be absorbed into the awaiting melody. Weill's swirling waltz refrain, with a hint of hesitation in the verse, provides the melodic release the audience has been primed for. In the song Weill strictly follows the standard AABA pattern he frequently disregards elsewhere. The B section (the bridge or release) connects the first two statements of the A melody with its final resolution, the singer's moment of self-recognition:

> *Ah, love used to touch me so lightly,*
> *Why will my heart betray me so?*
> *I would dance with a new lover nightly,*
> *But my foolish heart says no.*

Glinting with alternating light and shadow, "Foolish Heart" is a high point of Weill's Broadway portfolio, a number in which the German composer takes on and holds his own against not Mahler or Hindemith but Richard Rodgers, the master of the Broadway waltz. Knowing well they had a good thing going, Weill and de Mille prolonged the number with a dance. As Robert Pagent recalled, "First Mary sang the number, heartbreakingly; then Sono and I danced it in one, completing the story that we began in 'Forty Minutes for Lunch.' "[45]

"The Trouble with Women," a swell barbershop quartet (a natural, after all, in a show with a barber as the hero), represented Weill in high-mimicry mode. "Speak Low," a beguine that evoked the Latin American style popular at the time, sounds a little like Cole Porter, although the harmonies are distinctly Weill's. Sung first as alternating solos by Venus and Rodney and then as a duet, the song marked the moment in the show when the barber became utterly enchanted by the goddess. As a lovers' declaration, it is as poignant an ode as any in the literature of the American musical. Like "September Song," "Speak Low" is a Weill paean to the passing of time, to the fragility and the joy of romance. Like Weill's melody, Nash's lyrics are rich with sentiment. As Venus surmises in the elegant and arching bridge of the song, her romance with Rodney is destined to be fleeting:

> *Time is so old*
> *And love so brief,*
> *Love is pure gold*
> *And time a thief.*

And then she returns to the elegiac chorus of the song, which always begins in medias res above a touching G-minor harmony:

> *We're late,*
> *Darling, we're late,*
> *The curtain descends,*
> *Everything ends*
> *Too soon, too soon.*

Weill's rueful melody points to an impending loss. "Speak Low," like "September Song," is prime evidence that the caustic Weimar bard had a generous soft streak and an aching heart. Is it foolhardy, in retrospect, to read into the song the composer's intuition that length of years would not be among his gifts?

"Dr. Crippen" at the end of act 1 provided the requisite production number. Performed at a party by Whitelaw Savory and the ensemble, the song is not only a divertissement at a point where the creators felt the show needed one, it also has a connection to a twist in the plot. Rodney has been accused of killing his fiancée, Gloria, who has disappeared; the song tells about a Dr. Crippen, who killed Belle Elmore for the love of Ethel LeNave. "Dr. Crippen" was further evidence of Weill's team spirit, his willingness to provide sustenance wherever the show needed it—a possible hit song here, a novelty item there, a rousing ensemble number to end the act.

"Who Am I?" was the original opening number for act 2. A song in search of a tune about Savory's identity crisis and poorly performed by John Boles, it was cut out of town. Instead, the first song in the act was Molly's "Very, Very, Very," a wry look at the foibles of the very rich. Thematically tangential, the song, tailored to Paula Laurence's wisecracking urban persona, was another frame for Nash's lyrics. In the middle of the song, Weill pauses deliciously from the AABA formula he has pursued up to this point to have Molly half sing, half talk through two stanzas of gossip about the gentry:

> Since Sally ran off with her obstetrician
> Her hair's turned red and she looks like a Titian.
> Of course, I'd hate to swear in court
> What kind of Titian—beaut' or mort'.
> Have you paid your platina fur tax?
> I am up to my neck in surtax.

(Demanding on a first hearing, it was material like this that turned *One Touch of Venus* into a musical for connoisseurs, a boutique musical for the literati who might not normally have frequented Broadway showshops.)

In prison for allegedly killing Gloria, Rodney reprises "Speak Low." The following number, "Catch Hatch," after Rodney escapes from prison, may be Weill's most ambitious work in the show. Sung by Savory, Molly, and the ensemble on the trail of the escaped barber, it is a transition number that Weill turns into a fugue for chorus and orchestra. With its steadily escalating rhythm that captures the frenzied search for the missing hero, "Catch Hatch" ends with a massed vocal ensemble supported by strumming, densely textured orchestrations. In the show's musical lineup, this fully developed operetta-like finale was the act 2 production number.

"That's Him," as she knew the first time she heard it, was Mary Martin's chance to speak directly to the audience. This accounts for the song's unusual structure, which begins with the chorus, or refrain, as if it had no verse. Martin credited Mainbocher with teaching her how to sing the song, but de Mille claimed that Lotte Lenya was the star's muse. "Lenya had her bring her chair to the footlights and sit on it backwards and just talk to the audience. Mary was used to belting things with a high little voice that sounded like a boy soprano. But she whispered 'That's Him,' like a girl confessing she was in love for the first time. It was darling."[46] Her casual, confessional delivery, garnished with calculated but wonderfully comforting little laughs, complemented Weill's endearing melody and Nash's homespun lyrics. The song embodied a tribute to normality—in sentimental Broadway mode, composer and lyricist assured wartime audiences that after all it is the little everyday things that count and that endure.

Next up, Rodney's "Wooden Wedding" broke the spell. The descending notes and monotonous rhythm in which the mundane barber expresses his vision of wedded bliss contain the promise of an unhappy ending for the couple.

> *Golly how the time will fly*
> *Stealing kisses in the kitchen,*
> *Holding hands while the dishes dry,*

Rodney croons as Venus shudders. Her conflict is dramatized (and resolved) by de Mille's two-part ballet, which takes Venus from the boredom of suburban life to sensual revelry in a bacchanale, at the climax of which she is whisked home. This all-instrumental climax is not as musically accomplished as Weill believed it to be—he told de Mille it was "the finest piece of music he'd written since coming to America"[47]—but despite the inescapable tritones of the "divine" it certainly provided an adept and lively dance number.

If the show was to be a hit, it could not end with a pagan rite reserved for the gods and with Rodney deserted by Venus. The values of Ozone Heights had to be reaffirmed; the worthiness of a world accessible to the audience had to be validated. Once again Agnes de Mille came to the show's rescue when she supplied the idea for the finaletto in which Rodney meets Venus transformed into a (human) young woman from Ozone Heights. Having been instructed by the goddess of love, Rodney is now ready to recognize true romance. "The ending, which we dancers saw from the wings, when Rodney meets 'Venus,' was quite moving," Robert Pagent recalled.[48] At a subliminal level, the happy ending offered wartime audiences a love that transcended "death."

Mary Martin (with Kenny Baker) as Venus in a gown by Mainbocher. Martin accepted the lead in *One Touch of Venus* after Mainbocher assured her he would design her character's wardrobe. Paul du Pont and Kermit Love designed the costumes for the mortals.

. . .

One Touch of Venus began a tryout engagement in Boston on September 17, 1943, which was nearly destroyed by Howard Bay's set designs. "This light, bubbly champagne fantasy was set in what looked like a dirigible hangar," Paula Laurence recalled. "The stage was festooned with heavy gray drapes that looked like casket plush lining. It cost a fortune and it all had to be thrown out."[49] Mixed reviews cited the show's mixed intentions, its not fully integrated fusion of highbrow and popular elements. With new, airier settings and further cuts in the book and score, the show opened on Broadway at the Imperial Theatre on October 7. Some of the gripes from Boston remained. "One immediately got the impression that [the collaborators] had never been able to get together and decide what kind of a musical show *One Touch of Venus* was to be—something arty, sophisticated and abstract, or something like a Minsky burlesque, only more literate," according to Burton Rascoe in the October 8 *New York World-Telegraph*. Weill's score, hailed for its range and freshness; Nash's lyrics, by turns witty and contemplative; the sparkling performances of

Sono Osato, left, Kenny Baker, and Mary Martin in "Venus in Ozone Heights," Agnes de Mille's climactic ballet, which resolves the title character's conflict—should she remain on earth or return to the realm of the gods?—in *One Touch of Venus*

Mary Martin and Paula Laurence; and de Mille's dances were all widely praised. Following *Oklahoma!*, *One Touch of Venus* promoted de Mille to the catbird seat among Broadway choreographers. With her narrative dances in these two shows, Agnes de Mille turned the dream ballet into a prestige commodity that for a time in the 1940s any upscale musical felt obligated to include.

Like Gertrude Lawrence's Liza Elliott, Mary Martin's Venus was a performance of exact pitch in a role laced with land mines. Combining innocence with wisdom, her Venus was coy without being sticky, fetching without being sultry. The "skinny little Texan's" Venus was certainly not the remote, enigmatic, sexually ambidextrous, Teutonic goddess Dietrich would have played, but perky, direct, commonsensical, and American. Martin was preferable. In the last scene, when Venus "returns" as a young woman from the suburbs, Martin was dressed in a white piqué blouse, pink polka-dot skirt, and matching rolled-brim hat—the spitting image of the endearing all-American girl next door, just who the boys over there were fighting for. "At first we all wanted Dietrich," Maurice Abravanel recalled, "but we realized that Mary Martin was right. Because if Venus had been played by Marlene Dietrich in 1943, those scenes with Venus coming out, presumably naked, could never have gone. There would have been something very unproper and unpleasant. While with Mary it was very charming, exquisite, feminine, but sexless. Before a performance I would go to her dressing room or at intermission. She was usually in her negligee. But it never meant anything. With any sexy woman, it would have been—after all, you know—but not with Mary, ja?"[50] "The glamour girls would have been all wrong," Robert Pagent observed. "Mary had lovely posture and poise, plus the quality of the girl next door, and she was *not* all sweetness and light, which is why she became a star, after all."[51] Inspired by Mary Martin's appearance in the final scene, Oscar Hammerstein cast her as the wholesome nurse Nellie Forbush in *South Pacific.*

One Touch of Venus was a hit, the first one of the fledgling 1943–44 season, and the first important "modern" musical to open after the premiere of *Oklahoma!* on March 31, 1943. The period between *Oklahoma!* and *One Touch of Venus* was dominated by the return of antediluvian forms—three canonic operettas, *The Vagabond King, The Merry Widow,* and *Blossom Time* were revived, along with revue offerings of yesterday, *Chauve-Souris 1943* and *Artists and Models,* both unsuccessful repackagings. In the middle of the war, burlesque and vaudeville surged in popularity. Mike Todd's burlycue of 1942, *Star and Garter* with Gypsy Rose Lee, spurred a run on burlesque-style comics and revue sketches. *Follow the Girls* with Jackie Gleason was a hit 1944 girlie show. *Take a Bow,* a vaudeville with Chico Marx, fared poorly, however. Mike Todd, fabled big spender, was back at bat with *Mexican Hayride,* a colorful spectacle that starred beloved Broadway clown Bobby Clark and featured another middling Cole Porter score. The season was notable for the brief appearance of *What's Up,* a show by the new team of Alan Jay Lerner (a future Weill collaborator) and Frederick Loewe, like Weill a Berliner and former student of Busoni. The season's prestige hit was *Carmen Jones,* Oscar Hammerstein's adaptation of Bizet's *Carmen* into a Broadway-style musical. (In a revealing letter, S. J. Perelman wrote to Weill on December 8, 1944, that *Carmen Jones* was "an extremely beautiful and equally boring show BUT—Hassard Short and Raoul Pène DuBois have really made the visual end . . . a sheer delight. You never saw such richness and such colors; I realized what a milestone in the theatre *Venus* might have been had these two men done it. Our show is tasteless and dull (visually, of course, and always excepting Mary's costumes) by comparison. . . . As you said so often, this is what Gadget [Elia Kazan] never understood about musicals, and it's precisely what our show lacks.") Erich Wolfgang Korngold, Weill's fellow émigré, soon to have the kind of Hollywood success that would elude Weill, was represented by an adaptation of Offenbach's *La Belle Hélène* called *Helen Goes to Troy*. And at the end of the season a show called *Dream with Music,* with a dreary book by writers to become famous in other venues, Dorothy Kilgallen and Sidney Sheldon, seemed like a carbon copy of *One Touch of Venus*. The show's highlight was a dream ballet choreographed by de Mille's rival Balanchine and featuring his wife of the moment, Vera Zorina.

As *Venus* settled in for what was to be the longest Broadway run of any Weill show, the atmosphere backstage continued to be fractious. Cheryl Crawford and her partner, Jack Wildberg, quarreled bitterly. Weill was caught in the crossfire and also contributed to it. Before they had begun working on the show he had felt indebted to Crawford and thought of her fondly, but during rehearsals and after the show opened, his feelings underwent a major reversal. His first complaint to Crawford was about his billing, an always sensitive point for the composer. "I think everybody agrees that I have contributed more to the making and to the success of this show than anybody else. And now [to save money in the ads] you took away even the simple billing that every composer (even Fats Waller) is getting," he wrote to her on November 27, six weeks after the show opened. He also resented Crawford's approach to publicity. "As you know, the entire publicity for *Oklahoma!* was built around the show itself," he wrote on January 20, "but so far our publicity hasn't made the slightest attempt to hammer it into the people that we have an outstanding show. The consequence is that the name of our show has not become, like other shows in the same class, a symbol for high-class entertainment. So far it is just another musical or, at best, a good vehicle for Mary Martin." Weill's litany of complaints against Crawford was embellished by Perelman. After a meeting with the producer to "discuss things generally," Perelman concluded, as he wrote to Weill in a December 19 letter, that "nothing that Crawford ever does can ever have any real distinction; she is a third-rater, a safe, stingy, piddling little personality, and one of the least theatrical minds I do believe has ever managed on Broadway. You know, Kurt, there are some people who corrupt and spoil everything they touch. I am afraid we have a show which resists a good deal of mauling and still manages to get over."

Ill will festered elsewhere as well. Perelman loathed Kenny Baker, who "made some monstrous anti-Semitic cracks backstage. He is a no-good son-of-a-bitch," he wrote Weill on February 1, 1944. Mary Martin thought Jean Dalrymple was a busybody. Jean Dalrymple thought Mary Martin was haughty and stupid. No one liked Martin's husband, Richard Halliday. Sweet on stage, Martin could be high-handed off, and treated the supporting players like "plebes," according to ensemble member Jane Hoffman.[52] Everyone complained about Kazan's lack of interest. "The cast has been asking where he was and was hurt that he didn't seem to be very interested," Perelman wrote to Weill on December 8. "I think *Venus* is very much out of his mind. Gadge is a mercurial, restless guy who tires, like a child, of toys." When the show moved from the prestigious Imperial Theatre to the less exalted Forty-sixth Street, a new round of invective against management was unfurled. "It is the old, old story," Perelman wrote to Weill on January 16, 1944. "Half-measures, botched and insufficient actions, timidity, stinginess, and above all a sinister cabal composed of Crawford, Wildberg, and Jean Dalrymple. I can't begin to convey to you how these three serpents interlock, and how their points of view and taste match each other."

Weill, attentive as ever to backstage politics, appreciated Perelman's updates, but no amount of internecine conflict could dampen his pleasure in the fact that his perseverance had resulted in his second Broadway hit in a row. "This time I didn't have a Moss Hart or an Ira Gershwin next to me, but had to rely on my own judgment," the composer had written his parents on November 5. "I had to make all the decisions myself, often even against the wishes of my collaborators and had to collaborate on the libretto, the casting, scenic designs and the entire organization of a big Broadway show as well. During the seven weeks before opening, I never slept more than 2–3 hours a night."

TWELVE

Much Ado

A few weeks after *One Touch of Venus* opened, Weill was summoned to Hollywood to work with Ira Gershwin on an original musical. This time, Lenya accompanied her husband. Because she and Weill were keenly aware that her appearance, her accent, and her unique singing style made her virtually unemployable in the film factories—she did not conform to any recognizable type in a business dominated by type-casting—she kept an even lower profile in Hollywood than in New York. Like Weill, she was scornful of Los Angeles ("Lotusland" was their word for it) and of the Byzantine politics of the Hollywood studio system. Even the caressing winter climate could not compensate, and she couldn't wait to return to the familiar comforts of South Mountain Road. Weill had already been scorched by the movies—and worse was yet to come—but the new project was tempting. A time-travel fantasy that offered many spots for musical numbers, *Where Do We Go from Here?* had a screenplay by Morrie Ryskind, who had written for the Marx Brothers and collaborated with the Gershwins on their political operettas, and a producer, William Perlberg, who was promising creative elbow room.

Like *One Touch of Venus, Where Do We Go from Here?* is a story of a visitor from elsewhere (in this case a genie) who guides the destiny of a mortal. Here, the human is Bill Morgan, an average Joe who recalls Johnny Johnson in his eagerness to serve his country during wartime. But to his regret, Bill has been classified 4-F. The genie who promises to transport Bill to the battlefront has a faulty control of time, enlisting him in the army of the American Revolution, in the navy on Columbus's voyage to the New World, and as a soldier in the *Knickerbocker Holiday* era of Nieuw Amsterdam. Bill Morgan is another displaced person, like Venus and for that matter Kurt Weill, who survives on his skill as a quick-witted chameleon.

Weill and Gershwin were certainly aware of the quaint aspects of Ryskind's screenplay, essentially a morale booster for a country at war, but were enticed by the musical possibilities. The different period settings in each of the vaudeville-style sketches seemed an open-sesame to Weill's gifts for musical mimicry, the ethnic dialects—German, Italian, Dutch—a ready-made source for Ira's comic rhymes. The collaborators began working in November, and even with Ira's snail-like pace Weill completed their

The astonishing through-composed Columbus sequence, a ten-minute mini-opera, from Weill's only successful film, *Where Do We Go from Here?*, 1945. Here, Columbus (Fortunio Bonanova) confronts a possible mutiny.

Weill in Hollywood, the one "foreign" country to which he was
unable to adapt, posing with his new two-seater Oldsmobile coupe

score by early January. In a sense, they did their job too well. As Ira
recalled, William Perlberg was "so taken with the score and the story that
he asked Darryl Zanuck [head of Twentieth Century–Fox] to postpone the
shooting so that, with some slight changes in story and a few additional
numbers, he could produce it first as a Broadway musical."[1] And indeed,
as it had been shaped by the two theatre veterans, the material would
have made a zesty wartime Broadway show. But Zanuck had already
announced the project as a forthcoming release and ordered shooting to
move ahead on schedule.

"We are just finishing a little 'Italian opera' about the mutiny on
Columbus' ship, with arias, rezitativos and choruses," Weill wrote Maurice Abravanel on December 11, 1943. "Very funny and quite exciting.
God knows what they'll do with it." With their experiments for *Lady in the
Dark* as inspiration, the "little opera" the collaborators crafted was a three-
part, nine-and-a-half-minute musical scene that at the time was the
longest vocal number ever recorded in a Hollywood film. In part 1 the
sailors jockey with Columbus:

Your believing that the world is round
Is a belief that we believe unsound!
Our feet are on the ground,
And so far, we have found
The world is flat—like that!

as they announce a mutiny, a "nautical rebellion." In part 2, Weill's lusty send-up of an Italian eating song, the homesick sailors sing about the culinary and other delights back home. "Have you no loyalty to royalty?" Columbus counters. In part 3 Bill interjects. "The future you're failing / If you don't keep sailing / The *Nina,* the *Pinta,* and the *Santa Maria,*" he warns (one of several musical numbers in which the time traveler predicts the future to puzzled listeners). Bill's salute to the great American cities that will be built as a result of their voyage contains a reflexive bow to Hollywood, "the global cinematropolis." Remarkably, given its length and complexity, the studio "didn't touch" the "little opera," as a delighted Ira informed Weill in an undated letter. The through-composed Columbus sequence, designed as the template for a new kind of "Hollywood opera" that neither Weill (nor anybody else) had the chance to pursue further, remains the purest example on film of the kind of musical-theatre audacity that drove the composer's career. The film's credits list fourteen names responsible for musical arrangements and orchestrations, but the entire Weill-Gershwin score, including the separate numbers they wrote for the rest of the film, was substantially unmolested.

"There will be two pictures out with my music in the next few weeks," Kurt wrote his sister-in-law Ruth Weill on January 12, 1944. "I hear both are very good. People say that Ginger Rogers' singing 'Jenny' is terrific, and so is Charles Coburn's singing of 'September Song.' " (Both performances, in fact, are excruciating.) Although he was only minimally involved with the adaptations of *Lady in the Dark* and *Knickerbocker Holiday*—with interpolations by studio composers, the films either jettisoned or rearranged most of his work—Weill was nonetheless expecting a boost in his Hollywood rating. His hopes were soon to be smashed. The films were demolition derbies in which only faint traces of Weill's original concepts remained. Part misunderstood Broadway musicals, part stillborn Hollywood movies, the two adaptations did not satisfy the requirements of either medium, and more than anything else their utter failure proved that musicals conceived for the stage should most of the time remain there.

(When *One Touch of Venus* was sold to the movies, Weill with his agent, Leah Salisbury, hammered out a firm contract designed to protect him from further studio meddling. "Here is the content of the non-interpolation clause as I want it in the contract," Weill wrote in a September 4, 1944, letter to Salisbury. "All the songs in the picture have to be taken from the score, and the underscoring has to be based on themes from the original score." If new songs were to be added, Weill alone wanted to write them. He also wanted to "select and place the original songs," "to select themes and material for underscoring." And he wanted billing. "I want to make it absolutely clear that I will refuse to sign any contract which does not contain these conditions exactly as outlined in this letter." When the film of *One Touch of Venus,* which would be Weill's final collision with Hollywood, finally opened in October 1948, the terms of his contract were indeed honored. There were no interpolations, and all the scoring was based on themes from his score. But only three songs were used: "Speak Low," "That's Him," and, with new lyrics and a new title, "Foolish Heart." At a time when movie musicals were in their prime, *Venus* seems unaccountably embarrassed to break into song. The source of the film's curious and crippling resistance to Weill's score may have been its leading lady, Ava Gardner, a Universal contract player being groomed for stardom, who couldn't sing—she was dubbed by Eileen Wilson—or dance, or, for that matter, act. With a dull, coarse speaking voice, a plebeian slouch, and a complete absence of humor or charm, Ava Gardner made a singularly unpersuasive goddess. Her common touch completed the film's reduction of a sophisticated, ironic Broadway musical into a leaden romantic fantasy for postwar audiences.)

After four months in the movie colony Weill was chafing to return to New York and to the more congenial world of making musicals for Broadway. But the project he was offered did not entice him. In a February 27, 1944, letter to Ira Gershwin, Weill wrote that he was "unenthusiastic" about a musical based on *The Firebrand,* a hit 1924 play by Edwin Justus Mayer (for which Ira Gershwin had written lyrics to a song) about Benvenuto Cellini, the sixteenth-century Florentine sculptor, goldsmith, legendary lover, and bon vivant. "The people who are doing it as a musical called again to say that they have wonderful ideas to do it as a new kind of comic opera and that Elisabeth Layton and a Hungarian by the name of Szold are working on the book. After I hesitated again they finally asked would I be interested in case that you would do the lyrics—and I said yes." Two months later, in a typical flip-flop, Weill had convinced himself that the source material ("I am certainly glad I read it again") "is definitely one of the best written and best constructed comedies I have ever read. . . . I was amazed to what degree it is a ready made libretto for the kind of smart, intelligent, intimate romantic-satirical operetta for the international market which we always talked about. I see it as a small show with great touring possibilities, more a comic opera than a musical comedy," Weill wrote Ira on April 3.

Composing a comic opera would provide not only a welcome departure from the musical-comedy idiom of *One Touch of Venus;* it would require, as Weill informed his partner, "a great deal of music of all types: songs, duets, quartets and sextets, recitatives, underscored dialogue and some dancing." The one reservation he had was that "the love story is too cynical and hasn't got enough warmth and simplicity. This would be the main job for Eddie [Edwin Justus Mayer, who was now adapting his own play]," Weill suggested in his April 3 letter.

Cellini's *Autobiography* is "quite a fascinating book, full of intrigues, jealousies, fighting and f . . . ," Weill, en route to Los Angeles on the Santa Fe, reported to Lenya on June 25. "[Cellini] was a real big-mouth, bragging, lieing, cheating, but with a great feeling of independence and an utter disregard of any authority. The amazing discovery is how little life and manners have changed in those 400 years."[2] Once he arrived back in "Lotusland," Weill confronted Ira's preference for poker over working on the saga of a sixteenth-century rogue. "Ira, of course, is still trying to stall," Weill reported to Lenya on June 28, "but he has good ideas and I like his integrity and his knowledge (after Sid and Ogden [musical theatre neophytes]!). He says: let's make this a 'classic,' not a one season show for Broadway but something lasting—and you know that goes down like honey with me. So I'll keep fighting his laziness because it is worthwhile."[3] After a week of intensive work, Weill reported that "it looks more and more as if *Firebrand* might become what you and I have been waiting for: my first Broadway Opera. Ira, who keeps comparing it with *Rosenkavalier,* is getting really exciting [*sic*] every time I tell him that this show could be an entirely new combination of first class writing, music, singing and acting."[4] Two days later he reported that he and Ira would "treat great parts of the score in real opera style, without any attempt to write American pop songs. The part of Cellini will be treated in a kind of grandioso arioso style . . . [Ira] knows so much about style in words and music and he plays up to all my ambitions as a musician. The next thing I have to do now is to find a musical style for this score which, if I find it, will be quite different from anything that I or anybody else has done."[5]

By July 25, Ira had retreated again into his nonworking mode and Weill threatened to withdraw. This time Ira believed him, and "we wrote in one session an opening chorus which sets the character of the whole play. It is a song of the hangmen, preparing the gallows for Cellini [another Weill character facing execution!], written in a kind of Palestrina style," Weill wrote Lenya.[6] After quoting the opening lines Weill asked, "Doesn't that sound like *Dreigroschenoper?*" After they worked a few more days on the opening scene, Weill reported, "[Ira] said yesterday: if we keep the show on the scope of the opening scene it can become the greatest thing Broadway has ever seen. And you know what that means coming from him."[7] At this temporarily euphoric stage, Weill was also enthusiastic about his librettist. "Eddie has been ordered by me to stay home on Sunday and write a complete outline of the first scene. He came through beautifully. What a pleasure to work with a real writer! I am sure he will write my next opera; he has everything for it."[8]

Over the summer Weill began to lobby for a role in the show for Lenya, semiretired since her tour with Helen Hayes in *Candle in the Wind.* Perhaps feeling he hadn't done enough for her, perhaps sensing that despite her apparent diffidence and her stage fright Lenya wanted to return to performing, Weill aggressively promoted his wife for a role, and Lenya herself seemed to be caught up in the campaign. Winning the part of a lecherous Italian duchess for Mrs. Weill, however, was to be an uphill battle, and for good reason: Lenya was miscast.

Ira, who knew better, resisted. "If Ira wants to be bitchy in this matter, I am just in the mood to oblige him," Weill reported to Lenya on July 7.[9] When Ira wanted to cast Kitty Carlisle, Weill bristled. "Kitty Carlisle is impossible for the part. I will tell Ira today, that we might just as well give up right now, if that is the way he wants to cast the show. I am determined to fight this thing through, and please don't say I should not. You know I wouldn't do it if I wouldn't be convinced that you are ideal for the part."[10] Even after many weeks of working on a show that both Kurt and Ira had come to believe had the potential to chart a new course for the American musical, the contretemps over Lenya persisted. "Ira started talking about the casting of the Duchess again as if I had never mentioned you," Weill wrote on September 2. "There is a certain viciousness in his complete disregard of my desire in this respect—and that is so strange because Ira is

everything but vicious."[11]
Weill's growing suspicions
that Ira's wife, Leonore (called
Lee), was the snake in the
grass ignited one of the
Weills' most fevered vendet-
tas. "I wouldn't listen too
much what Lee is saying,"
Lenya assured Weill on
August 31. "She is a freak and
doesn't know anything anymore."[12] "Thank God, the
Queen of Roxbury Drive is
going to Mexico for two
weeks today," Weill reported
on September 6. "That might
help [in selling Ira on Lenya
for the Duchess]. [Lee] is such
a stupid cow. She tries to be
helpful, but she is too dumb
to understand the problems.
But [Ira] asks her . . . about
every line he is writing, but
what the hell, as long as he
turns out such first class
lyrics, it is alright with me."[13]

Weill urged Lenya to travel
to Los Angeles to audition for

Lenya and Weill at Brook House, around the time of
The Firebrand of Florence, 1945, in which Lenya costarred

Ira. "Darling, forget about Ira," Lenya advised Kurt on September 7, in
advance of her visit. "I will tell him, when I get out [to Los Angeles], that
he shouldn't carry on that much about that part and me playing it. I have
done more important parts and succeeded pretty well and if he doesn't
trust your judgment, he always can ask people like the Lunts or Helen
Hayes and so on. That'll fix him . . . he should shut up and wait. . . . If he
has no imagination, it's not our fault. After all, who knows him in
Europe?"[14] Working in tandem, Lenya and Weill succeeded—at least temporarily—in convincing Ira that she could play the part. Their campaign
to win Lenya the role revealed the deep sympathy between them; despite

Weill, lyricist Ira Gershwin, and librettist Edwin Justus Mayer, leering
at Catherine Littlefield, the choreographer of their show, *The Firebrand of
Florence.* Weill was rumored to be having an affair with Littlefield.

their seemingly successful adaptation to their new country, at heart they
remained two refugees huddling together against a world in which they
often felt misunderstood and unappreciated.

The leading role, written in a semioperatic range and requiring an actor
with a vibrant physical presence, was also proving hard to cast. Composer
and lyricist wanted opera star Lawrence Tibbett, but couldn't persuade
Max Gordon, their producer. When Weill, who should have known better,
suggested Nelson Eddy, Max Gordon in an August 30 letter wrote, "I am
not against him if you find that he can act. I have always been told that he
can't walk across the stage. We don't necessarily have to have names in this
show. Let's try to discover some people." Disregarding his own words,
however, for much of September Gordon was preoccupied trying to nab
Walter Slezak for the role of the Duke. Slezak, in fact, was a superb choice
for this Shakespearean-style buffoon, a compulsive poacher with a pen-

chant for malapropisms, and with his Viennese accent would provide pro-
tection for Lenya's otherwise anomalous presence as a duchess in Renaissance Florence. But Slezak wanted more money than Gordon was willing
to spend.

For Angela, the female lead, Susanna Foster and Kathryn Grayson, both
with trained soprano voices and attractive enough to justify the fact that
both Cellini and the Duke are infatuated with her, were sought but
unavailable. By mid-October, with Gordon hoping for a production by
early 1945, the show was still uncast, and Weill was faced with a fresh
round of objections to Lenya. "I read your letter to Ira and I was surprised
that you're still talking about Peggy Wood or Vivian [sic] Segal," Weill
wrote to his producer on October 17. "Neither of them would play the
part because it is too small, and it would be fatal if we would have to build
it up. I have made it very clear to you and everybody concerned that I want
Lotte Lenya (who happens to be Mrs. Weill) to play the part. I am sure this
is perfect casting, just as I was sure when I insisted on Mary Martin for
Venus. . . . The worst thing you could do to the show at this moment
would be to kill my enthousiasm which, up to now, has carried through
the whole project." Lenya was reinstated.

When the show, then called *Much Ado About Love,* began rehearsals in
December, Max Gordon batted a thousand in terms of his choice of director and performers: everyone was wrong. Because they had been impressed
by his openness to their musical experiments in *Lady in the Dark,* Weill
and Gershwin wanted Moss Hart to direct, but Gordon hired John Murray
Anderson, celebrated in the 1920s and 1930s for having conceived and
directed a series of opulent revues. Anderson had scant experience with
book shows and moreover seemed to have no sense of the style that was
needed for *this* show, a spoof of opéra comique. "Anderson was a charming
man, very amusing, but he tried to turn Weill's satirical operetta into a
circus," recalled Lys Symonette, a German-born musician Weill hired as
rehearsal pianist and general understudy, who was to work closely with
him for the remaining years of his life and who is now musical executive of
the Kurt Weill Foundation. "Like most Americans, including some theatre people at that time, Anderson didn't know who Weill was. He
thought he was just another Broadway composer. Anderson had worked at
Billy Rose's Diamond Horseshoe and with elephants for Barnum and Bai-
ley, and he wanted gorgeous showgirls."[15]

Because the producer was "so cheap—Gordon knew how to get money
but had no culture," according to Symonette—"he wouldn't spend the

money on Slezak" and hired a British actor, Melville Cooper, who didn't have Slezak's droll and juicy quality. "Cooper had no humor at all. He had such sad eyes, and big bags, and looked like a poor little beagle hound," Symonette said.[16] ("My style and Cooper's never ever jelled," Lenya recalled many years later, and repeated the mantra Weill had drilled into her, that if she had played opposite Walter Slezak "it would have been marvelous.")[17] Earl Wrightson and Beverly Tyler, the actors cast as Cellini and Angela, the hero's inamorata, a model who inspires one of his greatest statues, didn't have the magnetism to carry the show. "Wrightson was rather good-looking and he could sing, but his legs weren't so good, they were a little crooked, and he was always in tights. He had absolutely no sex appeal," Lys Symonette remembered.[18] Conductor Maurice Abravanel recalled that Wrightson's vocal coach told the actor, " 'You can't sing like that eight times a week. You have to control it, you have to be careful.' The moment he was careful vocally, he was careful in acting too. And instead of a dashing Cellini, he was a very passive one . . . a ninny. For Angela they hired a starlet who did not know the ABC of acting. And did not make up with a very good voice."[19] "Beverly Tyler was somebody's girlfriend, and she brought in money from MGM, which helped to get the show on," Lys Symonette said. "She was pretty, but not sexy, and couldn't sing."[20] "We resented her because she came from Hollywood; we thought the part should have been cast with a real New Yawker," Joan Bartels, a member of the chorus, recalled. "And Cellini should have been played by an actor with a strong sense of movement: in today's theatre, someone like Kevin Kline. Our star didn't have that."[21]

With mismatches everywhere, the performers stumbled through rehearsals. For Lenya, trapped opposite an incompatible Duke and stranded by the director and by her husband, the struggle was particularly acute. If Anderson wasn't helping Lenya, why didn't Weill, especially after he had fought so long to win her the role? "It was common knowledge that Lenya was going with one of the chorus boys, Paul Mario," Lys Symonette said.[22] Yet Weill would not have punished his wife for another amorous adventure—they had an understanding, after all, and a deep, enduring connection that transcended sex. Indeed, according to Symonette, Weill "hired Mario, who was rude and uncultured, really to keep Lenya happy. She was a sexy lady; for Weill, sex was in his music."[23] And besides, Weill was rumored to be having an affair with Catherine Littlefield, the show's choreographer. But still he did not come forward to protect or to help

Lenya. Although he was often blunt in his letters, it was Symonette's impression that face to face Weill "was not a fighter. At rehearsals, he was always very quiet, never made himself known that much. He wouldn't allow you to get close to him. He would look at you very, very sharply—really deep into your eyes. And he always had a little ironical smile, as if to say, 'Come on now.' He said very little; he never even made musical suggestions that anybody was aware of. He may have, on the side, to Maurice Abravanel, but in orchestra rehearsals he never made any remarks to the conductor in public."[24]

Along with the miscasting, Edwin Justus Mayer's book added to the doldrums. Mayer's original play, as Abravanel recalled, was "a big success, thanks partly to an incredible cast. Frank Morgan [the Wizard in *The Wizard of Oz*] played the Duke, Edward G. Robinson was the Duke's villainous scheming cousin, and Cellini was played by Joseph Schildkraut, who brought humor and gravity to the character. The book for our show didn't have the verve of the original. Mayer let them down. Kurt complained that he couldn't get him to work hard enough. Mayer needed insulin—diabetes. And in those days if you took insulin you had to take that much scotch. And so he was forever, you know, lit: in a haze."[25] Mayer nonetheless wrote characters—unlike Moss Hart's lady on the couch, for instance—who talked as if they might burst into song. But his Cellini was not the commanding antihero, the dashing Great Man of Destiny, he needed to be, and Mayer's clumsy farce plotting with its midsummer-night's-dream of romantic misalliances did not sustain dramatic momentum.

Adding insult to injury were the costumes. "The production was 'light' during rehearsals," Lenya recalled. "And then those cement costumes, it was like *Ziegfeld Follies* came in and drowned it musically. The costumes were heavy, they should have been floating. The production moved like glue. If that ever moves."[26] Perversely, the costumes covered up the showgirls Anderson had insisted on hiring.

But then there was the score—"marvelous, a comic opera in the Offenbach tradition of *The Grand Duchess of Gerolstein* or *Orpheus in the Underworld*," according to Abravanel[27]—the third and final collaboration of Kurt Weill and Ira Gershwin. "Whenever idiots talk about Weill going down in America, I have to scoff," Abravanel said. "Kaiser, even BB, was not a better lyric writer—I don't say poet—than Ira Gershwin, a very underrated guy."[28] "Ira and I played a lot of sixteenth century music (madrigals, Italian folk-dances etc.) and got very good ideas for the style of the score," Weill recalled.[29] And while the score is not precisely authentic to the sixteenth century—why should it have been?—the collaborators' homework paid off. The score not only evoked a Renaissance flavor, as well as the composer's comment on his sources; it also exhibited a melodic and harmonic unity that was rare in the composer's Broadway work. Melodic fragments that recur throughout—the Duchess, for instance, has her own entrance theme—achieve motivic force; and although it is not continuous, music supports the action to an unusual degree.

For the opening, Weill and Gershwin wrote what is one of the most enchanting and deftly constructed musical scenes in the entire literature of the American musical. Their act 1, scene 1—the dramatic conceit is the drawing-together of all the interested parties who await Cellini's imminent hanging—is a through-composed dazzler in which Weill knits together many disparate numbers: recitatives, ariosi, a funeral march, a dance, choral ensembles, and a full-blown aria for Cellini. The Hangman begins with a sturdy modal ballad; the gallows builders sing a contrasting madrigal in 6/8 time; there is some standard "traveling music" for sellers of souvenirs; and the Florentines sing paeans to their hometown. This last element brings a witty Gershwin text ("Praises in torrents / We shower on Florence") that Weill beautifully sets above a catchy bolero rhythm. When the locals segue into a brief dance break, Weill's sophisticated harmony and masterful polyrhythm could make you think you are hearing *West Side Story* twelve years before the fact. And this is all prior to the entrance of the villain, the reading of a will, the hero's culminating aria, the reprieve, and the reversal of the whole form—Florentines, souvenir sellers, gallows builders, Hangman, all in inverted order—that provides a flourishing finale. As Lenya exclaimed when she first heard Weill play through the scene, "You will have to keep the doors locked, so no late comers can disturb that beautiful first scene. And Cellini's song ["Life, Love, and Laughter"], that could be *Don Giovanni*."[30] The rest of the show, too often pausing for prose, never attained the radiance or the sheer musical-theatre cunning of the first scene.

In only two places besides the opening was Weill allowed to write extended musical scenes. At the end of act 1, as identities are confused and lovers traded, he wrote an operetta finaletto, marked as "finale alla Tarantella," in which he combined melodrama (music underlining and accenting dialogue), a dance number, brief reprises delivered as solos, duets, and massed ensembles. The only musical scene in act 2 is set during Cellini's trial, when once again the hero outwits a death sentence—and Weill had to campaign to be able to do it. "We are making a mistake just by musicalizing the first part of the trial," he wrote Ira on November 25, right before the start of rehearsals. "The whole trial scene should be another complete musical-lyrical conception, a complete equivalent (in form) to our opening scene." The trial scene isn't as closely worked as the bejeweled opening, but provided a needed balance to it; without a musical scene in act 2, as Weill realized, the show's structure would have become seriously skewed. Here again Weill weaves multiple numbers (some reprised from the opening scene) and adds a delicious blues snatched from the discard pile for *Lady in the Dark.* In this climactic number, which is to ensure his pardon, Cellini argues that "if you have to do what you do do / Whatever you do, you're not to blame."

> *Was Plato to blame for being Platonic?*
> *Or Babylon for being Babylonic?*
> *Was Caesar to blame for being Cesarian?*
> *Or the people for being proletarian?*[31]

"Am I to blame for acting like Benvenuto?" the firebrand concludes. What judge or jury, what audience, could resist the argument, couched in Weill's jazzlike rhythm (a breather from the faux-Renaissance syntax) and Ira's rhymes?

Conceived as separate numbers, the rest of the score pales against the musical scenes. Highlights include "You're Far Too Near Me," an elegant and sweeping waltz duet for Cellini and Angela. Weill thought the waltz "a peach . . . tailor made for the scene—and also a great song. And that combination, a great song in the right spot, is a nice thing to have. Ira calls [my] tune one of the great waltz melodies ever written!!!"[32] In the song, in which occasional shadows anticipate the show's bittersweet ending, Angela expresses her fears that the great man will ultimately leave her.

"We finished the Duke's entrance song yesterday which, I think, will rank next to any Offenbach or Gilbert and Sullivan song of that type," Weill crowed to Lenya.[33] But the entrance song proved in the production to be no more than serviceable stitching around a few clever lyrics, as when the courtiers encourage the plebeians by singing, "Hail the man you subsidize— / Alessandro the Wise!" In two other comic numbers Weill's music was no more than a neutral setting for Ira's wordplay. "I know where there's a nosy cook," the randy Duke courts Angela in "The Nozy Cook." "My lord, you mean a cozy nook," Angela corrects. "Yes, yes! Of course! A cozy nook for two. / And there we two can kill and boo." "A Rhyme for Angela" is again time out for Ira to spin ingenious rhymes. As Cellini muses,

> *If only her name were Olivia,*
> *She could be a cute bit of trivia;*
> *If she were tagged Maria,*
> *Or even Dorothea,*
> *She'd be my Sole Mia*
> *Divine.*

> *I can find a rhyme for Irma:*
> *She's Heaven on Terra Firma.*
> *But Angela has no patter—*
> *And yet, what does it matter*
> *If Angela's heart rhymes with mine!*

And "what does it matter," with rhymes like these, if the song is no more than a divertissement *en passant*?

If the show paused from time to time for Ira to show off, Weill was accorded a similar courtesy. A choral number, "Just in Case" ("We're soldiers of a duchy / Whose Duke is very touchy"), seemed introduced to prove that Weill could write a sturdy operetta march, even if it wasn't needed. And a big choral number, "When the Duchess Is Away," offered evidence of Weill's undimmed skill in writing complex vocal ensembles. A duet full of minor, chromatically twisted progressions, "Love Is My Enemy" clearly portended the end of the affair. The tense harmonies and the far-from-sparkling lyrics (Ira always resisted conventional love songs) result in a pretentious, self-consciously "big" number.

> *Love is my enemy, My beloved enemy,*
> *And you, my love, are love.*

In his November 25 letter to Ira, Weill described the number, then called "Man's Love," as "that song that Cellini needs in the second act because it expresses the whole idea of the show." And regrettably, indeed it did.

> *Love is my destiny; work is my enemy,*
> *Urging you onward, ever onward,*

as Angela summarized, seemingly endorsing the writers' conviction that man's destiny is work while romance is woman's domain.

Against Weill's objections, the show did not end with this bittersweet leavetaking (conventional in operettas about romances crossing class lines), but at John Murray Anderson's insistence included a final scene set in Versailles, where Cellini has become the court artist. Included only for the opulent spectacle that was the director's forte, the scene offered no new musical numbers, only some dances, principally a sarabande, an orchestral version of "Love Is My Enemy," and a full-company reprise of the opening number, "The bell of doom is clanging." Matched against the incandescent opening, the musically undernourished coda gave the show a broken-backed form, just as Weill feared it would.

For Lenya, Weill wrote only one song, "Sing Me Not a Ballad." The number had to be a showcase for Lenya's sui generis voice and style, and of a quality that would justify the composer's long campaign on her behalf. "We still haven't got the right idea for the Duchess' song," Weill had informed Lenya on August 27.[34] (And why only one song for the Duchess, when her counterpart, the foolish Duke, was given numerous musical spots, one or two more than were really needed?) Although they short-changed her, and it took them a long time to get the "right idea," Weill and Gershwin did write a strong comic song for Lenya, both ribald and rueful. In counterpoint to Ira's insouciant lyrics, Weill's melody and harmonies introduce a few autumnal shadings to inform the listener that the Duchess desires, but does not expect to win, love.

> *I am not like Circe,*
> *Who showed men no mercy;*
> *Men are most important in my life,*

the openly hot-to-trot Duchess declares. "Spare me your advances— / Just, oh just make love!" she concludes, lightly yet imploringly. Written for Lenya's limited range and the parlando style she had perfected in Berlin, the song was stitched to the measure of its unique performer. However, as it derided the Duchess as a lusty woman destined not to get the guy, it turned Lenya's homeliness and her sexual voracity into a comic spectacle with masochistic overtones. And unwittingly or not, Weill kept compounding the insult against his wife: "I had a wonderful idea for the entrance of the Duchess," he had written on July 20. "She is carried

A comic couple with eyes for others: the voracious Duke (Melville
Cooper) and Duchess (Lenya, miscast) in *The Firebrand of Florence*. Raoul
Pène DuBois designed the costumes; the show's set and lighting
designer was Jo Mielziner.

through the street in a sedan-chair . . . preceded by a little band of negro
boys; that's how she plays the first scene with Cellini. Good?"[35] No. "I saw
The Firebrand of Florence on opening night," Paula Laurence recalled.
"Lenya came in in a closed sedan chair—it was like an entrance from *Aida*.
When she stepped out, done up to look like Mary Martin, it was embar-
rassing, a travesty. After that entrance, she needed something wonderful to
sing or to speak, and they had left her empty-handed."[36]

. . .

When, as *Much Ado About Love,* the show opened a tryout engagement in Boston on February 23, 1945, the creators expected to be savaged. But to their surprise the reviews were mild. In his February 25 review, Elliott Norton called Weill's score "richly operatic in quality, yet melodic and full of wonderful popular songs . . . the loveliest score since *Oklahoma!*" Knowing well he had a show in trouble, however, Max Gordon summoned the usual brigade of play doctors, including George S. Kaufman and Elia Kazan. "Everyone who came up to Boston just threw up their hands," Lys Symonette recalled.[37] There was tinkering and trimming and a change of title from *Much Ado About Love* to *The Firebrand of Florence,* but when the show opened on Broadway on March 22 the reviews were much less approving. In the most damning notice, the curmudgeonly George Jean Nathan, no fan of musical theatre and especially not operetta, sneered that "it lacks only a little music by Wagner to constitute it a first rate funeral. . . . [Weill] is a lightly pleasant composer who at times, notably in *The Threepenny Opera,* has written proficiently. But he hasn't the strength or the fullness of musical imagination and resource to work any such miracle in this case. It takes music of an uncommon sort to make any stage costume show capture the necessary fragrant mood . . . and when the book is as sour as that of *The Firebrand of Florence,* it would require the service of Lehár, [Edmund] Eysler, Kálmán, and Victor Herbert operating in combination and in peak form to win over [contemporary] audiences to it, or to get them, at least, to suspend judgment regarding it."[38]

With no stars and mostly downbeat notices, the show's survival was out of the question. *The Firebrand of Florence* seemed like a back number. Rather than the new Broadway-opera form Weill and Gershwin had hoped to create, their show seemed antiquated, almost beside the point in both style and subject matter in an era beginning to be dominated by the Rodgers and Hammerstein musical play. Had the composer and lyricist been permitted to write a through-composed score, the show might still have failed to find an audience, but it would have realized Weill's ambition of introducing a new music-theatre language to Broadway. As it was, with a score continually pierced and deflated by a libretto that failed to turn Cellini into an antihero with something to say to audiences of the time, *The Firebrand of Florence* must be counted as Weill's one full-scale Broadway flop. The show expired after forty-three performances.

"Ouch!" Weill would say in later years whenever *The Firebrand of Florence* was mentioned. "The dramatist who had written the libretto was a total fiasco," Weill wrote in an April 30 letter to his parents. "Outside of Lenya (who gave a magnificent portrait of the Duchess of Florence) the cast wasn't very good and this time we didn't have any big star names." As to his own work, Weill boasted it was "the best I have written in years, a real opera with big choral and ensemble numbers full of melodic invention." "The failure hasn't touched me much," he protested. "I've gotten long since used to the ups and downs of success, and for a long time now I've been very conscious of the fact that, after the two gigantic successes, a setback has been overdue. Somehow I'm even glad that I'm not falling into the routine of a career of successes . . . as long as I'm trying to do something new with each work, which in many instances is ahead of its time."

"I am firmly convinced (and that is the official stand I take) that my score and your performance were the only interesting things in the show and that it was our bad luck that everything else went wrong," Weill wrote Lenya from Los Angeles on April 25. "So all we can do is to forget all about it. I had fun writing it and hearing the orchester [*sic*] and chorus and you had fun rehearsing—and a lot of people saw you playing comedy like nobody else can play it. And that's all we got out of it." But he added, "What is all this anyhow when you think that the Russians are in Berlin? Isn't is fantastic how unprepared those Nazis were for defeat?"[39] For the Kurt Weills, both by now American citizens—Weill had become a citizen on August 27, 1943; Lenya on May 5, 1944—Germany's resounding defeat was an occasion of great relief. But even the prospect of a Germany rid of Nazis did not make either of them long for their former home. They identified thoroughly with their new country, and continued to regard Germany as enemy territory they had no intention of revisiting. Weill continued to rail against the country and its citizens and refused as much as possible either to speak German or to socialize with Germans. Lenya shared his animosity.

Unfolding events in Europe—the defeat of the Third Reich, the liberation of the concentration camps—certainly superseded any news from the rialto, but perhaps because of the world-shaking headlines the theatre had a thriving season. There were two landmark musicals. The first, *On the Town*, had a score (his first for Broadway) by Leonard Bernstein, a composer, like Kurt Weill, from the other side of the musical street. His first time at bat, and for the most part camouflaging his classical background, Bernstein produced a remarkable pop score filled with ballads and comic numbers that remain among the choicest in the literature. (Weill, however, had not been enthusiastic when he saw *Fancy Free,* the ballet by Jerome Robbins and Bernstein that was the genesis of the musical. "That much heralded *Fancy Free* is what I suspected after those hysterical outbreaks of the critics: a phony," he wrote in an August 12, 1944, letter to Lenya. "It has a charming idea and is, on the whole, rather fresh and amusing, but seeing it after *Romeo and Juliet* is like hearing 'Oh, what a beautiful morning' after the *Mattheus-passion* [of Bach]."[40] Unfairly, Weill was guilty here of the highbrow condescension often directed against his own work.) A topical musical about sailors on twenty-four-hour leave, *On the Town* was a show for its own time, however, as a series of failed revivals have indicated. Bernstein's glorious score simply cannot compensate for the shallow, dated, blackout-sketch book by Betty Comden and Adolph Green. The other musical behemoth (and one that has been successfully revived) was Rodgers and Hammerstein's *Carousel,* a musical play that included extended musical scenes and a bravura soliloquy for its hero.

Musty operettas such as *Song of Norway,* with a score drawn from music by Edvard Grieg, and *Up in Central Park,* with a score by Sigmund Romberg, and splashy revues such as *The Seven Lively Arts* and *Concert Varieties,* both produced by Billy Rose, were less consequential offerings. Olsen and Johnson, the knockabout, low-rent vaudevillians, were back with *Laffing Room Only. Bloomer Girl,* set in the Civil War, with a score by Harold Arlen and lyrics by E. Y. Harburg and featuring another Agnes de Mille ballet, was a second-tier success; *Sadie Thompson,* a musical version of *Rain* with a score by Vernon Duke and lyrics by Howard Dietz, a second-tier failure. A peculiar footnote was provided by two musicals derived from *H.M.S. Pinafore* (oddly mirroring the rival *Mikado* musicals the season before): *Memphis Bound* and *Hollywood Pinafore,* the latter produced by Max Gordon, with a book by George S. Kaufman and a ballet by Antony Tudor. Both folded quickly. *The Firebrand of Florence* was the season's most prestigious failure, a distinguished misbegotten enterprise.

THIRTEEN

Street Opera

A few months after *The Firebrand of Florence* closed, Olin Downes, music critic of the *New York Times* since 1924, asked Weill if he would be interested in writing a short folk opera for radio. Downes, with a bias against European modernism and a strong interest in national and folk material, had sponsored *Railroads on Parade* when in 1938–39 he served as music director of the New York World's Fair and was therefore well aware of Weill's populist inclinations. Acting as matchmaker, Downes introduced Weill to a young playwright, Arnold Sundgaard, who had a strong interest in American folk music. (Ninety-three at this writing, Sundgaard is Weill's only living collaborator.) "When Downes called me in to meet with the composer of *The Threepenny Opera*, I had no idea what he was talking about," Sundgaard recalled. But after he became aware of Weill's European reputation, the modest writer was "daunted" by the assignment that had been handed to him. "I thought I had the germ of a story that would fit the kind of folk material Downes was looking for. When I had lived in the mountains of Virginia in 1939–40, among mountain people who would ask my wife and me to listen to string music, a cross between country music and folk song, among the songs I heard was 'Down in the Valley.' I felt that song suggested the kind of story we could write. Kurt had a volume of folk music he had studied—he was very predisposed; and when I got to know his work I realized that *Johnny Johnson* had a folk quality."[1]

The partners decided that the score would weave original music with traditional folk material, thereby casting Weill in a familiar role of musical ventriloquist. "Once we had agreed on a scenario, Kurt worked with amazing speed," Sundgaard recalled. "He preferred having the words first. I revised the lyrics for the traditional songs, sometimes adding a little bit, sometimes quite a bit. I would do three or four drafts before handing my work to Kurt—I seem to have had an innate sense of music—and he would make suggestions, such as a vowel sound is easier to sing than a consonant. I would write lyrics to my own dummy melodies, to which my words fit, and asked Kurt if he wanted to hear them. He was very definite about *not* wanting to hear them. 'Oh, God no,' he said. 'Not at all.' He said it would just throw him off. He said Brecht used to write tunes and impose them on him, and it drove him crazy. I always accepted the first melody he gave—it was flattering to hear your words set to music." Weill's confidence, surehandedness, and "very businesslike approach" put his young collaborator, "surprised at how easy it came," at ease.[2]

Because their short, twenty-six-minute work, intended to launch a series of radio ballad operas, needed a sponsor, the cowriters held "four or five auditions on Park Avenue in rather large apartments," as Sundgaard remembered. "Downes did a little introduction, Kurt played and sang, in his high, squeaky voice, and I did whatever the speaking parts were. When it was over, both of us were quite emotional about what we had written. It was always Weill's original music that would move me to tears," Sundgaard said. After the piano tryouts, the piece was orchestrated and recorded for audition purposes. "People seemed to like it, but nothing happened."[3]

Weill remained unshaken despite the failure to sell *Down in the Valley* or the projected radio series. "I wanted to tell you how proud I am to be connected with this project," he wrote Charles McArthur, an advertising executive who had had the idea for the series, on January 21, 1946.

I have been convinced for a long time that in a deeply democratic country like ours, art should belong to the people. It should come out of their thinking and their emotions and it should become part of their lives. It should be "popular" in the highest sense of the word. Only by making this our aim can we create an American art, as opposed to the art of the old countries which belonged to a selected class of aristocrats or "connoisseurs." The natural basis for the creation of an American music is the American folksong. *Down in the Valley* is a new way of making the folksong the basic element of an American art-form . . . a ballad-opera [which] exploit[s] the old American habit of storytelling and . . . present[s] the folksong in its most natural surroundings. . . . What could be a more natural medium for the presentation of these modern "ballad-operas" than the radio?

In this ringing manifesto, Weill embraced concepts of *Gebrauchsmusik* and *Lehrstück* he had pursued—and clearly not abandoned—in Berlin.

At the time he wrote to McArthur, however, Weill had put *Down in the Valley* in a drawer because he had become preoccupied with a larger project which had a greater professional stake. In Berlin in 1929 he had seen a play by Elmer Rice called *Street Scene* which had seemed to him intoxicatingly American. Taking place in front of a New York apartment house, Rice's verismo drama depicts the comings and goings of the building's ethnically diverse tenants. The characters are flatly conceived, little more than stage Irish, stage Italians, and stage Jews familiar from vaudeville. And the plot hinges on a melodramatic contrivance—an extramarital affair ends in tragedy when the husband, after discovering his wife's infidelity, kills her and her lover. Yet for all its limitations the play achieves a tragedy-of-the-common-man aura, and when he saw it Weill sensed the musical possibilities in Rice's urban cross-section. Now that he was in America he saw in the work the seeds for a new kind of Broadway opera that would rival the Rodgers and Hammerstein musical play. When he had first met the play's author at the time of *Knickerbocker Holiday,* Weill had mentioned his idea of turning *Street Scene* into a musical. Rice had abruptly rejected the notion, and since then had continued to turn down requests from other composers. But when Weill returned from Hollywood in the late spring of 1945, at a point when both he and Rice were without immediate projects, he repeated his interest in *Street Scene,* and this time Rice relented.

But in a letter he wrote on June 28 to William Schuman, another composer who had expressed interest in the play, Rice indicated strong reservations about turning *Street Scene* into a musical. "Whatever prestige value there would be in a successful musical version would rightfully accrue primarily to the composer and secondly to [the] author of lyrics, who would not be myself," he maintained. Rice admitted to Schuman, however, that

Weill, librettist Elmer Rice, and lyricist Langston Hughes are smiling in this publicity photo for *Street Scene,* but they were to have intense conflicts.

he had agreed in principle to work with Kurt Weill on what he just claimed he did not want to do. "Of course, the objections I have set forth to the whole idea of a musical version would apply to Kurt, who is an old friend and has had many years of experience in the theatre." Only a composer as confident as Weill, and one, moreover, schooled in navigating his way around egoistic writers (could Elmer Rice possibly be more difficult than the double-dealing Brecht?), would have entered the ring for round one against a living writer hovering possessively over his sacred text. Well aware of the problems that lay ahead working with the stubborn, brooding, truculent, widely disliked playwright—by all accounts, as Lys Symonette attested, "a thoroughly disagreeable man"[4]—Weill was unfazed.

Once Rice decided to move forward, an appropriate lyricist—the other cowriter who would be treading on Rice's closely watched property—had to be found. Though it is not possible to prove one way or the other, Weill and Rice each claimed the idea of asking Langston Hughes, the distinguished black poet who had been a prominent figure in the Harlem Renaissance. Whoever it was who asked him, Hughes needed no coaxing. "I am delighted at the prospect of working on a play that I remember as one of my great evenings in the theatre," he wrote Rice on October 23,

1945. "I think it will make a terrific music-drama in a form quite new to the American stage."

Because Rice was a member of the Playwrights Producing Company, *Street Scene* had a ready-made producer. But the problematic nature of the project, a Broadway opera with a tragic ending, made Rice's colleagues wary. This was going to be an expensive show with marginal commercial prospects, and to proceed the company informed Rice that an outside producer with deep pockets was a necessity. Rice was "bitter," as Walter Alford, associate publicist for the company, recalled. "The other members had more successful plays than he did, but Rice kept trying and as a courtesy they produced his works. But he always complained because he thought the others were getting preferential treatment. He was a very difficult man."[5] Weill, who took an active role in locating an outside producer, first approached Mary Pickford, who at that point was to produce the film of *One Touch of Venus*. Pickford agreed, but then withdrew. As he had done for *Down in the Valley,* Weill auditioned the score on the Park Avenue circuit. "This man had to sit at the piano and humiliate himself by having to play," Lys Symonette recalled. "He sang some of the songs, too, in his very high tenor that had a lovely quality. I remember one audition at Howard Cullman's, a very cultured man—people were rude, noisy, and drank a lot. As Weill sang 'Lonely House,' a dog came in and then a maid. And in a loud, drunken voice Billy Rose ordered, 'Play it again, Kurt, the one about the lonely heart.' You could feel Weill's tenseness, but he proceeded, because that's the way it was done here."[6] There were no takers, however, and *Street Scene* might have remained unseen if Dwight Deere Wiman, a wealthy investor who had backed numerous musicals, hadn't fallen in love with it. "His complete faith in the show kept it going," Lys Symonette observed.[7]

As he was scrambling for money and working closely with first-time Broadway lyricist Langston Hughes (Hughes had written an opera libretto for William Grant Still), Weill was invited to become a full-fledged member of the Playwrights Producing Company. "They were shorthanded," as Walter Alford recalled. Robert Sherwood had taken a leave of absence to write a book about Harry Hopkins; and S. N. Behrman bowed out because, according to Alford, "he just wanted to be a writer, not to attend endless meetings about money. Kurt Weill"—who accepted the invitation eagerly—"didn't seem to mind the endless money meetings."[8] Publicity releases called Weill the group's only nonplaywright member—an inaccurate assessment, because, as Maxwell Anderson, Behrman, and now Rice could attest, Weill was in fact a collaborative dramatist in the guise of a composer.

A man who did not have a light touch on the page or in personal relations, Rice had no sense of how to construct the book for a musical yet resented Weill's suggestions. Rice "did not want to drop one single line of his play," Maurice Abravanel, who would conduct, recalled. "Every time Kurt wanted to cut, Rice would thunder, 'Now this was a celebrated line.' To him, every line was a museum's item."[9] In order to protect his work from Rice, Weill was determined to select a director who would be sympathetic to the show's musical intentions. His first choice was Rouben Mamoulian, who had directed *Porgy and Bess,* Weill's favorite American show, as well as *Oklahoma!* and *Carousel.* "Excellent idea," Mamoulian, in Hollywood, wired Weill on January 19, 1946, after Weill offered him the job. "Have always loved *Street Scene* and think it can make exciting musical." Within hours of receiving his telegram, Weill wrote Mamoulian outlining the general approach he and Rice, after many months of heated discussions, had agreed on. "We will do it in one set like the original play (the whole form of the play, like in the ancient Greek tragedy, is based on unity of time, place and action), to avoid the conventional musical comedy technique and to work it out as a kind of popular Broadway opera (the dialogue will be spoken, but underscored, so that the audience should never know where the dialogue ends and the song starts—and by 'song' I mean arias, duets, trios and all forms of musical ensembles, and some real songs too). . . . I know how much you always have been interested in this form of musical theatre where music and drama are completely integrated, and I also know that you have the technique and the experience in staging this type of show like nobody else in this country." Weill informed Mamoulian that the love story, between the gentile heroine, Rose Maurrant, and a Jew, Sam Kaplan, would be "made more important and more passionate" than in the original play; that Rice's left-leaning political slant would be considerably softened (Hughes also had some notoriety as a leftist); that Sam, "instead of being always the beaten Jew, will be the young poet trying to adjust himself to the world and the hateful surroundings he is living in"; and that because of events in Europe anti-Semitic sentiments expressed by some of the neighbors would be eliminated. Mamoulian would have been an ideal director, but he turned down the project in favor of more lucrative offers from Hollywood.

Weill continued his search for a director who was neither Broadway lite, on the one hand, nor grand-opera heavy, on the other. But as he was immersed in the many problems of preparing *Street Scene*, in the late summer he received yet another call from Ben Hecht asking him to provide the music for another pageant. Hecht's *A Flag Is Born* was a propaganda piece commissioned by the American League for a Free Palestine and was to be staged within a month. Although preoccupied with his opera, Weill could not refuse a request from a friend for a cause he supported. Hecht's *We Will Never Die* had been a cry of protest and a warning; his new work was in effect a companion piece, another story of Jewish suffering etched with pride and resolve. In *A Flag Is Born* Hecht dramatized the urgency of founding a Jewish state for the survivors of Nazi persecution. Hecht asked for incidental music only, but notes in his script made significant demands. For the overture, for instance, he wanted "wild, bold music" that "cries out as if a world of torment and exultation were waiting behind the closed curtain." Under the circumstances, Weill could not devote more than perfunctory attention to the assignment. His incidental score, unpublished and lost, consisted of approximately fifteen numbers. Among them are the Kol Nidre theme, Jewish folk melodies, the "Hatikvah," the Kaddish, a medley of national songs (including the "Marseillaise," the Red Army March, and "Give My Regards to Broadway"!). And once again (and why not?) Weill used quotations from *The Eternal Road,* including motifs from the stories of Saul, David, and Solomon as well as the Wandering theme. Weill's scoring was divided between martial thunder—a pealing trumpet fanfare, a beating of cymbals, rolling drums, and fifes—and celestial repose, with lutes, lyres, and choral chants. In the climax, as Hecht's resolute young hero, David, turned toward "the shining bridge," holding high the flag of the nation yet to be born, Weill entwined the "Hatikvah" with strains of "Yankee Doodle" and "Over There." Because of the time pressure and the demands of *Street Scene,* Weill allowed Isaac van Grove, who had conducted *The Eternal Road,* to prepare the arrangements. *A Flag Is Born* opened on schedule at the Alvin Theatre on September 5, 1946. Directed by Luther Adler, it starred Paul Muni, Celia Adler, and a young Marlon Brando. In the *New York Herald-Tribune,* Howard Barnes called the enterprise "distinctly dubious," theatrically speaking, while Nat Kahn in the September 11 *Variety* cut to the chase: "The show socks hard as Palestine propaganda."

When *A Flag Is Born* opened, Weill was still looking for a director for *Street Scene.* He approached the relatively unknown Charles Friedman, who the previous season had directed *Carmen Jones,* Oscar Hammerstein's pop-opera version of Bizet's *Carmen.* Weill had had a mixed response to Hammerstein's adaptation and to the production, but noted appreciatively that Friedman had guided to commercial success a show in which opera merged with Broadway musical theatre. (When *Carmen Jones* rather than *One Touch of Venus* won a best score award from *Billboard,* Lenya delivered a pep talk to Kurt at the same time that she clobbered the competition. "I was so mad, when they gave *Carmen Jones* the award," she wrote on July 7, 1944. "Those snobs. Especially what they did with that score. It makes me furious to think, how little they know about you. But maybe after the war you will have the chance to write operas again and then see what will be left of that Hillbilly show *Oklahoma.*")[10] Charles

Opera singers adjusting to the demands of a Broadway musical, Norman Cordon and Polyna Stoska (who played Mr. and Mrs. Maurrant) discuss *Street Scene* with the show's conductor, Maurice Abravanel.

Friedman was indeed aware of the kind of balance needed for "opera" on Broadway. "In rehearsals he told Kurt that the show was too gray and needed some Rodgers and Hammerstein–type material," Lys Symonette recalled.[11]

For the starring roles, Weill wanted the hard-to-find combination of singers who had an operatic range and were also solid actors. Working closely with Friedman and Rice, Weill cast opera singers for the four major parts. Soprano Polyna Stoska from the New York City Opera (who later would appear at the Met) and the Met basso Norman Cordon were chosen to play the unhappily married Maurrants. Tenor Richard Manning, whom Weill had seen at the Met in a small role in *The Barber of Seville,* was cast as Sam, the Jewish intellectual. Only Anne Jeffreys, cast as the Maurrants' daughter, Rose, was not from a strictly operatic background, although she was a classically trained soprano. "I was under contract to RKO, but had gotten permission to sing in *Tosca* at the Brooklyn Academy of Music," Jeffreys said. "After *Tosca* opened, I received write-ups about 'starlet sings opera.' Following the second performance, Maurice [Abravanel] and Kurt came backstage to ask if I would be interested in doing a Broadway show. Kurt asked me to come to his producer's office, which was above the Adelphi Theatre, to listen to the score. He sat at a little upright piano and sang in his squeaky voice. His hair kind of stuck out on the sides a little bit, and he had funny little eyes with thick glasses and a funny little grin. He was small and oh, just so cute! I called him the koala bear; Maurice was big and blustery, and I called him the polar bear. Almost as soon as Kurt began to play and sing his score, I started to cry, and by the end I was dissolved in tears. From the office I called RKO and said I wanted an extension so I could do the show, and they granted it."[12]

Integrating opera-trained performers into a Broadway show presented many problems. "They would just stand and sing—there was no acting," Jeffreys said, admitting to a bias against opera singers she has continued to hold fifty years later. "In those days opera singers were interested only in themselves. Really, they were a little ridiculous, and so affected. Only four of us in the company were not of this opera cult. When they'd leave the theatre, the scarves were up to the eyes and they wouldn't talk to you when they were out in the cold. Unlike the opera people, I didn't have to pamper myself. I didn't have to rest before a show. I left that to the opera singers— there was enough of that to go around."[13]

In time Polyna Stoska managed to adjust to the Broadway schedule of eight performances a week, but the two men could not. From the beginning, Weill had been opposed to casting Cordon, an alcoholic, but, as Lys Symonette recalled, "Dwight Wiman wanted a Metropolitan Opera name, and so he hired Cordon against Weill's objections. Weill wanted my husband, Randolph Symonette, who played the Hangman in *The Firebrand of Florence,* to sing the role, and he wound up doing it after Cordon became incapacitated."[14] Richard Manning had to be replaced during tryouts. "His voice couldn't get over the orchestra," Lys Symonette said.[15] "He was physically right for the part, a frail, pasty-faced little thing, a typical tenor type, always with a scarf, looked like a puff of wind would knock him over," Anne Jeffreys said. "When they fired him, he was crushed. I cried for him. I heard that a few years later he committed suicide." He was replaced with Brian Sullivan, an operatically trained Irish-American tenor—not exactly ideal casting for a high-strung Jewish scholar. "He looked like a big bear, square and stodgy, and he was stolid in his singing and acting," according to Anne Jeffreys. "Certainly he was hired for his singing, not his acting. Flamboyant, noisy, rough—and when he sang he planted his feet on that floor; you couldn't have blown him over with a cyclone. He pounced on me, and I never trusted him again." "Don't ever touch me when I'm singing," he warned Jeffreys after she leaned on him one night when she was ill, just before he hit a high note. "Many years later, Brian was found floating in Lake Como, another suicide," Jeffreys said.[16]

During the long and difficult collaborative process, Weill's goal was to include as much music as he could get past Elmer Rice; during the equally troubled rehearsals, his concern was to achieve a musical balance between opera and Broadway. Aiming for a complete blend of music with words and action, the composer wanted to avoid "too many stops for applause, especially in the beginning when we should establish the form of the show." Instead of "the number technique of musical comedy" Weill sought a "flowing technique" in which breaks between the spoken and the sung word would be eliminated, as much as his colleagues would allow.[17] Remarkably, although many passages of Rice's original dialogue are untouched—or, as Rice might have argued, "uncontaminated"—by music, Weill's score has a through-composed texture. Underscoring links speech to song as it also enfolds the entire show in a web of musical echoes and cross-references—the movielike melodrama scenes, in which speech is delivered against musical underscoring, intentionally refute a conventional dialogue-number-dialogue format. Except, curiously, in the final scene, Weill does not compose *against* the text, as in epic opera, but rather to support its overheated emotions. The music's inner voice is psychological as opposed to social, and for this distinctly non-Brechtian street scene the composer banishes irony in favor of a direct emotional appeal—taking his cue from the original play, his score is a snapshot rather than an indictment of an American way of life. Managing, then, to seize an almost unbroken ground for his score, Weill accomplished exactly what Rice had feared: It is the music that is the show's first cause, its focus and motor.

Having won space for his music, Weill then had to defend its style(s).

The heavily hybridized score contains two blues numbers, "I Got a Marble and a Star" and "Lonely House"; a parody of Italian opera, the Ice-Cream Sextet; a mock-Straussian number, "We'll Go Away Together"; a soft-shoe number, "Wouldn't You Like to Be on Broadway?"; a jitterbug, "Moon-Faced, Starry-Eyed"; a slow fox torch song, "What Good Would the Moon Be?"; and two children's songs, "Fat, Fat, the Water Rat" and "Catch Me If You Can." Some of the numbers are composed in the traditional Broadway ABAB or AABA formats; many others are written in freer, irregular patterns with flowing lines that disregard most of the stencils for Broadway melody-making of the time. From the beginning of the project, in all his letters and public pronouncements, Weill always took special care to refer to the show as a Broadway—that is, a popular—opera. But of course Weill recognized that his "opera" would have to be adjusted to the realities of the Broadway market. As a result, lighter numbers that conform to Broadway formulas alternate throughout the show with material (labeled variously as aria, arioso, cavatina, arietta, and finaletto) with an operatic or semi-operatic caste.

The Broadway-style numbers have often been trotted out as prime evidence of Weill's concessions to American commercialism, on the one hand, and of the impossibility of writing a "pure" opera for Broadway, on the other. Of course *Street Scene* is *not* grand opera but, as Weill specified, an opera for Broadway; but did the self-imposed "opera" label, both at the time and ever since, however loosely Weill himself may have applied it, create unnecessary problems for critical reception of the work in America? "There was the agony what to call it," Maurice Abravanel recalled. "It is an opera. But you could not call it opera—that's poison for Broadway. I think it was called, finally, a musical play."[18] (It was called a "dramatic musical.") A hybrid of Broadway and opera, like *Mahagonny, Street Scene* requires opera singers and so is at home in an opera house. To be sure, the work's musical variety, its many "Rodgers and Hammerstein" touches violate standard opera etiquette in both a formal and a musical sense; but isn't that exactly Weill's point?

During rehearsals, often at the request of Charles Friedman, Weill was asked to bring in new material for exactly the kinds of theatrical considerations—pacing, contrast, production values—that are a standard part of creating the great hybrid called the Broadway musical. For a key spot in act 1, Weill began to compose a melting-pot ensemble he called "A Nation of Nations," in which each of the ethnic groups that comprise the street scene would be given music evocative of their national origins. To the composer, the pastiche number was to contain a musical and thematic résumé of the entire show. Right before it, Frank Maurrant, the wronged husband, was to perform an angry aria, "Let Things Be Like They Always Was," filled with gnarled Weillian chords, and Friedman felt that the melting-pot number lacked relief and contrast. " 'We need to brighten things up here,' the director told Weill," as Lys Symonette remembered. "So he added a song, 'Wrapped in a Ribbon and Tied in a Bow,' which sounds like R&H, and it became the big production number Friedman wanted, with people dancing in the street."[19] Outside Weill's usual range, "Wrapped in a Ribbon and Tied in a Bow" is a sweet, tinkly, up number sung by students celebrating their graduation—the title refers to the diplomas they have just received. It certainly "works," as it also fits into the setting. But it momentarily undoes the care Weill has taken to present the individual voices of his characters. Before and after this song, each character is defined by a specific sound—a characteristic musical palette. During "Wrapped in a Ribbon and Tied in a Bow," they lose their distinctiveness as they merge into a more generalized musical-comedy ensemble. Aware of the danger, Weill insisted during rehearsals that dialogue should interrupt the song before the ensemble could be posed for bows. Although he struggled to keep it from slickness, he entrusted the song's orchestration and arrangement to a professional orchestrator, Ted Royal.

Weill's second Broadway-style song, "Wouldn't You Like to Be on Broadway?" echoes Sportin' Life's temptation number, "There's a Boat Dat's Leavin' Soon for New York," in *Porgy and Bess*. It is a soft-shoe number, with a touch of tango in the bridge section, in which Rose's oily boss, Mr. Easter, sweet-talks her with the promise of stardom in return for her favors. Superbly performed by Don Saxon in an easy Broadway baritone, the silken show song threatened to stop the show. Weill counseled the director to take out the pose for applause at the end. And as another interruption he wanted Rose to sing a chorus of "What Good Would the Moon Be?" and "then have Easter answer her with a shortened version of the second chorus [of his song]."[20] The entwined songs would then dramatize the conflict between the characters, Easter's seduction rubbing against Rose's dewy romanticism, and thereby undercut the possibility of an unwanted break in the tension that a showstopping number would have caused.

"Moon-Faced, Starry-Eyed," a vigorous street dance in boogie-woogie rhythm, supplied a splash of local color near the end of the long first act. Written in a standard pop-song form, "Moon-Faced, Starry-Eyed" is first sung, then danced, by two street kids, the Jones family's trampy daughter,

Mae, and a neighbor swain, Dick McGann, with whom she goes out juk-
ing and drinking. "The number was positioned right," Danny Daniels,
who played Dick, recalled. "It gave the show a lift at the spot it needed
one. Anna [Sokolow, a pioneering figure in modern dance] worked with us
to make it look like street dancing—the style was expressive modern
dancing." Since the attempt was to make the dance look as much as possible a natural part of the street scene (and thereby anticipating *West Side
Story* ten years later), Daniels objected to the costume he had been given. "I
was very brash then, a hot young Broadway dancer, and I told the costume
designer, Lucinda Ballard, that the clothes she had for me made me look
like a dancer, when I was playing a kid down the block. They let me wear
what I had bought."[21]

"The characters were two young people who loved to dance, and it
didn't matter if they danced on the street or on top of the fire escape,"
Anna Sokolow recalled. Sokolow, one of the first choreographers to use
jazz, grew up on the Lower East Side in a Russian-Jewish working-class
family that could have lived in an apartment house like the one in the play.
"We heard jazz as something important and serious. When I began to use
jazz in my work, I first did it as a solo and called it *Ballad in a Popular Style.*
That *Street Scene* had an operatic dimension along with the jazz didn't affect
my dance, but I was full of respect for the operatic elements."[22]

Although their number was incorporated into the show as much as possible, the dancers themselves felt isolated. "I was in awe of the stars, and
we didn't socialize," said Sheila Bond, who played Mae. "I had no personal
contact with Kurt Weill, who was at rehearsals but never said anything to
us. We were a couple of kids with Anna, and we had no personal contact
with people of that stature."[23] And even though they had lines, the director "never gave us any instructions," Daniels said. As with "Wrapped in a
Ribbon and Tied in a Bow," Weill farmed out the number to Ted Royal to
orchestrate. "I was disappointed," Daniels said. "Perhaps Weill resented
having to do a jazzy number. And that may be why, even though we sang,
our song was never recorded for the original cast album. It was a double
whammy. We were apparently the most expendable number in the
show."[24]

"It wasn't one of Kurt's great songs," Sheila Bond felt. It wasn't meant
to be. With its intentionally banal lyrics, it was a song to be danced to.
Both Weill and Friedman were agreed that this time the song would be
performed to its completion, and that the show would stop long enough
for the audience to applaud the dancers. When she showed him the dance,

Sheila Bond and Danny Daniels in their showstopping number, "Moon-Faced,
Starry-Eyed," in *Street Scene.* Anna Sokolow choreographed.

as Sokolow recollected, Friedman told her, "That's no good. That won't
stop the show." Sokolow, who had never worked in a Broadway show
before, said nothing, but she remembered that Weill, throwing up his
hands, exclaimed, " 'Who knows what will stop the show?' And so, thanks
to Kurt, I was able to do it my way."[25] "We stopped the show every night,"
Sheila Bond boasted.[26] "This hot, sexy number," as Danny Daniels aptly
called it, became a high point in a show about the consequences of passion—in the show's calculated chiaroscuro, "Moon-Faced, Starry-Eyed"
was the light version of a theme that would develop tragically in act 2.

Following a nocturne that suggests orchestrally the movement from
night (ominous chords that anticipate the tragic events) to day (an orchestral swell; wake-up sounds that evoke Bernstein's energetic new-day opening of *On the Town*), the children's song that opens the second act is the last
of the show's critically vulnerable Broadway numbers. Another "charm"
song, "Children's Game" supplies social texture as working-class kids
mimic the behavior, or what they imagine to be the behavior, of Park
Avenue sophisticates. "Since we have taken out the relief material of the

second act, we should do a little more with the opening, which is full of possibilities," Weill wrote in his tryout production notes. Except for the bitter "Lullaby" near the end, this is indeed the only "relief" material in a street scene soon to be invaded by tragedy, and the entertainment the number offers deepens by contrast the impact of the events that follow.

Just as the foregoing numbers show off Weill's versatility, so too does the range of his operatic, or at least operatic-style, compositions. Reminding Broadway audiences that opera is not always about the grand gesture and the tragic passion, throughout the show Weill allies opera with comedy. Performed by a group of tenants, the opening ensemble, "Ain't It Awful, the Heat?" (a comic evocation of "Summertime," the glorious opening number of *Porgy and Bess*), has a whiny, repetitive melody, traded repartee, and slippery, chromatic string chords that comically express the enervating impact of the heat. The gossip trio, "Get a Load of That," which follows the janitor's blues-tinged reverie, "I Got a Marble and a Star," reprises the carping tone of the neighbors' dialogue. The composer uses canonic imitation between the voices to convey the effect of backbiting. An arietta, "When a Woman Has a Baby," sung by Mr. Buchanan, whose wife's offstage delivery will offset the deaths at the end of the play, supplies comic relief tucked into a simple, blueslike tune with operatic interjections. In the Ice-Cream Sextet, opera enters, and with a vengeance. *Rigoletto* and *Lucia* supply the principal grand-opera intertexts here as Weill indulges in sublime musical parody. He treats the light-as-air subject matter with an almost delirious overkill, as voices of many nations mingle in an ecstatic tribute to the favorite American summertime pleasure of eating ice cream.

Weill's sharpest and most controversial use of operatic comic relief occurs in the lullaby that is performed by two nursemaids after Maurrant has killed his wife and her lover. In a September 20 letter to Langston Hughes, Weill expressed his concern over the "problem of the whole last scene. What we do with the last scene, I am sure the nursemaids will be in, and we definitely need an amusing song for them. I know that this kind of lyric which should be gay and funny, is not easy to write, that's why I think you should start working on it, so that we won't get into trouble." Hughes's lyrics contain an acrid humor. "Hush, baby, hush, / Your daddy is a lush,"[27] the nurses sing to their infant charges. An attack on rich people, but also on the hard-bitten nurses themselves, the song contains a Brechtian social criticism and an epic-theatre detachment that play against the tragedy that has just occurred. Weill entrusts the only other music surrounding the killings to other outsiders, a chorus of sympathetic observers of someone else's tragedy.

In writing the mordant "Lullaby" as the major musical offering after the double murder, Weill seemed to be retreating into the familiar security of epic-theatre irony. However skillfully conceived on its own terms as social satire that marks the unconcern of the outside world, "Lullaby" is a forcible reminder that *Street Scene* is indeed not a conventional opera, where the murders and their impact on those left behind would surely be the show's commanding musical statement. Yet here, in a show where he has been "talking" in a variety of musical accents almost without a pause, Weill curiously elected silence. Understandably, a number of music critics faulted Weill for appearing to duck the challenges of the last scene by failing either to musicalize it entirely or to provide the principals with impassioned arias.

Representing a fusion of operatic and Broadway idioms, a few of the songs can be tilted either "upward" to opera or "downward" to pop. The show's two blues numbers, "Lonely House" and "I Got a Marble and a Star," are prime examples of the kinds of musical slippage Weill was working with. A comparison of the two demonstrates how much better his handling of the blues was when he allowed himself freedom to develop such material along operatic lines. The blues never came naturally to him, the way they did to other show composers, like Gershwin and Harold Arlen. In "I Got a Marble and a Star" he tries to hew closely to the traditional form, but his melody is based upon an unidiomatic alternation between "regular" and "blue" notes which gives the whole number a touristy, unconvincing feel. "Lonely House" is another matter. From the beginning, "Lonely House" was marked as Sam's aria and so described in all the early preproduction meetings. "Sam's aria (unless you have a better idea) should be about the house," Weill wrote to Langston Hughes on January 22, "as Elmer lined it out the last time we all met—the house being a prison for the spirit etc. It could almost become a theme song for the show. It should be passionate and very moving, but as personal as we can make it, that means: not abstract!!!" In this, Weill succeeded splendidly. The blues provide a vocabulary and an aura, but the song develops operatically. Its famous verse is a microcosm of *Street Scene* as a whole: the night noises, the distant traffic, the layers of unconnected sound-events are presented as polytonal splashes over a slow, chromatic riff. Sam's voice is spare, chant-like. The slow riff, jazzy and foreboding, which will later become incidental music for Anna's offstage tryst, portends the climactic murders. (And it was evocative enough to become an instant musical icon of "cool" and of danger. Years later, it was put to use in the James Bond theme song!) The song's chorus and bridge artfully combine the "lonely" harmonies of the blues with a searching, expressive vocal line. The return of the chorus is unusual in that it brings back the harmony of "lonely house, lonely me!" but not the tune or the words. Instead, Weill, in an elegant adaptation of jazz tradition, gives Sam a variant of the melody (as if he were a saxophone player, blowing above the chord changes), and Langston Hughes delivers his best lyrics of the show: "The night for me is not romantic: / Unhook the stars and take them down." The song then concludes with a musical fade-out over the ominous riff and the forlorn night sounds. In "Lonely House" Weill was able to fuse jazz and opera into a powerful musical chiaroscuro.

Anna Maurrant's major second-act number, "A Boy Like You," is decidedly a song rather than an aria. Notably less heavy than her act 1 aria, the song, with irregular lines, conforms to the "either/or" flow of much of Weill's musical signature for the show. Indeed, Lenya later sang a touching version adapted with complete conviction to her own cabaret range. Rose's "What Good Would the Moon Be?" is a torch song in a dreamy, wistful slow fox rhythm with semioperatic touches. Its ending, with a poignant insistence on diminished and half-diminished chords, recalls the hesitant bridge section of "September Song." "It was more or less in the popular range," Anne Jeffreys recalled. "They had hoped it would have some popularity on record, and through playing it on the airwaves, it did. But it was very rangy. The intervals were sometimes difficult and certainly not the norm. If you knew Kurt Weill's music, however, it was typical."[28]

"We'll Go Away Together," an operetta duet for Sam and Rose sung just before the tragedy erupts, "sounded like a Strauss waltz," Maurice Abravanel recalled. "Lenya came to me and said, 'Maurice, that goes too far, that's like such and such of Johann Strauss.' [The song, which is not strictly a waltz, recalls a number from a standard Romberg or Lehár operetta.] She was very, very upset. I didn't feel so badly because even if Kurt worked with a model, by the time he had put his touch on it, it was 100% Kurt."[29]

Weill took care to prevent the romantic duet at the climax of act 2, Sam and Rose's "Remember That I Care," from escaping the net of character and situation. Rather than writing for melody primarily, he wanted his music to serve the lyrics. "[Rice and I] feel [the lyrics for] the love duet can be improved," he told Langston Hughes in a January 22 letter. "Sam should start out (as you have it) in the mood of his aria ["Lonely House"], but then through Rose's optimism he should be more and more carried away." Weill wanted the duet to reflect the singers' contrasting and evolving moods. The song "should build into a beautiful duet which reaches the climax . . . when Sam asks her to kiss him, and here the lilac-bush theme [a lilac bush has become a symbol of their feelings for each other] should sing out in the orchestra."

In some of the material for Mr. and Mrs. Maurrant, Weill daringly replaces "Broadway" with full-fledged opera. In act 1, the characters have one aria each, Anna's "Somehow I Never Could Believe," Frank's "Let Things Be Like They Always Was," which define the conflict that has poisoned their marriage, Anna's romanticism against Frank's reactionary macho intransigence. (In act 2, "grand" opera is confined to a quartet performed by Anna, Frank, Rose, and Wille, "There'll Be Trouble"; Frank's tortured "I Loved Her Too"; and two big choral numbers with opera solos—arias *con coro.*) For Weill, Anna's act 1 aria became the reason he did the show, and a preview of the kind of American opera he hoped to continue to write. The aria lasts for six and a half minutes—dangerously long, as Weill knew. It is constructed of eight different sections, through which the singer recounts her youthful optimism, her loveless, constricting marriage, and her hopes for a better future, all embodied in tortuous Weillian harmonies that foreshadow her fate. More complex in its musical language than anything else in the score, the aria nonetheless, as Weill worked hard to ensure, was not an isolated tour de force. He urged Langston Hughes to rewrite his original lyrics in order to achieve a style that would be "more singable, smoother, and easier on the ear."[30] And nowhere in the score did Hughes heed his composer more conscientiously than here. Like Weill, Hughes, in Anna's aria as throughout, is unafraid of banality; his lyrics for Anna's lament contain many plainspoken phrases that border on cliché but are truthful to the character. Anna expresses her memories and her dreams in a direct style that has the rhythm of everyday speech.

> *Somehow I never could believe*
> *That life was meant to be all dull and gray.*
> *Somehow I always will believe*
> *There'll be a brighter day.*
> . . . .
> *So I went wand'ring down the pavements of New York,*
> *And through the subway's roaring tunnels underground,*
> *Hoping I'd discover some wonderful lover.*
> *Frank was the one that I found.*

Weill's compliance with the "American way" has become legendary, but on Anna's aria he wouldn't budge. When Friedman asked him to trim it, he refused. When Billy Rose told him, as Lenya recalled, " 'Kurt, you're crazy! That aria is too long,' Kurt very quietly said, 'Billy, if this aria goes over, it will prove to me that I have written the opera I wanted to write.' "[31] Among the collaborators, only Dwight Deere Wiman supported the composer. The aria stayed as Weill wrote it, magnificently performed by Polyna Stoska. (But as Anne Jeffreys noted, "Polyna Stoska had a Germanically trained voice, and she sang everything on one level. I had been trained oppositely—you interpreted the word and you sang with the word, but she had that one tonal thing.")[32]

Heading into the home stretch, Weill wrote his parents in a September 9, 1946, letter that *Street Scene* was "the biggest and most daring project I have undertaken over here so far, because this time I'm writing a real opera for the Broadway theatre. If this succeeds, it will open up a large new vista for me, because today I'm almost without competition in the field of popular opera." The composer's supreme self-confidence was to be sorely tested during the show's tryout in Philadelphia.

Street Scene, billed as a "dramatic musical," opened there at the Shubert Theatre on December 16, 1946, to brutally sparse audiences and an indifferent critical reception. "It was the most disastrous opening I have ever attended," Lenya remembered. "Right next door was some stupid show, *Finian's Rainbow,* standing room only. Three weeks of *Street Scene,* twenty people in the audience, thirty." Only Weill and Wiman continued to believe wholeheartedly in the show. "One reviewer in Philadelphia wrote that it was tired Puccini," as Lenya recalled. "Kurt said, 'Well, he wasn't a bad composer.' He was never shaken by any bad reviews. He was so sure of himself, that's what he wanted to do with his life."[33] Famously reticent during rehearsals, Weill broke his pattern during this calamitous tryout. "The one time he talked to the cast—'talk' is too much—he said a few words," Lys Symonette recalled. " 'Kids, I believe in this show and I'll fight for it. Just have faith.' "[34]

Just before the opening in New York, on January 9 at the Adelphi Theatre, on Playwrights Producing Company stationery, Weill wrote to the cast that "the show we are giving tonight is to me the fulfillment of an old dream—the dream of a serious, dramatic musical for the Broadway stage. . . . I want you to go out tonight in the spirit of fighting an important battle." "In New York the rumor had spread that we were a flop, and

Brian Sullivan (Sam) and Anne Jeffreys (Rose) are at center stage in this full-cast
publicity photo for *Street Scene.* Jo Mielziner designed the famous set;
Lucinda Ballard designed the costumes.

they were preparing for a first-class burial," Weill wrote Caspar Neher on
February 16. "But as soon as the music started at the premiere, the entire
picture changed, and after ten minutes I knew I had the audience in the
palm of my hand."

"A musical play of magnificence and glory," Brooks Atkinson wrote in
the January 10 *New York Times.* "Weill is a Broadway virtuoso with a love
for the trivia as well as the grandeur of his theme." "It has all the enchant-
ments of a memorable theatrical achievement and none of the operatic pos-
turing which so often mars operetta offerings," Howard Barnes wrote in
the *New York Herald-Tribune. Street Scene* is "the most important step
toward significantly American opera that I have yet encountered in the
musical theatre," Olin Downes wrote in the *New York Times* on January 26,
contrasting the show's "direct and unacademic" approach to the "artificial
and unrooted" American opera *The Warrior,* by Norman Corwin (libretto)
and Bernard Rogers, which had opened the week before at the Metropoli-

tan Opera. There were some naysayers. In *PM,* Louis Kronenberger grumbled about "the strictly operatic side" that "some of it seems rather pretentious, and some of it is as facilely florid as movie music." He objected particularly to a disparity between the "palpitant music [which] sometimes collides with the prosaic words to the point of bathos."

When a feature photo spread in *Life* called him a German composer, Weill wrote a letter on February 12 to the magazine in which he declared his national allegiance. "I do not consider myself a 'German composer.' The Nazis obviously did not consider me as such either, and I left their country (an arrangement which suited both me and my rulers admirably) in 1933. I am an American citizen, and have composed exclusively for the American stage [since my arrival in America in 1935]."

Street Scene was the most serious and ambitious musical of the season. More than fifty years later it ranks as one of the most serious and ambitious of all American musicals—a great, problematic work, and one of Kurt Weill's hardest-to-categorize hybrids. By its very existence, the work testified to the elasticity and range of the Broadway musical. The same season a double bill by Gian Carlo Menotti, *The Telephone* and *The Medium,* offered another enticing version of Broadway opera. Menotti's style was closer to "the real thing" than Weill's impure crossbreed, but Broadway at the time was receptive to operatic invasions, and Menotti's double bill ran for an astonishing 212 performances. As Miles Kreuger passionately argued, *Street Scene* is "a Broadway musical play of its era which fits into the evolutionary cycle of musical theatre, which at that time was open to expanding the spectrum of emotion that Broadway musicals started to embrace. The so-called Broadway numbers seem out of place when opera companies do *Street Scene,* when in the original production they were integrated. It was a beautifully conceived, beautifully staged and acted *Broadway* show, and it does not need the patina of legitimacy by being performed on an opera stage."[35] Nonetheless, *Street Scene* has found a permanent home not on Broadway, but on opera-house stages in America and Europe, where, in good productions, Weill's opera for Broadway has been notably comfortable.

At the time, both Weill's and Menotti's operas were overshadowed by two commercial blockbusters, *Finian's Rainbow* (with a score by Burton Lane and lyrics by E. Y. Harburg and Fred Saidy), and *Brigadoon* (with a score by Frederick Loewe and lyrics by Alan Jay Lerner), both fantasies that took place in settings far removed from postwar America. Other noteworthy shows in the 1946–47 season included *Beggar's Holiday,* an Americanized version of *The Beggar's Opera* with a score by Duke Ellington and starring Alfred Drake playing Macheath as an American gangster, and Nunnally Johnson and George S. Kaufman's *Park Avenue,* Ira Gershwin's disappointing Broadway swan song, in which he supplied lyrics for a score by Arthur Schwartz. These modern-style musicals were offset by revivals of old-fashioned operettas that included Oscar Straus's *Chocolate Soldier* and Victor Herbert's *Gypsy Lady.*

The reviews on the whole, which were more positive than those for *Porgy and Bess,* recognized the merit and the courage of Weill's achievement in *Street Scene,* but his troubles with the show were not over. Business was robust for two months but started to flag by March, when to save the show Weill and Rice agreed to a 40 percent royalty cut. When Langston Hughes apparently did not accept the cut, Weill sent him a blistering letter. "Don't be mad at ME," Hughes wrote back on April 21, "because at this distance I haven't the least idea what is going on up there." "Langston at no time refused to go along with Elmer and yourself on the 40 percent royalty cut," Maxim Lieber, Hughes's agent, wrote Kurt on April 22, before launching a counteraccusation: "You are so determined to squeeze every cent out of the play for yourself that you would rather see the play closed if Langston does not agree to a reduction pro-rated in accordance with the existing contract," Lieber snapped. Weill lashed out at his publisher, Chappell, falling back on the accusation that they had not properly exploited the score, even though he had not written *Street Scene* to yield separate numbers with Hit Parade potential.

But no sacrifice or accusations of blame could stem the financial losses the show was incurring; and after 148 performances, with great reluctance, Wiman and the Playwrights Producing Company closed it. "At the last performance," Victor Samrock, the publicist for the Playwrights Company, wrote Weill in Palestine in a May 22 letter, "the excitement generated was something no one had ever seen before in a theatre. The audience got up and cheered for fully ten minutes. They threw their programs in the air, the orchestra struck up 'Auld Lang Syne,' and the cast, with arms locked, sang the song to the audience. When the cast finished, the audience joined in, and when it was all over, the people in the theatre kept on cheering for another ten minutes."

As Weill predicted, *Street Scene* is the most enduring of his American works. It has had more revivals than any other show of his and has done more to realize the composer's lifelong goal of confounding rigid distinctions between the opera house and the commercial musical theatre.

FOURTEEN

Before Sondheim

I am intending to go to London and Paris to arrange for productions in England and France of my plays *Lady in the Dark, One Touch of Venus, and Street Scene,*" Weill wrote the Playwrights Producing Company on March 28, 1947, after *Street Scene* had settled into what was clearly going to be a disappointing run. In an aside, he mentioned that he would also be going to Palestine "to visit my parents who live there." It was to be the first time he had seen his parents since his arrival in America twelve years earlier (in 1941 he had tried to bring them to the United States) and the first time he had traveled outside the borders of his new country. Throughout the long separation, Weill had been a dutiful son who regularly sent money and letters; but he had kept his distance emotionally as well as physically. His parents were outsiders to the world that mattered most to him, just as he was an outsider to their religious beliefs. (Weill, however, was not indifferent to his heritage or to the problems of the Jewish Diaspora, and in the fall of 1947, a few months after his return from Palestine, he proudly accepted Meyer Weisgal's request to orchestrate the "Hatikvah." "It is a very good orchestration," Weill boasted to his parents in a November 29 letter. "The Boston orchestra will bring it out on a record and today [Chaim] Weizmann [to become the first president of the new state of Israel] wrote to me that it will be played as the official 'Hatikvah' at the opening of the first Jewish Parliament. . . . Weizmann asked me to come and see him again, when I am back in Palestine." Surely no other letter from their famous son pleased the elder Weills as much.)

When he returned from his visit to Palestine—Weill would not see either the country or his parents again—he was in creative limbo, an uncomfortable spot for an artist with a near-monastic dedication to his career. "The two projects . . . that have been suggested to me lately are still very vague," he wrote Maxwell Anderson on July 25. One of them was "an interesting idea which [Alan Jay] Lerner [a New City neighbor] brought to me last week and which we are investigating now." The previous season, working with Frederick Loewe, Lerner had had a huge hit,

Brigadoon, which was produced by Cheryl Crawford; and it was Crawford, after obtaining Loewe's consent, who brought Lerner to Weill. At this point, Weill had mixed feelings about Crawford—he had been furious with her for her stinginess and her general mismanagement of *One Touch of Venus,* and he and Lenya made snappish comments behind her back about her mannish appearance and her deranged partner, Dorothy Patten, whom they called "the pick-axe beast." But Weill and Lenya were not ingrates. They remembered that soon after their arrival in America, Crawford had been a crucial and well-placed ally. Weill respected

Weill in 1947 working with lyricist and librettist Alan Jay Lerner on *Love Life*

Crawford's taste in musical theatre; and if she thought Lerner had a potentially worthy idea, he was prepared to listen.

Heir to the Lerner dress shops, Alan Jay was wealthy, cultivated, talented, and ambitious. Weill, who knew Lerner casually, had high regard for his intellect, and he also liked him—indeed, Lerner was to join the rarefied list of those who miraculously managed to escape any barbed comments from either Mr. or Mrs. Weill. "The first impression was very sympathetic," Lenya recalled. "Alan is well-bred and charming; he looked like a college kid, alert, clever. He had a head much too big for his body, hair grew quickly so he can look like a nineteenth century poet . . . he had a sensual mouth. Kurt liked Alan right away because he was very flexible, excited by ideas, and a wonderful listener with a great sense of humor, just like Kurt had. They made each other laugh."[1] But Lerner was also a full-fledged neurotic. Miles Kreuger, who was Lerner's press agent in the 1960s, recalled him as "a pill-popping hypochondriac who compulsively applied unguents on his hands to keep his skin from cracking. He was a true eccentric, nervous and insecure, who bit his fingernails and never stood still. Back and forth he paced relentlessly. He was terrifically judgmental about his work, very self-analytical, never self-satisfied."[2]

At first sight, Weill, outwardly calm, self-contained, deeply private, and facing the world with his bemused gaze, and Lerner, high-strung and seemingly always on the verge of coming apart, made an odd couple. But both temperamentally and creatively Lerner was to be the most deeply compatible of all Weill's American colleagues. "He was a real partner, one who was up to Weill's standard," as Lys Symonette observed. "Anderson certainly wasn't, and Rice for sure wasn't. But Weill felt that Lerner could have been his American Brecht, so to speak. With Lerner, he came closest to the level he had worked on with Brecht—the big tragedy was that Weill couldn't live with Brecht, but he couldn't live without him either."[3] Unlike Brecht, however, Lerner was genuinely interested in musical theatre. As on *Lady in the Dark,* Weill would be working with an author in the process of intense psychoanalysis. The neuroses that were the driving impulse behind both shows—Moss Hart's sexual ambivalence, Lerner's issues about marriage (he was to marry seven times)—were certainly not Weill's, a confirmed heterosexual who had only one wife. But just as Weill mastered a variety of musical styles, he was also able imaginatively to identify with the psychological problems of his book writers and lyricists when those issues were at the core of the material he was working on. His muse sparked by collaboration, Kurt Weill, in effect, was a "Method" composer.

Lerner wanted to tell the history of a marriage, an unremarkable subject, to be sure; but his novel idea, which immediately delighted Weill, was to examine that marriage over a period of more than 150 years, from 1791 to 1947, during which the married couple does not age. Sam and Susan Cooper and their two children, Lerner's all-American family, would have the leading roles in a kind of national allegory—changes in American life would be reflected by changes in the Coopers' love life. The "fantastic" marriage was to begin in a bucolic late-eighteenth-century New England community, Lerner's version of an American Utopia, in which Susan is content to be a homemaker and Sam works at home as a furniture maker. Bit by bit, Progress (industrialization, capitalism, women's suffrage, the media) chips away at the Coopers' domestic paradise. The Coopers divorce, but attempt to reunite at the end of the show.

Cheryl Crawford had been right on the money in suggesting Weill for the project. As he could see at once, Lerner's chronicle format would place such large narrative and thematic demands on the music that, in effect, he would be required to function as a cowriter. And the historical sweep would necessitate the use of many kinds of popular American music. Weill also liked the tone that Lerner seemed to be taking: sentiment laced with hefty doses of cynicism. He plunged in with great enthusiasm, working with Lerner almost uninterruptedly from July 1947 through January 1948 as they grappled with telling a new kind of story in a new way. In a real sense, they were pioneers trekking where no one had ventured before; and since they were carving out an original story, rather than working on an adaptation, they were writing without a net.

Early on, the collaborators subtitled their show "a vaudeville," and like an old-fashioned vaudeville program it was set up as a series of individual turns. The revuelike structure echoed *Mahagonny*, but happily for Weill Lerner welcomed his assistance more than Brecht had—Lerner knew in general outline what he wanted, but needed Weill to help him build the show scene by scene. Because of the fluid architecture—this was a show of movable parts—the collaborators rewrote a number of the sketches many times, and the musical went through more drafts, revisions, and out-of-town surgery than any other Kurt Weill project.

To guide the audience through the show's unconventional form, Lerner felt he needed some sort of master of ceremonies. And, working with

Weill, he devised a then novel kind of narration: From time to time a chorus would perform vaudeville-style numbers designed to stop the show in
the *Threepenny Opera* sense. But at the same time that they wanted to find a
way of binding the episodes, the cowriters also did not want to connect all
the dots. "Let the audience work a little" was to be their implicit motto in
designing the commentary numbers, which were shaping up as mini
learning pieces in the Brecht-Weill tradition.

While their show was radically innovative in a formal sense, musically
the collaborators intended to remain well within standard Broadway patterns. This was not to be any kind of opera, but almost, like *Show Boat,* a
résumé of popular American styles. It was not at any point Weill's intention, however, to imitate or to compose valentines to bygone modes.
Rather, after extensive research, he sifted elements of old-time music into
modern-sounding numbers sprinkled with historical grace notes and a
touch of Weill that, inevitably, offered a European slant on the American
musical scene. In places throughout the score, his style is often strongly
influenced by the "prairie" or Americana style of Aaron Copland. (Weill's
achievement theatrically, however, is much stronger than Copland's in his
problematic 1954 opera, *The Tender Land.*) Weill's first-draft score, pitted
with quotations from many musical forms, included a polka, a blues, a
czardas, a fox-trot, a rumba, a torch song, a patter song, a madrigal,
romantic ballads, a ballet, a mini–minstrel show, and a Broadway aria. On
the show's bumpy road from original concept to opening night on Broadway, the czardas and the rumba wound up among the sizable discard
section.

The first draft, clunkily called *A Dish for the Gods,* is often too bitter.
Ominously, the show opens with the Coopers' marriage already shattered
beyond repair, and the first number, an ironic hymn to "Progress," the
effects of which have contaminated the marriage, gives away too much too
soon. Two entirely misconceived scenes, removed root and branch in later
drafts, added to the sour flavor. In the first of them, scene 7, a mostly sung,
self-enclosed revue sketch called "Murder at the Museum," Susan, a newly
minted suffragette firebrand, storms a museum with a cadre of militant
feminists to smash a statue of Venus. (Was Weill indulging in a little
inside joke, slyly deconstructing his early and more conventional musical?) The blatant scene expresses a level of feminist rage the play cannot
absorb. In scene 9, set on a cruise ship on New Year's Eve in the jazz age,
Sam has become a lower-level corporate player, a desperate bottom feeder,
willing to do almost anything to curry favor. He and Susan, each of them

engaged in an affair, sing "You Understand Me So" to their new partners. Dialogue and situation boil with venom. If he was going to have the hit he wanted, Lerner began to realize, he would have to curb his anger and restrain the demons that may have been gnawing at him during his sessions with his analyst.

The cocreators reconfigured *A Dish for the Gods* as *Love Life.* They softened the tone while keeping sharp, provocative edges, and set the history of the Coopers' marriage within the framework of a memory play. The show opens with Sam and Susan, circa 1948, as participants in a magic show. Susan is sawed in half; Sam levitates. In their transformed states, they reminisce about "what we once had together"[4] 150 years ago.

In Mayville, 1791, in the age of plenty, the score speaks in an American folk style with modal harmonizations right out of Aaron Copland's populist phase. (Copland's great ballets, *Billy the Kid, Rodeo,* and *Appalachian Spring,* spanned the years 1938–1944.) "Who Is Samuel Cooper?" and "My Name Is Samuel Cooper" share the same basic melodic line. The first song, in a brisk, forthright, unvarying rhythm, is a question about a newcomer framed by the community; the second song, the hero's answer, is Weill's bravura version of a standard entrance aria.

> *My name is Samu'l Cooper,*
> *There's none but God I fear.*
> *I came from Massachusetts*
> *And headed straight for here.*

"Here I'll Stay," the following duet for the Coopers, expresses their utter contentment in a pretty, well-wrought number that is one of Weill's underappreciated creations. The poise of Weill's romantic ballad perfectly embodies Lerner's idealized vision of late-eighteenth-century New England as a bright and shining place—Brigadoon and Camelot rolled into one.

Having established an American paradise, the cowriters can now introduce the complications of "Progress," a vaudeville number performed by a group called the Eight Go-Getters in a limbo area in front of the curtain.

> *What is this thing*
> *That's better than Spring?*
> *What thing is this*
> *That's greater than a kiss?*

The Go-Getters perform "Progress," one of the ironic,
vaudeville-style comment numbers staged in one
in *Love Life,* 1948, a pioneering concept musical.

What is the "X"
That's bigger than sex?
What could it be?

As they answer the question, "It's Progress! Where ev'ry man can be a
king," they perform a soft-shoe routine. Here, as throughout, Lerner and
Weill throw an ironic twist into a familiar musical style.

"Progress" sets up the next scene, "The Farewell—Mayville 1821," in
which, as a result of that thing that's "bigger than sex," Sam has to go to
work outside his home. "I Remember It Well," Sam and Susan reminisce,
although their recollections collide. (Ten years later, in *Gigi,* with a new
melody by Frederick Loewe, Lerner will reuse the lyric as a comic number
for Maurice Chevalier and Hermione Gingold.) "Green-Up Time," a hymn
to spring phrased as a high-spirited community polka, provides the requisite act 1 production number. It's a quasi-operatic winner, the vocal hoe-

down that Copland never wrote. The fragility of this last happy moment for the Coopers is underlined by Weill's minor chords, which send flickering shadows across the sunburst of his melody.

"Economics," performed by a black quartet in one, announces changes in the Coopers' domestic life and in the fabric of their community.

> *Man and Woman you got to admire*
> *They conquered cold and they conquered fire. . . .*
>
> *But there's one thing that's beat 'em,*
> *That they just can't subdue;*
> *One thing that defeats 'em,*
> *And splits 'em up in two.*
> *And that love-defyin' thing*
> *About which we's gonna sing*
> *Is Economics!*

The jazzy uptempo refrain—"That's good economics; That's good economics, / But awful bad for love!"—is more firmly American in pitch and timbre than any of Weill's European-based sorties into jazz in the 1920s. But intentionally he gives the black-based "Economics" and the soft-shoe "Progress" a Broadway rinse that separates them from authentic versions of their genres.

The musicless scene 3, "The New Baby," in which Susan is frustrated in her desire to conceive, is followed by a comic vaudeville clog dance, "Mother's Getting Nervous," performed by a Trapeze Artist and Three Tots, who comment retrospectively on Susan's "condition" without seeming to grasp the import of their theme. "Oh, we'd like to know / What's wrong with mother." Like "Progress," the number concludes with a dance specialty of yesteryear, here a fine Dixieland routine, a tap dance of the waltz-clog school. Scene 4, the replacement for the original suffragette scene, offers a ripe display of the cowriters' theatrical ingenuity. Sam sings "My Kind of Night," a ballad that recalls the musical equilibrium of "Here I'll Stay"; Weill's wistful, soothing melody, his lulling rhythm, and Lerner's lyrics establish a man at peace with himself and his world.

> *What a pleasant evening, just rocking to and fro.*
> *It makes you wonder why a man has to roam.*

In *Love Life,* Susan (Nanette Fabray) leads the chorus in a rousing
feminist salute, "Women's Club Blues," as Sam (Ray Middleton), who has
just sung "My Kind of Night," reclines contentedly on the porch.
Boris Aronson's two-part set underscored the characters' estrangement.

Sam's lovely song on his porch is bisected by the strident feminist complaint of Susan's "Women's Club Blues." The blues Weill wrote for this spot and Lerner's lyrics are an awkward charade—Weill's approximation of a blues number is curiously perfunctory, and Lerner's lyrics sink to bald declaration, as in Susan's "And when the moon is out at night / I start to dream about the right / To work!" "We've got to be free!" announce Susan and the members of her club, their polemics unleavened by wit or poetry. It may have been that neither writer in this prefeminist era was a confirmed feminist, hence the hollow sound of the treatment of women's rights. But the placement of the number is shrewd, a theatrical tour de force, in fact, that offers a vivid stage image of gender separation, with Sam rocking obliviously on the porch as Susan conducts a fiery meeting inside the house.

The next vaudeville number, "Love Song," performed by a hobo, was reminiscent of "Johnny's Song" in *Johnny Johnson*. The hobo's haunting number expresses a sentiment, "Hear me, I only sing a love song," a preoccupied, self-destructive world ignores. Placed between the split-screen scene separating male from female, and the following episode, in which the Coopers' marriage begins to unravel, the hobo's unheeded message provides a pungent comment. For the hard-to-crack cruise-ship scene that ends act 1, Weill wrote three songs, but only one was finally used, Sam's desperately repeated "I'm Your Man," a deft patter song in which the character tries to ingratiate himself with his rich fellow passengers.

> *If it's home you believe in, then how do you do,*
> *I'm your man! I'm your man!*
> *If it's women you're after, then how do you do,*
> *I'm your man! I'm your man!*

"Ho, Billy O!" the madrigal that opens act 2, is a Weill novelty item, a bit of showing off which adds another genre to the show's motley musical program. Sixteen singers straggle through a litany of modern ailments—neurosis, aggression, manic depression, self-destruction, alcoholism, obesity—that interfere with love. More detached from the immediate narrative context than any of the other choral-comment songs, the number goes on too long, but with its catalogue of obstacles to true romance leaves a lingering acerbic trace on the remainder of the show. Although the following sketch, set in a locker room where men who act like boys boast of their sexual exploits, also had a tangential narrative link, it was a musical-theatre bonanza. The hard-driving rhythms of Weill's musical setting—a

cross between his "Cannon Song" from *The Threepenny Opera* and a hearty
male chorus from a Sigmund Romberg operetta—play deliriously against
Lerner's winking lyrics.

> *We're the sexiest men you can find,*
> *But all of it's here in the mind.*
> *We're the sexiest men women know;*
> *We pay them to act like it's so.*

In the scene without music that follows, everyone in the family wants to
listen to a different radio program—Lerner's heavy-handed lesson on how
a new medium of mass communication strains private life. After the Coopers agree to call it quits, Susan performs a no-more-than-passable torch
song that (too many times) asks the blunt question "Is It Him or Is It Me?"
Living on his own, Sam sings "This Is the Life," one of the composer's stur-
diest Broadway arias. While his model may seem to be Billy Bigelow's celebrated "Soliloquy" in Rodgers and Hammerstein's recent *Carousel,* Weill
creates a different mold, in effect declaring, "This is how it should be
done." Pretending to savor his freedom from marriage and family, Sam is
in fact miserable; his confusion is reflected in Weill's knotty harmonies
and in the agitated inner voice of the song.

> *This is the life, the life for me!*
> *This is the way that life should be!*
> *I'm free!*

he announces. Beneath his bravado is a melancholic tremor. A sudden,
unwanted change of mood—

> *I still have thoughts of her I can't forget.*
> *But that's a thing they say that time will heal.*
> *I wonder why it hasn't done it yet—*

is embodied in a new melody. Impulsively, Sam cancels his dinner order,
then sings a brief reprise of "My Name Is Samuel Cooper." This song,
which once embodied a gentle confidence, is now colored by the arrogance
of the self-made man, and with a shock we realize how far Sam has sunk.
When he ventures out on his own into the nighttime city, each stabbing

declaration of his delusional freedom is musically expressed as a cry from the heart.

> *I got my freedom,*
> *The perfect life!*
> *Don't have a family,*
> *A home, a wife!*
> *This is the life, the life for me!*
> *This is the way it ought to be!*
> *I'm free! Free! Free!*

The climactic "Minstrel Show," which remarkably remained intact throughout the show's many rewrites, is an extended musical scene alternating between underscoring, as characters converse in rhythmic patter, and songs that flow in and out of the dialogue. Comparisons to the "Circus Dream" of *Lady in the Dark* are inescapable. A carnival barker, playing the end man in a traditional minstrel show, tries to sell Sam and Susan Mysticism, Cynicism, the Ideal Man—illusions by which they can avoid reality. In the first illusion, sung by Miss Horoscope and Miss Mysticism, the Fortune Telling Sisters, Weill's whining, monotonous melody topples the singers' belief in "cards and fate" "rul[ing] what you do." Mr. Cynic takes the next spot in the olio to serenade the Coopers with a deliberately awkward banjo ditty that endorses nihilism:

> *This is a world full of nothin',*
> *And nothin's worth trying to save.*

Shifting to coloratura vocal pyrotechnics, Weill introduces a brief opera parody in the song for Miss Ideal Man. The singer assures Susan that

> *Love is really what they say it is*
> *On the screen—on the screen,*

and that she must learn "to wait and wait, / Until you find your ideal mate." Inspired about finding her "Mr. Right," Susan performs a deliberately over-the-top number "in the hyper-romantic style of a star-struck nightclub singer." In its too-vivid lyrics and melody, "Mr. Right" is a parody of a torch song, an ironic counterpoint to Susan's earlier, genuine (if not first-rate) torch song, "Is It Him or Is It Me?" and at the same time a rousing eleven o'clock number, which is what it needs to be at this point in the show.

> *He'll be a perfect dream of manhood.*
> *He'll be everything and more a man should.*
> *Tender as a flower,*
> *He'll look like Tyrone Power—*
> *That's all I want of Mister Right.*

In her epiphany she realizes she and Sam must face "Reality," a song with short, jittery phrases and jarring harmonies performed by the interlocutor and his minstrels. One epiphany being insufficient underlining for this show, the interlocutor sums it up for us in dialogue: "You gotta have illusions to get along in the world." "The Minstrel Show," in effect, has been a kind of *Lehrstück* that through negative examples forces the protagonists to change their point of view.

At the beginning of "The Minstrel Show," Sam and Susan are naïve outsiders eager to be hoodwinked. By the end, they are ready to repair their marriage. The change is expressed entirely through musical means, including underscoring. However forced it is dramatically, in their show-within-the-show format Weill and Lerner devised an exciting new paradigm for the musical theatre. (With neater stitching, Stephen Sondheim and his book writer, James Goldman, used the same basic ground plan twenty-two years later in the Loveland sequence in *Follies,* in which a show-within-the-show leads to a change in the characters.) When "The Minstrel Show" ends, Sam and Susan are on opposite sides of a tightrope. As their children watch, and the music (a reprise of "Here I'll Stay") swells, they begin walking toward each other. They are a short distance from each other, reaching out, when there is a shivering, evanescent orchestral dissonance and the curtain falls.

After working for several months over the summer of 1947, Weill and Lerner felt secure enough by early fall to begin thinking of casting for a projected opening in March or April. For the role of the quintessentially American Susan Cooper, Weill had the odd notion of Gertrude Lawrence—British, brittle, and more vocally challenged than ever. Blinded by her box-office clout, he and Lerner offered her a role for which she was totally unsuited; and apparently no wiser than her would-be employers in assessing her limits, the star accepted. The production was spared Lawrence's presence only because of a technicality: she would not sign unless a summer hiatus was written into the contract, the same issue that caused havoc during the run of *Lady in the Dark.* "It never occurred to me that you would expect us to open a show in March and close it on June 1," Weill wrote to Lawrence on October 11. "I am more than sorry that things developed this way because there is no doubt in my mind that it would have been one of the great parts in your career." "As far as I am concerned, Kurt, I would work for love to have another success with you. (Well, *almost* love!!)," Gertrude Lawrence wrote back on October 21. But she remained adamant about not performing "through the heat of a New York summer. So damn sorry we have reached this impasse."

In November Weill pursued a far more appropriate diva, Mary Martin, who had the down-to-earth charm as well as the vocal capacity the part required. With Lerner, Weill went to see Martin in Chicago, where she was on tour with *Annie Get Your Gun.* But, curiously, Martin did not care for the score. Weill then had the foolish idea of approaching another *Lady in the Dark* veteran, Ginger Rogers, who had given a leaden, charmless performance in the film and whose hard-bitten quality had the wrong kind of common touch for Susan Cooper. Rogers, fortunately, was not available. The final choice was Nanette Fabray, a young performer who had just had a hit in *High Button Shoes* and who projected warmth, gusto, and a comforting, everyday quality that effectively countered Lerner's often acerbic material. And Fabray could handle Weill's pastiche score. "I had such a big vocal range I could sing anywhere," Fabray claimed.[5] The first choice for Sam Cooper was Ray Middleton, another Weill veteran (Washington Irving in *Knickerbocker Holiday*), who, like Fabray, had just had a big Broadway hit—he had been Ethel Merman's costar in *Annie Get Your Gun.* With his rich Broadway baritone—"he had a booming voice, and Weill loved booming voices," as Lys Symonette recalled[6]—Middleton would be able to handle Sam's demanding second-act aria. "Middleton had a very masculine strength," Miles Kreuger said. "Like other baritones of that era, he was a little stiff—but the show, like others of the 1940s, was tilted toward the female lead."[7]

Cracking *Love Life* proved more toilsome than either Weill or Lerner had imagined, and by early 1948 they realized they would not be ready to open until the fall. Throughout the spring and into the summer the collaborators continued to add to and subtract from the show's open-ended vaudeville structure. "I'm working like a savage on my new work," Weill wrote his parents on June 24. "It's called *Love Life* (*Liebesleben*) and this time I have a very good librettist, who just bought himself a house very close to mine, so that we can constantly work together. For a few weeks I've been orchestrating, which means that I'm sitting by my desk for approximately ten hours a day."

In April, and then again in late June and July, Weill took time out to work on another show. The previous September 4 he had received a request from Hans Heinsheimer, now head of Schirmer's, to try "[his] hand again in the field of educational music and write a school opera." Heinsheimer suggested that if the work were to be a success, it would vindicate Weill's theories that American opera has a future. "It could make history." Weill thought of *Down in the Valley*. When Weill played it for him, Heinsheimer liked it but wanted another fifteen minutes added to the original thirty minutes. In April, after Heinsheimer had arranged for the work to be given a premiere in July at Indiana University in Bloomington, Weill reteamed with Arnold Sundgaard. As Sundgaard recalled, "We wrote two new songs for Heinsheimer, a very autocratic man. I was terrified of him, but Kurt was not. We wrote 'Brack Weaver, My True Love,' and 'Where Is

Elia Kazan directing Ray Middleton, Nanette Fabray, and a group of children in *Love Life*. Kazan, who postponed rehearsals of *Death of a Salesman,* was unhappy directing a musical.

the One Who Will Mourn Me When I'm Gone?' "[8] " 'Neo-folk,' it might be called out of kindness; 'pseudo-folk,' it should be called in all honesty," Sundgaard said about his and Weill's interpolations.[9] Indeed, the stitching shows, and Weill's labored chordal progressions between melodies, his bridge material, sound like transitions.

The original version contained stretches of dialogue with no musical accompaniment, but for the expanded piece Weill provided continuous musical underpinning—doubtless a carryover from his experiments with *Street Scene.* As Sundgaard said, Weill "punctuated the dialogue with carefully cued chords on the piano and explained how all of it would be underscored by the orchestra. I saw at once that a composer with a gift for opera is a talented stage director as well. His music informs every moment of the action, how each scene should be felt, what its pace shall be, what its nuances are."[10] Weill's annotations, however, lack the deft touch he brought to the melodrama sections of *Street Scene.* The result is sometimes heavy-handed, as if in writing a school opera for amateur performers he felt he had to prescribe the proper response to each turn of the action.

Although some of the techniques Weill used were familiar from his German school operas and *Lehrstück,* in its basic intention *Down in the Valley,* a tragic folk opera, has no common boundaries with the earlier pieces. Far from being didactic or detached, the work is merely—and only—sentimental. The story's dark outcome, however, is unearned. For killing his romantic rival at a dance in front of many witnesses who could truthfully testify that he acted in self-defense, Brack Weaver is found guilty and (unlike other Weill protagonists facing the same fate) hanged. Characterization and motive in this hillbilly tragedy count less than the authors' clear intention of wringing tears from the audience. As Sundgaard claimed, "Its unfolding as a tragic romance was intended to follow in extended form the shape and progression of a traditional ballad."[11] When *Down in the Valley* was presented in New York the summer of 1949 by a company with the delightful name of the Lemonade Opera, Weill, who attended rehearsals, on June 29 wrote a revealing cautionary letter to the director, Max Leavitt. "[The opera's] effect has always been a highly emotional one. It has moved people and excited them," he wrote as his preface to urging the director to replace the "highly formalized and stylized" approach he had taken to the work in order to play it in the way it was written, as a "red-hot piece of theatre."

For all (perhaps even because of?) its aesthetic misjudgments, *Down in the Valley* packed a wallop. The school production in July 1948 at the University of Indiana, led by a superb Marion Bell (who had starred on Broadway in *Brigadoon* and was to marry Alan Jay Lerner), was wildly successful. Heinsheimer was deluged by requests from school and amateur groups for performance rights. "We have created without any doubt the most successful school opera ever presented in this country," he wrote Weill on February 14, 1949. "It has been given in 100 American cities," Weill bragged to his parents on July 11, 1949. "The newspapers greeted my opera as the great event in America's musical life. The critic of the *New York Times* compares it to *The Beggar's Opera,* which did become the origin of English opera and says that *Valley* will enter history as the fountainhead of American opera. Another critic starts his review: 'Kurt Weill . . . will someday be called the founder of American opera.' You can imagine what this means to me, since this recognition allows me to work once more in the field of opera, which really always has been my proper field of activity."

The show was far from an unqualified critical hit, however. In this most deeply American of his subjects, Weill's European roots, his Puccini-esque imitations, his polyphonic writing and chromaticism, are more pronounced than in any of his Broadway works—the score might well be subtitled "Kurt Weill's European Essays on Mountain Music." "[Weill's] whole treatment . . . is in essence foreign to the nature of the story," as Harold Schonberg wrote in the *New York Times* on July 15, 1948. "The theme is American. Weill's setting is based on European concepts. The story is simple, whereas Weill's treatment is slick and sophisticated." "A sumptuous noise, but overwritten and spurious," Cecil Smith wrote in the August 1949 edition of *Musical America.* "The innocent folk melodies are subjected to chromatic harmonizations that artificialize and cheapen them . . . a tissue of vulgarisms. By comparison the best of his Broadway works—*Lady in the Dark, One Touch of Venus*—are Mozartean. . . . If *Down in the Valley* represents the ultimate Americanization of Mr. Weill, the news is bad, for he has thrown away his fine-grained sandpaper and reached for a trowel."

Audiences didn't care. The American counterpart to *Der Jasager, Down in the Valley* was Weill's biggest commercial success since *Die Dreigroschenoper.* In less than a decade, there were over fifteen hundred productions. On January 4, 1950, when it was broadcast on NBC Television, it became the first television opera. With the simply conceived characters and story line and the flexible orchestration, Weill, unlike many other composers, had succeeded in creating an accessible, popular opera for schools and amateurs that touched audiences from all parts of the country.

. . .

Weill worked with unusual speed on the expanded *Down in the Valley* because he had already thought through the material with Arnold Sundgaard a few years before, and because *Love Life,* now planned for a September opening, required continued stitching. A number of the problems were caused by Cheryl Crawford, who again, as for *One Touch of Venus,* managed to compile a mismatched team. For this innovative musical she hired Elia Kazan, who had no ear for music and no sense of musical staging. *One Touch of Venus* could, and did, carry itself; but *Love Life* needed a maestro with a secure grasp of musical-theatre rhythm. In the fall of 1948, acclaimed for his staging of last season's *Streetcar Named Desire,* Kazan was in a different niche than at the time of *Venus* five years earlier. With a masterly gift for working with actors—in 1947, along with Crawford and Robert Lewis, he had cofounded the Actors Studio, home of the Method—he was now the pre-eminent director of the postwar American theatre. Yet none of the techniques of Actors Studio naturalism—improvisation, sense and emotional memory, private moments, substitutions—were relevant to the needs of a concept musical with a tricky tongue-in-cheek style. Crawford, and Kazan himself, should have noticed what everybody else seemed to: that he was the wrong person to nurture Lerner and Weill's demanding work.

"I didn't like him," Lys Symonette said, voicing the feelings of virtually everyone connected with the show. "He really messed it up—he didn't have any idea about how to stage the musical numbers," she recalled.[12] "Kazan was one of the big problems," Nanette Fabray remembered. "He was not a man with a light touch, he was not a man of fun and magic. He directed with a heavy hand. I went in the light direction and he was enchanted. But you have to have the chorus and other people with you."[13] What Kazan could do was to stage the intimate scenes without music: the bedroom scene when Susan tells Sam she wants another child and Sam has to consult his work schedule; the scene in which the family quarrels over which radio show to listen to. But in *Love Life* the chamber scenes are placed against a large historical canvas painted primarily through musical numbers. To turn the show into a fluidly paced vaudeville which moved seamlessly from close-ups of Susan and Sam to long-shot comment numbers from the ensemble required a choreographer. And here, too, Crawford stumbled.

She chose Michael Kidd, a brilliant choreographer, who was "too young and didn't have the guts to stand up to Kazan," according to Lys Symonette.[14] "Kazan tried hard to stage some of the musical numbers," Kidd said, trying to be fair. "Where it was a realistic number he did beautifully; where it was a highly stylized number like the minstrel show, he was really not in his element. When it came to actually staging musical movements, he was mistaken and should not have done it."[15] Where Kazan and Weill communicated across a cultural and aesthetic gulf, Weill and Kidd talked the same language. Quite unlike Kazan, Kidd recognized the show's importance. "It was a very original, experimental show," Kidd said. "And it was very daring at the time. It was a testimonial to Kurt Weill's extraordinary ability because the show had such a wide range of musical concepts. The songs and dances had a feel as if they occurred during that period, not literally, a theatricalized version. We didn't do authentic folk dances, the songs weren't authentic folk songs."[16]

The rapport between choreographer and composer, which was strictly professional ("I wouldn't call him a warm man. No small talk. Very efficient, a job to get done," Kidd recalled),[17] led to some payoffs in the production numbers in both acts. For the spot in act 1 where the community would celebrate the arrival of spring, Lerner had asked Weill for "a really happy song," but as Lerner recalled, "there was a minor strain in everything Kurt wrote, even in this 'happy' song."[18] Weill's happy-sad melody seemed to resist Kidd's numerous attempts to transform it into the jubilant production number the show needed at this point. "Finally, I hit on the idea of converting it into a polka," Kidd said. "Weill dropped into rehearsal one day, watched, and turned to me and said, 'I didn't know you wanted a polka, I would have written one.' I said, 'Kurt, I didn't know either, but I tried so many forms, this seemed to me to have the most life to it. He proceeded to orchestrate it in a superb fashion. He was very pragmatic, very skillful, very businesslike. Made very quick decisions and executed them with great expertise. He tried to make 'Green-Up Time' the best polka that could be done."[19]

The production number for act 2, which was to grow out of Sam and Susan's divorce, seemed to stump both Weill and Kidd. Deep into rehearsals, no song existed for the spot. "I came up with an idea for a Punch and Judy ballet," Kidd said. "A dancer [would play] Sam Cooper in the ballet, but it was not [to be] as directly representative as the ballet in *Oklahoma!* It was a completely theatricalized version of a divorce. It was not a substitution. It symbolized the husband in a comparable parallel situation." Weill was the only one who liked Kidd's idea, and he succeeded in convincing his colleagues that a ballet would add the right mix to the show. (Writing ballet music would also give him the chance to play with symphonic forms, as he had in his ballets for *One Touch of Venus*. He based his ballet score on motifs from *Love Life* and a fragment of war music from *Die Bürgschaft*. Surprisingly, he allowed his assistant, Irving Schlein, to arrange the ballet music.)[20] "There was a [danced] prologue to the divorce scene in court, in a hotel room when they're caught in an adulterous situation—others wanted to take it out," Kidd said, "but Kurt spoke up, 'Mike's right. It works and I don't see why we're questioning it. I also thought it wasn't necessary, but I think I'm wrong.' And he was the key decisive vote in keeping it in."[21]

Because of its peculiar structure, the show continued to remain in a perilously fluid state throughout rehearsals and into the Boston and New Haven tryouts in September. "As always when one tries something new, we were unable to foresee how the audience would react," Weill wrote his parents. "When we opened in New Haven, we found that some parts of which we had promised each other a great deal, were not as effective and vice versa. Which meant that already before the opening in Boston we had to make changes within a few days' time. In Boston we got very good notices and the play was a great success with audiences, but we made use of the three weeks to make drastic changes; new music had to be written, and each change we made daily during rehearsals meant I had to sit up at night and orchestrate."[22] Throughout the rehearsal and tryout period, Weill was ruthless in cutting his own material. The original suffragette scene with five musical spots—out. "Susan's Dream," performed by a black quartet right after "Progress"—out, because Weill felt it was holding up the show. A drinking song set in a Temperance League—out. In the cruise-ship scene at the end of act 1, a terrific rumba sung by a chanteuse—deemed irrelevant; out. In the same scene, a smashing ballad, "You Understand Me So," which Susan and Sam sing to new lovers—too bitter; deleted. At the last minute, a torch song for Susan in act 2, "Where Do I Belong?," sung right after Sam leaves, was replaced by "Is It Him or Is It Me?" In two places, the hobo's "Love Song" and the locker-room scene, Weill agreed to cuts when he shouldn't have. "Love Song" was reinstated in New York, but the locker-room scene, which offended some bluenoses in Boston, was not.

Weill and Lerner were willing to listen to criticism and to make adjustments, but on one matter they wouldn't budge. Regardless of audience response, they wanted to retain the vaudeville numbers that commented, sometimes obliquely, on the dissolution of the Coopers' love life. In a daring conceptual move that recalled the separation-of-elements in the

Brecht-Weill pieces, the cowriters wanted to preserve a cleavage between book scenes and the vaudeville numbers. They wanted these ironic numbers, staged in one, to present a bit of an obstacle course for those spectators looking to be carried away by easy sentiment. American vaudeville brushed with Weimar *Lehrstück, Love Life* has dual national and aesthetic identities—the irony that saturates every level of the show, beginning with the title, mandated a split-focus response unusual for Broadway. "Audiences were confused by it," Michael Kidd maintained. "The idea of making musical comments upon preceding scenes and in between scenes perplexed them. Almost revue-like in its format, there was no carry over of emotion from one scene to another. People had to start over again with each scene. Do audiences identify with the characters on stage or do they identify with the author's comment on what went on on the stage?" Kidd asked.[23] "As a producer, Cheryl Crawford should have said, 'The public is confused,' but she was so in awe of Kazan and of Lerner and of Weill that she never spoke up," Nanette Fabray said. "Weill wouldn't have been that onto what the American public's feeling was about it. But he would have wanted to do whatever would make a hit. Another problem was that Lerner would not give us some indication of the time changes. It was hard for the audience to recognize that we'd gone from 1609 [sic] to 1700 [sic] to 1820."[24] Miles Kreuger disagreed: " 'The audience' didn't have trouble with this strange and beautiful show. Theatregoers, then as now, were more nimble in accepting innovations than revisionists would have you believe. Brooks Atkinson, who always had trouble accepting innovations in the musical theatre—i.e., his myopic reactions to *Porgy and Bess* and *Pal Joey*—had trouble with *Love Life*."[25]

Out of town and then when it opened in New York on October 7 at the Forty-sixth Street Theatre, *Love Life* elicited contending reactions. "The most mature musical play the American stage has yet produced . . . a dream of a show about the American dream," Elliott Norton wrote in the *Boston Post* on September 14, giving Cheryl Crawford two highly quotable quotes for ads. Norton predicted correctly that, like the previous season's *Allegro* (an unusual musical by Rodgers and Hammerstein), it would "create controversy and perhaps some indignation, for it uses some of the old conventional show techniques for unconventional ends; and it even points a moral." But Elinor Hughes in the *Boston Globe* grumbled about the "broken narrative line, and more symbolism and commentary than people, story and music," and regretted the "sardonic symbolism" that "harked back to Weill's early *Threepenny Opera*" and "seemed to overload the basically simple story." "Complex and joyless," Brooks Atkinson declared in the *New York Times* on October 8. "A general gripe masquerading as an entertainment . . . gets lost in some strange, cerebral labyrinth, and the pretense that it is vaudeville is a pose. . . . Most of the show's pleasures come from Mr. Weill's music box. He has never produced a more versatile score with agreeable music in so many moods—hot, comic, blue, satiric, lush and romantic." "Iconoclastic in every direction," George Freedley raved in the *New York Telegraph* on October 9, calling it "the most intelligent and adult musical yet offered on the American stage" while assuring prospective patrons that they could have "just as much fun at *Love Life* as at *Annie Get Your Gun.*"

Despite the mixed notices, the show ran for 252 performances, a thoroughly respectable run for the time. But a musicians' union strike called the "Petrillo Ban" prevented an original cast recording, and an ASCAP strike prevented the songs from being played on radio, and what is in many ways Kurt Weill's most ambitious American show has lapsed into obscurity. The seemingly bland, all-purpose title—only in context does its sting become apparent—may have contributed to the show's lack of name value. And Lerner's refusal during his lifetime to permit a revival was also responsible for its unwarranted burial. "I told Alan that of all the musicals in the entire literature I should most like to direct *Love Life,*" Miles Kreuger recalled. "Alan looked at me closely before saying that he could never allow it to be done because he felt he had turned into everything he had satirized in the show."[26]

To the general public *Love Life* may well be the Weill musical that got away, but many theatre professionals are well aware of the show's significance. "*Love Life* and *Allegro* were the first concept musicals," said Hal Prince, who directed a series of landmark concept musicals, including *Cabaret* (1966), *Company* (1970), *Follies* (1971), and *Pacific Overtures* (1976). "They were the first of their kind. Subconsciously, when I first saw them, I noted that they were shows driven by concepts. They didn't work, though I was too young at the time to realize that. (Weill's score is swell, by the way.) Were the shows upstaged by their concepts? In both cases you were so aware of the concept and the craft."[27] Fred Ebb, the lyricist of *Cabaret* and *Chicago,* recalled *Love Life* as "a marvelous piece and a major influence. I was amazed it wasn't a bigger success."[28] "Kurt and Alan tried to pull it off [build a musical around commentary numbers] and it didn't work; the m.c. in *Cabaret* functions like the vaudeville choruses in *Love Life,* it's the same basic idea, and it worked," Michael Kidd observed. "I told this to

Country squire: Weill at Brook House, ca. 1948

Lenya when I visited her backstage after seeing her in *Cabaret,* and she said, 'You're absolutely right. It was the idea that Kurt tried to do a long time ago.' "[29] (The vaudeville-show format in *Chicago* also has a strong similarity to *Love Life.*)

The first major musical of what was to be a historic Broadway season for musical theatre, *Love Life* was compared to *Allegro,* which had opened almost exactly a year earlier, on October 10, 1947. Covering a vast span of time, and with an experimental Greek chorus placed at the side of the stage, setting the scenes and providing comment, *Allegro* was also a musical in the form of a chronicle play. Its 315-performance run surpassed that of *Love Life,* but like the Weill-Lerner show it too has slipped into a historical limbo as a prestige musical with an avant-garde trim. And apparently, in the heavily revived Rodgers and Hammerstein canon, it remains an untouchable. Frank Loesser's *Where's Charley?,* a star vehicle for Ray Bolger, had a regulation musical comedy score by a composer who was to become one of Broadway's most renowned. *My Romance,* the last score by Sigmund Romberg and the last show produced by J. J. Shubert (Weill's *Street Scene* star, Anne Jeffreys, had the lead), was a valentine to old-fashioned operetta, Mr. J. J.'s favored genre. Mike Todd continued his streak of brash, teasingly erotic musicals with *As the Girls Go,* an old-fashioned show on a newfangled subject, the first woman president. Authentic opera appeared on Broadway (but not for long) when Benjamin Britten's *Rape of Lucretia* opened at the Ziegfeld. Nineteen forty-eight ended with Cole Porter's one great musical, *Kiss Me, Kate,* the one Porter show with a durable, witty book (by Sam Spewack and his wife, the dreaded Bella), the one Porter show fully equal to the sum of its parts. The spring semester was dominated by a musical that boasted what was at the time the largest advance sale in Broadway history, Rodgers and Hammerstein's behemoth *South Pacific*—schmaltz raised to the level of art.

Two songs from *Love Life,* "Here I'll Stay" and "Green-Up Time," had a life outside the show. Nanette Fabray won a Tony Award. And in a modest but genuine way, Lerner and Weill's concept musical became a conversation piece among Broadway professionals and sophisticated theatregoers, generating debate about its ambitious form and content. Nine times out of ten, Weill's pastiche score rises to the steep goals the cowriters set for themselves; nine times out of ten, Lerner's book fails to. In a work with Brechtian aspirations, Lerner missed not only the master's astringent poetic touch but also, and more crucially, his keen, cold social observation. The show founders on two facile premises: that America's love life has been contaminated by its materialistic urges, and that there was a town of immaculate conception in New England in the late eighteenth century. As an image of an ideal world, Lerner's Mayville is much less potent than either Brigadoon or Camelot, the fantasy realms Lerner created for two other shows. A New England town doubtless pitted with racism, religious intolerance, and sexual repression can hardly serve as an icon of prelapsarian perfection or as a model with which to indict modern American values, as Lerner seeks to do. His Eden is thinly conceived, as is his depiction of what he considers America's long fall from a state of grace. As a social observer, Lerner is terminally superficial. Nonetheless, although *Love Life* may fail as thesis drama, it is a work of notable musical-theatre intelligence. And despite the seams, the lack of fit between figure and ground, the thematic scope that exceeds Lerner's grasp, this courageous, unjustly neglected work has had a major influence on some of the most innovative musicals of the past fifty years.

FIFTEEN

Cry, the Beloved Country

Only a few weeks after *Love Life* opened, Weill and Lerner wrote a treatment for a film musical called *Miss Memory,* and within a month they traveled to Hollywood to try to sell it. This was to be Weill's final trip to "Lotusland," and like all the others it was filled with failure for the Broadway composer. But this time, the usually optimistic Weill did not seem to have any illusions. "The movie industry is practically dead," he reported to Lenya in a November 13, 1948, letter. "There are only two studios still making a few musicals. One is MGM—there the ruler is Arthur Freed who said, after reading *Miss Memory:* 'this is no time for sophisticated stuff; what we need is meat and potatoes.' " Apparently Darryl Zanuck at Twentieth Century–Fox, the other studio still making musicals on a regular basis, expressed some interest in the treatment, but as a wised-up Weill commented to Lenya, "I am pretty doubtful about the chances, not only for *Miss Memory* but for anything halfway good, in this town." By the end of the month, he and Lerner returned to New York, having made, as Weill expected, no sale.

In January 1949, just as he was preparing to begin work on what would be his last musical (another collaboration with Maxwell Anderson, his favorite writing partner), Weill had another run-in with Brecht, his most difficult collaborator. Brecht had sent Weill changes he had made in the script and the lyrics of *Die Dreigroschenoper* for an upcoming production in Munich. Weill disapproved. "I must confess that I don't understand what you intend to achieve with these changes," he wrote Brecht on January 17. "It's possible that I can't judge the situation in Germany sufficiently from over here, but it seems clear to me that from your point of view, as the lyricist of *Die Dreigroschenoper,* these new texts represent a weakening of the original text, since the more cabaret-style allusions to 'current' events are simply not on the level of *Die Dreigroschenoper.*" Brecht wrote back on January 28, adopting the conciliatory tone he always used in writing to Weill. "It is a question of temporary changes, valid *only* at this particular point in time (and not to appear in print)," Brecht assured his erstwhile partner. "You can take my word that I will undertake nothing, absolutely nothing, against your interests and will in every instance consult with you, if only because I'm still hoping for further collaboration between us." In the event, Brecht used his revised script and lyrics without Weill's permission.

Weill also received no royalties from the Munich production, as he complained in a January 7, 1950, letter to Brecht. "I have not heard from you in a very long time," he wrote, making no attempt to conceal his exasperation. "The entire legal situation of *Die Dreigroschenoper* remains unresolved. . . . [You told me] that you intended to hand over the stage representation of *Dreigroschenoper* to Suhrkamp Verlag. I answered you at the time that I would agree to such a solution, provided that I could come to terms with Suhrkamp about the conditions of the contract. Unfortunately, I have heard nothing at all either from you or from Suhrkamp. Now I think that we cannot let this situation drag on any longer. . . . Any further performances of this work [at this time] are illegal." For what were to be the remaining three months of his life, Weill did not hear from Brecht.

"For years I've wanted to write something which would state the position and perhaps illuminate the tragedy of our own negroes," Maxwell Anderson had written to Alan Paton on March 15, 1948, after, urged by Weill, he had read Paton's novel *Cry, the Beloved Country.* "Now that I've read your story I think you have said as much as can be said both for your country and ours." Anderson was writing to ask Paton's permission for him and Weill to turn the novel, about race relations in South Africa, into a Broadway musical. "It would be our task—as we see it—to translate into stage form without dulling its edge or losing its poetry, this extraordinarily moving tale of lost men clinging to odds and ends of faith in the darkness of our modern earth," Anderson concluded on a grandiloquent note.[1] In a decision he was later to regret, Paton agreed to allow Anderson and Weill to musicalize his novel.

At the time that Anderson obtained Paton's permission, Weill was still preoccupied with revisions of *Love Life* but was relieved to have an exciting new project in the works. Because they were neighbors and best friends, Anderson and Weill conferred over many months about their plans for adapting Paton's novel. And as a result, when they finally set to work in earnest—in two intense gallops concentrated around February and March 1949 and then again in August and September, right before rehearsals were scheduled to begin—they wrote with remarkable speed. Ten years earlier, they had worked on another show with black characters, *Ulysses Africanus,* from which they rescued a few songs that had been waiting for a new berth, but they knew each other's working habits so intimately that they would have worked quickly in any event. Often within twenty-four hours after Anderson had handed him a lyric, Weill would walk through the woods connecting their properties carrying drafts of several melodies from which Anderson could choose.

For Weill, composing a musical tragedy offered both a radical change of pace from *Love Life* and a set of challenges that were to be unique in his Broadway career. The first concern he and Anderson had was in preserving the tone of Paton's poetic novel in which a worried father, the Reverend Stephen Kumalo, journeys to Johannesburg from his home in the country to find his wayward son, Absalom. At just the moment of Stephen's arrival, Absalom during a robbery kills a white man, Arthur Jarvis, whose father, James, is Stephen's neighbor. Absalom is arrested, tried, and executed as, across the great gulf of apartheid, Stephen and James reach out in tentative friendship. The awkward plotting, strewn with coincidence, is redeemed by a majestic authorial voice rich in philosophical asides and lyrical descriptions of the South African landscape, an eloquent silent witness to racial division. If they were to honor their commitment to Paton, the collaborators would have to find a way to preserve at least an echo of the novel's commanding narrative presence.

From the beginning, Anderson and Weill were agreed that the way to retain Paton's chief "character" would be through a chorus. "To keep the plot and the dialogue in the form you gave them would only be possible if a chorus—a sort of Greek chorus—were used to tie together the great number of scenes, and to comment on the action as you comment in the philosophic and descriptive passages," Anderson notified the author.[2]

Most of Weill's choruses—such as the one that mocks the greedy capitalists of Mahagonny, for instance—had been ironic observers, but a black chorus singing of the racial tragedy in South Africa could have no trace of Berlin badinage. Weill's writing, for the character numbers as well as for the chorus, would have to vibrate with the deep emotion that infuses the novel.

If Weill's challenge in *Love Life* had been to assimilate a cavalcade of popular American musical forms, here his assignment was to interpret a musical language that was further from his training and background than any he had ever worked on. As always, he was an eager student and sent to Africa for recordings of different kinds of native idioms. About Zulu music, which he studied closely, he

An uneasy collaboration: Maxwell Anderson, Rouben Mamoulian, and Kurt Weill working on the score for *Lost in the Stars*, 1949

observed, "It's not harmony and it's not melody, and it relies on a great many quarter-tones."[3] Certainly Weill could have supplied a convincing simulacrum of African sonorities for a Broadway audience that could not have told the difference between the original and a skillful copy. Drums, tom-toms, an assortment of native rhythms and movements might have been the basis of a new kind of Broadway score, heavily percussive, sensual, and vibrant. But just as his minstrel show in *Love Life* was no more than a loose interpretation of authentic minstrelsy, Weill decided that his score for what was to be called *Lost in the Stars* would be "African" only in a general sense, would, in fact, be more American than African. "American spirituals are closer to African music than many people realize," Weill said. "There must be tom-toms in the score at times," he said,[4] but as a practical man of the theatre Weill never lost sight of the fact that he was writing for the New York stage, not for a tribal pageant. His score would be "African" molded to the requirements of a Broadway musical, a decision that matched Anderson's that the black actors in the cast would speak in unembellished American accents rather than attempting to re-create a black South African dialect.

The composer's own distance from the sources of black music was part of a larger issue, one that he and Anderson had failed to confront adequately in their patriarchal, condescending treatment of black characters in the aborted *Ulysses Africanus.* As white Americans, they were of course telling someone else's story, and the only honest way they could approach it was through emphasizing its universality. "The breaking of the tribe is only a symbol of the breaking of all tribes and all the old ways and beliefs," Anderson wrote Paton.[5] And as Weill announced before the opening, "We [want to] give a picture of the whole world today."[6]

Featuring a crucial and sustaining role for the chorus and a chorus leader—an unusual strategy that underlines the show's departure from Broadway conventions—along with several extended musical scenes and arias in which Reverend Kumalo expresses his anguish, Weill's score defies boundaries between opera and musical theatre. Even more thoroughly than in *Street Scene,* and despite the fact that he borrows epic-theatre conventions and writes primarily in the neoclassic format of a choral play, Weill eliminates virtually all traces of the angular, caustic style of his Brecht period. His score, openly and frankly, is written to tug at the heart. And yet, as in *Street Scene,* his other musical tragedy, he faced a delicate balancing act. For contrast and for pacing, he knew he needed to find spots for lighter material. And at the same time, as he was aware, too much relief would undermine the momentum of a story that moves inexorably toward Absalom's execution.

In adjusting the chiaroscuro Weill had the help of Rouben Mamoulian, who this time accepted Weill's job offer. Mamoulian, in effect, became the show's third author—a circumstance for which Weill, but not Maxwell Anderson, was grateful. Like Charles Friedman, the director of *Street Scene,* Mamoulian pushed for greater contrasts, especially in act 1, before the tragic action is set in motion. "Rewrite [act 1, scene 1] for a different treat-

Lost in the Stars, Kurt Weill's *Porgy and Bess.* White and black choruses, on different sides of the stage, register their responses to the murder of a white man in the song "Fear!"
Setting by George Jenkins

ment of Stephen's character," he requested. "We want to show him as he was before all the tragic events came into his life and caused him to lose his faith and hit the rock bottom of despair. In this scene he should be a man of clear and happy convictions. Give him a serene and kindly sense of humor." Mamoulian urged a lighter mood throughout the early part of act 1, before Stephen discovers his son's fall: "Stephen is starting out on a bright adventure." "Put a few smiles and chuckles into the scene between Alex [Stephen's grandson] and Stephen," he advised. "The child should serve the purpose of brightening the mood and relieving the intensifying drama of Stephen."[7] "Every laugh, chuckle or smile that can be honestly brought into our play will be like a drink of water in the desert," Mamoulian counseled, for once Stephen must confront what has become of his son, "no light strokes can be applied to him, so we must make the most with other characters, especially with the children."[8]

From first to last, and to an unprecedented degree for a Broadway show, choral writing dominates. "There is a lovely road that runs from Ixopo into the hills,"[9] the chorus leader sings in the opening number, in which

Anderson, wisely, has preserved the lyrical opening lines of the novel. "The Hills of Ixopo" is a free-flowing melody that at once establishes the score's abandonment of the traditional AABA song form. The number's undulating movement suggests the geographical divisions between the rich upper hills, where the white families live, and the parched lower hills, "red and bare," occupied by blacks. The escalating rhythm of "Train to Johannesburg," introduced by accordion—a novel touch—and sung by the Leader and the chorus, evokes a chugging locomotive picking up speed as it moves from the country to the city. It sounds very much like a Negro spiritual. "White man go to Johannesburg, / He come back. / Black man go to Johannesburg, / Never come back," the chorus intones as Anderson's plainspoken lyric again underlines the great divide between the races. "The Search," written in a semioperatic idiom, is one of several musical montages in the show. Providing connections among many brief scenes that sketch Stephen's search for Absalom in the city's black underworld, the music serves as a kind of cinematic editing device. The chorus supplies both factual information (the addresses where Absalom has lived) and comment ("Make no doubt! / It is fear that you see in her eyes! / It is fear!"), and in the climax it voices Stephen's inner monologue: "This is heavy, heavy for me." Unfortunately, Weill has supplied the chorus with utterly banal "traveling" music, its main motif a trite blues fragment transposed to many keys and repeated too many times.

Interlocked musical scenes, "Murder in Parkwold" and "Fear!," which dramatize the sudden murder of a white man and the reactions from white and black bystanders, are more skillful. For this musical montage, Mamoulian offered a number of ideas. "It should be composed as a series of short-clipped statements about the murder, by various members of the chorus, black and white, in a near-reportorial manner," Mamoulian advised—a good suggestion that was not, in fact, implemented. "In between these, newsboys' voices would shout 'Murder in Parkwold,' in a kind of sharp, staccato punctuation. Over all this, and tying it into a rhythmic musical pattern, there could be an obligato of humming by the chorus, a moaning chant. This interlude will prepare for the 'Fear' number."[10]

Yes, it is fear!
Fear of the few for the many,
Fear of the many for the few,

The Reverend Stephen Kumalo (Todd Duncan) marries his
imprisoned son (Julian Mayfield) to Irina (Inez Matthews)
in *Lost in the Stars.*

both white and black choruses chant antiphonally. The call-and-response form, a staple of African music, is given a chilling melodic twist. "What is there you have not taken from us / Except hate and fear?" the black chorus intones. "Men are not safe in the streets, / Not safe in their houses," the white chorus rejoins. Voicing communal emotions, the chorus becomes the concrete embodiment of a tragic racial conflict.

At the beginning of act 2, in "The Wild Justice," the chorus returns to a more detached role, questioning, in some of Maxwell Anderson's most powerful and poetic lyrics, the elusive justice that is part of the beloved country's cry.

Have you fished for a fixed star with the lines of its light?
Have you dipped the moon from the sea with the cup of night?
Have you caught the rain's bow in a pool and shut it in?
Go, hunt the wild justice down to walk with men.

"Were the ends of justice met?" the chorus asks. "Not yet, / No, not quite yet," it solemnly answers. This is strong material. One only wishes, at moments like these, that Weill had abandoned his concept of African song as a simplified precursor of Negro spirituals, which in a misguided attempt at "primitivism" leads him to undercompose. The lackluster result is a series of parallel fifths for the chorus that can only be described as Broadway Cherokee.

Following the Judge's announcement "Absalom Kumalo, you are sentenced to be hanged by the neck until you are dead. And may the Lord have mercy on your soul," the chorus bursts into "Cry, the Beloved Country," Weill's psalm for a benighted land. Now the choral writing is powerful, universal, freed from programmatic restraints. (Did the song's enormous emotive force spring from the composer's feelings about another country blasted apart by hatred, his own lost Germany?) In the anthem, the chorus leader equates the fate of "the wasted man," "the lost son," to "the broken tribes" and "the broken hills." The threnody is interrupted by dialogue—Stephen marries Absalom to his loyal girlfriend, Irina, who is carrying his child, and Absalom expresses his fear—before the chorus returns to its final benediction on "the lost." In "A Bird of Passage," as in Greek tragedy, the chorus provides a panoramic perspective:

This is the life of men on earth;
Out of darkness we come at birth
Into a lamplit room and then
Go forward into dark again.

"Four o'clock, it will soon be four," the chorus chants, providing the musical ground against which Stephen and Irina wait for Absalom's execution. There is a bit of ill-considered musical word painting on the clock motif, dispelling some of the tension that should be building. The execution itself is musically unmarked. Weill's silence ends with a stirring reprise of the refrain of "Thousands of Miles," Stephen's first song in the show. As it blesses the connection the black and white fathers have begun to forge, the chorus claims the last word:

Each lives alone in a world of dark,
Crossing the skies in a lonely arc,
Save when love leaps out like a leaping spark,
Over thousands, thousands of miles.

Entrusting the chorus with most of the show's musical and narrative high points, Weill was guilty of underwriting for the principals. Only Stephen, with five songs, has substantial musical responsibilities. Todd Duncan, the original Porgy, who was cast, as he said, after "they had heard over sixty Negroes for the role,"[11] worked closely with Weill, Anderson, and Mamoulian on shaping his character's songs. "Mr. Weill was very pliable, and I found I could make suggestions and that I would be heard," Duncan recalled. "He was a quiet man . . . I better just stick to that. I can't say that he ever made me laugh. Anderson was arrogant. He looked and acted like he was angry all the time. He had such a sour-looking face. Mr. Mamoulian really ran the show; he was the director in every sense. That first song I sang, 'Thousands of Miles' "—which expresses Stephen's essential optimism, his belief in the power of love to close the distances between people, including those that separate husband from wife, parent from child—"had a great sense of drama and the turn of a phrase that only Kurt Weill would do." But Duncan objected to Stephen's second song. "I didn't like the lullaby, 'The Little Gray House.' It was too jazzy, not calm or pastoral enough. 'I hope you don't think I'm difficult,' I told Kurt Weill, who said—he was so calm—'Don't worry, let's wait two days, I have a melody that fits this beautifully.' He was right. The difference was in the tessitura, and in the rhythmic approach. I wanted something that was earth, like a folk song, quiet and nostalgic. And that's what I think we got."[12]

Stephen concludes act 1 with the title song, a hymn that rumbles with the character's torment. "I loved the song, which had been written before [for *Ulysses Africanus*], then used again for our show," Duncan said. "I don't think it will ever die. It's monumental. It's not ethnic, it's all mankind, an image of the Oppressed."[13] Alan Paton, however, objected to Anderson's lyric. "The song . . . sung . . . by the humble and unsophisticated black priest . . . was highly sophisticated, and it was extremely painful for me to hear my humble hero in a role that he could never have taken. It was made more painful for me by the fact that the song belonged to the death-of-God genre, or to put it more accurately, to the desertion-of-God genre. God had created the universe . . . but now He had gone away. . . . So 'we are lost out here in the stars.' "[14]

In a rowdy Johannesburg bar, Linda (Sheila Guyse) performs
"Who'll Buy?" a Broadway number that momentarily "interrupts" Weill and Anderson's musical tragedy. Costumes designed
by Anna Hill Johnstone

In act 2, Stephen's big number was "O Tixo, Tixo, Help Me" ("Tixo" is
the word for God in native dialect), a soliloquy in the tradition of the one
from *Carousel,* but even more ambitious. Weill may have been aware of the
ironic parallelism: Billy Bigelow's soliloquy deals with the expected birth
of a son; Stephen's with the expected death of one. Mamoulian encouraged
Weill and Anderson to go deeper than they had in their first draft. "Here is
a chance for Kurt's score to rise to a high operatic level," the director
urged. "With Todd Duncan playing the part let's have a sweeping powerful aria, deeply emotional and of tragic dimensions, which should conclude with the cry of a loving, bleeding heart, biblical in stature. 'Oh,
Tixo, Tixo, help me!' This should be a musical line of utter beauty; prayer-

ful, humble and full of sorrow. . . . This line of prayer, repeated three times, could emotionally remind us of Christ's passion in the Garden of Gethsemane."[15] Rising to the call, Weill composed a true *recitativo accompagnato,* in which virtuosic writing for orchestra illuminates the inner turmoil of Stephen on the eve of the execution. True to the tradition of this form, the number never breaks into full-blown song. Instead, Stephen's tormented thoughts, prayers, and recollections are constantly seeking, never finding, resolution. His despair can only lead him to greater despair. The song's winding, tortuous melodic motifs demand operatic range and intensity. "For quite a while I felt I hadn't touched bottom on it," Duncan said. "Or hadn't touched God with it. I felt, most of the time, that I was a little too academic, too intellectual rather than being organic. I think once or twice I touched the Lord with it."[16]

For Irina, Weill wrote "Stay Well" and "Trouble Man" (with a surprising harp introduction), two songs of bluesy emotion strongly reminiscent of *Porgy and Bess.* Their boiling intensity, which expresses the great joy and equally great pain her lover has given, answered Mamoulian's plea for the writers to "build up" Irina, "who does not convey any feeling of love for Absalom. This should be expressed more vividly, so that both Stephen and the audience are impressed by the depth of her feeling for the boy, and her hunger for his 'presence.' "[17] For minor characters Weill supplied two Broadway-style numbers for which he was later to take some critical heat. "Who'll Buy?" is a Bessie Smith–style slow drag written on a Bessie Smith–style conceit: food as metaphor for female sexuality. (It was Bessie Smith, after all, who once sang, "I need a little sugar in my bowl, / I need a little hot dog in my roll.") Here Linda, a singer in a shantytown dive where Absalom and his rough friends congregate, belts the question, "Who'll buy my juicy rutabagas?" Alan Paton objected that "the drinking dive in Shanty Town was like nothing to be seen in Johannesburg and the dialogue was like nothing to be heard there."[18] But here, as throughout, Anderson and Weill were attempting only to create a "South Africa" of the Broadway imagination. A more pertinent criticism of the song is that the creators' imaginations fell a little short; neither the words nor the music get truly down-and-dirty, and enticing as it is, the song is also never quite as much fun or quite as naughty as it needs to be.

"Big Mole," on the other hand, is a terrific children's song, written for Stephen's grandson. Anderson's young daughter, Hesper, chose "Big Mole." " 'Which one do you like, Max?' Kurt asked, when he brought in three melodies he had written to lyrics my father had handed him the day before. Kurt always deferred to my father's judgment, but because 'Big Mole' was a child's song, this time I was allowed to choose. I liked all three, but of course I adored the one I chose. And in the play, little Herbert Coleman, with a big, big voice, stopped the show when he sang it. The number was very well placed near the end of the show when the audience needed a release."[19]

Weill also wrote one brief song, "The Little Tin God," for Stephen's corrupt brother, John, which was cut. Surprisingly, there are no songs at all for Absalom or for the white father and son. Leslie Banks, cast as James Jarvis, was not a singer, but that had never stopped Weill before. (At one point over the summer, Weill thought another nonsinger, Rex Harrison, who was to have the greatest success of his career in a singing role in *My Fair Lady,* would be playing Jarvis.) "We had very great difficulty with the actor playing the white father," Duncan recalled. "After Weill wrote this powerful musical soliloquy for me, our director wanted a soliloquy by the white father to balance that. And Anderson and Weill wrote one, but it just didn't hit: the actor couldn't do it. It was the cause of turbulence between Mamoulian and Anderson."[20]

Indeed, director and book writer never quite adjusted their differing visions, and tensions between them simmered throughout rehearsals. In all the battles, the strong-willed, take-charge director prevailed. "Mamoulian wanted my part played sweet, Anderson wanted a brick in the hand," Todd Duncan remembered. "I think Mamoulian was right, because honey will do the job better than vinegar."[21] The playwright's son Alan, who was production coordinator—"I was the go-between between the director and the authors"—recalled Mamoulian as a "flamboyant, overpowering Hollywood character, overwhelming for Max, and for Kurt, too, who were both quiet and shy. He was an autocrat who wanted a larger-than-life quality. He wanted the chorus to be bombastic; Dad and Kurt saw it as a more modest group, the voice of simple folk. I had stage-managed *Knickerbocker Holiday* and observed that Joshua Logan became very emotionally involved with the actors, but Mamoulian could have had a megaphone."[22] "Mamoulian didn't appreciate the show's blend of poetry and reality and made it all too stylized," Hesper Anderson commented. "And nobody liked the Mamoulians. He was so weird."[23]

Weill had to confront another personnel problem when, to his chagrin, his usual conductor, Maurice Abravanel, decamped in order to conduct a rival Broadway opera, Marc Blitzstein's *Regina.* (Abravanel had also been unable to conduct *Love Life* and had been replaced by Joseph Littau.)

Weill, who disliked Blitzstein personally and professionally, felt betrayed. Against the protests of his colleagues in the Playwrights Producing Company, who wanted a well-known conductor like Lehman Engel, Weill insisted on hiring Maurice Levine. (In gratitude, Levine named his son, born a year later, Michael Kurt, after his benefactor.) But when Levine wanted to hire someone to take Lys Symonette's usual job of rehearsal pianist and musical assistant, Weill came to her defense. "He wanted me to have a contract—I had never had one before—and he came in from New City to be with me when I had a meeting at the Playwrights Company office," Symonette recalled. "He had no other reason for coming in that day except to protect me: that is a measure of how humane and caring he was."[24]

"This was and is a conductor's score," Levine, who led a small chamber orchestra of twelve musicians, observed. Weill fought bitterly with the musicians' union to retain the small ensemble, unique to Broadway at the time. As in each of his works, he had insisted on doing his own orchestrations in order to create a particular "sound world," which he felt for this show required a chamber rather than a conventional-sized orchestra. "If you're conducting a popular type Broadway show where they lock into basic rhythms, you'll find as a conductor you can lean on the drummer a lot. As long as he has the groove and the rhythm section is grooved. When you get a score like [that of] *Lost in the Stars,* you have to conduct every note and every bar, you give inflections and nuances and breathe with the performers. It's like opera." (Levine recalled that Weill came to the first few performances after opening night. Following the show, he would go over the score with his conductor, giving "the most specific indications which only two musicians would understand. 'When you go from the G to the G sharp in the second viola, bring that note out so that we can feel the resolution all the more.' " Weill continued to comment, and to hover, for about six weeks. "He would just show up. And then one day he said, 'I just want to tell you I have no more notes. This is it. Do your best to keep it that way.' ")[25]

To add to the pressure, the production, in financial straits from the beginning, was still short of money as opening night loomed. Since both Anderson and Weill were members, the Playwrights Producing Company would of course produce. But as the group informed the coauthors, who were urged to seek additional capital, a musical tragedy with no stars and featuring a score in which most of the music would be performed by a semioperatic chorus was clearly going to be a box-office risk. Weill had led the drive for outside money, but after receiving numerous negative responses he and Anderson, on July 18, had formed a limited-partnership agreement: Weill put in $3,000, Anderson $7,500. It wasn't enough, and the harried composer was forced to seek additional funding right up to the opening. "It's a distinguished job and a fine thing for the theatre," Billy Rose wrote Weill on October 12, responding negatively, as most people had, to a request for money. "In addition to a moving libretto, Maxwell Anderson has written some of the finest lyrics I've ever read. Do I want to invest in the show? I hardly think so. I'm afraid, everything considered, that its commercial chances are only so-so."

As he scrambled for money and ran interference between Anderson and Mamoulian, Weill had to deal with another kind of unpleasantness. Over the summer the director Dino Yannopoulos had asked him for permission to stage *The Czar Has His Photograph Taken* as part of a series of short operas to be presented by the Metropolitan Opera Studio at the Juilliard School of Music. Weill did not want any work from his German catalogue staged in America, and certainly not this short opera written in the early difficult style he had abandoned by the late 1920s—*The Czar* was a reminder of a world he had left behind. Nonetheless, he reluctantly granted permission and agreed to one meeting with the director, at Brook House. "We went through the whole score. No changes were made," Yannopoulos recalled. "Weill told me, 'You can do anything you want. Please. It's yours. I give it to you. Don't pay me any royalties.' Kurt Adler, who was to conduct, came with me and asked, 'You want this slower? Faster?' Weill just sat there."[26] The composer's firm don't-look-back policy had clearly kicked in.

He may have consented to a production because a performance at Juilliard, then way uptown at Claremont Avenue and 121st Street, could have little impact on his Broadway reputation and in all likelihood would amount to no more than a passing curiosity: a historical footnote. He wanted no part in the staging and had no interest in attending a performance. "I was given the job of translating the opera into English," Lys Symonette said. "When I told Weill, the reaction was icy. He just froze up—almost annoyed." Preoccupied with rehearsals for *Lost in the Stars,* he brusquely turned down an invitation to attend a dress rehearsal, but agreed only after Symonette, at Yannopoulos's request, told him, "The kids worked so hard, and it would mean so much to them to meet you." He conceded, and asked Lys, following a *Stars* rehearsal, to accompany him in a taxi up to Juilliard. "Going uptown from the Broadway district he said not one word, and on the way back downtown after the show, not one word, and with a face that just told me, 'Don't talk to me.' "[27] During the run-through, as Yannopoulos recalled, Weill sat with no expression whatever. "I went over to him and asked if he liked it. He got up and said, 'I must congratulate you—the singers, not me. You did a marvelous job, but I must apologize for having written that kind of music."[28]

Because of the tight budget, there were no out-of-town tryouts for *Lost in the Stars.* After a short preview season, in which "there were practically no changes made," according to Symonette,[29] the show opened at the Music Box on October 30, 1949. "Beautiful," "moving," "important," were words of praise that appeared in a number of reviews. "Out of a memorable novel has come a memorable musical drama," Brooks Atkinson reported in the *New York Times* on October 31. "It is difficult to remember anything from Kurt Weill's portfolio that is as eloquent as this richly orchestrated singing musical." Objections tended to focus on the show's temperature. "It doesn't tug at your emotions as it should," Robert Coleman noted in the *Daily Mirror,* voicing a recurrent puzzlement. Virgil Thomson, usually cool toward Weill, saluted the composer's solos, choruses, and set pieces for their "variety" and "their movement toward a goal. It is a play with musical numbers, a *singspiel.* Whether one 'likes' Mr. Weill's numbers or not, their relation to the play is a model of procedure," he wrote in his column in the *New York Herald-Tribune.*

But among the general acclamation was a reproving voice that for Weill carried a particular sting. In a long article in the December 31 *Saturday Review of Recordings* huffily entitled "Lost in the Stars of Broadway," Weill's first American mentor, Harold Clurman, cast a critical eye on the scope of the composer's American career. "The *Lost in the Stars* score is certainly good in that it performs its theatrical function (it makes Maxwell Anderson's words go down easily and . . . it helps the play's sad tale seem elevating as well as touching). . . . The fact that the music is not particularly original—that it is, indeed, full of obvious reminiscences—is not in itself as damaging as certain connoisseurs would have us believe." Clurman praised Weill's "unerring sense of the theatre." But "of music as music" Clurman raised doubts. "At no time does the music [of the show] penetrate my consciousness as a living element." He opposed the "synthetic" quality of the present work to Weill's *Threepenny Opera* score. To Clurman, Weill's career since *Johnny Johnson,* "always on a high level of craftsmanship," reflected "an adaptation toward an increasingly facile . . . artistically nondescript goal. The result has been, naturally, a decline in real quality, an ever more conventional musicality and an increase in journalistic praise as well as box office receipts."

Another displeased viewer opening night was Alan Paton. Personal relations between Paton and Maxwell Anderson had never improved. "Anderson was—to me—a withdrawn and taciturn man, and he was to stay that way," Paton recalled.[30] And as Victor Samrock, the Playwrights Producing Company business manager, noted, "We knew that Paton felt Maxwell Anderson had softened the impact of the race problem for the sake of Broadway, had softened the unlikelihood of the blacks and whites getting together. (We didn't have a big black audience. The blacks had so many problems that they didn't relate to Africa, at least at the time.)"[31] "I may say that this terrible evening was made more endurable by the beauty of the singing, and by Kurt Weill's music," Paton reported. "The chorus, 'Cry, the Beloved Country,' was powerful and beautiful, and moved me deeply, but these were not the words of a stranger, they were my own."[32]

"Of course, as always when one has a big success," Weill wrote to his parents on January 20, 1950, "there are also a lot of attacks from composers or dramatists who are less successful." Not for the first time, Weill was jumping the gun—*Lost in the Stars* did brisk business for the first two months, but by January audiences began to dwindle. Weill worked as hard promoting the musical after it opened as he had during the tense rehearsals, but despite his efforts *Lost in the Stars* limped through the spring before closing in May. It then toured briefly. The racially divided America of 1950 did not reflect the spirit of racial reconciliation depicted on stage, and in some cities black actors had difficulty finding accommodations. In protest, Todd Duncan withdrew before the end of the tour.

"It must be somewhat surprising indeed to find a serious subject treated in a form which (in this country at least) has been used so far only for a lighter form of entertainment," Weill wrote on November 14 to Olin Downes, thanking the *New York Times* music critic for his review, in which he had praised Weill's score as "another important step toward an American musical theatre." "The nature of my experiment," Weill continued, "was to do a 'musical tragedy' for the American theatre so that the typical American audience (not a specialized audience) can accept it; and the real success of the piece to me is the fact that the audience did accept it without hesitation, that they accepted a lot of very serious, tragic, quite un-Broadway-ish music of operatic dimensions, together with some songs written in a more familiar style." In a follow-up letter, on December 19,

Downes wrote to express his objection to those songs "in a more familiar style. No doubt a Broadway spectacle simply has to have numbers in the form of song hits, and that kind of formalism disturbs me a little bit. . . . But I am still waiting for the day when you get exactly the subject which you can treat without the faintest consideration of public taste or expediency of any sort." Weill was quick to defend his use of popular song. "It seems to me that the American popular song, growing out of the American folk-music, is the basis of American musical theatre (just as the Italian song was the basis of Italian opera), and that in this early state of the development, and considering the audiences we are writing for, it is quite legitimate to use the form of the popular song and gradually fill it with new musical content," he responded to Downes on December 20.

In writing his most solemn Broadway score, did Weill capitulate to the perceived tastes of the madding crowd, as his letter seems to indicate? Agnes de Mille, among others, thought so. "I felt the score was pretty cheap," she grumbled. "I was just shocked. [For the climax] Beethoven would have been hard pressed and Kurt delivered a dear little sentimental ditty."[33] But to be true to his quest of founding an American opera based on American popular song, the idioms he employed for *Lost in the Stars* were exactly the right ones, with accessible melodies embedded in larger and more complex forms than the standard AABA structure. Continuing his self-appointed role of musical educator, begun in Berlin, Weill composed in a way intended to welcome as well as to challenge a broad audience. There are some lapses, however. The absence of music in the climactic scene between the fathers, and the musical silence of Absalom and the white characters throughout the show, suggest a curious failure of creative nerve. Despite his frequent filmic underscoring and extended musical scenes, Weill's musical gaps confer an unfinished glaze on his score. "In this kind of work the intensity must never slacken and all elements of the theatre—words, music and movement—have to be molded into one unity," Weill wrote his parents on November 5, 1949. "In this I have succeeded better than in any of my earlier works." But had he? With its sometimes lazy use of musical primitivism, and its notable diffidence in regard to all the characters except Stephen, the score does not consistently sustain the high pitch, "the intensity [that] must never slacken," that the material requires. And strong as it is, Anderson's dialogue, which sometimes retains, word for word, the novel's severe, formal, almost ritualistic rhythms, breaks the tension that the best of Weill's writing builds. This musical tragedy cries out for a through-composed score. Even so, in terms of the composer's own goal of writing musicals that stretched formal, thematic, and generic boundaries, *Lost in the Stars* must be rated as a success—in fact, as Kurt Weill's most fully achieved "Broadway opera." As Miles Kreuger noted, "The show has—it had to have—a dramatic unity, one that *Street Scene* doesn't have or need. For that reason—because it is so unrelieved by other elements—it comes closer than *Street Scene* to the 'opera' label. *Street Scene* has a greater spectrum of emotion and of musical styles, but *Lost in the Stars* would be better in an opera house."[34] (Despite the fact that there is far more dialogue than in traditional operas, *Lost in the Stars,* like *Street Scene,* has had numerous, successful opera-house productions.)

If by and large the show holds up musically, really through no fault of its own it has become ideologically problematic. "It has succumbed to history: the world has gone by it," Quentin Anderson said.[35] From a contemporary perspective, the play's emblematic reconciliation between two fathers who nonetheless keep their places in the South African chain of being as dictated by apartheid is an antiquated fiction—well-meaning but irrelevant. Apartheid, inevitably, had to be ended through violence rather than a paternalistic gesture of the white father. It would seem that, overtaken by the realities of a postapartheid South Africa, Anderson's beautifully written history lesson might have been relegated to an example of yesterday's liberalism; but from the mid-1980s to the early 1990s the show had several revivals.

The 1949–50 season had some disappointments: *Miss Liberty,* a highly anticipated new musical by Irving Berlin, fizzled; and the one runaway hit, *Gentlemen Prefer Blondes,* was no more than a brisk, low-consciousness musical-comedy hootenanny. But in addition to *Lost in the Stars,* the season boasted two other important opera–musical theatre hybrids: *Regina,* Marc Blitzstein's adaptation of Lillian Hellman's *Little Foxes,* which opened the night after the Anderson-Weill show; and *The Consul,* by Gian Carlo Menotti, voted best musical by the New York Drama Critics Circle. To Weill, the existence of *Regina* seemed to confirm his often-repeated claims that Blitzstein was forever nipping at his heels, trying to imitate him and to poach on his territory as a musical-theatre firebrand. "[*Regina*] could have been a better success if Blitzstein's attempts at writing songs would have been more successful," Weill grumbled in a November 14 letter to Olin Downes. "Awfully bad and dramatically false," Downes fired back in his December 9 letter. Both were wrong. *Regina* is a luminous work by an unfairly neglected master. It is fully equal to Weill's strongest American work and, as much as *Street Scene* and *Lost in the Stars,* represents a significant experiment in melding opera with Broadway.

In January, February, and March of 1950, in what were to be the final three months of his life, Weill as coproducer oversaw *Lost in the Stars,* prepared the orchestrations for the original cast recording, supervised the NBC-TV production of *Down in the Valley,* and began to collaborate with Maxwell Anderson on a musical of Mark Twain's *Adventures of Huckleberry Finn*—like *Lost in the Stars,* a story about a friendship between a black and a white character who must overcome ingrained prejudice. The work was part of Weill's long-range project of musicalizing American literary classics; he had plans, down the line, to tackle *Moby-Dick.* For *Huck Finn,* Weill had no reformist agenda. The show was conceived as a conventionally structured Broadway musical rather than a folk opera, and his score was to comprise separable numbers rather than extended musical scenes. The five songs he was working on in rough-draft form are enchanting— airy, light-filled, and suffused with a rolling American gait. "River Chanty," an ode to the river sung by Jim and Huck on their raft as it moves from side to side, starboard to leeward, suggests the river's undulations and its timeless power. The song, evoking a majestic American landscape, has a remarkable spaciousness. "Apple Jack" and "Catfish Song," as fresh as all outdoors, are vibrant backwoods numbers with a pungent folk-music flavor. Infused with a child's sense of wonder at the natural world, and containing a hint of the grand adventure to come, "Come In, Mornin'" is Huck's greeting for a new day. In "This Time Next Year," the last song Weill was to write, Jim anticipates his freedom. Rippling with yearning and expectation, this was a fitting swan song for an optimist.

At the end of February, Weill's health began suddenly to fail, and it remained uncertain into March. (The previous July, Weill had collapsed on Alan Jay Lerner's tennis court, but he recovered quickly and asked Lerner not to mention the incident to anyone.) On March 16, his heartbeat became irregular. Lenya, worried, checked him into a local hospital on March 19. He seemed to rally and, sitting up in bed in his hospital room, was able to accept visits from Maxwell Anderson. But on March 23, he suffered a relapse. Lenya had him moved to a hospital in New York for intensive care. Rallying once again, he continued to meet with Anderson for discussions about *Huck Finn.* But as April began he took a final turn. On April 3, his heart stopped.

With so little time to prepare for the shock of his death, Lenya was inconsolable, weeping uncontrollably and wondering if she had the strength to go on without the partner she had shared her life with for the past quarter of a century. And Maxwell Anderson, the best friend Weill had ever had, was equally "shattered," as Hesper Anderson recalled. "There had been such an enormous connection between them."[36] "Kurt's death, so sudden, was a terrible shock to Dad," Alan Anderson said. "People told him he had to finish *Huck Finn,* and he went to Irving Berlin. But he couldn't find another collaborator. His work wasn't going anywhere at the time, and he was discouraged. If he and Kurt had been able to work together, my father would have lived longer."[37]

In April 1950 Lotte Lenya was uncertain about her husband's place in the American theatre and fearful that he would soon be forgotten. She little suspected that she would devote the remaining thirty-one years of her life to seeing that he wasn't.

SIXTEEN

The Widow Weill

W ith her usual passion and extravagance, Lenya leaned down over Kurt's coffin, which was laid out downstairs in Brook House, and kissed his penis," Quentin Anderson recalled. "And then she said to me, out on the terrace, 'It doesn't really matter what we did, does it?' I understood she was saying she had an unbroken devotion. It had not been meant that she was to be sexually faithful, but it had been a profounder bond than any other. I saw them often, and I was never conscious either of differences or of manifestations of affection. It was as if they were partners who knew each other so well and so relied on each other that they hardly needed exchange of words."[1] Now, with Weill's death, the strongest and most enduring relationship of Lenya's life had been abruptly ruptured. "Her grief, her fear after Kurt's death were all-consuming," Hesper Anderson said. "And it went on and on and on. She cried endlessly. She didn't want to live. She didn't see how she *could* live."[2]

After her failure in *The Firebrand of Florence* in 1945, Lenya once again had become Mrs. Kurt Weill of South Mountain Road. For the last five years of her husband's life, when "Lotte Lenya" in effect had ceased to exist, Mrs. Weill cooked and cleaned for her husband (Arnold Sundgaard remembered her bringing in trays of excellent home-baked chocolate cookies)[3] and played cards nightly with a group of neighbors. "She never got the strength inside her to be an independent woman," observed Hesper Anderson. "She was a generation before. Lenya had made a decision that for those early years she was going to back Kurt—Kurt always came first with her."[4] Now Kurt was gone, and without children or a career, and the nightly ritual of cards as her major activity, Lenya seemed married to her mourning.

When Ernst Josef Aufricht, the producer of the original Berlin production of *Die Dreigroschenoper,* asked Lenya to sing in a tribute to Weill that he would be presenting at Town Hall on February 3, 1951, she turned him down. But George Davis, an editor and writer who had befriended Lenya (and whom she would marry on July 7, 1951), convinced her that it was her duty as the composer's widow to participate in the tribute. Davis was determined that neither Kurt Weill nor Lotte Lenya would be forgotten. But up to the last moment, seized by periodic bouts of nerves and insecurity, Lenya threatened to withdraw, as Davis continued to remind her of her obligation to Weill. When she stepped onto the stage at Town Hall ten months after Weill's death, "she was shaking," as Hesper Anderson

Composer Marc Blitzstein, who adapted Brecht's libretto and lyrics, coproducer Stanley Chase, Lenya, and producer-director Carmen Capalbo discuss the upcoming production of *The Threepenny Opera* at the Theatre de Lys, 1954.

recalled. "When she started, her voice was quavery and she was trembling. But once she got going, she was magnetic, magic, spellbinding. After going through all the grief . . . it was an inspiration."[5] Many in the audience were German refugees, for whom Lenya's appearance was a powerful reminder of Berlin in the 1920s. For the American spectators, most of whom would never have seen or heard any of the music from Weill's German period, Lenya was a revelation. In Berlin over twenty years earlier, her voice had been higher and lighter, with intimations of an almost-legitimate, almost-soprano quality; now, at the half-century point, it had taken on a sandpapery roughness. But "it didn't matter that she sounded like a crow . . . approaching shrapnel," composer David Raksin said,[6] because her lack of technical finish, her raw *Sprechgesang* style flecked with a thrumming vibrato, was the source of her unique appeal. "What is your intuition about how Kurt Weill's music should be sung?" Lenya was asked near the end of her life. "The way I sing it," she snapped.[7] She was right, as her legendary performance at Town Hall indicated.

After the concert, Lenya was eager to retreat once again to Brook House. But Maxwell Anderson, about whom she had "very mixed feelings," according to his daughter, Hesper, wrote a part for her as Socrates' wife, Xantippe, in his new play, *Barefoot in Athens,* about Socrates' final days, when he faced charges of treason. Lenya was not interested, but Anderson and a number of her neighbors urged her to return to work. The play opened on October 31, 1951, and after it closed thirty performances later Lenya seemed intent on retiring once again.

Her next performance, however, was to have long-range consequences both for her and for Weill. As part of a four-day Festival of Creative Arts at Brandeis University, Lenya was persuaded to re-create her original role of Jenny for a concert performance on June 14, 1952, of *The Threepenny Opera.* In 1933, in its only prior professional production in America, the show had been performed in a stilted translation that made the raffish characters seem like exiles from *The Student Prince* or *Blossom Time.* At Brandeis, conducted by Leonard Bernstein, professor of music and director of the School of the Creative Arts, the work was performed in a vigorous, idiomatic translation by Marc Blitzstein. "The lyrics are a miracle—nineteenth century slanginess [with] a touch of twentieth century detachment," Cecil Smith raved in the July 1952 number of *Musical America.* "To make the characters more immediate, Blitzstein has chosen a new locale, New York in the 1870s, the unbridled days of gangsterism in the unsavory neighborhood of the notorious Five Points. The characters have a spontaneous, ver-

Lenya, at fifty-four, playing Jenny, the role she originated
in 1928, and Scott Merrill as Macheath,
in the de Lys *Threepenny Opera*

nacular quality . . . [and] all translation retains all the rough-and-ready, seedy vigor of the original Gay-Pepusch opera and Weill's cynical, post-World War I Teutonic transmutation."

The show attracted the interest of a number of would-be producers. Because they wanted to do something to alter or to "improve" the original, however, Lenya rejected all the offers. A full year after the concert, with many New York theatre professionals convinced of the work's commercial prospects, the show still did not have a producer. Carmen Capalbo, a young theatre director who had studied with John Gassner at Yale, knew the show from the Telefunken recordings and from a prompt copy of the 1933 New York production he had located at the New York Public Library. "It was a horrendous translation, I couldn't figure it out," Capalbo said, but he was determined that "someday [he] would do the play properly."[8] (The first publication of *The Threepenny Opera* in English was Eric Bentley's 1949 translation.) He called Marc Blitzstein to inquire about the rights. "You're a day too late—we just signed with another producer," Blitzstein informed Capalbo, who ignored the information. "I call Marc ten days in a row—I was a pest, and after the tenth call he asked me not to call again. I went into a funk. The next morning, he called me. 'Do you still want to do it? Come to my apartment to meet Lotte Lenya and me.'" Capalbo attended with Stanley Chase, his new producing partner, with whom he had taken a twelve-week lease on the Theatre de Lys, located on Christopher Street in Greenwich Village around the corner from where he lived. "Marc ran the meeting; Lenya, accompanied by George Davis, seemed very nervous, and didn't say much,"[9] as Capalbo recalled. "That first day Marc played for us a number of the songs," Stanley Chase said, "I really got chills. He always had a cigarette dangling from his mouth. He had this upright piano and he was just alive with Weill."[10] "How would you do this?" Lenya asked the two young men. "Exactly as written," Capalbo responded. "That seemed to impress her," Capalbo remembered. "Many of the people who had approached her had wanted to do something *to* it. When I said I wanted to direct, Marc and Lenya were nodding to each other. Then he asked me to sing the score!" Capalbo, who had a deep baritone, clearly understood the style, "off-handed and against the beat: it's an American vaudeville, music-hall style. Fred Astaire, who had no voice yet was a great singer, had it. The voice is secondary: the words are everything. After two or three songs, Lenya stopped me and said, 'Where did you learn to sing like that?' . . . 'From you,' I said."[11] Chase also felt that George Davis, who was at Lenya's side, "may have been the deciding factor in our getting it . . . a sheer guess that he sensed something, our eagerness, our innocence. Many people, after all, including Billy Rose and Roger Stevens, had approached them."[12]

Lenya decided to entrust the work to a young and little-known director who was offering a production in an out-of-the-way theatre on a street she had never heard of. When Capalbo showed her the de Lys, she liked both the theatre and the neighborhood: "nothing but tenements and garbage pails; it wasn't chic," according to Capalbo. And as Lenya was quick to realize, the intimate, modest de Lys (which then as now, as the Lucille Lortel, has no architectural style whatever), situated far from the slick uptown Broadway showshops, was a more appropriate setting for *The Threepenny Opera* than the inappropriately elegant Schiffbauerdamm had been.

Capalbo's next job was to convince Lenya to reprise her role as Jenny. " 'I'm an ugly old German lady with an accent,' " she told Capalbo. "She was very insecure, and basically felt that American audiences would never understand what she was about. And she was worried about age—she was fifty-four, the rest of us were kids. I told her Jenny could be any age." It took three weeks for Capalbo, aided by George Davis, to smash Lenya's resistance. "You have to trust me," he told her.

The show opened with no stars other than Lenya—on their minuscule budget, Capalbo and Chase could hardly afford name performers, and didn't really want them anyway. For his Macheath he cast the little-known Scott Merrill. "I knew nothing about *The Threepenny Opera* when I went to a cattle-call audition," Merrill remembered. "I knew Kurt Weill had written 'September Song,' and I knew *One Touch of Venus*. I thought Lotte Lenya might be Cheryl Crawford. At the time I was involved mostly in dancing:

Competing for Macheath (Scott Merrill): Beatrice Arthur as Lucy and Jo Sullivan as Polly perform "The Jealousy Duet" in *The Threepenny Opera*. Costumes by Saul Bolasni

I don't sing that well, and I certainly wasn't vocally trained. My voice was natural; my movement was like poetry, and it was the movement that Lenya liked. In the final audition, Marc Blitzstein played 'Death Message' ["Call from the Grave"], and Lenya said, 'I want you to "vomit" on me,' and after I sang the song they told me I had the part. I was on top of the world: I knew it was quite an event." Blitzstein "was not happy with their choice of me," Merrill recalled, "so I worked with him three times a week. 'If you want to talk it, do,' Marc told me. He wanted me to do every syllable correctly. And Lenya told me, 'Tell a story with each song.' That was really the secret of her success with 'Pirate Jenny': she told a story, not caring what her voice was like." Insecure at first, Merrill took a "heavy-hammer attitude, which wasn't right and wasn't working. After several weeks Lenya took me out to dinner and said, 'Go out and be campy: have a ball.' After that I began to have more fun with it."[13]

For Polly, Capalbo hired Jo Sullivan, who had appeared in the Brandeis concert. "She had a steely ingenue quality that was right for the character," Capalbo said. And Sullivan could sing, in a smooth, trained lyric soprano that provided a contrast to the untrained voices of some of the other performers. For her rival, Lucy, Capalbo cast a young, unknown Beatrice Arthur—tart, tall, tough in manner and appearance. As Mrs. Peachum, Charlotte Rae, who had studied for opera (and who had played the role in a college production of the show at Northwestern University in 1946, had the most powerful lungs in the cast. "When she sang 'The Dependency Song' at the ironing board it blew the rafters off," the show's costume designer, Saul Bolasni, remembered. "Lenya was not amused. 'It's not necessary to have a voice like that for this part,' she said. It was jealousy. I sensed Lenya wasn't too happy with any of the ladies, but she was crazy about Scott Merrill."[14]

Although Capalbo had mixed feelings about Lenya ("She could be vicious whenever she was backed into a corner or perceived that she was being backed into a corner, but she could also be terrifically charming"), he was relieved that she trusted his approach and did not try to codirect. "I wanted to capture the work's spirit of youthful rebellion in the Brecht-Weill style of epic-theatre detachment," Capalbo said, and because his actors were "Strasberg-brainwashed," he had to pull them from the sway of Actors Studio realism that dominated the American stage at the time. "They wanted to act as if there *was* no audience, and at first they resisted my instructions to turn and talk to the house. This isn't the real thing, after all, but actors only half-pretending to play characters from a time and place different from the reality outside the theatre. Brecht and Weill's obvious estrangement from an English tone and setting is part of what lends the work its fabled alienation. We made no attempt at English accents, and although nominally the play is set in Victorian London we didn't play it in a specific period. And the look I was after was a grab bag out of a trunk. I wanted it to have the wonderment of kids dressing up and creating a style of their own."[15] Capalbo's job was made easier because, with Lenya present, he could show his actors a prime example of epic style. As Lenya said, "I was trained in the Brecht-Weill style. You step in and out of your performance—if somebody would ask me in the middle of 'Pirate Jenny' a question, I would answer and go right on just the same, because I don't need any mood to create. I don't have to get into a trance. I'm like a ditch digger, digging the ditch."[16]

If Lenya kept her promise not to interfere with Capalbo's directing, Capalbo honored his word about being faithful to Kurt Weill. "We followed the original orchestrations. Not a note was changed, except to transpose for voices," he said—a claim that Kim Kowalke, president of the Kurt Weill Foundation for Music, vigorously disputes. Because in its original form, however, the show was something of a musical smorgasbord, its songs a movable feast, Capalbo felt entitled to some reassigning. Although Lenya had sung "Pirate Jenny" in the 1931 film version and was certainly identified with the song, in 1928 it had been performed by Polly as her wedding song. Understandably, Capalbo wanted Lenya to sing "Pirate Jenny," and at Lenya's suggestion he imported "Bilbao-Song" from *Happy End* as the number Polly performs at her wedding. (With new lyrics, it was called "The "Bide-A-Wee Song.") Happily, Capalbo restored Lenya's "Solomon Song," cut in 1928, and because Beatrice Arthur was practically a baritone Blitzstein had to transpose her part in the "Jealousy Duet," written originally as a vocal sparring match between two sopranos. Although it violated Weill's original intentions, "the contrast between the high and low voices worked, and their number stopped the show every night," Capalbo said.[17]

Lenya, on the whole, treated Capalbo well, because she felt he was working to honor her husband's achievement. Toward Marc Blitzstein, however, she was often abusive. " 'Damn him, he's a dirty little Jewish tailor who thinks he's a composer,' " she griped, according to Capalbo. And as Maurice Abravanel said, "Kurt had never liked Blitzstein personally or as a composer, and Lenya carried on with those feelings."[18] Lenya and George Davis were adamant that on the marquee and in all advertising and promotion the show should be announced as " 'Kurt Weill's *Threepenny Opera.*' George Davis told me we had to be clear that Marc Blitzstein was not to be thought of as the composer," Capalbo said. And following Lenya's orders, not only was Blitzstein put in his proper place, with his name and function ("translated by") below the title and in smaller type than Weill's, but so was Bertolt Brecht, whose name appeared in even smaller type than the translator's. Working out an ancient grievance against her least favorite of her late husband's collaborators, Lenya was determined to give Brecht modest billing. Brecht, "who wrote the book on shrewdness," as Capalbo claimed, "had given Lenya full authority to act for him. He knew the production would be good for him, regardless of how big his name appeared." But there was hell to pay when, just before the opening, a *New York Times* headline announced, "Marc Blitzstein Work to Be Performed." "Lenya called Marc that night, screaming and swearing. 'I didn't write that, the *Times* assigns a headline writer,' Marc, crestfallen, explained to her," Capalbo recalled.

Regardless of how she treated him, Blitzstein, according to Capalbo, "adored her. He was very protective of her, as though she were his mother, and was respectful of her as Kurt's widow."[19] For all her resentment, Lenya praised Blitzstein's translation. "He has come closest to capturing the power of Brecht's book and lyrics," she maintained. "He has kept the slang and the sting."[20] Decades later she cited the translation's "great integrity.

It's a masterpiece of adaptation, because he doesn't change. On rare occasions he had to change just a slight bit, adding or taking away a little note." And both at the time of the production and for the rest of her life she defended Blitzstein from the most frequent criticism directed against his work, that he had softened—defanged—Brecht's acrid original. "English is softer than German, you can't get away from that. You will find that even in *Seven Deadly Sins,* translated by a great poet, Auden, as close as anyone can come to Brecht, but it is still sharper sounding in German."[21]

After they paid $600 down for a twelve-week rental of the Theatre de Lys, Capalbo and Chase raised the money, "well under $10,000, about $8700–8800," according to Stanley Chase, "mostly from a phone in Cromwell's drug store. There were forty-two investors in all—$400 from my mother, $600 here, $500 there." Like the original production, the Off-Broadway *Threepenny Opera* was not expected to be a hit. "Our attorney said, 'You guys are crazy. Only a few German refugees will see it,' " Chase recalled.[22] " 'Are you kidding?' people would tell me, warning me that we wouldn't get eight people to schlepp down to Christopher Street to see it," Capalbo said.[23]

The Threepenny Opera opened on March 10, 1954. Marlene Dietrich was in the audience and, as Chase recollected, "mostly older people, who were familiar with the recordings and the Pabst film, and German refugees who had seen the original."[24] Reviews were decidedly mixed. "Falls flat on its arch face," Robert Coleman grumbled in the *New York Daily Mirror* on March 12. In the *New York Journal-American* on March 11, John McLean offered the curious suggestion that the show "should be painted on a larger and more expensive canvas; it doesn't seem to lend itself to the restrictions of an intimate production." Other reviews were more encouraging. Virgil Thomson, an ambivalent Weill watcher and a powerful music critic, conferred his influential stamp of approval. "A classic work of music and poetry, Blitzstein's [!] *Threepenny Opera* does not get a luxurious production at the Theatre de Lys," he reported in the *New York Herald-Tribune* on March 21. "But it doesn't need one. It belongs to the theatre of revolt, to the literature of social and political satire, and needs only indignation, compassion and conviction to make it come off. The simpler the presentation the better. . . . So much of [the original spirit] comes through that this listener found himself transported to post–World War I Berlin." Both Brooks Atkinson in the drama department and Olin Downes in the music department of the *New York Times* wrote raves. But even without the

ABOVE: Lenya in her riveting performance of "Pirate Jenny" in the long-running
Threepenny Opera at the Theatre de Lys

BELOW: Scott Merrill, Jo Sullivan, and Lenya in *The Threepenny Opera*

imprimatur of the *Times* the show might well have survived on its ecstatic word-of-mouth. At first primarily older people and refugees revisiting their youth in another country came to the show, but as Stanley Chase recalled, "eventually we attracted the *Guys and Dolls* crowd as well as tourists."[25]

The show paid off in six weeks, but because another production had been booked into the theatre it had to close at the end of the scheduled twelve-week run. "We could have taken it uptown, but I never believed it would have made it there," Capalbo claimed. "No other Off-Broadway theatre was available, but I made a vow to bring the show back. We put the scenery in my basement at 13 Gay Street, and the big pieces up in the Bronx. It took fifteen months, but we reopened at the de Lys as I had promised."[26] Capalbo's campaign had been helped by Brooks Atkinson, who would write "Bring back *The Threepenny Opera*" at the end of every review of the string of mediocre shows that opened at the de Lys following *Threepenny Opera*'s enforced departure. In association with Lucille Lortel, who now owned the theatre, Capalbo and Chase reopened the show on September 20, 1955, with Lenya, Scott Merrill, Jo Sullivan, Beatrice Arthur, and William Duell (in the dual roles of Filch and the Messenger) reprising their original roles. Samuel Matlowsky continued to conduct the eight-piece orchestra placed stage right (in the original production there had been seven pieces).

The de Lys *Threepenny Opera* rescued Weill from the oblivion that Lenya feared was about to engulf him at the time of his death. Even the reviews that criticized the play or the performance praised the score—for its wit, its melodic appeal, its theatrical cunning. There was no doubt that Weill was the show's star attraction. And at the same time that it inaugurated the Weill revival in America, the show also marked the true beginning of Lenya's American career. Certainly not of her own design, her appearance in her original role transformed her into an icon of the country she had fled more than twenty years earlier. With her tousled, now red hair (she had become a redhead at the suggestion of George Davis) and her jagged, harsh features, at fifty-four she had come more than ever to resemble an expressionist portrait by Jawlensky or Kokoschka. She was a mask that seemed to express the unrest and cynicism that the show reflected and by which it was inspired. "What happens on stage in Act II is simply hair-raising," Jerry Tallmer reported in the *Village Voice.* "Miss Lenya shambles front and center to exhale the first weary, husky, terrible notes of her husband's famous song about the black freighter. Her voice lifts and hardens into the reprise, and suddenly . . . we are stark up face to face against a kind of world and a kind of half-century that no one born this side of the water can ever quite fully make, or want to make, his own. Hogarth and Gay, Goya and Lautrec, Koestler, Malraux, Traven, and even such as Remarque and George Grosz—all of it, all of them and a hundred others, are packed into this one hot, hellish instant, with the smoke still rising from the cremato-ries and Bert Brecht's old friend Uncle Joe Stalin just sitting there, wait-ing, far to the north. In Miss Lenya's hands, truth gets annealed . . . after twenty-five years, into a weapon of blinding strength and beauty."[27]

Lenya protested that Jenny is only "a minor role, and if she ever becomes a major role then there's something goddamn wrong with the whole production."[28] But her "Pirate Jenny," her droll "Solomon Song," and her ribald, scathing "Tango Ballad" duet with Macheath were incan-descent. "No matter how many times I saw the show I made sure, if I was upstairs in the office, to see her sing 'Pirate Jenny,' " Capalbo recalled. "It always gave me gooseflesh. We had better-trained voices in the show, but Lenya captured the feeling of Weill by just a sheer economy of gestures." Capalbo had decided that he would not stage the number. He had Lenya come to center stage and in a presentational style confront the audience. "She took a stance and focused. A single light was on her—and until the end, she remained still, absolutely unmoving. It was as close to a close-up as I could come. At the end, she lifted her arm, as a cheer rang the air."[29]

With a few breaks, Lenya remained in the show for two years. "When I left for the last time," she recalled, "they were all heartbroken and fright-ened, and horrified. They said: 'Miss Lenya, look—we have to close the show.' I said: 'You will not. Don't be silly. This is a marvelous work, and it would be a poor sign for Brecht and Weill if this would only depend on a minor role.' "[30]

Setting records at the time for longevity and profit, *The Threepenny Opera* played at the Theatre de Lys for the next six years, closing finally at the end of 1961. During the marathon run it was seen by over 750,000 patrons who paid three million dollars to sit in the 299-seat theatre. Seven hun-dred and nine actors performed twenty-two roles. The landmark produc-tion, one of a handful of shows responsible for creating the modern Off-Broadway movement, helped to change the demographics of New York theatre.

Why did a 1928 German musical set long-run records and win the affec-tion of New York theatregoers? "A great many elements came together for-tuitously," Carmen Capalbo speculated. "We were in rehearsal during the

McCarthy hearings: the show has to be put in that context. Then the success of Louis Armstrong's recording of 'Mack the Knife' opened the show to the world. CBS Radio banned Armstrong's record, claiming it was conducive to juvenile delinquency because it glorified a gangster. When Armstrong's record was banned, MGM put out a single with no lyrics, with Louis whistling the first few bars. It sold a million. Once that happened, the original record was no longer banned. The song became ingrained, and our job was to connect the show with the song, which we did. Then out of the blue came the record by Bobby Darin, on an Atlantic album. One cut was 'Mack the Knife.' It went to number one and added a good year on the run."[31] Capalbo also had the idea of cutting a cast album, a first for an Off-Broadway show. "Nobody thought it would work," he recalled. "Lenya, who was afraid of rejection, for Kurt as well as for herself, would not let me offer the show to the logical person to record it, Goddard Lieberson at Columbia, so I went to MGM." The album, released in July 1954 and a long-running best-seller, cleaned up some of Blitzstein's rawer lyrics. Nonetheless, the recording captures the show's essence.

Like the original Berlin production, which to this day evokes sighs of pure pleasure from very elderly Berliners, New York theatregoers who saw the raffish, handmade de Lys production recall it with high regard. A show about a corrupt, topsy-turvy society had an obvious mirroring effect in late-Weimar Germany, but its timeless satire of some of the seven deadly sins also resonated for audiences in economically prosperous, conformity-ridden Eisenhower America. In a superficially stable postwar America, in which rebels played by Marlon Brando and James Dean were a new kind of movie hero, the lowlife characters in *The Threepenny Opera* had a brash renegade appeal. Kurt Weill, a classically trained composer who wanted to speak to a mass audience, would surely have been delighted.

After Lenya left the cast, George Davis supervised the next phase of her career. He persuaded her to return to Germany to arrange for recordings of her first husband's German works. "She absolutely did not want to go," Hesper Anderson recalled. "She felt about Germany the same way that Kurt did—she hated Germany, she hated Germans—but she did go, because George, who had a mission, convinced her that she would be furthering Kurt Weill's music."[32] In Hamburg in 1955 she recorded *Lotte Lenya Sings Berlin Theater Songs by Kurt Weill.* Included were numbers she herself had performed in Germany, including her signature "Seeräuber-jenny," and from *Mahagonny,* "Havanna-Lied" (Havana Song), "Alabama-Song," and "Wie Man Sich-Bettet." The "Moritat" and "Barbara-Song" from *Die Dreigroschenoper,* three songs from *Happy End* ("Bilbao-Song," "Surabaya-Johnny," and "Was Die Herren Matrosen sagen-Tango"), and three unusual selections, "Vom Ertrunkenen Mädchen" ("The Ballad of a Drowned Girl") from *Berlin Requiem* and "Lied der Fennimore" ("Fennimore's Song") and "Cäsar's Tod" ("Caesar's Death") from *Der Silbersee* completed the program. With orchestra and chorus under the direction of Wilhelm Brückner-Rüggeberg, Lenya subsequently supervised recordings of and sang her original roles in *Mahagonny* (1956), *Die Dreigroschenoper* (1958), and *The Seven Deadly Sins* (1956) and, in a departure, sang almost all of the songs from *Happy End* (1960), with a chorus performing a few of the Salvation Army numbers. Although the recordings provoked divided opinions, there can be no debate about the singer's own performances. By the mid-1950s, Lenya's voice had ripened into a deep huskiness, and with age the insolence, mockery, and existential wisdom that had always been part of her repertoire had an authoritative patina. In July and August 1957 she recorded *"September Song" and Other American Theatre Songs of Kurt Weill.* If she made the Berlin theatre songs partly to preserve a record of her own original performances, the American theatre songs were chosen solely to pay tribute to Weill and to remind listeners, who by 1957 may have begun to forget, of the range of Weill's American oeuvre. From the comic "Saga of Jenny" from *Lady in the Dark* and "Sing Me Not a Ballad" from *The Firebrand of Florence* (the only song on the album Lenya had originated) to the joyful lilt of "Green-Up Time" from *Love Life* to the rueful romantic notes struck in "Foolish Heart" and "Speak Low" from *One Touch of Venus* to the wistful "September Song" and "It Never Was You" from *Knickerbocker Holiday* to the mournful dissonance of "Lonely House" and "A Boy Like You" from *Street Scene* to a trio of numbers from *Lost in the Stars,* "Trouble Man," "Stay Well," and the title song, Lenya performed material that veered far from her usual world-weary mode. Highlights are her "Green-Up Time," in which her voice bubbles with unshadowed mirth; her bluesy, downbeat "Lonely House"; and her delicate and wry "Foolish Heart." Notably, the American theatre songs have a greater range than the German songs.

In Berlin in November 1957, as she was negotiating for the recording of *Die Dreigroschenoper,* George Davis had a heart attack as he and Lenya were leaving a performance at the Staatsoper. "I took him in a taxi back to his apartment," music critic and family friend Paul Moor recalled, "and then to a hospital. George didn't speak German. Later the hospital called me to tell me he had died, and I told Lenya, who collapsed into uncontrollable sobbing. It was the same cause of death as Kurt's, and she was all too aware

that George had been responsible for her second career."
Although it had been "a marriage of convenience," as Hesper Anderson said[33]—Davis, a
homosexual, had called himself "the husband of the
Widow Weill"[34]—Lenya had
grown deeply dependent on
her second husband. "She
kept a photograph of George,
and treated it like an icon," as
Paul Moor recalled. "I saw her
talk to it, saying, 'You did it.
You got it back.'"[35] After
Davis's death Lenya refused to
capitalize on her growing
renown. Often without an
agent, and without George
Davis to prod her, she neither
sought work nor waited for
offers. But she was always
eager to promote Weill.

Mr. and Mrs. George Davis, on the porch
at Brook House, early 1950s

In Julius Rudel, a Viennese refugee from Hitler and general director
and principal conductor of the New York City Opera from 1957 to 1979,
she gained an important champion of her first husband's work. In October
1957 the Ford Foundation awarded Rudel's company a $105,000 grant for
a five-week season, to be performed in the spring of 1958, devoted exclusively to the contemporary American opera. From the more than two hundred scores submitted to him, Julius Rudel selected ten. Weill's *Lost in the
Stars* was to be seen in a season that included Blitzstein's *Regina,* Menotti's
Old Maid and the Thief, Robert Kurka's *Good Soldier Schweik,* Douglas
Moore's *Ballad of Baby Doe,* Leonard Bernstein's *Trouble in Tahiti,* and
Carlisle Floyd's *Susannah.* "Is *Lost in the Stars* 'pure' opera? No," Julius
Rudel maintained. "But I felt that it was sufficiently operatic to be
included in my season. Weill had his own standards and he lived by them.
He admired the Broadway techniques, and he was canny enough to see
that, to reach the audience he wanted to, Broadway was where he had to
be. Gian Carlo Menotti, who also wanted longer runs and a larger audience

than any opera house could offer, also went to Broadway, like Weill avoiding the opera stage altogether. Weill had to change here, but he didn't change all that much: *Threepenny Opera* is a Broadway show. Weill did not sell out in America but remained true to himself."[36] Rudel presented *Lost in the Stars* not only in order to expand the operatic repertoire—"I offered opera-house 'takes' on material like Gilbert and Sullivan, *Show Boat, Porgy and Bess,* which normally did not appear there"—but also because at the time he felt that Weill was "an important composer in danger of being overlooked. In the 1950s and 1960s it was an almost all-Mahler world," and in presenting Weill at City Opera Rudel hoped to "correct the imbalance."[37]

In 1958, most of the music and drama critics did not share Rudel's belief that *Lost in the Stars* belonged on an opera-house stage. "It is not an opera because the music is incidental and illustrative—opera is made of different stuff and in a different manner," Paul Henry Lang pronounced in the *Herald-Tribune* on April 11. "All characterization is done in prose and the protagonists are fully formed before they break into music. . . . The music is of a rather low grade, at times embarrassingly so, and full of very ordinary tricks. . . . Every one gets some nice songs, but they are tacked onto the characters and do not spring from a musico-dramatic impulse." Nonetheless, Lang called it "a good show, though not an opera." "Everything of real importance in the work is expressed in Mr. Anderson's eloquent prose. . . . Weill's music is a mere decoration, so irrelevant and trivial that one suspects it could be left out without damage to the production as a whole," huffed Winthrop Sargent in the *New Yorker* of April 19, adding that "the inclusion of *Lost in the Stars* in what is supposed to be a season of American opera makes me wonder whether the sponsors of this worthy undertaking have any clear notion of what they are trying to do." Disregarding the carping reviews, audiences responded warmly to *Lost in the Stars,* and the show became the one popular success of Rudel's American opera season.

Rudel included *Street Scene* in his 1959 season. Again, reviews for the most part were skeptical or reproving. "Since *Street Scene* is a Broadway-slick musical it is possible to question its inclusion in a season devoted exclusively to American opera," Jay Harrison wrote in the *New York Herald-Tribune* of April 3, adding that the New York City Opera "mounted the work as though it had been in the business of giving musicals since the Shuberts were in grade school." "Wrapped in an operatic ribbon and tied in a Broadway bow, the package is a hybrid," Miles Kastendieck argued in the *Christian Science Monitor* on April 4. On Broadway, Weill's hybrid shows had been saluted for their operatic elements, but on an opera-house stage they were dismissed by and large as intruders. In truth, both shows, with their mixed musical programs, are superior Broadway musicals of their time more than they are American operas. Nonetheless, Rudel's inclusion of them in his seasons of American opera was a pioneering effort to erode the barriers that continue to separate Broadway from opera. Lenya was immensely grateful to him for reviving Weill shows that might otherwise have had to wait decades for recognition, and when she set up the Kurt Weill Foundation near the end of her life, she appointed Rudel to her board of trustees.

At the same time that Rudel was resurrecting Weill's Broadway "operas" at City Opera, George Balanchine asked Lenya to re-create her original role for the American premiere of *The Seven Deadly Sins,* to be presented by the New York City Ballet. This time, Lenya needed no persuading: performing Brecht and Weill's *ballet chanté* under the direction of its original choreographer on a ballet stage would confer the kind of legitimacy she was seeking to secure for Weill's legacy. To Lenya's immense satisfaction, both dance and theatre critics recognized the significance of this peculiar masterwork, an idiosyncratic blend of café jazz and art song spiked with Weill's acrid harmonies. Jay Harrison, music critic for the *New York Herald-Tribune,* in his December 4, 1958, review, aptly described Weill's score as "a personal distillation of all the music that floated like blue smoke through the beer halls, nightclubs and dives of Berlin in the late 1920s and Paris of the early 1930s. . . . It was one of Weill's greatest gifts that with a chord he could sum up an era, with a tune bring back an epoch only half remembered." "The present production is better, profounder, and generally more important than the original," pronounced John Martin, dance critic of the *New York Times.* "The most complete event of the theatre season . . . a new species . . . clearly identifiable as a classic," Jerry Tallmer wrote in the June 1959 *Evergreen Review.*

Despite herself, Lotte Lenya at long last had become a celebrity in America. But she appeared only infrequently. Highlights included her return to the Theatre de Lys in *Brecht on Brecht* in 1962 and her appearances on film in 1961 in *The Roman Spring of Mrs. Stone* as a "countess" dripping with decadence who runs a brothel of nubile young men and in 1963 as a lesbian spy who battles James Bond with a pair of knife-sprouting shoes in *From Russia with Love,* and three concerts at Carnegie Hall.

The final success in her strange on-again, off-again career, as the landlady, Fräulein Schneider, in *Cabaret,* the 1966 Broadway musical based on Christopher Isherwood's *Berlin Stories,* set in a time and place for which Lenya had a become a living symbol, had a deep connection to her first husband's work. From the first the show's entire creative team—director Hal Prince, composer John Kander, lyricist Fred Ebb, and librettist Joe Masteroff—had thought only of Lenya for the role. Prince invited Lenya to Fred Ebb's apartment to hear the four songs that had been written for the character. "We were a little nervous about some of what we were playing for her, especially 'What Would You Do?' [in which Fräulein Schneider defends her decision to break off her engagement to a Jewish tenant, and thus accommodate herself to National Socialism]," Fred Ebb recalled. "In real life, of course, she had been married to a Jew and she had chosen to leave. We hoped she wouldn't be offended."[38] But after she heard "So What?," which expresses the wry detachment that helps the landlady to survive, and which seems saturated in Lenya-like irony and common sense, she said, "Very good, I'll do it." ("Not so fast," snapped her hard-bitten agent, Bertha Case, who had come with her.)[39]

Composing the score for a show set in Weimar Berlin with Weill's widow as their star, Kander and Ebb were concerned that their work would be measured against Weill's. "Kander and Ebb knew they were influenced by Kurt Weill, but appropriately, they wrote a Kander and Ebb score that is an homage to Weill but not an imitation," Hal Prince said. "Take Lenya's song 'What Would You Do?' It says what's on its mind clearly. Placed against a song Brecht and Weill might have written for the same situation, it isn't anywhere near off-center enough. Brecht would have obfuscated it."[40] Like many Broadway professionals, Kander and Ebb were more familiar with—and seemed to prefer—the American to the German Kurt Weill. "At the time I was working on *Cabaret,* I made the conscious decision not to listen to Weill's German music," John Kander said. "Of course I had seen *The Threepenny Opera* downtown, but I didn't study the score; rather, I listened to Berlin cabaret music and to popular music of the period—music that had influenced Weill. Weill's American work had a greater impact on me," Kander claimed. "The fantastic form of *Lady in the Dark,* the fact that *Street Scene* is an opera—these were great models for us."[41] "In no way were we trying to imitate or go one better," Fred Ebb said. "Brecht and Weill were geniuses. The important thing was that we had our individual voice."[42]

"During rehearsals I urged Lenya to tell us if we had gotten anything wrong," Prince said. "After all, she was there; we weren't. Of course, as she perfectly understood—she was smart, straightforward, ruthless and sentimental, with herself as much as anybody else—*Cabaret* is not authentic to Weimar but to Broadway."[43] "When the show opened, her presence onstage ratified our work. If she was there, we had to be doing it right," Fred Ebb claimed.[44]

A musical about Berlin on the eve of the Nazi takeover, with Lotte Lenya in a leading role and a demonic master of ceremonies who periodically interrupts to offer oblique and mordant musical commentaries, *Cabaret* certainly has many of the insignia of a Brecht-Weill music-theatre work, and of the Brechtian-style *Love Life*. Half conventional book musical, built around contrasting romantic partners, half experimental concept musical, *Cabaret* was a beautifully constructed hybrid

Lenya and her third husband, painter Russell Detwiler, in the mid-1960s. Detwiler, who died in 1969, painted the German expressionist portrait of Lenya.

and a decidedly new kind of show for its time and place. The spirit of Kurt Weill, musical-theatre reformer, hovers over the show, although finally there is no doubt that *Cabaret* is what Hal Prince claimed it was, a Broadway musical written by Kander and Ebb rather than Brecht and Weill—and as remote from the real Berlin of the period as some of Brecht and Weill's imaginary approximations of "Amerika" in the 1920s had been from the real America. Ironically, through the immense popular success of the original production, of the 1972 film directed by Bob Fosse, and of the 1998 Broadway revival directed by Sam Mendes, Kander and Ebb's

Margo Harris, with whom Lenya had the last intimate relationship of her life,
looking, with apparent delight, at one of her own sculptures

Cabaret, more than any of Brecht-Weill's less realistic but more trenchant
and pained musical metaphors of a city in turmoil, has become, in popular
discourse, the dominant image of decadent late-Weimar Berlin. A view by
outsiders has coopted any of the representations by those who were there.

For Lenya, *Cabaret* was the last hurrah of her peculiar, truncated American career. In a handmade role, in which to her usual crustiness was added
a streak of Broadway sentimentality, she finally embraced a persona she
had always seemed to avoid, that of Broadway diva. "In that role in our
show, she was absolutely authentic: nobody will ever again be as good in
that part as she was," Hal Prince said. "In *Threepenny Opera* downtown, she
was as charismatic as you can get. Yet there were limitations, which she
was keenly aware of. She was more a personality than an actress, but it
didn't matter. Just as it didn't matter if her notes weren't 'beautiful'—they
were 'beautiful' in their interpretation. She knew her shortcomings, and
indeed never thought of herself as a star. Yet paradoxically—and she was
full of contradictions—she comported herself like a woman who knew just
how good she was."[45]

Following *Cabaret* there was only one other major Lenya performance, as
Mother Courage in a student production at the University of California at

Irvine in 1971 directed by her friend Herbert Machiz. (Lenya had performed the role in Germany in 1965; both performances were notable failures.) She continued, as ever, to tend to Weill affairs, overseeing major productions and offering the benefits of her experience and symbiotic connection to her first husband's music. Much of her time, however, was taken up with her disastrous third and fourth marriages. During the time she was appearing in *Cabaret,* she was married to an artist, Russell Detwiler, an alcoholic homosexual many years her junior. "I am not very good at being Mr. Lotte Lenya," Detwiler claimed, in a statement resonating with the ill will that infected the marriage. "I do not have the genius of Kurt, or the imagination of George."[46] South Mountain Road neighbor Milton Caniff observed that Detwiler was "a very personable guy when he was sober. And a pain in the neck when he wasn't. Lenya needed a pet around the house and I guess he served that purpose. I don't believe many tears were shed over his death from a heart attack [on October 30, 1969]. I think she was rather relieved to wrap it up."[47] Many among Lenya's circle of friends and acquaintances did not even know of her fourth marriage, to Richard Siemanowski, yet another homosexual with a drinking problem who died young from a heart attack. "They were totally drunk when they got married," Lys Symonette recalled. "Lenya did not spend her wedding night with him. She just wanted to see if she could get him. But then she found out he liked his hairdresser boyfriend more. When they got back from Europe, he was in the hospital. She looked in the register to see who he listed as next of kin. When she found out it was his boyfriend, she told me, 'That's it. We're finished.' "[48]

Her disastrous choice of husbands naturally provoked speculation among her friends. What was she doing? Was she punishing herself for having betrayed Kurt? For all her fabled sensuality, did she really resent sex? Longtime friend Paul Moor observed: "Her attitude to male homosexuals was a very definite product of her own early mistreatment sexually, some of it voluntary, part of it when she went whoring at the age of eleven. She was terrified of male aggressiveness, but had a very strong sexual appetite. A homosexual male partner didn't threaten her because it left the initiative to her. She could more or less control the situation. Her very appreciative narcissism was fed by the fact 'If I can get him to get it up, what a triumph!' "[49]

The final intimate relationship in Lenya's life was with a woman named Margo Harris. Harris, a sculptor, was a lesbian who for a time was married to a German psychiatrist named Ernst Hammerschlag. Lenya met Harris in the mid-1970s at one of the frequent card parties hosted by Lenya's agent, Bertha Case. The two women began an affair. By the time Lenya was diagnosed with cancer in 1979, Harris, who separated Lenya from her friends and forced her to change her will, had made herself indispensable. "With all her tentacles, Margo had taken control," Paul Moor said. "Lenya was by then too weak to resist, even though, like everyone else, she had turned against Margo. She didn't want the sexual relationship Margo wanted, and she detested—and who could blame her?—Margo's circle of New York lesbians, Bertha Case, Dorothy Patten, Cheryl Crawford."[50] "Lenya was so insecure in many ways that when somebody very powerfully strong came on and gave her a bill of goods, she fell for it," Lys Symonette observed. "Out of . . . fear. She really didn't like Margo, who was absolutely nuts about Lenya. But how *could* she have liked Margo, who was dreadful?"[51]

One of Lenya's final actions—one of the few that Margo did not obstruct—was to appoint Kim Kowalke as president of the Kurt Weill Foundation. Kowalke had gotten to know Lenya casually when he was writing his dissertation, *Kurt Weill in Europe,* at Yale. In 1979, he was invited to join the board of trustees for an expanded and reorganized foundation, which, although it had been set up in 1962 by John Wharton, was "a shell Lenya never used," Kowalke said.[52] In November 1981 Margo Harris summoned Kowalke to her apartment, where Lenya was staying. " 'Lenya's dying and wants to see you,' Margo told me in her brutal way," Kowalke recalled. "Lenya, on morphine, took my hand and said, 'I want you to take over as president of the foundation.' 'I'm not the right person,' I protested. 'I'm a scholar, not a businessman.' 'You've never asked for anything; you're the only one I can trust.' She would not take no for an answer. Although Lenya had no time for academics and stuffed shirts, she did respect knowledge, and she was grateful that I had written my dissertation on Weill at a time when nobody would deal with him as a serious composer. ('I like "September Song," too, Mr. Kowalke, but I wouldn't write a dissertation on it, heh, heh,' the chair of the Yale music department had told me.) Margo would have had a great influence in who was chosen," Kowalke said, convinced he passed precisely because of his status as an outsider, as someone who had never been close to Lenya and therefore was not a threat to Margo. "Lys and David Drew, both very close to Lenya, would not have been acceptable to Margo, who kept an enemies list, a list of rivals. Margo was terribly jealous of Weill and was irritated to no end because she was unable to replace him in Lenya's affection. I was a Midwest farmboy, a former graduate student untainted by previous skirmishes. I was chosen for my 'naiveté'—and because I was less of a threat to Margo than anybody else."[53]

Utterly in the control of a woman she had grown to despise, Lenya died on November 27, 1981, in the small, bare maid's room at the back of Margo Harris's apartment. It was virtually a pauper's death for a woman who left millions, yet with the searing memory of her childhood poverty never seemed to know how wealthy she was. "Whenever I would meet Lenya at Rumpelmeyer's for ice cream I always paid, because I thought she was poor," Kowalke recalled. "It never dawned on me she was rich"—an impression the wily Lenya surely wished to foster. "She asked her attorney if she could afford a new dress for the opening night of *Mahagonny* at the Met [in 1979]—she could have afforded hundreds."[54]

On her deathbed Lenya told Kowalke she was "leaving everything to the foundation." But it turned out that she did not leave everything to the foundation. There were protracted battles with Margo Harris (who died in 1998), and "after one and a half years, once we cleared up legal and copyright issues, in 1983 I laid out a ten-year plan," Kowalke said. An academic who loves and honors all of Weill's work ("Only Eurocentric snobbishness would dismiss the American work, some of which in fact is better than the earlier work," he said),[55] Kowalke runs the foundation in a no-nonsense manner. With Lys Symonette as the musical executor ("I was for Lenya the last link to Kurt Weill, and with the music she trusted me, that's why she put me in her will as the musical executor," Lys Symonette said),[56] Kowalke "plays by the book. We're a charitable organization, under IRS supervision. People think we're particular, but remember that we're dealing with a composer who wanted his orchestrations followed exactly as he wrote them. All we ask is that you play and sing the notes that Weill wrote: and you should hear the howling! Outside the theatre Weill didn't care about arrangements, but he was a purist inside the theatre, and we insist that theatre performances or recordings have to be done as Weill wrote them."[57] Kim Kowalke and Lys Symonette oversee Kurt Weill's musical legacy with the same loyalty that Lenya demonstrated during her lengthy and superbly played run as the Widow Weill.

SEVENTEEN

Coda

A s for myself, I write for today. I don't give a damn about writing for posterity," Kurt Weill maintained. At his death in 1950, "posterity" seemed inclined to return his assessment. The obituary notice in the *New York Times* on April 4, 1950, was notably measured and made no large claims for either the merit or the impact of his work. "Weill wrote music for *One Touch of Venus, Lady in the Dark,* and Other Broadway Hits," the first of three subheadings proclaimed. Was this an example of American provincialism or a prescient view of how Weill was to be rated in the future? "Also turned out operas," the second heading mentioned casually. "*Der Protagonist* and *Tsar Has Himself Photographed* His Best-Known Works," the third claimed foolishly, casting doubt on the reliability of the first two subheadings. Flagrantly missing were attempts to place Weill within the cultural contexts in which he composed, to summarize his stature, or to predict the contours of his legacy. An air of dismissal hovered over the obituary, whose theme seemed to be that Kurt Weill wrote some popular songs for Broadway, and now he's gone. An appraiser of his musical estate, who might have been working in collusion with the *New York Times,* concluded that only *Down in the Valley* and a few songs had monetary value or would be likely to endure.

Only Virgil Thomson, often waspish about Weill's work during the composer's lifetime, struck a note of proper appreciation and tribute. "He was probably the most original single workman in the whole musical theatre, internationally considered, during the last quarter century," Thomson wrote in the *New York Herald-Tribune* on April 9, 1950. But, as throughout his remarks over the years, Thomson was quick to qualify his praise. "He was not a natural melodist like Richard Rodgers or George Gershwin. . . . Nor was he a master of thematic development. . . . He was an architect, a master of musico-dramatic design, whose structures, built for function and solidity, constitute a repertory of models that have not only served well their original purpose but also had wide influence on composers as examples of procedure. . . . Weill came to the light musical theatre, for which most of his American works were conceived, from a classical training . . . and long experience of the artistic, the experimental theatre." Thomson cited Weill's collaboration with Bertolt Brecht as "epoch-making . . . [they] transformed the German opera." "Whether Weill's American works will carry as far as his German ones I cannot say," he wrote disingenuously, for his tone implied his conclusion: The American works are not as good. "They lack the mordant and touching humanity of Brecht's poetry. They also lack a certain acidity in the musical characterization that gave a cutting edge to Weill's musical style when he worked in the German language." "Nevertheless, they are important to history," he stated—inferring that "history" is where they belong. For Thomson, Weill was "the last of our local light theatre men to orchestrate his own scores and the last to have full mastery of composition. Just at present the American musical theatre is rising in power . . . [and it has] lost . . . a workman who might have bridged for us the gap, as he did in Germany"—but, according to Thomson, had not yet in America— "between grand opera and the *singspiel.*"

The contemporary assessment from Germany was bleaker. In an influential and widely quoted obituary in the *Frankfurter Rundschau* on April 15, 1950, Theodor Adorno dismissed Weill as a deluded artist who had tried to convince himself that he could function as a serious composer within a commercial arena and from Adorno's elitist perspective, had inevitably failed. Adorno, who unlike Weill returned to Germany after the war, seemed to be voicing the consensus of German intellectuals—and by and large, despite more nuanced readings since, his opinion remains in force to the present.

If in 1950 Weill seemed headed toward obscurity, to be remembered if at all as an interesting special case of an émigré classicist who had improbably achieved a modest but genuine success on Broadway, fifty years on Weill is generally acclaimed as one of the seminal theatre composers of the twentieth century. Nonetheless, since his death Weill's work has had an uneven, frequently disappointing production history in his second country. No subsequent staging has matched the impact or the influence of the de Lys *Threepenny Opera.* Although *Mahagonny* failed as a musical (in 1970) and had a highly qualified "success" at the Met in 1979, it has been well staged at opera houses in Boston, Washington, and Minneapolis, among others. Revived fairly often at New York City Opera and a number of regional opera stages, including the Chicago Lyric Opera, *Street Scene* has had the happiest production history of any of Weill's works. *Johnny Johnson* was a one-performance Off-Broadway casualty in 1971. The musical and lyrical pleasures of *Knickerbocker Holiday* were not realized in a lackluster 1971 production in Los Angeles and San Francisco with a miscast Burt Lancaster. A well-received 1972 revival of *Lost in the Stars,* the only American work of Weill's to appear on Broadway since his death, had a disappointingly short run. The Yale Repertory Theatre in the 1970s presented important productions from the Brecht-Weill catalogue, including the American premieres of the *Mahagonny-Songspiel* (as *The Little Mahagonny*) and *Happy End,* along with *Seven Deadly Sins* and another fizzled pop *Mahagonny.* After being taken over by the Chelsea Theatre Center, the Yale Rep's *Happy End* appeared on Broadway in 1977 in a misguided production starring Meryl Streep. For Joseph Papp's Public Theatre, Richard Foreman staged a strikingly humorless and wrongheaded *Threepenny Opera* in 1976. Weill's last Broadway outing to date was a disastrous *Threepenny Opera* in 1989 starring Sting and (mis)directed by John Dexter. (See the appendix for detailed accounts of these significant, if rarely successful, productions.)

In 1999, anticipating the composer's centenary and launching a process of reassessment that will continue well into the future, two major productions rescued rare Weill works from oblivion. The American premiere of *Die Bürgschaft* in June at the Spoleto Festival USA in Charleston, South Carolina, occurred because of the persistence of a longtime Weill advocate, conductor Julius Rudel, and director Jonathan Eaton, a specialist in staging Weill's early German work. "I've been selling the opera for fifteen years," said Eaton, who in 1998 had directed a well-received production of *Die Bürgschaft* in Bielefeld, Germany. "Not many American companies would be interested. I brought it to the attention of Steven Sloane [the music director, opera and orchestra, of the Spoleto Festival USA], who had the courage to say yes."[1] Resisting a trendy revisionist updating, Eaton created a mise-en-scène that might have come out of an epic-theatre production of Weill's era. "Epic theatre is, after all, nonnaturalistic theatre, and I was guided by elements of the Japanese Noh style, which had had such a marked influence on Brecht and Weill," Eaton said. "I used faceless masks for the double chorus: we wanted to suggest Chinese Communists, faceless masses, as well as concentration camp victims. The piece is big enough to work as a commentary on Russia, China, Yugoslavia, America's crass commercialism. 'Where are our value systems?' is the question the opera asks."[2] By turns "alienated" and impassioned to just the right temperature, the production honored Weill's entwined commitment to instruction and entertainment.

"After *Der Protagonist* Weill felt music has to be written to a large public, a creed he did not forget even in so solemn a piece as *Die Bürgschaft,* where he uses popular musical forms, a tango, a fox-trot," Julius Rudel noted. "At the same time, at the start of the second act, he uses three-part invention in a strictly academic style. And at the end of act 1, strict counterpoint and imitation, the sequencing of vocal lines, the Handelian fugato, are all academic, but couched in terms such that nobody will be frightened. On the other hand, the Gang of Three [who accommodate to each shift in the ideological winds, always poised to make a killing] are cabaret, and played for dark comedy."[3] The Three, weaving in and out of the work like sinister, cheeky lords of misrule, troubadours who want to rob you blind, were a highlight of the production. "They are theatrically successful, there to seduce you with their musical turns and to hit you with meaning," Eaton said. "Without those three, the piece would be harder to swallow; with them, it's great entertainment."[4] Offering cabaret turns en route to an apocalyptic climax, the production certified the long-unheard opera as a major work.

But to call *Die Bürgschaft* the kind of writing Weill should have and would have continued to pursue if Hitler hadn't come to power, to describe it, as some critics did following the Spoleto premiere, as his masterpiece, the fulfillment of his highest aspirations, only feeds a Eurocentric high-culture bias against the American musical theatre. Periodically, Lenya would claim that Weill wrote for Broadway only in order to obtain the financial security that would allow him to compose "real" operas like *Die Bürgschaft,* which had minimal commercial prospects. But Weill became so deeply committed to Broadway and its flexible possibilities that it is unlikely he would have returned to writing "real" or "pure" operas. What he began to do instead, however, threading later Broadway works such as *Street Scene* and *Lost in the Stars* with operatic elements, may have produced works with a wider, longer reach and a greater variety than any he might have modeled on the example of *Die Bürgschaft*. The admirable Spoleto production performed a valuable service, but it did not consign the composer's Broadway portfolio to the category of lesser, compromised work—work written, so to speak, in the shadow of this commanding didactic opera. Rather, the production paradoxically reinforced the strength, the integrity, and the astonishing versatility of Weill's music (in Julius Rudel's phrase) "written to a large public."

On June 14, 1999, two weeks after the American premiere of *Die Bürgschaft,* a provincial opera house in Chemnitz, Germany, provided another occasion for evaluating a rare Weill work in a fresh and historically important context. The Chemnitz Opera's world premiere of *Der Weg der Verheissung,* the German version of the work produced in New York in 1937 as *The Eternal Road,* was the fulfillment of a four-year quest. In 1995, the chief dramaturg of the Chemnitz Opera, Karl-Hans Möller, expressed interest to the Kurt Weill Foundation in looking at their material on *The Eternal Road.* Möller and his colleagues realized that their chances of gaining rights for a production were slim. "Chemnitz is not well known, and we hadn't had our name from 1953 to 1990, when, as part of East Germany, we were called Karl Marx Stadt. (We got our name back in 1990 by plebiscite, after the breakdown of the Wall but before reunification.)" As Möller had expected, the foundation, "looking for a big theatre in Berlin and Vienna," was "not very enthusiastic about Chemnitz."[5] There the matter rested until, early in 1997, Möller received a letter from Edward Harsh at the Kurt Weill Foundation inviting him to a meeting in Frankfurt with others potentially interested in producing the work. At the end of the session, as Möller noted, the foundation was "alerted to our unknown town," and the Chemnitz Opera was mindful that to present a production of the magnitude of *The Eternal Road* would require a partner or even a consortium of partners.

"You have the rights," Kim Kowalke informed Möller after three days of intense meetings in June 1997. "But we must be sure the production will have international recognition. We believe your theatre is able to do it, but you need to link up with opera houses in Israel, New York, and one other place in Europe. Also, the actors playing the rabbi, Moses, and Jeremiah, as well as the conductor, the director, and the designer must have international recognition and be approved by us."[6] Determined to be the mouse that roared, the management of the Chemnitz Opera, with help from the Ministry of Foreign Affairs and from the state government, lined up an impressive team of coproducers that included the New Israeli Opera in Tel Aviv, the Brooklyn Academy of Music, and the Opera Kraków in Poland, and an international creative team that included an American conductor, John Mauceri; a German director, Michael Heinicke; and an Israeli set and costume designer, David Sharir.

Profound respect for Jewish religious traditions was the production's guiding principle. "Nobody, for one moment, thought of any other way to present this material," Möller said. "We felt we must do it as if we were in an Israeli synagogue. Our fathers wanted to have Jews banned from the world, and to correct that our first promise and obligation was to be very sensitive. There can be no other way to present a Jewish house of worship on a German stage. One newspaper said we drove political correctness to excess: yes, we certainly did."[7] Gerhard Müller, the dramaturg who prepared the stage version for Chemnitz, made some cuts in Werfel's prolix libretto, but only one significant change. "In the 1930s, Werfel was spared the knowledge of where the road was to lead in the decade that followed, and so the original production ended on an optimistic note," Kowalke pointed out. "But in 1999 that knowledge had to be read back into the material. We know what happened, and a teleological approach was unavoidable."[8] Instead of marching out of the synagogue, as in 1937, in the Chemnitz production the congregants stood frozen in place as Nazi storm troopers invaded their sanctuary. In a chilling image, shadows descended on the huddling Jews, their fate transformed suddenly into a premonition of the Final Solution. "Because we didn't want the ending to be without any hope," Kowalke said, one character, the Son, a Survivor, stepped out from the engulfing darkness.

Weill's score was handled scrupulously. A few passages of recitative were trimmed, but songs, arias, and choral writing were preserved exactly as Weill had written them; and since most of the music had been composed to Werfel's German text rather than to the English adaptation by Ludwig Lewisohn, the Chemnitz performance was closer to Weill's original intentions. In addition, act 4, which was never performed in New York, was reinstated. "In Chemnitz, the score was restored to almost to its complete version, although there is still about thirty minutes of unheard material, and was probably better sung than in 1937, and certainly better played now that the music was live rather than on disc," as Kim Kowalke maintained.[9]

But something more than the restoration of Weill's score was at stake in Chemnitz. Because of the persistence fifty years after his death of a little-known opera house in his native country, Weill's belief in music's "usefulness" was tested in extraordinary circumstances. And in Chemnitz the audience—or rather, the impact of the show *on* the audience—was more significant than the show itself. Watching a sixty-three-year-old Jewish pageant in profound silence—"a cough was an event," conductor John Mauceri noted[10]—became an act of atonement and an implicit vow "to see that such things never happen again," as Karl-Hans Möller observed.[11] (When it was presented in New York at the Brooklyn Academy of Music in March 2000, stripped of the German dialogue between the stage and the audience, shortcomings in both production and text were more evident.)

Die Bürgschaft in Spoleto and *Der Weg der Verheissung* in Germany and New York were significant occasions for re-examining a key aspect of the Kurt Weill portfolio. When more of the composer's German catalogue is seen in America, in regional and university theatres and opera companies as well as in New York, and the American Weill becomes more familiar to German audiences on stage, where Weill's work must be seen in order to be fully savored, the scope of his contributions to the theatrical culture of both countries, as well as the essential continuity of his entire career, will be revealed. And perhaps in this way, the shadows that continue to trail his legacy—the accusations of compromise, the caveats that would label him a songwriter rather than a composer—would begin further to recede.

However, to begin to frame answers to the questions that must be asked—how and why has Weill's work survived, and how can his influence be measured?—it must be acknowledged that yes, Weill did sometimes compromise, and yes, he wrote some great songs, and both these facts are part of the reason for his continuing popularity *as well as* for the stature of his work. Weill's original "compromise"—his original fall from pure classical grace—occurred not in America but in Germany, when he became the century's first major crossover composer. In tentative ways from 1925 on, but with full commitment beginning with *Die Dreigroschenoper* in 1928, Weill incorporated popular idioms—dance music and jazz—and shimmering melody into his classically based work. He married disparate elements into a particular sound that, in the late 1920s, was fresh, defiant, tart—a sound that has come to be identified as synonymous with Weimar cabaret but which was a distinctly Weillian hybrid that retains its bewitching appeal. The Brecht-Weill Weimar sound mutated, though never entirely disappeared, as Weill's collaborators and circumstances shifted, but the composer's mix-and-match eclecticism remained. Confounding distinctions between high and popular musical forms, between the concert hall and the music hall, between opera and cabaret, he dedicated his career, in Germany as in America, to shattering hierarchies and borders. He was influenced by Mozart and Louis Armstrong, by Alban Berg and Cole Porter, by Bach and Richard Rodgers, by Mahler and George Gershwin, by Handel and folk music. In Berlin as later on Broadway, his work does indeed swirl with the kind of "compromise" mandated by his lifelong project of integrating many different kinds of music.

In self-defense against critics who accused him of selling out, Weill often claimed that the only categories of music he recognized were "good" and "bad" rather than "serious" and "light." Whereas "serious" and "light" are usually easy to distinguish and "good" and "bad" are not firmly predefined categories, nonetheless Weill's assertion underscores his career-long refutation of musical absolutism. Properly to measure Weill's accomplishment, the nagging, simplistic contrast between the European Kurt Weill, austere, rigorous avant-gardist, and the American Kurt Weill, Broadway boulevardier, must be abandoned once and for all. Assessment needs to be disentangled from an elitist Eurocentric perspective that scorns Weill's Broadway accomplishments and clucks over his abandonment of compositional complexity. Of course, *One Touch of Venus* is not the same kind of show as *Die Bürgschaft,* but then neither is *Happy End.* Weill's changing his tune was both characteristic and habitual, but his commitment to reforming and advancing the way music is used in the theatre did not alter. As Kim Kowalke maintained, "If there is more than 'one' Kurt Weill, there are also many more than two. He was many different composers. He believed a composer creates a new work each time out. *Happy End* was a flop because it was a copy of *Threepenny Opera.* In 1934 alone, he wrote totally dissimilar works in *Marie Galante, The Eternal Road,* and *A Kingdom for a Cow.* Are there three Kurt Weills in this list? Isn't there a greater distance between *Marie Galante* and *The Eternal Road* than, say, between *Love Life* and *The Threepenny Opera?* Weill himself claimed that *Street Scene* was close to *Die Bürgschaft,* and *Love Life* has many evident resemblances to some of the Berlin pieces. *The Firebrand of Florence,* an American work, and *A Kingdom for a Cow,* a European one, have a great deal in common. Did he change? Yes, certainly. From the beginning he had been interested in moving toward something new and different. Had he lived another twenty-five years, he would have amazed us with changes. Finally, however, there really was only one Weill, dedicated to the theatre, to reaching a wide audience, and to using his work to reflect and comment on social issues. Those commitments meant he had to change as the circumstances around him changed."[12]

On Broadway, as in Berlin, Weill sought the best writers he could find, and then explored ways in which his theatre songs could speak to, illuminate, or productively quarrel with their narrative contexts. He was a born collaborator with the ability to adjust to local customs without abandoning his own standards—he teased, prodded, stretched, but did not dismantle the conventions of whatever musical-theatre tradition he was working in. Writing for Broadway, he sensed he could continue rather than short-circuit the kind of career he had pursued in Berlin. It was his strategy, brilliantly accomplished, to bend the American musical theatre to his own exacting measure while at the same time writing with enough of a protective coating to guarantee that his work would be produced.

The greatest Weill is the caustic, sly, potent yet world-weary Weill of Brecht-Weill—the music for *The Threepenny Opera* is one of the wittiest, cheekiest, most delightfully insulting scores ever written for the theatre. But if Weill did some of his keenest writing in Berlin, he also composed in an early, tormented style, that of an avant-garde aesthete, that he decisively rejected. Although it never reaches the level of his collaborations with Brecht (what else in the musical theatre of the twentieth century has?), Weill's American work, judged as compositions for the theatre, is of a quality that is comparable to his European catalogue, and is arguably more diverse. *Street Scene* shares almost nothing in common with *One Touch of Venus;* far more than their respective South African and New England settings separate *Lost in the Stars* from *Love Life.* And what do *Johnny Johnson* and *The Firebrand of Florence* have in common except the name of their composer?

"The arrogance of the European experts to say, 'We have only one important Weill, after we have thrown him out, his work was not important anymore.' This is a second killing," said German composer and conductor H. K. Gruber. "It's so unfair. I hate hearing it, and I still hear it often from important people running international festivals."[13] If many European critics have tended to be disdainful of the post-German Weill, many American theatre professionals have long recognized the importance of Weill's innovative American musicals, which have served as both model

and inspiration for many of the strongest shows in the half-century since his death. "Leonard Bernstein knows every note of Kurt Weill," Lotte Lenya said, "and I think he liked Kurt Weill's music very much. He is the one who continued where Kurt Weill left off. He is the closest. His *West Side Story*—lovely—his *Candide,* a marvelous score. Those are things Kurt Weill would have done, if he would have lived, you know?"[14] "Kurt Weill's place in the American musical theatre is very high. He has had an enormous influence on our work," said Hal Prince,[15] who in *Cabaret* and in a series of musicals with Stephen Sondheim, including *Company, Follies, Pacific Overtures, Sweeney Todd,* and *A Little Night Music,* developed ideas about the so-called concept musical Weill had begun to articulate with some of his American collaborators. John Kander and Fred Ebb, composer and lyricist of *Cabaret* and *Chicago,* musicals heavily influenced by Weill's example, have acknowledged their debt. "Kurt Weill's work set a model for us to follow," Ebb said.[16]

In the face of a career of such sustained and protean achievement, why erect rigid judgmental divisions—between serious and light, between opera and musicals, between Europe and America, Berlin and Broadway—which Weill spent his life trying to abolish? Let Lenya have the final word. "There is no American Weill, there is no German Weill. There is no difference between them. There is only *a* Weill."[17]

Appendix

The following is not intended to be a complete catalogue of all the major Weill productions since the composer's death; what follows is a highly selective sampling, mostly of productions in New York.

Despite the long-running success of the de Lys *Threepenny Opera,* Weill's work was rarely produced in America in the 1960s. After that show finally closed at the end of 1961, the next major Weill production in America was the long-delayed premiere of *Mahagonny,* produced and directed by Carmen Capalbo, which went into rehearsal at the end of 1969. "From the time I first talked to Lenya about wanting to present *Mahagonny* until the time it appeared was thirteen years," Capalbo recalled in an interview with the author on June 2, 1999. The director had first mentioned his interest in the show early in 1956, after *The Threepenny Opera* had reopened downtown. "Lenya said I could have the rights, and it was given that Marc Blitzstein would do the adaptation. Before his death he had worked out a rough first draft." But when Blitzstein was killed in an alley in Martinique in 1964, Capalbo was left with a half-finished adaptation, which was rejected by Brecht's son, Stefan, and a long struggle to clear the rights. "Stefan controlled the American rights for all of his father's works, and it became clear that he and Lenya had to marry their rights to allow me to do an American production. At first, Stefan's negative aspect wasn't apparent, at least to me, but Lenya hated him. I heard her say to him, in one of our early meetings, 'You used to sit on my lap and piss on my dress.' She couldn't take Stefan as being an equal to her."

Now, with Blitzstein's work deemed unusable, Capalbo had "to start from ground zero." Finding an adequate translation, never easy for Brecht's vernacular German, became "part of the long, winding road. And like a fool I committed my life to it." At Stefan Brecht's suggestion, Arnold Weinstein prepared an adaptation. Capalbo (who found Weinstein's first draft "unusable in every respect. It didn't sing; Marc's version sings") worked closely with Weinstein for many months. Finally, he felt he had a version he could "go with." But Stefan Brecht began to be obstructive. "He'd shake hands, then you'd get a call from a lawyer." At a certain point, Lenya, "who was not uncooperative," according to Capalbo, told him that it looked as if they would have to forget the production. But enticed by the goal of presenting the American premiere of a work he "idolized," Capalbo refused to retreat. He went directly to Weill's original publishers, Universal Edition in Vienna, who were "very good." Finally, after years of delay, Capalbo secured the legal rights for the American premiere.

And then "the bloodbath" began. Approaching *Mahagonny* as a work with "a contemporary spirit, written by two young people, two kids, really, who weren't in the museums yet, for God's sake," Capalbo was eager to address a New York audience of 1969. "Don't forget what was happening on the streets then. Protest was in the air." Because the theatre and the surrounding neighborhood had "the right feel" for his vision of the show, Capalbo booked the run-down, barnlike 1,700-seat Anderson Theatre on lower Second Avenue. (*"Mahagonny* can't be done in a small theatre: it has a thirty-five-piece orchestra," Capalbo, who nonetheless used a rock band, pointed out.) Located two blocks south of Fillmore East, Bill Graham's rock emporium, the Anderson was in an area that at the time was the East Coast equivalent of San Francisco's Haight-Ashbury: a haven for hippies. "I had no intention to do it as a rock opera, but I bet that if Weill and Brecht had written the work in 1969, they would have used a rock band instead of a jazz band," Capalbo speculated, voicing a sentiment that three decades later continues to rile many Weill aficionados. "Rock in the 1960s evoked the same kind of resonance that jazz had for Brecht and Weill in Weimar Germany. Rock was the lingua franca of America at the time, and later of the world, and it meant something different then than it would today. I wasn't ahead of the curve, I was *on* the curve. The Doors' version of the 'Alabama-Song' had come out in 1967. There was a precedent for what I was trying to do, and that was the Berlin production, where the creators wanted a more relaxed, cabaret, musical-theatre sound than they had had in Leipzig, and that's the spirit in the work I wanted to capture. Lenya agreed with me—at first." ("The Berlin production was *not* a cabaret or pop version; rather, Weill was insistent on maintaining the highest musical standards, and it was cast, by and large, with performers who had legitimate opera or operetta voices," Kim Kowalke said, in an interview with the author on January 7, 2001.)

Capalbo auditioned rock and pop stars, including Cher, James Taylor, and Linda Ronstadt, and hired a rock band. "Stefan Brecht at the time thought it was a brilliant idea to use a rock group. Rock was the instrumentation—there were *no* reorchestrations, only minor transpositions for voices, which Kurt Weill did all the time." "The precedent for what I was attempting was sitting in front of me: Lenya herself. Jenny, as written, is for a high soprano; it had to be changed when Lenya played it. I didn't want to change a note of that score: I worship that score," Capalbo said. (Lys Symonette, the musical executive of the Kurt Weill Foundation, and Kim Kowalke, president of the foundation, firmly dispute Capalbo's claim. "There were major changes made in the score," Symonette said in an interview with the author on November 17, 2000. "It was a massacre."

"The score was mangled almost beyond recognition," Kowalke said in an interview with the author on November 29, 2000.)

Although he hired a rock band and "talked himself sick trying to get rock singers," Capalbo cast nonrock voices for the leading roles. Each of the actors had particular problems. Estelle Parsons, who had recently won an Academy Award for *Bonnie and Clyde,* was Begbick, cofounder of the City of Nets, a role Capalbo had promised her when Parsons had appeared in his Los Angeles production of *The Threepenny Opera* ten years earlier. "The piece is really in this middle range that nobody can do successfully," Parsons claimed in an interview with the author on September 23, 1999. "The music is extremely difficult; it isn't like *Threepenny.* You need opera singers who can also act it: Where are they? Trained singers are instruments. Teresa Stratas [who was to play Jenny in the Met's 1979 production] would never have a harsh or natural note: it's external acting, another kind of acting altogether from what an actor is trained to do. There's no connection between the gut and sounds as an expression of emotion. Certainly I couldn't sing in an opera-house *Mahagonny,* and according to some of the reviews, which claimed I shrieked, I couldn't sing in a musical-theatre version, either. My singing was self-expression: I acted the songs, letting the music come out as it will. I would never sacrifice the drama for purely musical values; a trained voice doesn't do that. For *Threepenny Opera* natural voices can be used; for *Mahagonny* that is more problematic," Parsons said.

In Lenya's role of Jenny, Capalbo cast Barbara Harris, another strong actress, like Parsons, and also a seasoned performer in Broadway musicals. "She wasn't as good as she should have been because she couldn't accept the fact that Jenny would sell Jimmy out for money," Capalbo recalled. "I told her it wasn't our job to rewrite the philosophy of the play. But she wanted to be loved, like most American actors, and was afraid audiences would perceive Jenny as the villain. She never unsheathed the knife because she said Jenny sells him out because she loved him. She never quite got Brecht's flavor. Estelle, on the other hand, got the play's spirit fully; her problem was vocal." "Barbara Harris was wonderful, but Lenya should have played Jenny," Estelle Parsons said. "What she could have offered to Carmen and to all of us in that production! When you worked with her on Brecht and Weill material, you know how it has to be done: with hard edges and non-naturalistically. She was better at that style than anybody could possibly be, but she never came around." "We couldn't find anybody to play Jimmy, even from the opera," Capalbo recalled. "One night at Elaine's [restaurant] I heard a huge male voice coming from the back. The singer, who looked like Robert Mitchum—like a guy who had worked in the Yukon—was the physical prototype." Henry "Chick" Madden, however, had a drinking problem. " 'I'm staking my life on you,' I told him. 'This play could make a star of you.' He said he would stop drinking. I spent weeks with him before the first rehearsal." Madden seemed to be holding himself together, but looked nervous at the dress rehearsal. "In the hurricane scene a young dancer grazed him and he went nuts, hurling a chair into the auditorium. We all agreed we would have to replace him." The director recast a week before the first scheduled preview. But this second choice, Mort Shuman, also did not work out. "He had a pleasant operetta voice, which sounded silly for the role," as Estelle Parsons recalled. "The third Jimmy, Frank Porretta, was the best."

When Lenya and Stefan Brecht saw the show for the first time at the first preview, they were appalled. Lys Symonette, who accompanied them (and who later became, to Capalbo's chagrin, a phantom figure in the balcony, seeing that every note of Weill was restored and respected), recalled in an interview with the author on May 15, 1999, that "what you saw there you couldn't believe. It was *not Mahagonny.* Lenya started to fall under her seat. Stefan, who had approved the Weinstein translation, which was vulgar, was shocked to death." Lenya never confronted Capalbo directly, and continued to talk to him ("She appeared to be on my side"). But Stefan Brecht, who objected to the rock band, to the quality of the voices, to Capalbo's use of live closed-circuit TV and of a porno clip in the brothel scene, "tried every legal means to stop the show." He carried the dispute to arbitration, where "all three adjudicators, including their guy, voted for me," Capalbo said. But it was a Pyrrhic victory. The besieged director had to contend with Stefan Brecht's nonstop campaign against the show, "a combination of World War II, impeachment, and dirty tricks—he was willing to go down with the ship," and with an unfinished production. "If only, after that first preview (and there were a million things wrong with that first preview), Lenya and I had sat down and worked through the problems. If only I had been allowed to finish my work in peace," Capalbo felt he could have delivered a powerful and valid interpretation. "I thought then, and I think now, that I was on the right track. And after I saw the 1979 Met production, I *knew* I was on the right track."

Over the course of the previews, Capalbo restored the original jazz band ("reaction to the rock band was fifty-fifty"). "We hired top jazz musicians, and the thirty-five-piece orchestra was under the same conductor we had for *Threepenny,* Sandy Matlowsky, universally respected for his musicianship and his understanding of Weill." Also removed was the porno clip. The show, which had a strong advance and did nearly sell-out business early in what was to be a historically protracted preview season of 69 performances, finally opened on April 28, 1970, and closed eight performances later. It lost around $350,000, an Off-Broadway record at the time.

Most but not all of the reviews were as poisonous as Capalbo had anticipated. "Outright butchery," thundered Martin Gottfried in the April 20 *Women's Wear Daily.* "We waited forty years for this production; must we wait another forty for a performance that will carry this great work entire into our eyes, ears, heart and mind?" queried Albert Goldman on May 10 in the *New York Times. Mahagonny* is a difficult liminal work, a radical mixture of jazz and opera that switches gears in ways that continue to seem daring more than seven decades after it was written. And quite unlike *The Threepenny Opera,* it seems designed to repel a loving response. "If audiences don't, in a sense, 'detest' the show, you failed," Capalbo claimed. His downtown, rough-and-ready, antiopera *Mahagonny* was a valid (though not, of course, the only) approach to this great, problematic, contentious piece of outlaw music theatre. For many nonpurists, the Second Avenue *Mahagonny* performed as a play with a great jazz score was, for all its faults, a memorable event. "It was a wonderful experience," Estelle Parsons said. "I just loved doing the show, working on that incredibly rich material. I don't care what the critics said about me: I'm glad I did that great piece of theatre." Lenya later claimed that she had to stay in bed for a week after she saw it. But she and Stefan Brecht had only themselves to blame. They had given their permission, had been invited, indeed urged, to attend every audition and every rehearsal, and had chosen to stay away—until it was too late. "It was her and Weill's loss," Capalbo said. "As a show, *Mahagonny* is doomed in this country. It can only be done in an opera house."

Many would argue, however, that an opera house is precisely the place where *Mahagonny* belongs. "*Mahagonny* needs opera singers, rather than singing actors like me," Lenya said in a televised intermission interview during the opening night of *Mahagonny* at the Metropolitan Opera House on November 17, 1979. Once the work finally appeared on an American opera stage, however, it ignited a critical firestorm about whether it belonged there. In 1979, as in 1930, Brecht's libretto and Weill's mixed score still had the power to irritate, unnerve, or bore many viewers, and critics and audiences had no trouble finding something to gripe about. "A pretty dated example of dialectical materialism, and to these ears much of the music is dated too," Harold C. Schonberg, music critic for the *New York Times,* scoffed in a November 18 review. "Even if better than I think, given the stop-start nature of the score and the endless pages of dialogue"—there is hardly any dialogue at all—"the work is entirely wrong for the Met," Byron Belt pronounced in the *New Jersey Star-Ledger* on November 20. "Thoughtfully prepared and carefully executed, but curiously tame and lacking the vividness which no other *Mahagonny* I've ever come across has missed," wrote Andrew Porter in *The New Yorker* on December 3. In the *New York* of December 24, Alan Rich reviewed the critics, calling the production New York's "first honest conversational controversy in years."

Although gorgeously sung, John Dexter's ponderously paced, solemn, stiff-in-every-joint opera-house staging utterly lacked the raw theatrical energy of Carmen Capalbo's maligned Second Avenue venture. Dexter's stately approach violated the work's fluid movement between speech and song and its clipped, almost cinematic pacing. As Hal Prince commented in a June 4, 1998, interview with the author, "It looked silly on that vast stage. The homemade legends and banners, the attempt to look poor in that rich, sumptuous environment did not work. The Chicago Lyric asked me to direct *Mahagonny,* but I turned it down. I cannot see it on any giant opera-house stage. How abrasive can you be on such a huge stage? The lunacy and boldness of the characters are made for small theatres."

Only one component of the production pleased everyone. As Jenny, the role Lenya had played in the 1930 Berlin production, Teresa Stratas was a dose of double dynamite: a compact, dark, fiercely intense opera singer who was at the same time a powerful actress. Unlike any of her colleagues, she seemed to appreciate the synergy of the Brecht-Weill collaboration, the fact that Weill must be approached *through* Brecht. "In *Mahagonny,* as in *Lulu,* there was reflected the alienation and degeneration of Berlin at that time, the decadence and that hard sort of German look and that dry kind of sound," Stratas observed in an interview with Alan Rich in 1980 (WLRC, series 60). "I found that in Brecht and Weill, but that's not all I found. If you take only the Brecht text, that's the spirit of the whole . . . until you add Weill's music. In its simplicity and beautiful melodies there is great nobility and an elegance. His music assures me that in spite of all these negatives and excesses and greed and selfishness there is something very noble in the spirit and the human being can be something better than these other things." Playing the double-edged quality she found in Brecht-Weill, Stratas created the only character on the stage. Her Jenny vibrated with anger, bitterness, and passion; she was hard-boiled through and through, but Stratas understood that tarts who betray their clients and lovers for money also have feelings and a past that made them as they are, which she illuminated without ever reducing Jenny to the cliché of the good-hearted prostitute. (Lenya befriended Stratas and in effect chose her to carry the torch for Weill. And indeed, in a radically different style from Lenya's—a testament to the range that Weill's theatre songs can support—Stratas became the world's foremost interpreter of Kurt Weill. Her recordings *The Unknown Kurt Weill* and *Stratas Sings Weill* are as definitive as Lenya's albums of Berlin and American theatre songs.)

A year after the Second Avenue *Mahagonny*, a Weill work suffered another Off-Broadway failure. Directed by José Quintero, a revival of *Johnny Johnson* opened and closed on April 11, 1971, at the Edison Theatre. "Lenya was really the artistic overseer of the production," recalled Bob Lidiard, who played Johann, the sniper (John Garfield's role in the original Group Theatre production), in an interview with the author on June 7, 1999. "She would speak at the production meetings. She certainly helped me to understand what I was saying. 'You're a sniper, but you don't hate: it's just your job, what you were told to do.' With her help I could see the character's conflict. And she taught me German for the role. She was happy with the way the score was sung. Our company was vocally trained; some even had opera training. She felt we were doing Weill correctly." Reviewers agreed, but by and large dismissed Paul Green's book. "I am convinced that Weill is the most underestimated of twentieth century composers . . . [and] he was very possibly the finest composer ever to be associated with the Broadway musical," Clive Barnes wrote in his April 4 review in the *New York Times*. "But the literary and political tediums of *Johnny Johnson* will do little to set the record straight." Recalling the demise of *Mahagonny* and now the failure of *Johnny Johnson*, Richard Watts in the April 24 *New York Post* wrote that "in the process of dismissing their books there was no reviewer who failed to express enthusiasm for the Weill music. Instead of fading from memory it is evident that the truly great anti-Nazi composer is growing in a fame that is unfortunately posthumous. When Brecht and Weill first became famous as a collaborative team, it was Brecht who was regarded as the more eminent but I think it was Weill who was the more gifted and enduring creative artist."

In February 1972 the Kennedy Center kicked off a retrospective program of American musicals with a production of *Lost in the Stars*. Directed by Gene Frankel and starring Brock Peters as Stephen Kumalo, the show was so well received it was transferred to Broadway, where it opened on April 18, 1972, the first time a Weill work had appeared on the Main Stem since the original production of the show had closed twenty-two years earlier. Reviews of Weill's score surpassed any he had received during his Broadway years. Two decades after his death, he was coming to be regarded as a Broadway master: "the greatest composer of theatre songs in this century," "the greatest composer ever to write for Broadway." On October 1, 1972, *Berlin to Broadway with Kurt Weill: A Musical Voyage*, Weill's only major posthumous revue, began a successful run at the Lucille Lortel Theatre (formerly the Theatre de Lys). Act 1 was devoted to the Berlin catalogue, act 2 to the American.

The impetus for the Yale Repertory Theatre performances of works by Brecht and Weill came from Michael Feingold, who had graduated from the Yale School of Drama in 1969 and whose fascination with the Brecht-Weill canon had been ignited by the superb original-cast album of Carmen Capalbo's *Threepenny Opera*. Feingold suggested a production of *The Seven Deadly Sins* to Robert Brustein, dean of the drama school, who, as Feingold recalled in an interview with the author on May 21, 1999, "countered by saying we should do it with *Little Mahagonny*, which at the time I thought was one of Weill's lost German works." As the double bill went into production in 1972, with Alvin Epstein directing *The Seven Deadly Sins* and Michael Posnick staging the American premiere of *Little Mahagonny*, Feingold received "a frantic call" from the Yale Rep: the scores had arrived but there was no translation of *Little Mahagonny*. Feingold suggested they use a translation by Arnold Weinstein. But when Brustein sent the translation to Lenya, she rejected it. "She wanted everybody to do right by the work—she was naturally protective of a rare piece she had appeared in so many years before, and she found Weinstein's translation offensive." Brustein asked Feingold to prepare a translation. "This was baptism by fire: I was working to please Lenya, who didn't know me, and I was also aware of the difficulties of translating Brecht. He was the maker of a kind of language reform because he writes such pure, simple German it's almost biblical. It's common speech, which can be very simple and grave at the same time that it can be low-down. In English you can only get the same effect by using slang. Weill gives you the outline, because you have to follow his music, and you can never subdivide a beat. With its strong beat, his music is based on an ostinato. Everything comes from the bass line. You cannot violate the rhythmic shape of the phrase; the least eighth-note extra is a defilement. That's why jazz and rock musicians love his work over that of almost any other classical composer." To his great relief, when Feingold presented his first Brecht translation to Lenya, she accepted it.

Rather than re-creating the original European productions, the directors of both short works wanted to examine them from new angles. Alvin Epstein attempted a kind of "rewriting" of the only previous American production of *The Seven Deadly Sins*, Balanchine's with Lenya. "That was a danced production," Epstein said in an interview with the author on June 12, 1999. "I wanted to make it a more theatrical production. I staged a lot of action, in mime, for the whole company; you have to invent a lot from the basic, stingy stage directions Brecht gives you." Rather than following Brecht's boxing-ring staging, Michael Posnick presented *Little Mahagonny* as a vaudeville show. "The vaudeville concept worked because the piece, like vaudeville, consists of detachable parts,"

Feingold observed. "It's a number opera with no plot but with a musical and emotional continuity about the life of the city. It was a pivotal piece for the company and for me. Lenya came, with her agent, Bertha Case, and was thrilled. When I met her I was too terrified to have a first impression: her *Berlin Theatre Songs* recording was my bible. Here was this little wrinkled lady with red hair who was very matter-of-fact and not without cunning. Brustein asked her why *Happy End* had never been done in this country. 'No one ever asked,' she said. 'Well, I'm asking,' Brustein said. At that point I was hired as literary manager of Yale Rep and as the translator of *Happy End*."

This time Feingold would not be reworking a prior translation; he would be starting from scratch, because there was no version of the play in English. Like all Brecht-Weill aficionados, Feingold knew Lenya's 1960 recording of songs from *Happy End* (sung in German), "at least five of which are among the greatest ever written for a musical." But when he began to study Elisabeth Hauptmann's book he realized how much work had to be done. "It could have been *Guys and Dolls* if it had been coherent. It is a 1920s musical, which means the book isn't quite right: you have to keep repairing it, to make a home for the songs. Lenya knew I could translate the lyrics, but she also trusted me with the book. She said, 'I give you carte blanche.' I worked hard to put an American sound in it." When he showed Lenya his work, she approved. The American premiere of *Happy End* on April 6, 1972, helped to gain for the Yale Rep its place as an important regional theatre. And in April 1973 the Yale Rep's *Little Mahagonny* was well received in a limited guest run at the Manhattan Theatre Club.

Next up, at Feingold's suggestion, was a staging of the full-length *Mahagonny*. "We knew in advance we were crazy, but we forged ahead, not quite realizing the marathon demands, musically," Feingold noted. Since the company consisted of trained actors rather than singers, an opera-house version was out of the question; but neither Feingold, who would write a new translation, nor the director, Alvin Epstein, saw the piece as operatic. Much like Carmen Capalbo's production four years earlier, this second American *Mahagonny* was performed in a Broadway style. "Voices alone simply don't make it," Epstein observed. "We had singing actors, like Kurt Kasznar, not a great singer, and Jeremy Geidt, who can sing if he has to, and did, and Sigourney Weaver, who played one of the whores: they were all basic growlers who can carry the tune. We didn't do it grand opera; we did the music as written [in that in-between zone that makes it peculiarly problematic]. Because our conductor, Otto-Werner Mueller, was a Teutonic tyrant, no changes were allowed." Electing not to set their production in a 1920s German milieu, Epstein and his scene designer, Tony Straiges, "found the 'correct' scenic environment, in the Gold Rush days in the American West." "We thought, because of the disaster on Second Avenue, that we should start clean, with a new approach," Feingold said.

"The leads at Yale were all singers, imported to the company," Kim Kowalke, a graduate student at Yale at the time, recalled in an interview with the author on January 7, 2001. "Except for two actors, Jeremy Geidt and Kurt Kasznar, who were miscast and got terrible reviews, it was musically excellent." Lenya seemed to like Epstein's approach more than Capalbo's, and the production was better reviewed. But it was only a stab at a knotty, stubborn, peculiarly unyielding work that, as its creators had intended, will never have the popular success of *The Threepenny Opera.*

As the original producer of *Hair* and *A Chorus Line,* New York Shakespeare Festival producer Joseph Papp clearly had an eye for unusual and timely musicals, and in 1976 he decided to present a new version of *The Threepenny Opera.* "The Blitzstein *Threepenny Opera* swept me into an experience which I still account as one of the most moving of my life," Papp wrote in liner notes for the original-cast album of his production. "Lenya was brilliant . . . and the entire production was extraordinary. Although World War II was over, the devastation that Hitler had wrought was still with us, and to me the show was a horrendous reminder of the days and the climate that brought him to power." For years Papp had felt that it was time to bring back *The Threepenny Opera,* but given his zest for reinvestigating classics he was not interested in simply copying Capalbo's production, much as he had admired it. Obtaining the rights from Lenya and Stefan Brecht became a prolonged and frustrating experience. "After long negotiations Lenya gave her approval, but Brecht exacted a condition that I heartily embraced: he insisted that Richard Foreman direct," Papp recalled. Foreman, the director and playwright of his own experimental Ontological-Hysteric Theatre, was a prominent figure in New York's theatrical avant-garde with a recurrent stylistic syllabus that included harsh lighting, strings running across the stage, and a feisty deconstructive approach to language. If dictatorial, Stefan Brecht's choice of Foreman was nonetheless not inapt. Using a new translation by Ralph Manheim and John Willett—"abrasive and faithful," according to Papp—Foreman stripped the work of its sneaky reserves of humor, wit, and sentiment and turned it into a chilly German expressionist nightmare in which all the characters moved like robots. Emblematic of Foreman's heavy hand was Raul Julia's dead-eyed, deadpan, sexless Macheath. A more joyless or unmusical interpretation of Weill's score would be difficult to imagine. Nonetheless, Foreman's self-infatuated cutting-edge take on the work of German theatre radicals of the past received mostly praising notices. The most informed of all possible spectators, however, detested the production. "Humorless—no charm, no naughtiness, no sex: they ruined it," Lenya told Lys Symonette (who recounted the comment in an interview with the author on May 14, 1999).

Encouraged by the reception of Foreman's strictly DOA *Threepenny Opera,* and still on a Brecht-Weill roll, Yale Rep revived their successful *Happy End* in 1976. And this time, the production was to have a commercial afterlife. In the spring of 1977, the show moved to the Chelsea Theatre Center, then housed at the Brooklyn Academy of Music, whose famously difficult director, Robert Kalfin, according to Michael Feingold, "made notes on how he could fix it." The problems started with the casting of Shirley Knight as Lilian Holiday. "Shirley was brought in for New York star luster," Feingold said in an interview with the author on May 26, 1999. "But, mysteriously, her mind was channeled so she could either sing or act. One night her singing was bell-like and in the acting department no one was home. The next night she acted beautifully and was off-key. Her Method training couldn't get her through this. She was Little Mary Sunshine: when you invite people for bratwurst, you don't give them McDonald's." Kalfin fired Michael Posnick, who had directed the Yale Rep production, and later Shirley Knight, replacing her with Meryl Streep, who had played the role for a few performances in the second production at Yale. "He also decided he was the author, and asked for percentages," Feingold claimed. "His idea was to make the show a Brechtian whorehouse, and he cheapened and vulgarized everything. He also pulled gobs from a literal translation of the original text and spread it over my adaptation, making it bloated and incoherent. Meryl was wonderful—she could act *and* sing and on the same night. But I was miserably unhappy." Most of the critics were not, however, and the show, with only a remote link to its Yale Rep origins and now ominously billed as a "Chelsea Theatre Center Production newly conceived by Robert Kalfin," was transferred to the Martin Beck Theatre for a Broadway run. "The marvel of the evening is the Kurt Weill score, arguably superior to that of *The Threepenny Opera,*" T. E. Kalem wrote in *Time* on June 13, 1977. "One word of joyous warning," he added. "In *Happy End* Brecht dropped agitprop. The show has no redeeming social value save delight." Even so, as with every production of Brecht to this day that has been mounted on Broadway, *Happy End* came to an untimely end, and the second posthumous appearance of a Weill show on the street where he had earned his living added no significant income to his widow's estate.

In 1980, *Der Silbersee,* the last work Weill had composed in Germany, had a belated American opera-house premiere. "I had to change the original for an American audience," said Hal Prince (in an interview with the author on June 4, 1999), who directed the production for the New York City Opera at the request of Julius Rudel. "I'm not a purist, and I knew American audiences would not sit through Kaiser's long-winded three-act play, which contained only one hour of Weill's music. I loved some of Weill's themes, and adapted the material to honor the eloquent way he brought together opera and musical-theatre tradition. We were putting on the show in an opera house, and I wanted it to be an opera, with a more or less continuous musical underscoring, which the original did not have. Hugh Wheeler [who adapted—Americanized—Kaiser's play] and I tried to be practical." "The original play is so difficult and highfalutin' I could barely make out what it was all about," Hugh Wheeler said in liner notes for the recording. "I'm so bored with that 1930-ish, pissy-assed socialism that I can't take it. Hal Prince, Lys Symonette [who served as the musical editor], and I were confronted by a simple choice. Either, puristically, we return the work to oblivion or, at the risk of being accused of 'artistic blasphemy,' we could rescue these musical jewels from their intractable matrix. We chose the latter course and by removing over two hours from the spoken dialogue we 're-created' *Silver Lake.*"

De-Kaisering *Der Silbersee,* Wheeler and Prince reduced the libretto to two acts, eliminated passages of lengthy literary dialogue, trimmed the contemporary political implications, and supplied an unambiguously happy ending for its two male protagonists. All but one of Weill's twenty-three original musical segments were preserved. Prince added a dancing character, the personification of

Hunger, who wove in and out of the action; reassigned "The Ballad of Caesar's Death" from the innocent mystic Fennimore to the tyrant, Frau von Luber; and embellished the play with incidental music arranged by Symonette, who borrowed material Weill had composed in 1927 for Strindberg's *Gustav III.* Prince's melding of opera with musical theatre was apparent in the casting. Severin, the outcast who has several agitation arias that attain a Verdian force, was played by opera singer William Neill. For the much less musically demanding role of Officer Olim—in the original, the character has only one duet—Prince cast Joel Grey, his emcee from *Cabaret,* whose voice is sheer Broadway razzle-dazzle. Coming from such differing backgrounds, the two leads reflected the musical dialectic within the work. As a practical man of the theatre, Weill himself would surely have conceded the wisdom of this shorter, lighter, less pious and more affirmative version. "It was a marvelous job," Maurice Abravanel said in an interview with David Farneth and Lys Symonette on August 8, 1984 (WLRC, series 60). "The language of Kaiser would not go in New York, it might not even go in Germany today. It's what we call elevated language, *gehobene Sprache.* Prince knew to put music underneath the language: you speak more poetically that way. You speak in a different tempo. While without music this becomes—what we on Broadway say 'realistic'—which wouldn't go. Prince knew what he was doing: he made it palatable." Lenya also approved, and appointed Prince to the board of trustees of the Kurt Weill Foundation.

John Dexter's 1989 production of *The Threepenny Opera* is to date the last production of a Kurt Weill show on Broadway. "One day, out of the blue, I got a call from [Hollywood producer] Jerome Hellman," Michael Feingold recalled in an interview with the author on May 28, 1999. Hellman was planning to produce *The Threepenny Opera* on Broadway as a vehicle for his Los Angeles neighbor the rock star Sting and wanted to commission a new translation. He was calling to request a writing sample from Feingold, whose free adaptation of *Happy End* was by then the standard version of the play produced in English. As his audition piece Feingold decided to translate Mrs. Peachum's song of sexual dependency, which Rosa Valetti, who originated the role, had refused to sing because she had been offended by the lyric in the act 3 reprise that "a woman's hole was Macheath's last resting place." "Well, the lyrics were intended to be offensive," Feingold said. His translation, more rough-edged than Blitzstein's, got him the job.

When he hired Feingold, Hellman, making his Broadway producing debut, did not yet have a director or a concept. Hellman, on unfamiliar turf, asked Feingold, the longtime drama critic for the *Village Voice,* to recommend a director. "I suggested Ingmar Bergman, who loves *Threepenny Opera,* but Jerry Hellman was afraid of Bergman, 'a director of such somber movies.' The Shuberts were pushing Trevor Nunn, and I put a doubt in their minds. Then I suggested John Dexter. I knew he was dangerous, but I also knew that he was familiar with the score and understood what the work was about." Once Hellman and the Shuberts agreed on Dexter, however, the project was doomed. "I hadn't realized at the time that Dexter [who had AIDS] was essentially dead, his system worn out from his avid consumption of drugs, alcohol, and young men," Feingold reflected. "He was Frankenstein's monster with a rivet in his neck." "John Dexter was unforgettably nasty—a meaner man I have never met," Alvin Epstein, cast as Mr. Peachum, said in an interview with the author on June 28, 1999. With a dying director "devoting a lot of his energy to proving he was in control of the show when he wasn't," as Feingold claimed, a poisonous atmosphere saturated the production from the start.

With no director in charge, but with the producer and Dexter's minions indulging a sick and unspeakably cruel man with the trappings of tyranny, the ill-assorted cast was left to fend for themselves. The ill will was increased by the misconduct of Georgia Brown, cast as Mrs. Peachum, "a shameless scene-stealer who, abetted by Dexter, undermined the work of many people," according to Alvin Epstein. Brecht and Weill had not conceived the show as a vehicle for a star, but this time a star was the reason for the production—and the star needed help. Sting was making his theatrical debut singing material with longer, denser lyrics than he was accustomed to. "He could have been good," Alvin Epstein recalled, "but he needed coaching in acting and singing this kind of material. He never got it. Dexter believed in giving external, mechanical direction only, he was dealing with traffic and refused to deal with what actors are supposed to be doing." The production was so unlucky that even its one ace in the hole fizzled. In the pit, making his Broadway debut, was Julius Rudel, who restored and orchestrated Lucy's aria, cut in 1928, and presented the songs in the exact order of the original production. Rudel, who admired Weill's "fantastic use of a small orchestra," expanded the number of musicians from eight to fifteen for a soupier, less mordant Broadway sound. "I did the show to have the Broadway experience one time, and because, really, *The Threepenny Opera* is a Broadway show," Rudel remembered in an interview with the author on June 4, 1999. "But it was not a happy experience. The less said about it, the better."

"Sting just simply doesn't have enough sting, and neither does the show," wrote Jerome Weeks in the *Dallas Morning News* of December 6, 1989, expressing a widely held opinion. "Without a sense of outrage, of dark irony, the Bertolt Brecht/Kurt Weill masterpiece seems as harmless as a community production of *H.M.S. Pinafore,*" Howard Kissel chided in the *New York Daily News* of November 6. Taking a long-distance view of the show's reception, Ross Wetzsteon in the November 21 *Village Voice* noted the "ironic spectacle of our leading 'culinary' critics virtually unanimous in calling for a more acerbic, excoriating, politicized *Threepenny Opera* [that] reminds us of the familiar irony that Brecht, to his ambivalent astonishment, created a wildly popular bourgeois entertainment out of the most explicitly anti-bourgeois sentiment—but also leads to the somewhat less astringent irony that Dexter's production, in attempting to appease those sentiments, has met with widespread bourgeois disappointment. *Threepenny Opera* may have unintentionally become one of the century's most endearing musicals, but that doesn't mean it works when turned, as it is here, into just another bland Broadway show . . . no growl, no snarl, no snap, no sarcasm—nothing but the lethargic high spirits of show biz."

In May 1999, for its twenty-first season, the Ohio Light Opera, the resident professional company that performs each summer at the College of Wooster in northern Ohio and the only company of its kind in the United States, got a jump start on centennial tributes in presenting the most obscure work of Weill's Broadway years. "Thomas Hampson's record of Kurt Weill songs [which includes all of the extraordinary through-composed opening scene] made me interested in looking at *The Firebrand of Florence,*" said James Stuart, founder and longtime director of the company, in an interview with the author on June 2, 1999. "Although the material I received from the Kurt Weill Foundation was in a chaotic state—it was hard for me to understand the show—I saw, when they sent the vocal score, that it was something my troupe could do. The foundation gave me some leeway. I took out the last scene, set in Fontainebleau; Weill himself had suggested that there be no Fontainebleau spectacular at the end, for which he had not written any new music. He wanted the show to end as we did it, a bittersweet finale in which the hero leaves the heroine." Three-quarters mock operetta that teases a genre long past its prime when the show was presented in 1945, and one-quarter sincere operetta romance in the Romberg-Friml-Herbert vein, *The Firebrand of Florence* demands an ironic edge that was beyond the earnest, old-fashioned Ohio Light Opera production, well sung but poorly acted. The valuable performance revealed the failure of the show's creators to follow through on the promise of their intoxicating twenty-minute opening scene.

Notes

The Weill-Lenya Research Center, housed at the Kurt Weill Foundation for Music in New York, holds an extensive collection of letters to and from Kurt Weill as well as letters by others that pertain to Weill's professional activities. The dates of each letter that is quoted from are cited in the text, and unless otherwise indicated, the letters are in the holdings of the Weill-Lenya Research Center (abbreviated as WLRC throughout the notes). Correspondence between Weill and his Viennese publisher, Universal Edition, comprises series 41 of the collection; other letters to and from Weill are in series 40. Apart from the interviews conducted by the author, and unless otherwise noted, all interviews cited are part of WLRC, series 60.

CHAPTER ONE • OVERTURE

1. Eric Bentley, interview with the author, June 30, 1999.
2. Harold Prince, interview with the author, June 4, 1998.

CHAPTER TWO • ENTER BB

1. Translation by Michael Feingold, typescript, WLRC, series 20.
2. Hans Heinsheimer, interview with Alan Rich, October 10, 1981.
3. Lotte Lenya, interview with David Beams, 1962.
4. Felix Jackson, interview with Alan Rich and Kim Kowalke, 1979.
5. Hans Heinsheimer, interview with Alan Rich, October 1981.
6. Ernst Krenek, interview with Alan Rich, n.d.
7. Kurt Weill, quoted in Kim Kowalke, *Kurt Weill in Europe,* p. 27.
8. Felix Jackson, *Portrait of a Quiet Man: Kurt Weill, His Life and Times,* unpublished typescript, WLRC, p. 221.
9. Hans Heinsheimer, interview with Alan Rich, October 1981.
10. Margarethe Kaiser, interview with Horst Koegler, n.d.

11. Lotte Lenya, interview with Alan Rich, 1981.
12. Felix Jackson, *Portrait of a Quiet Man,* p. 39.
13. Kurt Weill, quoted in Jackson, *Portrait of a Quiet Man,* p. 26.
14. Felix Jackson, interview with David Farneth, April 5, 1985.
15. Lotte Lenya, interview with Alan Rich, 1981.
16. Maurice Abravanel, quoted in Kowalke, *Kurt Weill in Europe,* p. 43.
17. Claire Goll, interview with George Davis, November 13, 1954, WLRC, series 37.
18. Ibid.
19. Kurt Weill, *Der deutsche Rundfunk,* March 13, 1927, quoted in Kowalke, *Kurt Weill in Europe,* p. 55.
20. Bertolt Brecht, "On the Use of Music in Epic Theatre," 1935, published in *Schriften zum Theater,* 1957, collected by Siegfried Unseld.
21. Lotte Lenya, interview with George Davis, n.d., WLRC Ser.37.
22. Ibid.
23. Ibid.

CHAPTER THREE • NIGHT SOUNDS

1. Margot Aufricht, interview with Alan Rich and Kim Kowalke, n.d.
2. Ibid.
3. Ibid.
4. In an interview with the author on June 29, 1999, John Fuegi claimed that "Brecht himself wrote no more than one-quarter of his signed work." Eric Bentley, in an interview with the author on June 30, 1999, suggested that line-counting and attribution aside, what Brecht contributed in the final analysis to the work of his assistants was a commodity that cannot be strictly measured— the force of his poetic genius. "Elisabeth Hauptmann was part American, which is why she knew English. Her English, not perfect, was a foreigner's 'good' English. She was a scholarly and brainy woman, but was she the great creative force John Fuegi suggests? Fuegi originally was a hero worshiper of Brecht, then lost it when he decided to write an anti-Brecht book from a feminist perspective: all the good things are by women, and he asserted that Brecht couldn't create a good female character. It's naïve to think a woman has to write a good female role. When Fuegi contends that Hauptmann wrote 80 percent and Brecht 20 percent, that 20 percent could make the difference between dead and alive. It isn't the right way to measure creative work. Brecht became like a dybbuk inside Elisabeth Hauptmann; she and Helene Weigel knew all Brecht's work by heart. Proving that Hauptmann went to the typewriter doesn't prove Brecht didn't put it in her head. I was witness to Hauptmann making a change in a Brecht script, a political change to bring a scene in line with party doctrine; there was nothing creative about it: Fuegi has misrepresented the issue. Brecht was accused of plagiarism in his use of Kipling poems for ballads in *The Threepenny Opera,* but in fact he altered Kipling quite a lot, just as Brecht's conception of Marlowe's *Edward II* is fundamentally different from the original. Postmodern theorists who announce the death of the author are wrongheaded; the individual is an

unfashionable concept now, but Brecht was an original—his work has a strong individual voice, and he made others' work into his own."

5. Kurt Weill, "About *The Threepenny Opera,*" reprinted in *The Threepenny Opera,* translated by Ralph Manheim and John Willett, 1979, p. 98.

6. Margot Aufricht, interview with Alan Rich and Kim Kowalke, n.d.

7. Ibid.

8. Bertolt Brecht, "Notes to *The Threepenny Opera,*" reprinted in Manheim and Willett, p. 96.

9. Kurt Weill, "About *The Threepenny Opera,*" reprinted in Manheim and Willett, p. 99.

10. Margot Aufricht, interview with Alan Rich and Kim Kowalke, n.d.

11. Marta Feuchtwanger, interview with David Farneth, 1984.

12. Felix Jackson, *Portrait of a Quiet Man,* pp. 163–164.

13. Ibid., p. 164.

14. Ibid., p. 64.

15. Norbert Gingold, interview with David Farneth, April 12, 1985.

16. Lotte Lenya, interview with David Beams, 1962.

17. Margot Aufricht, interview with Alan Rich and Kim Kowalke, n.d.

18. Ibid.

19. Ibid.

20. Ibid.

21. Marta Feuchtwanger, interview with Alan Rich, 1984.

22. Eric Bentley, interview with the author, June 30, 1999.

23. Margot Aufricht, interview with Alan Rich and Kim Kowalke, n.d.

24. Ibid.

25. Hans Heinsheimer, interview with Alan Rich, October 1981.

26. Robbie Lantz, interview with the author, June 7, 1999.

27. Ibid.

28. Virgil Thomson, interview with Alan Rich, 1983.

29. Kurt Weill, "*Die neue Oper,*" 1926, quoted in Stephen Hinton, "Misunderstanding *The Threepenny Opera,*" in Hinton, ed., *The Threepenny Opera,* p. 182.

30. Listed in Geoffrey Abbott, "The *Dreigroschen* Sound," in Hinton, ed., *The Threepenny Opera,* pp. 162–163.

31. Lyrics from the translation by Ralph Manheim and John Willett, 1979.

32. John Oser, interview with David Farneth, February 12, 1990.

33. Maurice Abravanel, interview with Alan Rich, Kim Kowalke, and Lys Symonette, August 26, 1979.

CHAPTER FOUR • THE SECOND TIME AROUND

1. Bertolt Brecht, "An Example of Pedagogics (Notes to *Der Flug des Lindberghs*)," 1930, reprinted in John Willett, *Brecht on Theater,* 1964, p. 31.

2. Elisabeth Hauptmann, interview with George Davis, May 25, 1955, WLRC, series 37.

3. Margot Aufricht, interview with Alan Rich and Kim Kowalke, n.d.

4. Ibid.

5. Ernst Aufricht, quoted in Felix Jackson, *Portrait of a Quiet Man,* p. 175.

6. Translated by Michael Feingold, freely adapted from the original German by "Dorothy Lane," 1972.

7. Ibid.

8. Ibid.

9. Felix Jackson, *Portrait of a Quiet Man,* p. 121.

CHAPTER FIVE • SLOUCHING TOWARD ARMAGEDDON

1. Letter from Kurt Weill to Universal Edition, November 18, 1927, WLRC, series 41.

2. Kurt Weill, "Notes to My Opera *Mahagonny,*" excerpt, translated by Kim Kowalke, in Lee et al., *"Mahagonny": A Sourcebook,* 1995, p. v.

3. Lyrics are from the translation by W. H. Auden and Chester Kallman, published by Arcade, 1996.

4. David Drew, *Kurt Weill: A Handbook,* p. 177.

5. Kurt Weill, "Foreword to the Production Book of the Opera *Aufstieg und Fall der Stadt Mahagonny,*" excerpted in Lee et al., *"Mahagonny": A Sourcebook,* 1995, p. v, translated by Kim Kowalke.

6. Bertolt Brecht, "Notes to the Opera *The Rise and Fall of the City of Mahagonny,*" originally published over the names Brecht and (Peter) Suhrkamp in *Versuche* 2, 1931, later reprinted in *Brecht on Theatre* as "The Modern Theatre Is the Epic Theatre." Excerpted in John Willett and Ralph Manheim, eds., *The Rise and Fall of the City of Mahagonny,* 1988, p. 88.

7. Ibid., p. 89.

8. Kurt Weill, "Notes to My Opera *Mahagonny,*" loc. cit.

9. Brecht, "Notes to the Opera *The Rise and Fall of the City of Mahagonny,*" loc. cit., p. 89.

10. Ibid., p. 88.

11. Hans Heinsheimer, "Best Regards to Aida," excerpt, in Lee et al., *"Mahagonny": A Sourcebook,* p. 31.

12. Alfred Polgar, *Das Tagebuch,* March 22, 1930, excerpt in Lee et al., *"Mahagonny": A Sourcebook,* p. 31.

13. Kurt Drabek, interview with Bernd Kortländer, n.d.

14. David Drew, *Kurt Weill: A Handbook,* p. 229.

15. Translation [of *Der Jasager*] by Larry Lash (CD booklet, Polydor 893-727-2).

16. In the late summer and fall of 1930, as they were enjoying the success of *Der Jasager,* Brecht and Weill had become increasingly estranged. But they formed a united front against a motion-picture company, Nero, planning an adaptation of *Die Dreigroschenoper.* Despite the growing differences between them, each adopted a sneering attitude to the film industry as manufacturers of bourgeois kitsch. "With the help of a lawyer we have finally succeeded in securing satisfactory contractual assurances that we will be given effective collaborative rights," Weill informed Universal Edition in a letter of August 6, 1930. "Nero, purely

commercial in orientation and curiously disorganized, apparently wanted to make a harmless operetta film. We had and have to use every means at our disposal to guard against that." Their distrust only deepened at their first meeting when the film's director, G. W. Pabst, one of the leading figures in postwar German cinema, whom they certainly ought to have regarded as a kindred spirit, said that he saw *The Threepenny Opera* as "a modern fairy tale." "Brecht exploded, because this was not a fairy tale to him," recalled an eyewitness, the film's sound editor, John Oser, in an interview with David Farneth on February 12, 1990 (WLRC, series 60).

As the film was in production over the following months, Weill continued to regard the filmmakers as cultural enemies. "Our every attempt to protest against the kitsch which is manufactured there will be suppressed by use of deliberate force and methods one only thought possible in the wild west novels," he reported in a October 6, 1930, letter to Universal Edition. Brecht, by 1930 a fully committed Marxist, wanted to rewrite the script in order to bring it up to Marxist speed, and on a daily basis he would bring to the studio suggestions for "strengthening" the material. If the filmmakers had incorporated his revisions, the work would have become a shrill and humorless tract. Weill had a much stronger case against the filmmakers than Brecht, as most of his score was not going to be used. Appalled at a project that was slipping out of their control, Brecht and Weill sued. The well-publicized trial, however, only helped to gain preopening publicity. "Weill won. And Brecht lost," Lenya recalled in a 1962 interview (with David Beams, WLRC, series 60), although, as she admitted, "the violation of Brecht's script was not as drastic as the violation of the music." What Weill "won," as he reported in a January 14, 1932, letter to Universal Edition, was the fact that "there isn't a single piece of music in the whole film— there are 28.5 minutes of music in the film—which isn't also in the original." But what he lost was the reinstatement of his entire score with the numbers sung in their original theatrical order and context. What Brecht "lost" was much, but by no means all, of his revised takes on the play. In Pabst's film there is really more Brecht than Weill. Indeed, more than Brecht was ever willing to concede, the film deepens the play's political implications. On film, for instance, Peachum's fake beggars are a more prominent and menacing presence—a potentially revolutionary mob, in fact. In a new ending, Peachum and Macheath form an alliance to exploit the power of the poor, who don't realize how powerful they are or how much they are needed by those in power. Disgruntled nonetheless, Brecht wrote *The Threepenny Novel,* in which at merciless length and with none of the biting humor of the play he transformed the material into a Marxist apologia. It is easily the worst writing of his career.

If the film is not Brecht's play, it certainly isn't Weill's musical, either. Only a few numbers are retained, but they are performed in a cryptic, offhanded style, with lean jazz orchestrations and a primitive hurdy-gurdy underscoring, that has an authentic ring. To the gratitude of posterity, "Pirate Jenny" was reassigned to Lotte Lenya as Jenny. For this one song only, the film pauses fully, as the camera regards Lenya with a transfixed gaze: and just as Brecht and Weill had intended, a song is allowed to stop the show. Although Weill had sided with Brecht against Nero Films, once the film opened late in 1931 he was thrilled at the "tumultuous response from public and press," as he wrote Universal Edition in a letter on December 1.

17. Margot Aufricht, interview with Alan Rich and Kim Kowalke, n.d.
18. Maurice Abravanel, interview with Alan Rich and Armen Guzelimian, August 23, 1978.
19. Margot Aufricht, interview with Alan Rich and Kim Kowalke, n.d.
20. Ernst Aufricht, quoted in Felix Jackson, *Portrait of a Quiet Man,* p. 177.
21. Gerhard Henschke, interview with the author, June 1, 1999.
22. Felix Jackson, *Portrait of a Quiet Man,* p. 177.
23. Kurt Weill, quoted ibid., p. 178.
24. Margot Aufricht, interview with Alan Rich and Kim Kowalke, n.d.
25. Theodor W. Adorno, "*Mahagonny* in Berlin," 1931, translated by John Andrus, reprinted in Lee et al., "*Mahagonny*": *A Sourcebook,* p. 41.

CHAPTER SIX • LAST RITES

1. Maurice Abravanel, interview with David Farneth and Lys Symonette, August 8, 1984.
2. Lotte Lenya, interview with David Beams, 1962.
3. Translated by Jonathan Eaton, typescript at WLRC, series 20.
4. Translated by Hugh Wheeler and Lys Symonette, typescript at WLRC, series 20.
5. Laura McCann, interview with the author, May 15, 1999.
6. Quoted in Jon Halliday, *Sirk on Sirk,* 1972, excerpted in Lee et al., "*Der Silbersee*": *A Sourcebook,* pp. 27–29.
7. Letter from Lotte Lenya to Caspar Neher, February 15, 1953, WLRC, series 43.

CHAPTER SEVEN • IN TRANSIT

1. Maurice Abravanel, interview with Alan Rich, Kim Kowalke, and Lys Symonette, August 26, 1979.
2. Lotte Lenya, interview with Alan Rich, 1981.
3. Maurice Abravanel, interview with David Farneth and Lys Symonette, August 7, 1984.
4. Ibid.
5. Harry Kessler, *In the Twenties: The Diaries of Harry Kessler,* p. 458.
6. Ibid., p. 459.
7. Maurice Abravanel, interview with David Farneth and Lys Symonette, August 8, 1984.
8. Ibid.
9. Letter from Kurt Weill to Lotte Lenya, *Speak Low (When You Speak Love),* p. 106.
10. Ibid., p. 112.
11. Ibid., p. 123.
12. Ibid., p. 112.

13. David Drew, *Kurt Weill: A Handbook,* p. 271.
14. Translated by John Mucci and Richard Felnagle, typescript at WLRC, series 20.
15. Letter from Kurt Weill to Lotte Lenya, *Speak Low,* p. 151.
16. Ibid., p. 152.
17. Ibid., p. 184.

CHAPTER EIGHT • THE ROAD TO AMERICA

1. Meyer Weisgal, *Meyer Weisgal . . . So Far,* p. 117.
2. Gottfried Reinhardt, *The Genius,* p. 245.
3. Michael Wager, interview with the author, June 1, 1999.
4. Gottfried Reinhardt, *The Genius,* p. 247.
5. Meyer Weisgal, *Meyer Weisgal . . . So Far,* p. 120.
6. Ibid.
7. Ibid.
8. Letter from Kurt Weill to Lotte Lenya, *Speak Low,* p. 125.
9. Letter from Kurt Weill to Max Reinhardt, October 6, 1934, WLRC, series 40.
10. Letter from Kurt Weill to Lotte Lenya, *Speak Low,* p. 187.
11. Ibid., p. 182.
12. Ibid., p. 188.
13. Ibid., p. 189.
14. Meyer Weisgal, *Meyer Weisgal . . . So Far,* p. 126.
15. Ibid.
16. Michael Wager, interview with the author, June 1, 1999.
17. Meyer Weisgal, *Meyer Weisgal . . . So Far,* p. 126.
18. Cheryl Crawford, *One Naked Individual,* p. 94.
19. Ibid.
20. Letter from Kurt Weill to Lotte Lenya, *Speak Low,* p. 193.
21. Ibid., p. 194.
22. Paul Green, production notes for *Johnny Johnson,* copy held at WLRC, series 30, of the original on deposit with the University of North Carolina at Chapel Hill as part of the Paul Green papers.
23. Ibid.
24. Phoebe Brand, interview with the author, May 20, 1999.
25. Kurt Weill, interview with *Brooklyn Eagle,* December 20, 1936.
26. Phoebe Brand, interview with the author, May 20, 1999.
27. Kurt Weill, interview with *Brooklyn Eagle,* December 20, 1936.
28. Phoebe Brand, interview with the author, May 20, 1999.
29. Paul Green, production notes for *Johnny Johnson,* loc. cit.
30. Phoebe Brand, interview with the author, May 20, 1999.
31. Ibid.
32. Robert Lewis, notes on Kurt Weill's lectures to the Group Theatre, July 27, 1936, WLRC, series 80.
33. Ibid.
34. Phoebe Brand, interview with the author, May 20, 1999.
35. Ibid.

36. Robert Lewis, interview with Peggy Sherry, May 29, 1991.
37. Phoebe Brand, interview with the author, May 20, 1999.
38. Robert Lewis, interview with Peggy Sherry, May 29, 1991.
39. Phoebe Brand, interview with the author, May 20, 1999.
40. Morris Carnovsky and Phoebe Brand, interview with John Mucci, September 1987.
41. Harold Clurman, *The Fervent Years,* p. 188.
42. Phoebe Brand, interview with the author, May 20, 1999.
43. Morris Carnovsky, interview with Peggy Sherry, September 14, 1987.
44. Phoebe Brand, interview with the author, May 20, 1999.
45. Harold Clurman, *The Fervent Years,* p. 188.
46. Ibid.
47. Ibid., p. 189.
48. Phoebe Brand, interview with the author, May 20, 1999.
49. Cheryl Crawford, *One Naked Individual,* p. 96.
50. Robert Lewis, interview with Peggy Sherry, May 29, 1991.
51. Ibid.
52. David Drew, *Kurt Weill: A Handbook,* p. 267.
53. Ibid., p. 280.
54. Benjamin Zemach, interview with Kim Kowalke and Lys Symonette, September 3, 1987.
55. Maurice Abravanel, interview with David Farneth and Lys Symonette, August 7, 1984.
56. Maurice Abravanel, interview with David Farneth and Lys Symonette, August 8, 1984.
57. Michael Wager, interview with the author, June 1, 1999.
58. Meyer Weisgal, *Meyer Weisgal . . . So Far,* p. 122.
59. *The Eternal Road,* New York, 1936, xi.
60. Michael Wager, interview with the author, June 1, 1999.
61. Letter from Kurt Weill to Lotte Lenya, *Speak Low,* p. 206.
62. Lotte Lenya, interview with David Beams, 1962.

CHAPTER NINE • HOW CAN YOU TELL AN AMERICAN?

1. Letter from Kurt Weill to Lotte Lenya, *Speak Low,* p. 228.
2. David Drew, *Kurt Weill: A Handbook,* p. 289.
3. Letter from Kurt Weill to Lotte Lenya, *Speak Low,* p. 235.
4. Ibid., p. 243.
5. Ibid., p. 248.
6. Burgess Meredith, *So Far, So Good,* pp. 59–60, WLRC, series 60.
7. David Drew, *Kurt Weill: A Handbook,* p. 300.
8. Hesper Anderson, interview with the author, June 8, 1999.
9. Ibid.
10. Quentin Anderson, interview with the author, May 28, 1999.
11. Burgess Meredith, *So Far, So Good,* pp. 60–61.
12. Quentin Anderson, interview with the author, May 28, 1999.

13. Ibid.
14. Hesper Anderson, interview with the author, June 8, 1999.
15. Quentin Anderson, interview with the author, May 28, 1999.
16. Alan Anderson, interview with the author, June 1, 1999.
17. Quentin Anderson, interview with the author, May 28, 1999.
18. Burgess Meredith, *So Far, So Good,* p. 61.
19. Alan Anderson, interview with the author, June 1, 1999.
20. Joshua Logan, quoted in Shivers, *The Life of Maxwell Anderson,* p. 174.
21. Ibid.
22. Kurt Weill, interview with Elinor Hughes, *Boston Herald,* January 4, 1941.
23. Maurice Abravanel, interview with David Farneth and Lys Symonette, August 7, 1984.
24. Lyrics from typescript of *Knickerbocker Holiday* at WLRC, series 20.
25. Miles Kreuger, interview with the author, June 29, 1999.
26. Carl Nicholas, interview with Dave Stein, August 14, 1996.
27. Maurice Abravanel, interview with David Farneth and Lys Symonette, August 7, 1984.
28. Gerald Bordman, *The American Musical Theatre,* p. 512.
29. Jean Dalrymple, interview with unidentified man, January 27, 1989.
30. Miles Kreuger, liner notes, *One Touch of Venus with Mary Martin,* Decca 9122.
31. Carl Nicholas, interview with Dave Stein, August 14, 1996.
32. Typescript of *Ulysses Africanus* at WLRC, series 20.
33. Ronald Sanders, *The Days Grow Short,* p. 285.

CHAPTER TEN • LIMELIGHT

1. Moss Hart, preface to the Chappell piano/vocal score of *Lady in the Dark,* quoted in mcclung et al., *"Lady in the Dark": A Sourcebook,* 1997, p. 6.
2. Kurt Weill, "Notes About My Career," from the Playwrights Producing Company press release for *Lost in the Stars* (1949), quoted in mcclung et al., *"Lady in the Dark": A Sourcebook,* p. 7.
3. Ira Gershwin, "A Living Liner," issued with *The Two Worlds of Kurt Weill,* RCA LSC-2863, quoted in mcclung et al., *"Lady in the Dark": A Sourcebook,* p. 7.
4. Kurt Weill, "Notes About My Career," loc. cit.
5. Maurice Abravanel, interview with David Farneth and Lys Symonette, August 8, 1984.
6. Ira Gershwin, notes written on July 12, 1967, as a response to Kurt Weill's letter to him of September 2, 1940, WLRC, series 40.
7. Ibid.
8. Lyrics from typescript at WLRC, series 20.
9. Paula Laurence, interview with the author, July 12, 1999.
10. Moss Hart, "Thirty-five Years of Broadway Musicals," interview with Brooks Atkinson, June 17, 1960, WQXR radio (New York), quoted in mcclung et al., *"Lady in the Dark": A Sourcebook,* p. 21.
11. Maurice Abravanel, interview with Alan Rich, Kim Kowalke, and Lys Symonette, August 26, 1979.

12. Letter from Ira Gershwin to Kurt Weill, August 26, 1940, WLRC, series 45.
13. Harry Horner, typescript, n.d., WLRC.
14. Maurice Abravanel, interview with Alan Rich, Kim Kowalke, and Lys Symonette, August 26, 1979.
15. Danny Kaye, quoted in Singer, *The Danny Kaye Story,* p. 80.
16. Ibid.
17. Ira Gershwin, *Lyrics on Several Occasions,* p. 209.
18. Ann Ronell, interview with Kim Kowalke and Lys Symonette, June 23, 1988.
19. Letter from Kurt Weill to Lotte Lenya, *Speak Low,* p. 325.
20. Virgil Thomson's February 23, 1941, review, reprinted in mcclung et al., *"Lady in the Dark": A Sourcebook,* p. 31.
21. "Dr. Brooks," preface to *Lady in the Dark,* New York, 1942, viii.
22. Kitty Carlisle Hart, interview with the author, June 9, 1998.
23. "Dr. Brooks," preface to *Lady in the Dark,* loc. cit.

CHAPTER ELEVEN • I'M A STRANGER HERE MYSELF

1. Hesper Anderson, interview with the author, June 8, 1999.
2. Helen Hayes, interview with Peggy Sherry, July 25, 1991.
3. Gigi Gilpin, interview with Lys Symonette and David Farneth, n.d.
4. Letter from Kurt Weill to Lotte Lenya, *Speak Low,* p. 334.
5. Ibid., p. 343.
6. Ibid., p. 322.
7. Ibid., pp. 328–329.
8. Ibid., p. 332.
9. Letter from Marlene Dietrich to Cheryl Crawford, July 31, 1942, WLRC, series 47.
10. Letter from Kurt Weill to Lotte Lenya, *Speak Low,* p. 364.
11. Ibid., p. 366.
12. Ibid., p. 367.
13. Cheryl Crawford, *One Naked Individual,* p. 119.
14. David Drew, *Kurt Weill: A Handbook,* p. 332.
15. Ben Hecht, *PM,* February 22, 1943.
16. Lyrics from typescript at WLRC, series 20.
17. Cheryl Crawford, *One Naked Individual,* p. 124.
18. Letter from Kurt Weill to Lotte Lenya, *Speak Low,* p. 369.
19. Kitty Carlisle Hart, interview with the author, June 9, 1998.
20. Jean Dalrymple, interview with Peggy Sherry, June 6, 1991.
21. Mary Martin, interview with Helen Ormsbee, n.d., unsourced.
22. Mary Martin, *My Heart Belongs,* p. 108.
23. Mary Martin, interview with Helen Ormsbee, loc. cit.
24. Mary Martin, *My Heart Belongs,* p. 32.
25. Paula Laurence, interview with the author, May 21, 1999.
26. Agnes de Mille, interview with Peggy Sherry, August 9, 1991.
27. Mary Martin, *My Heart Belongs,* p. 113.
28. Paula Laurence, interview with the author, May 21, 1999.

29. Ibid.
30. Agnes de Mille, interview with Peggy Sherry, August 9, 1991.
31. Paula Laurence, interview with the author, May 21, 1999.
32. Ibid.
33. Robert Pagent, interview with the author, July 28, 1998.
34. Agnes de Mille, interview with Peggy Sherry, August 9, 1991.
35. Allyn Ann McLerie, interview with the author, July 28, 1998.
36. Robert Pagent, interview with the author, July 28, 1998.
37. Allyn Ann McLerie, interview with the author, July 28, 1998.
38. Robert Pagent, interview with the author, July 28, 1998.
39. Attributed anonymously.
40. Robert Pagent, interview with the author, July 28, 1998.
41. Allyn Ann McLerie, interview with the author, July 28, 1998.
42. Agnes de Mille, interview with Peggy Sherry, August 9, 1991.
43. Ibid.
44. Ibid.
45. Robert Pagent, interview with the author, July 28, 1998.
46. Agnes de Mille, interview with Peggy Sherry, August 9, 1991.
47. Ibid.
48. Robert Pagent, interview with the author, July 28, 1998.
49. Paula Laurence, interview with the author, July 12, 1991.
50. Maurice Abravanel, interview with David Farneth and Lys Symonette, August 7, 1984.
51. Robert Pagent, interview with the author, July 28, 1998.
52. Jane Hoffman, interview with the author, June 12, 1998.

CHAPTER TWELVE • MUCH ADO

1. Ira Gershwin, notes in response to past correspondence, July 31, 1967, WLRC, series 47.
2. Letter from Kurt Weill to Lotte Lenya, *Speak Low,* pp. 370–371.
3. Ibid., p. 374.
4. Ibid., p. 388.
5. Ibid., p. 391.
6. Ibid., p. 401.
7. Ibid., p. 403.
8. Ibid., p. 401.
9. Ibid., p. 393.
10. Ibid., p. 393.
11. Ibid., p. 438.
12. Ibid., p. 437.
13. Ibid., pp. 440–441.
14. Ibid., p. 442.
15. Lys Symonette, interview with the author, May 14, 1999.
16. Ibid.
17. Lotte Lenya, interview with David Beams, 1962.

18. Lys Symonette, interview with the author, May 14, 1999.
19. Maurice Abravanel, interview with David Farneth and Lys Symonette, August 7, 1984.
20. Lys Symonette, interview with the author, May 14, 1999.
21. Joan Bartels Kobin, interview with the author, April 3, 2000.
22. Lys Symonette, interview with the author, November 17, 2000.
23. Ibid.
24. Lys Symonette, interview with the author, May 14, 1999.
25. Maurice Abravanel, interview with David Farneth and Lys Symonette, August 8, 1984.
26. Lotte Lenya, interview with David Beams, 1962.
27. Maurice Abravanel, interview with David Farneth and Lys Symonette, August 8, 1984.
28. Ibid.
29. Letter from Kurt Weill to Lotte Lenya, *Speak Low,* p. 376.
30. Letter from Lotta Lenya to Kurt Weill, *Speak Low,* p. 416.
31. Lyrics from typescript at WLRC, series 20.
32. Letter from Kurt Weill to Lotte Lenya, *Speak Low,* p. 426.
33. Ibid., p. 432.
34. Ibid.
35. Ibid., p. 396.
36. Paula Laurence, interview with the author, July 12, 1999.
37. Lys Symonette, interview with the author, May 14, 1999.
38. George Jean Nathan, unsourced, n.d.
39. Letter from Kurt Weill to Lotte Lenya, *Speak Low,* p. 453.
40. Ibid., p. 418.

CHAPTER THIRTEEN • STREET OPERA

1. Arnold Sundgaard, interview with the author, August 3, 1999.
2. Ibid.
3. Ibid.
4. Lys Symonette, interview with the author, May 14, 1999.
5. Walter Alford, interview with the author, August 4, 1999.
6. Lys Symonette, interview with the author, May 14, 1999.
7. Ibid.
8. Walter Alford, interview with the author, August 4, 1999.
9. Maurice Abravanel, interview with Alan Rich, Kim Kowalke, and Lys Symonette, August 26, 1979.
10. Letter from Lotte Lenya to Kurt Weill, *Speak Low,* p. 382.
11. Lys Symonette, interview with the author, May 14, 1999.
12. Anne Jeffreys, interview with the author, May 19, 1999.
13. Ibid.
14. Lys Symonette, interview with the author, May 14, 1999.
15. Ibid.
16. Anne Jeffreys, interview with the author, May 19, 1999.

17. Kurt Weill, notes to creative team during Philadelphia tryout, December 1946, WLRC, series 31.
18. Maurice Abravanel, interview with David Farneth and Lys Symonette, August 8, 1984.
19. Lys Symonette, interview with the author, November 17, 2000.
20. Kurt Weill to Charles Friedman, notes during Philadelphia tryout, WLRC, series 31.
21. Danny Daniels, interview with the author, June 9, 1999.
22. Anna Sokolow, interview with the author, June 11, 1999.
23. Sheila Bond, interview with the author, June 8, 1999.
24. Danny Daniels, interview with the author, June 9, 1999.
25. Anna Sokolow, interview with Peggy Sherry, May 10, 1991.
26. Sheila Bond, interview with the author, June 8, 1999.
27. Lyrics from typescript at WLRC.
28. Anne Jeffreys, interview with the author, May 19, 1999.
29. Maurice Abravanel, interview with David Farneth and Lys Symonette, August 7, 1984.
30. Letter from Kurt Weill to Langston Hughes, January 22, 1946, WLRC, series 40.
31. Lotte Lenya, interview with unidentified man, 1960.
32. Anne Jeffreys, interview with the author, May 19, 1999.
33. Lotte Lenya, interview with Alan Rich, 1981.
34. Lys Symonette, interview with the author, May 14, 1999.
35. Miles Kreuger, interview with the author, June 29, 1999.

CHAPTER FOURTEEN • BEFORE SONDHEIM

1. Lotte Lenya, interview with George Davis, n.d., WLRC, series 37.
2. Miles Kreuger, interview with the author, June 29, 1999.
3. Lys Symonette, interview with the author, May 14, 1999.
4. Lyrics from typescript at WLRC, series 20.
5. Nanette Fabray, interview with Peggy Sherry, October 1, 1991.
6. Lys Symonette, interview with the author, May 14, 1999.
7. Miles Kreuger, interview with the author, June 29, 1999.
8. Arnold Sundgaard, interview with the author, August 3, 1999.
9. Arnold Sundgaard, "Portrait of the Librettist as a Silenced Composer," *Dramatists Guild Quarterly,* Winter 1980, p. 29.
10. Ibid., p. 24.
11. Ibid., p. 25.
12. Lys Symonette, interview with the author, May 14, 1999.
13. Nanette Fabray, interview with Peggy Sherry, October 1, 1991.
14. Lys Symonette, interview with the author, May 14, 1999.
15. Michael Kidd, interview with Peggy Sherry, October 1, 1991.
16. Ibid.
17. Ibid.
18. Alan Jay Lerner, quoted in Lees, *Inventing Champagne,* p. 61.

19. Michael Kidd, interview with Peggy Sherry, October 1, 1991.
20. David Drew, *Kurt Weill: A Handbook,* p. 361.
21. Michael Kidd, interview with Peggy Sherry, October 1, 1991.
22. Letter from Kurt Weill to Albert and Emma Weill, October 17, 1948, WLRC, series 46.
23. Michael Kidd, interview with Peggy Sherry, October 1, 1991.
24. Nanette Fabray, interview with Peggy Sherry, October 1, 1991.
25. Miles Kreuger, interview with the author, June 29, 1999.
26. Ibid.
27. Harold Prince, interview with the author, June 4, 1998.
28. Fred Ebb, interview with the author, June 5, 1999.
29. Michael Kidd, interview with Peggy Sherry, October 1, 1991.

CHAPTER FIFTEEN • CRY, THE BELOVED COUNTRY

1. Letter from Maxwell Anderson to Alan Paton, March 15, 1948, WLRC, series 47.
2. Ibid.
3. Kurt Weill, quoted in *New York Times,* October 30, 1949.
4. Ibid.
5. Letter from Maxwell Anderson to Alan Paton, March 15, 1948, WLRC, series 47.
6. Kurt Weill, quoted in *New York Times,* October 30, 1949.
7. Rouben Mamoulian, production notes to Kurt Weill and Maxwell Anderson for *Lost in the Stars,* WLRC, series 20.
8. Ibid.
9. Lyrics from typescript at WLRC, series 20.
10. Rouben Mamoulian, production notes, WLRC, series 20.
11. Todd Duncan, interview with Peggy Sherry, May 2, 1991.
12. Ibid.
13. Ibid.
14. Alan Paton, *Journey Continued,* p. 20.
15. Rouben Mamoulian, production notes, WLRC, series 20.
16. Todd Duncan, interview with Peggy Sherry, May 2, 1991.
17. Rouben Mamoulian, production notes, WLRC.
18. Alan Paton, *Journey Continued,* p. 20.
19. Hesper Anderson, interview with the author, June 8, 1999.
20. Todd Duncan, interview with Peggy Sherry, May 2, 1991.
21. Ibid.
22. Alan Anderson, interview with the author, June 1, 1999.
23. Hesper Anderson, interview with the author, June 8, 1999.
24. Lys Symonette, interview with the author, November 17, 2000.
25. Maurice Levine, interview with David Garland, December 20, 1988.
26. Dino Yannopoulos, interview with Peggy Sherry, May 4, 1991.
27. Lys Symonette, interview with the author, May 14, 1999.
28. Dino Yannopoulos, interview with Peggy Sherry, May 4, 1991.
29. Lys Symonette, interview with the author, May 14, 1999.

30. Alan Paton, *Journey Continued,* p. 21.
31. Victor Samrock, interview with David Farneth and Peggy Sherry, June 14, 1991.
32. Alan Paton, *Journey Continued,* p. 21.
33. Agnes de Mille, interview with Peggy Sherry, August 9, 1991.
34. Miles Kreuger, interview with the author, June 29, 1999.
35. Quentin Anderson, interview with the author, May 28, 1999.
36. Hesper Anderson, interview with the author, June 8, 1999.
37. Alan Anderson, interview with the author, June 1, 1999.

CHAPTER SIXTEEN • THE WIDOW WEILL

1. Quentin Anderson, interview with the author, May 28, 1999.
2. Hesper Anderson, interview with the author, June 8, 1999.
3. Arnold Sundgaard, interview with the author, August 3, 1999.
4. Hesper Anderson, interview with the author, June 8, 1999.
5. Ibid.
6. David Raksin, interview with Peggy Sherry, October 2, 1991.
7. Lotte Lenya, interview with Alan Rich, 1981.
8. Carmen Capalbo, interview with the author, May 26, 1999.
9. Ibid.
10. Stanley Chase, interview with Donald Spoto, March 24, 1987.
11. Carmen Capalbo, interview with the author, May 26, 1999.
12. Stanley Chase, interview with Donald Spoto, March 24, 1987.
13. Scott Merrill, interview with the author, June 8, 1999.
14. Saul Bolasni, interview with David Farneth and Peggy Sherry, April 18, 1991.
15. Carmen Capalbo, interview with the author, May 26, 1999.
16. Lotte Lenya, interview with David Beams, 1962.
17. Carmen Capalbo, interview with the author, May 26, 1999.
18. Maurice Abravanel, interview with David Farneth and Lys Symonette, August 7, 1984.
19. Carmen Capalbo, interview with the author, May 26, 1999.
20. Lotte Lenya, quoted by Emory Lewis, *Cue,* April 3, 1954.
21. Lotte Lenya, interview with David Beams, 1962.
22. Stanley Chase, interview with Donald Spoto, March 24, 1987.
23. Carmen Capalbo, interview with the author, May 26, 1999.
24. Stanley Chase, interview with Donald Spoto, March 24, 1987.
25. Ibid.
26. Carmen Capalbo, interview with the author, May 26, 1999.
27. Jerry Tallmer, *Village Voice,* October 26, 1955.
28. Lotte Lenya, interview with David Beams, 1962.
29. Carmen Capalbo, interview with the author, May 26, 1999.
30. Lotte Lenya, interview with David Beams, 1962.
31. Carmen Capalbo, interview with the author, May 26, 1999.
32. Hesper Anderson, interview with the author, June 8, 1999.
33. Ibid.

34. Milton Caniff, interview with Donald Spoto, October 15, 1985.
35. Paul Moor, interview with Donald Spoto, August 19, 1986.
36. Julius Rudel, interview with the author, June 4, 1999.
37. Ibid.
38. Fred Ebb, interview with Donald Spoto, February 6, 1986.
39. Ibid.
40. Harold Prince, interview with the author, June 4, 1998.
41. John Kander, interview with the author, June 1, 1999.
42. Fred Ebb, interview with the author, June 7, 1999.
43. Harold Prince, interview with the author, June 4, 1999.
44. Fred Ebb, interview with the author, June 7, 1999.
45. Harold Prince, interview with the author, June 4, 1998.
46. Letter from Russell Detwiler to Helen Harvey, read by Donald Spoto in an interview with Helen Harvey, November 5, 1985.
47. Milton Caniff, interview with Donald Spoto, October 15, 1985.
48. Lys Symonette, interview with the author, May 14, 1999.
49. Paul Moor, interview with Donald Spoto, August 19, 1986.
50. Ibid.
51. Lys Symonette, interview with the author, May 14, 1999.
52. Kim Kowalke, interview with the author, July 21, 1999.
53. Ibid.
54. Ibid.
55. Ibid.
56. Lys Symonette, interview with the author, May 14, 1999.
57. Kim Kowalke, interview with the author, July 21, 1999.

CHAPTER SEVENTEEN • CODA

1. Jonathan Eaton, interview with the author, June 5, 1999.
2. Ibid.
3. Julius Rudel, interview with the author, June 4, 1999.
4. Jonathan Eaton, interview with the author, June 5, 1999.
5. Karl-Hans Möller, interview with the author, June 16, 1999.
6. Ibid.
7. Ibid.
8. Kim Kowalke, interview with the author, June 16, 1999.
9. Ibid.
10. John Mauceri, interview with the author, June 16, 1999.
11. Karl-Hans Möller, interview with the author, June 16, 1999.
12. Kim Kowalke, interview with the author, June 16, 1999.
13. H. K. Gruber, interview with David Farneth, February 21, 1997.
14. Lotte Lenya, interview with David Beams, 1962.
15. Harold Prince, interview with the author, June 4, 1998.
16. Fred Ebb, interview with the author, June 7, 1999.
17. Lotte Lenya, interview with Alan Rich, 1981.

Bibliography

Bentley, Eric. *Bentley on Brecht.* New York: Applause Books, 1998.

——. *The Brecht Commentaries. 1943–1986.* New York: Grove Press, 1987.

Betz, Albrecht. *Hanns Eisler: Political Musician.* Cambridge, England: Cambridge University Press, 1982.

Bordman, Gerald. *American Musical Theatre: A Chronicle.* New York: Oxford University Press, 1978.

Brecht, Bertolt. *Brecht on Theatre.* Selected and translated by John Willett. New York: Hill and Wang, 1964.

——. *Selected Poems.* New York: Grove Press, 1959.

Buckle, Richard. *George Balanchine: Ballet Master.* New York: Random House, 1988.

Busoni, Ferruccio. *The Essence of Music and Other Papers.* London: Salisbury Square, 1956.

Citron, Atay. "Pageantry and Theatre in the Service of Jewish Nationalism in the United States: 1933–1947." Ph.D. dissertation, New York University, 1989.

Clurman, Harold. *The Fervent Years: The Story of the Group Theatre and the Thirties.* New York: Harcourt, Brace, Jovanich, 1975.

Cook, Susan C. *Opera for a New Republic: The Zeitopern of Krenek, Weill, and Hindemith.* Ann Arbor: UMI Research Press, 1988.

Copland, Aaron. *What to Listen For in Music.* New York: Mentor, 1953.

Crawford, Cheryl. *One Naked Individual: My Fifty Years in the Theatre.* Indianapolis: Bobbs Merrill, 1977.

Davis, Sheila. *The Craft of Lyric Writing.* Cincinnati: Writer's Digest Books, 1985.

Dent, Edward J. *Ferruccio Busoni.* London: Eulenburg Books, 1974.

Dizikes, John. *Opera in America: A Cultural History.* New Haven: Yale University Press, 1993.

Drew, David. *Kurt Weill: A Handbook.* Berkeley: University of California Press, 1987.

Eisner, Lotte H. *The Haunted Screen: Expressionism in the German Cinema and the Influence of Max Reinhardt.* Berkeley: University of California Press, 1973.

Farneth, David, with Elmar Juchem and Dave Stein. *Kurt Weill: A Life in Pictures and Documents.* New York: Overlook Press, 2000.

Farneth, David, ed. *Lenya the Legend.* New York: Overlook Press, 1998.

Fermi, Laura. *Illustrious Immigrants: The Intellectual Migration from Europe, 1930–1941.* Chicago: University of Chicago Press, 1968.

Friedrich, Otto. *Before the Deluge: A Portrait of Berlin in the 1920s.* New York: Fromm International, 1986.

Fuegi, John. *Bertolt Brecht: Chaos, According to Plan.* Cambridge, England: Cambridge University Press, 1987.

———. *Brecht & Co.: Sex, Politics, and the Making of Modern Drama.* New York: Grove Press, 1994.

Furia, Philip. *Ira Gershwin: The Art of the Lyricist.* New York: Oxford University Press, 1996.

Gay, Peter. *Weimar Culture: The Outsider as Insider.* New York: Harper & Row, 1968.

Gershwin, Ira. *Lyrics on Several Occasions.* New York: Alfred A. Knopf, 1959.

Gillian, Bryan, ed. *Music and Performance During the Weimar Republic.* Cambridge, England: Cambridge University Press, 1994.

Goldhagen, Daniel Jonah. *Hitler's Willing Executioners: Ordinary Germans and the Holocaust.* New York: Alfred A. Knopf, 1996.

Goldstein, Malcolm. *The Political Stage: American Drama and Theatre of the Great Depression.* New York: Oxford University Press, 1974.

Gordon, Eric A. *Mark the Music: The Life and Work of Marc Blitzstein.* New York: St. Martin's Press, 1989.

Grismer, Kay L. *Cheryl Crawford Presents: A History of Her Broadway Musical Productions, 1936–1949.* Ann Arbor: UMI Research Press, 1993.

Grosz, George. *A Little Yes and a Big No.* New York: Dial Press, 1946.

Harden, Susan Clydette. "The Music for the Stage Collaborations of Weill and Brecht." Ph.D. dissertation, University of North Carolina, Chapel Hill, 1972.

Haxthausen, Charles W., and Heindrun Suh, eds. *Berlin: Culture and Metropolis.* Minneapolis and Oxford: University of Minnesota Press, 1990.

Hecht, Ben. *A Child of the Century.* New York: Simon and Schuster, 1954.

Hinton, Stephen, ed. *The Threepenny Opera.* Cambridge, England: Cambridge University Press, 1990.

Hirsch, Foster. *Harold Prince and the American Musical Theatre.* Cambridge, England: Cambridge University Press, 1989.

———. *A Method to Their Madness: The History of the Actors Studio.* New York: W. W. Norton and Co., 1984.

Hoffman, Paul. *The Viennese: Splendor, Twilight, and Exile.* New York: Doubleday, 1988.

Jackson, Felix. *Portrait of a Quiet Man: Kurt Weill, His Life and Times.* Unpublished; typescript at WLRC.

Jarman, Douglas. *Kurt Weill: An Illustrated Biography.* Indianapolis: Indiana University Press, 1982.

Jelavich, Peter. *Berlin Cabaret.* Cambridge, Massachusetts: Harvard University Press, 1993.

Jungk, Peter Stephan. *Franz Werfel: A Life in Prague, Vienna, and Hollywood.* New York: Grove Weidenfeld, 1987.

Kater, Michael. *The Twisted Muse: Musicians and Their Music in the Third Reich.* New York: Oxford University Press, 1997.

Kazan, Elia. *Elia Kazan: A Life.* New York: Alfred A. Knopf, 1988.

Kessler, Harry. *In the Twenties: The Diaries of Harry Kessler.* London: Weidenfeld and Nicolson, 1971.

Kilroy, David Michael. "Kurt Weill on Broadway: The Postwar Years (1945–50)." Ph.D. dissertation, Harvard University Press, 1992.

Kowalke, Kim H. *Kurt Weill in Europe.* Ann Arbor: UMI Research Press, 1979.

Kowalke, Kim H., ed. *A New Orpheus: Essays on Kurt Weill.* New Haven: Yale University Press, 1986.

Kowalke, Kim H., and Horst Edler, eds. *A Stranger Here Myself: Kurt Weill-Studien.* Hildesheim: Olms Verlag, 1993.

Lareau, Alan. *The Wild Stage: Literary Cabarets of the Weimar Republic.* Columbia, South Carolina: Camden House, 1995.

Lee, Joanna, Edward Harsh, and Kim Kowalke, eds. *"Mahagonny": A Sourcebook.* New York: Kurt Weill Foundation for Music, 1997.

———. *"Der Silbersee": A Sourcebook.* New York: Kurt Weill Foundation for Music, 1996.

———. *"Street Scene": A Sourcebook.* New York: Kurt Weill Foundation for Music, 1996.

Lee, Joanna, and Kim Kowalke, eds. *"The Seven Deadly Sins": A Sourcebook.* New York: Kurt Weill Foundation for Music, 1997.

Lees, Gene. *Inventing Champagne: The Worlds of Lerner and Loewe.* New York: St. Martin's Press, 1990.

Lerner, Alan Jay. *The Street Where I Live.* New York: W. W. Norton & Co., 1978.

Lewis, Robert. *Slings and Arrows: Theater in My Life.* New York: Stein and Day, 1984.

Lindenberger, Herbert. *Opera. The Extravagant Art.* Ithaca: Cornell University Press, 1984.

Logan, Joshua. *Josh: My Up and Down, In and Out Life.* New York: Delacorte Press, 1976.

Martin, Mary. *My Heart Belongs.* New York: Quill, 1984.

mcclung, bruce d. "American Dreams: Analyzing Moss Hart, Ira Gershwin, and Kurt Weill's *Lady in the Dark.*" Ph.D. dissertation, Eastman School of Music, University of Rochester, 1994.

mcclung, bruce d., Joanna Lee, and Kim Kowalke, eds. *"Lady in the Dark": A Sourcebook.* New York: Kurt Weill Foundation for Music, 1996.

Meredith, Burgess. *So Far, So Good.* Boston: Little, Brown and Co., 1994.

Morley, Sheridan. *Gertrude Lawrence.* New York: McGraw-Hill, 1981.

Münsterer, Hanns Otto. *The Young Brecht.* London: Libris, 1992.

Osato, Sono. *Distant Dances.* New York: Alfred A. Knopf, 1980.

Palmer, Christopher. *The Composer in Hollywood.* New York: Marion Boyars, 1990.

Parmalee, Patty Lee. *Brecht's America.* Cincinnati: Ohio University Press, 1981.

Paton, Alan. *Journey Continued.* New York: Oxford University, 1988.

Potter, Pamela M. *Most German of the Arts: Musicology and Society from the Weimar Republic to the End of Hitler's Reich.* New Haven: Yale University Press, 1998.

Reinhardt, Gottfried. *The Genius: A Memoir of Max Reinhardt.* New York: Alfred A. Knopf, 1979.

Rice, Elmer. *Minority Report: An Autobiography.* New York: Simon and Schuster, 1963.

Sanders, Ronald. *The Days Grow Short: The Life and Music of Kurt Weill.* New York: Holt, Rinehart, and Winston, 1980.

Schebera, Jürgen. *Kurt Weill: An Illustrated Life.* New Haven: Yale University Press, 1995.

Shivers, Alfred S. *The Life of Maxwell Anderson.* New York: Stein and Day, 1983.

Singer, Kurt. *The Danny Kaye Story.* New York: Thomas Nelson and Sons, 1958.

Smith, Wendy. *Real Life Drama: The Group Theatre and America, 1931–1940.* New York: Alfred A. Knopf, 1990.

Spiel, Hilda. *Vienna's Golden Autumn: From the Watershed Year 1866 to Hitler's Anschluss, 1938.* New York: Weidenfeld and Nicolson, 1987.

Spoto, Donald. *Lenya: A Life.* Boston: Little, Brown and Company, 1989.

Stern, Fritz. *Einstein's German World.* Princeton: Princeton University Press, 1999.

Stewart, John. *Ernst Krenek: The Man and His Music.* Berkeley: University of California Press, 1991.

Stuckenschmidt, H. H. *Arnold Schoenberg: His Life, World and Work.* New York: Schirmer Books, 1977.

Symonette, Lys, and Kim H. Kowalke, eds. *Speak Low (When You Speak Love): The Letters of Kurt Weill and Lotte Lenya.* Berkeley: University of California Press, 1996.

Taylor, John Russell. *Strangers in Paradise: The Hollywood Emigrés, 1933–1950.* New York: Holt, Rinehart and Winston, 1983.

Taylor, Ronald. *Berlin and Its Culture.* New Haven: Yale University Press, 1997.

———. *Kurt Weill: Composer in a Divided World.* Boston: Northeastern University Press, 1999.

Thomson, Virgil. *Virgil Thomson.* New York: Alfred A. Knopf, 1966.

———. *Words with Music.* New Haven: Yale University Press, 1989.

Thornhill, William. "Kurt Weill's *Street Scene.*" Ph.D. dissertation, University of North Carolina, 1990.

Viertel, Salka. *The Kindness of Strangers.* New York: Holt, Rinehart and Winston, 1969.

Von Eckardt, Wolf, and Sander L. Gilman. *Bertolt Brecht's Berlin.* Garden City, New York: Anchor Press, 1975.

Wagner, Gottfried. *Twilight of the Wagners: The Unveiling of a Family's Legacy.* New York: Picador USA, 1999.

Watson, Steven. *Prepare for Saints: Gertrude Stein, Virgil Thomson, and the Mainstreaming of American Modernism.* New York: Random House, 1998.

Weisgal, Meyer. *Meyer Weisgal . . . So Far: An Autobiography.* New York: Random House, 1971.

Wharton, John F. *Life Among the Playwrights: Being Mostly the Story of the Playwrights Producing Company.* New York: Quadrangle, 1974.

Whitford, Frank, ed. *The Bauhaus: Masters and Students by Themselves.* Woodstock: Overlook Press, 1993.

Willett, John. *Art and Politics in the Weimar Period: The New Sobriety, 1917–1933.* New York: Pantheon, 1978.

———. *Caspar Neher: Brecht's Designer.* London: Methuen, 1986.

———. *The Theatre of the Weimar Republic.* New York: Holmes & Meier, 1988.

Williams, Jay. *Stage Left.* New York: Charles Scribner's Sons, 1974.

Index

Note: Page numbers in *italics* refer to illustrations.

A NOTE ON THE TYPE

The text of this book was set in Garamond No. 3. It is not a true copy of any of the designs of Claude Garamond (ca. 1480–1561), but an adaptation of his types, which set the European standard for two centuries. It probably owes as much to the designs of Jean Jannon, a Protestant printer working in Sedan in the early seventeenth century, who had worked with Garamond's romans earlier, in Paris, but who was denied their use because of Catholic censorship. Jannon's matrices came into the possession of the Imprimerie Nationale, where they were thought to be by Garamond himself, and were so described when the Imprimerie revived the type in 1900. This particular version is based on an adaptation by Morris Fuller Benton.

Composed by North Market Street Graphics, Lancaster, Pennsylvania

Printed and bound by QuebecorWorld, Fairfield, Pennsylvania

Designed by Iris Weinstein